Django REST APIs Demystified

Simplifying API Development with Django

Ganeshkumar Patil

Apress®

Django REST APIs Demystified: Simplifying API Development with Django

Ganeshkumar Patil
Stafford, UK

ISBN-13 (pbk): 979-8-8688-1849-3 ISBN-13 (electronic): 979-8-8688-1850-9
https://doi.org/10.1007/979-8-8688-1850-9

Managing Director, Apress Media LLC: Welmoed Spahr
Acquisitions Editor: Anandadeep Roy
Coordinating Editor: Jessica Vakili

Cover image by Freepik.com

Distributed to the book trade worldwide by Springer Science+Business Media New York, 1 New York Plaza, New York, NY 10004. Phone 1-800-SPRINGER, fax (201) 348-4505, e-mail orders-ny@springer-sbm.com, or visit www.springeronline.com. Apress Media, LLC is a Delaware LLC and the sole member (owner) is Springer Science + Business Media Finance Inc (SSBM Finance Inc). SSBM Finance Inc is a **Delaware** corporation.

For information on translations, please e-mail booktranslations@springernature.com; for reprint, paperback, or audio rights, please e-mail bookpermissions@springernature.com.

Apress titles may be purchased in bulk for academic, corporate, or promotional use. eBook versions and licenses are also available for most titles. For more information, reference our Print and eBook Bulk Sales web page at http://www.apress.com/bulk-sales.

Any source code or other supplementary material referenced by the author in this book is available to readers on GitHub (https://github.com/Apress). For more detailed information, please visit https://www.apress.com/gp/services/source-code.

If disposing of this product, please recycle the paper

To my wife, Seema, and daughter, Siya, whose patience and encouragement fueled every page.

To my parents, whose love and guidance shaped me. And to my late father—your values continue to light my way.

Table of Contents

About the Author

Ganeshkumar Patil has over 20 years of experience in the software industry, having worked extensively with programming languages such as C, C++, Python, JavaScript, and React, alongside various technology stacks. His career spans full-stack development, enterprise software solutions, and deep dives into modern API architectures. Over the last four years, he has focused on Django and Django REST Framework while transitioning to full-stack development.

About the Technical Reviewer

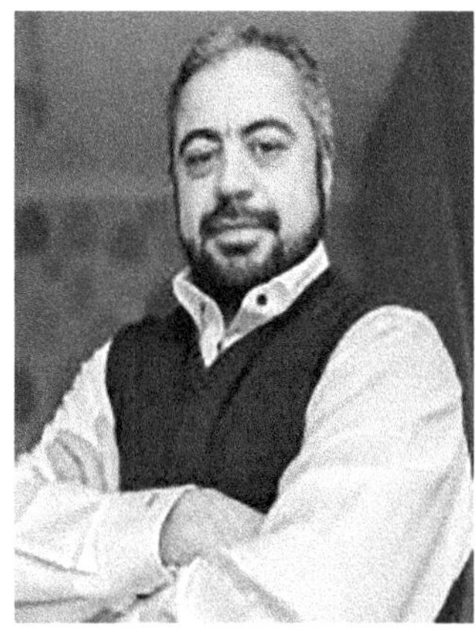

Norair Arutshyan is a software engineer with a strong focus on back-end development and API design, specializing in Python, Django, and Django REST Framework. He holds a master's degree in applied mathematics and applies a rigorous, analytical approach to building and maintaining scalable, high-quality systems.

Dedicated to continuous learning and professional growth, Norair actively seeks opportunities to expand his technical expertise and stay current with modern development practices. His areas of interest include software architecture, automated testing, and performance optimization.

As a technical reviewer for this book, he contributed his practical experience and critical insight to ensure the material is accurate, clear, and aligned with real-world software development needs.

Acknowledgments

Writing this book has been a deeply rewarding experience, and I am grateful to many individuals whose support, guidance, and encouragement made it possible.

First and foremost, I would like to express my sincere thanks to **Apress** for giving me the opportunity to bring this work to life. I am especially thankful to **Anandadeep Roy**, who first reached out to me and encouraged the idea of writing this book. Your belief in the value of this content helped set everything in motion.

My heartfelt appreciation goes to **Nirmal Selvaraj**, my production editor at Apress, for your consistent support and thoughtful communication throughout the publishing process. Your guidance helped shape the manuscript and navigate the complexities of production smoothly.

I would also like to acknowledge **Norair Arutshyan**, the technical reviewer for this book. Your detailed feedback and insightful comments strengthened the technical accuracy of the content and helped make it more useful for readers.

A special thanks to my colleagues **Mathew Bryan** and **Peter Campbell** for offering early feedback and reviewing initial drafts. Your informal input helped validate the direction of the content and provided much-needed encouragement during the early stages.

Finally, and most importantly, I would like to thank my **family**. To my **wife**, for her constant support and understanding during the long hours spent writing. To my **daughter**, whose presence brought joy even during the most challenging moments. To my **mother**, for her unwavering love and encouragement. And to my **late father**, whose values, strength, and belief in lifelong learning continue to guide me. Though you are no longer here, your influence remains ever-present. This book is dedicated in part to your memory.

Thank you all for being a part of this journey.

Introduction

Django REST APIs Demystified is designed to provide a comprehensive guide to building RESTful APIs using the Django REST Framework (DRF). This book covers everything from fundamental concepts to advanced features, enabling developers to create scalable, secure, and maintainable APIs with confidence.

The book begins by introducing the core principles of REST and how DRF implements these concepts to simplify API development. You'll learn how to structure Django projects, design models, create serializers, and build views to handle client requests. As you progress, the book dives into advanced topics such as authentication and permissions, request throttling, caching strategies, API versioning, and schema generation. Each chapter presents these concepts through stand-alone applications that demonstrate practical implementation and reinforce learning in a modular way.

Who This Book Is For

This book is ideal for a broad audience:

- **Beginners** who are new to RESTful API development and want to learn how to use Django REST Framework effectively
- **Intermediate developers** who have experience with Django and want to expand their skill set by mastering API design and development
- **Advanced developers** looking to deepen their understanding of DRF's more sophisticated features and optimize their APIs for real-world scenarios
- **Team leads and architects** responsible for designing scalable and secure APIs and guiding development teams in best practices

While no prior experience with Django REST Framework is required, familiarity with Python and basic Django development will help you follow the material more easily.

How This Book Is Structured

The book is organized into chapters, each focusing on a specific aspect of DRF:

- **Getting Started:** Introduction to REST principles, Django project setup, and fundamental API building blocks
- **Core Components:** Detailed exploration of models, serializers, views, and routers
- **Advanced Features:** Covers authentication, permissions, throttling, caching, and versioning
- **Customization and Testing:** Guides on customizing DRF's behavior and writing tests for robust APIs
- **Integration:** How to work with third-party tools and extend DRF for complex use cases

Each chapter includes hands-on examples and practical code to illustrate concepts clearly, enabling you to apply what you learn immediately.

What You Need to Know Before You Begin

To get the most out of this book, it's helpful to have a basic understanding of Python and Django fundamentals. If you're new to Django, it is recommended to familiarize yourself with its basic concepts through introductory resources before diving into this book. This foundation will make it easier to grasp the API-specific content covered here.

By the end of this book, you'll have the knowledge and practical experience to build secure, efficient, and maintainable REST APIs suitable for a wide range of applications—from small projects to enterprise-grade systems.

CHAPTER 1

Introduction to APIs

API stands for Application Programming Interface. It is a set of rules and protocols that allows different software applications to communicate with each other without having to know how they are implemented. It defines how different components of software systems can interact and exchange data. It acts as a middleman or agent for transferring data from one application to another.

APIs use a common format, JSON, to interact with applications. Front-end applications may be mobile applications developed by React Native or web applications developed by React; they all can get their required data by interacting with server application using an API. For example, mobile application may require data from a database that can be retrieved by using an API from a server. Similarly, a web application also gets the same data from the database using the same API. The figure below shows how different applications can get their required data using APIs:

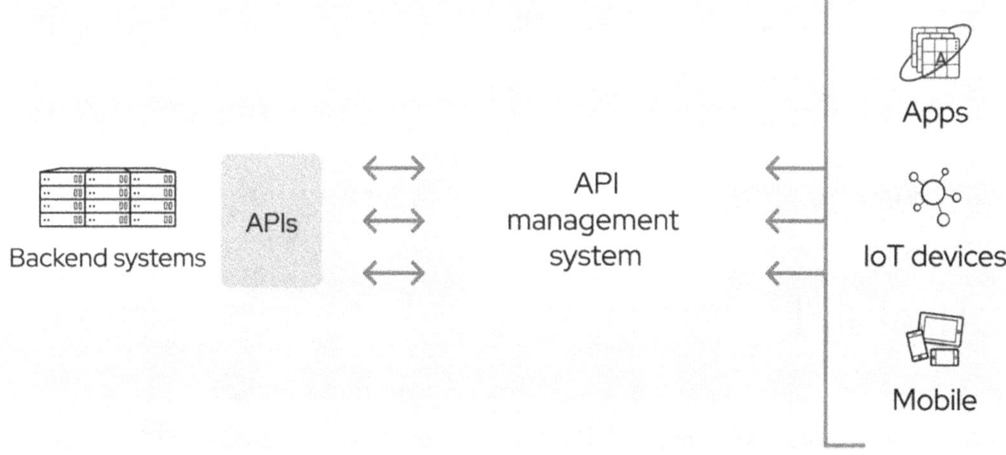

G. Patil, *Django REST APIs Demystified*, https://doi.org/10.1007/979-8-8688-1850-9_1

APIs can be classified into three types:

1. Private
2. Public
3. Partner

Private API

Private APIs are APIs that are intended for internal use within an organization or a specific application. They are not publicly available or accessible to external developers or users. Private APIs are commonly used to enable communication between different components or services within a system or to expose functionality within an organization's infrastructure.

Public API

Public APIs, also known as Open APIs, are APIs that are made available to external developers and the general public. Public APIs allow third-party developers to integrate their applications, services, or platforms with the API provider's system or data. They typically have documentation, usage guidelines, and developer resources to facilitate integration by external parties.

Examples of public APIs include social media APIs (e.g., Twitter API, Facebook Graph API), payment gateway APIs (e.g., PayPal API), and mapping APIs (e.g., Google Maps API).

Partner API

Partner APIs are APIs that are provided to specific partners or trusted entities for integration purposes. They are accessible only to authorized partners who have a business relationship or agreement with the API provider. They may offer additional features or privileged access compared to public APIs. Partner APIs are commonly used for integrating with trusted third-party services, building value-added services, or enabling collaboration between organizations.

It's important to note that the specific definitions and distinctions between these types of APIs can vary depending on the context and the organization providing the APIs. The access levels and capabilities of an API can be defined and managed by the API provider based on their specific requirements and policies.

There are several types of APIs based on their architectural styles and communication protocols. Here are some common types of APIs.

RESTful APIs (Representational State Transfer)

RESTful APIs are based on the principles of REST, which is an architectural style for designing networked applications. They use standard HTTP methods like GET, POST, PUT, and DELETE to perform operations on resources identified by URLs (Uniform Resource Locators).

RESTful APIs typically return data in formats like JSON (JavaScript Object Notation) or XML (Extensible Markup Language). They are widely used for web development due to their simplicity, scalability, and statelessness.

SOAP APIs (Simple Object Access Protocol)

SOAP is a protocol for exchanging structured information in web services using XML. SOAP APIs define an XML-based message format and communication protocol for remote procedure calls (RPC) between systems. They often use the HTTP or HTTPS protocol for transport and provide functionality for defining complex data structures, security, and error handling.

GraphQL APIs

GraphQL is a query language and runtime for APIs developed by Facebook. They allow clients to request specific data fields and shape the response according to their needs. Clients can send a single request to the GraphQL API endpoint, specifying the desired data structure, and receive a response containing exactly what was requested. GraphQL APIs provide more flexibility to clients by reducing over-fetching or under-fetching of data.

JSON-RPC and XML-RPC APIs

JSON-RPC (JavaScript Object Notation-RPC) and XML-RPC (Extensible Markup Language-RPC) are remote procedure call (RPC) protocols using JSON and XML formats, respectively. They allow clients to invoke methods on a remote server by sending requests with method names and parameters and receiving responses with results. JSON-RPC and XML-RPC APIs are relatively simple and lightweight compared to other API types.

WebSocket APIs

WebSocket APIs provide full-duplex communication channels over a single TCP connection. They enable real-time, bidirectional communication between clients and servers, allowing server-initiated updates and eliminating the need for frequent polling. WebSocket APIs are commonly used for applications requiring real-time data updates, such as chat applications or live dashboards.

gRPC APIs

gRPC stands for Google Remote Procedure Call, and it is an open source framework developed by Google for building high-performance, language-agnostic APIs. It uses Protocol Buffers (protobuf) as the interface definition language and provides features like bidirectional streaming, authentication, and flow control. gRPC APIs are designed for efficient communication between microservices and can be used in a wide range of programming languages.

These are some of the most widely used types of APIs. Each type has its own strengths and use cases, and the choice of API type depends on the specific requirements of your application.

In this book, we are concentrating on developing REST API using the Django framework.

CHAPTER 2

REST API Concepts

REST is an acronym for Representational State Transfer. REST API is an architectural style for designing networked applications, particularly web services. It defines a set of constraints and principles that enable communication between different systems over the internet. If we design an API using REST architecture, that API is called REST API.

Before getting into REST APIs, let us understand some of the terms commonly used in REST Framework.

Web APIs

Web APIs, also known as HTTP APIs or RESTful APIs, are APIs that are accessed over the web using the HTTP protocol. They allow applications to request and exchange data using standard HTTP methods such as GET, POST, PUT, and DELETE. Web APIs are widely used for building web applications, mobile apps, and integrating different systems.

Endpoint

It is a specific URL or URI (Uniform Resource Identifier) that corresponds to a specific resource or functionality of the API. Each endpoint typically represents a specific operation or data entity that the API provides access to.

The API might have an endpoint like `https://api.weather.com/forecast`. This endpoint is responsible for retrieving weather forecasts.

G. Patil, *Django REST APIs Demystified*, https://doi.org/10.1007/979-8-8688-1850-9_2

HTTP Methods

HTTP methods, also known as HTTP verbs, are used to indicate the type of operation being performed on a resource through an API.

The most common HTTP methods used in web APIs are as follows.

GET Method

The primary purpose of an HTTP GET request is to retrieve data from a server. It is used when a client wants to access or fetch a specific resource or information from a server. GET requests commonly include parameters appended to the URL as a query string. Parameters are key-value pairs separated by ampersands (&).

For example: `https://example.com/api/data?key1=value1&key2=value2`. The server can use these parameters to provide specific data or filter the response.

Unlike other HTTP methods like POST or PUT, a GET request does not include a request body. The parameters or data associated with the request are usually sent as part of the URL itself.

POST Method

The primary purpose of an HTTP POST request is to submit or send data to a server for processing or storage. It is used when a client wants to create a new resource, update an existing resource, or perform other actions that involve sending data to the server.

Unlike an HTTP GET request, a POST request includes a request body that carries the data being sent to the server. The data can be in various formats such as JSON, XML, form data, or binary data, depending on the requirements of the server-side application. The data to be sent is encapsulated within the request body. It can contain any necessary parameters, fields, or content that the server expects for the requested action or operation.

POST requests are commonly used when submitting sensitive or confidential data, such as user credentials or payment information. It is important to ensure the use of secure connections (HTTPS) and proper authentication and authorization mechanisms to protect the transmitted data.

PUT Method

The primary purpose of an HTTP PUT request is to update or replace an existing resource on the server. It is used when a client wants to modify the state or content of a resource with a new representation provided in the request.

Similar to an HTTP POST request, a PUT request includes a request body that carries the data being sent to the server. The data contains the new representation of the resource to be updated or replaced. When making a PUT request, the client typically sends the complete representation of the resource, including any unchanged fields. The server uses this complete representation to update or replace the existing resource.

PATCH Method

The primary purpose of an HTTP PATCH request is to perform a partial update on an existing resource. It is used when a client wants to modify specific fields or properties of a resource without sending the complete representation of the resource.

Similar to an HTTP PUT request, a PATCH request includes a request body that carries the data being sent to the server. The data contains the changes or updates to be applied to the resource. Unlike a PUT request, which typically replaces the entire resource, a PATCH request only modifies the specific fields or properties specified in the request body. Other fields or properties not included in the request body remain unchanged. When making a PATCH request, the client does not need to provide the complete representation of the resource. It can send only the fields or properties that require updating, minimizing the amount of data sent over the network.

DELETE Method

The primary purpose of an HTTP DELETE request is to request the removal or deletion of a specific resource on the server. It is used when a client wants to delete a resource permanently. An HTTP DELETE request typically does not include a request body. Since the request is focused on resource deletion, no additional data is needed in the request body. The DELETE request is sent to a specific URL that represents the resource to be deleted. The server identifies and deletes the corresponding resource based on the URL provided.

Other Methods

In addition to the commonly used HTTP methods described above, there are other methods defined by the HTTP specification, such as HEAD and OPTIONS. These methods are typically used in more advanced scenarios—for example, HEAD is used to fetch response headers without the response body, and OPTIONS is used to determine what HTTP methods and operations are supported by the server at a specific endpoint.

These methods are less commonly used in everyday API development and are therefore not covered in depth in this book. Readers interested in these methods can refer to the HTTP specification or relevant API documentation for further details.

HTTP Request

An HTTP request is a message sent by a client to a server using the Hypertext Transfer Protocol (HTTP). It is the fundamental means of communication between clients (such as web browsers or applications) and servers on the World Wide Web.

An HTTP request consists of several components:

1. **HTTP Methods**
2. **Request URL**: The Uniform Resource Locator (URL) or Uniform Resource Identifier (URI) specifies the location and identifier of the requested resource. It typically consists of a protocol (e.g., "http://" or "https://"), domain name or IP address, and optional path, query parameters, or fragment identifier.
3. **Request Headers**: HTTP headers provide additional information about the request or the client to the server. They include details such as the client's User-Agent, Accept-Language, Content-Type, and more. Headers can be used for authentication, content negotiation, caching directives, and other purposes.
4. **Request Body (Optional)**: In certain HTTP methods like POST, PUT, or PATCH, a request body can be included to send data to the server. The request body contains the payload or content being sent, typically in a specified format such as JSON, XML, or form data.

5. **Cookies (Optional)**: HTTP requests can include cookies, which are small pieces of data stored by the client and sent to the server with each request. Cookies are often used for session management, user authentication, and tracking user preferences.

HTTP Response

An HTTP response is a message sent by a server to a client in response to an HTTP request. It is the server's way of communicating the outcome of the request and providing the requested data or other relevant information.

An HTTP response consists of several components:

1. **Response Status Line**: The response status line includes the HTTP version, a numeric status code, and a brief textual description of the status. The status code indicates the outcome of the request, such as success, redirection, client or server errors, or other conditions.

2. **Response Headers**: HTTP response headers provide additional information about the response, server, and requested resource. They include details such as Content-Type, Content-Length, Cache-Control, Set-Cookie, and more. Headers can provide instructions for caching, content negotiation, security, and other purposes.

3. **Response Body**: The response body contains the actual content or data requested by the client. The format and content of the response body depend on the server's implementation and the nature of the requested resource. It can be HTML, JSON, XML, binary data, or any other supported format.

4. **Cookies (Optional)**: HTTP responses can include cookies, which are small pieces of data sent by the server and stored by the client. Cookies can be used for session management, user authentication, and other purposes. The client typically includes these cookies in subsequent requests.

5. **Other Meta-information**: Depending on the specific circumstances and server configuration, an HTTP response may include additional meta-information. This can include response time, server version details, security-related headers, and more.

Request Parameters

API endpoints often accept parameters that provide additional information to customize the request or specify the desired data. Parameters can be sent as part of the URL (query parameters) or in the body of the request (request body parameters).

For example, the location=NewYork part in the URL is a query parameter that specifies the location for which the forecast is requested. API endpoints often accept various parameters to customize the request.

Overall, REST architecture follows a certain set of rules for endpoints, methods, headers, and data. Whenever an API interaction occurs, the client sends a request and the server sends a response. Request may be any of the above-specified HTTP methods. APIs can be configured to send a response in any configured format, either JSON or XML format. We will look into them using examples in the later chapters.

REST APIs are stateless, meaning that the server does not store any client session information. Each request from the client to the server contains all the necessary information for the server to understand and process the request. The server does not maintain any client context between requests. These APIs expose resources, which are the fundamental entities or data entities that clients can interact with. Resources are typically identified by unique URLs (Uniform Resource Locators) or URIs (Uniform Resource Identifiers).

REST APIs follow the four basic CRUD operations: Create, Read, Update, and Delete. These operations map to the standard HTTP methods such as POST, GET, PUT/PATCH, and DELETE, respectively. Each method performs a specific action on a resource. They use a uniform and consistent interface for interacting with resources. They adhere to standard HTTP methods and utilize HTTP status codes to indicate the result of a request. They also leverage standard data formats, such as JSON (JavaScript Object Notation) or XML (Extensible Markup Language), for representing and exchanging data. REST APIs separate the concerns between the client and the server. The server is responsible for handling requests and processing data, while the client is responsible for the user interface and user experience.

REST APIs provide a scalable and interoperable approach to building distributed systems. They are widely used in web development to expose and consume data and services across different platforms, devices, and technologies. APIs that adhere to the principles of REST are commonly referred to as RESTful APIs.

CHAPTER 3

Project Configuration

In this section, we start our journey into Django REST Framework. In this chapter, we are setting up the project for API development using Django.

Environment

We are using the following environment for the project setup:

Ubuntu 22.04.5 LTS

Python 3.12

Django 5.1.2

Django REST Framework 3.15.2

VSCode

Below extensions on VSCode:

- Python Extension Pack
- Tabnine AI Code Completion For Enterprise

Please make sure the above virtual environment is set up and the required packages are installed. We provided requirements.txt along with the project in the GitHub repository for your reference for the list of modules installed for the project.

The repository is organized to refer to each chapter. As we go through each chapter, you can refer to the corresponding Django apps in the repo. For example, for this chapter, you can refer to the chapter3 app on the repo.

G. Patil, *Django REST APIs Demystified*, https://doi.org/10.1007/979-8-8688-1850-9_3

Project Overview

The Django REST Framework project used throughout this book is structured to progressively demonstrate key DRF concepts. The base project is named drfproject, and it contains an application called chapter3_project_setup, which defines the core data models: StreamPlatform, WatchList, and Review. These models represent a simple streaming service domain and serve as the foundation for all subsequent examples. As new chapters are introduced, additional applications are created to explain specific DRF features such as serialization, authentication, permissions, throttling, pagination, and viewsets. However, all these features are demonstrated using the base models defined in the chapter3_project_setup app to maintain consistency and focus on the DRF concepts rather than expanding the data model itself.

Project Setup

Follow the below steps to create a project on your machine:

1. Create a virtual environment on Ubuntu with the below command:

   ```
   conda create --name drf_book_env python=3.12
   ```

2. Activate the virtual environment:

   ```
   conda activate drf_book_env
   ```

3. Install the packages:

   ```
   pip install django==5.1.2
   pip install djangorestframework==3.15.2
   ```

4. Create a Django project:

   ```
   django-admin startproject drfproject
   ```

5. Get into the drfproject directory, and create an app chapter3_project_setup as below:

```
cd drfproject
python manage.py startapp chapter3_project_setup
```

6. Make sure that "rest_framework" and the created app name are added to INSTALLED_APPS in drfproject/settings.py as below:

```
INSTALLED_APPS = [
    'django.contrib.admin',
    'django.contrib.auth',
    'django.contrib.contenttypes',
    'django.contrib.sessions',
    'django.contrib.messages',
    'django.contrib.staticfiles',
    'rest_framework',
    "chapter3_project_setup",
]
```

7. Perform migrations:

```
Python manage.py migrate
```

8. Create a super user using the required details like username, email, and password, so you can log in to the admin to see the created objects:

```
python manage.py createsuperuser apiuser
```

9. Now go to the watchlist_app/models.py file, and create the below models:

```
from django.db import models
from django.core.validators import MinValueValidator,
MaxValueValidator
from django.contrib.auth.models import User

CATEGORY_CHOICES = (
```

```
        ("MOVIE", "MOVIE"),
        ("SERIES", "SERIES"),
    )

    # Create your models here.
    class StreamPlatform(models.Model):
        name = models.CharField(max_length=30)
        about = models.CharField(max_length=150)
        website = models.URLField(max_length=100)

        class Meta:
            verbose_name = "Stream Platform"
            verbose_name_plural = "Stream Platforms"

        def __str__(self):
            return self.name

    class WatchList(models.Model):
        title = models.CharField(max_length=50)
        storyline = models.CharField(max_length=200)
        platform = models.ForeignKey("StreamPlatform",
        on_delete=models.CASCADE, related_name="watchlist")
        active = models.BooleanField(default=True)
        imdb_rating = models.FloatField(default=0)
        created = models.DateTimeField(auto_now_add=True)
        episodes = models.IntegerField(default=0)
        category = models.CharField("Category",
                                    max_length=30,
                                    blank=True,
                                    null=True,
                                    choices=CATEGORY_CHOICES,
                                    help_text="Watchlist
                                    category")

        class Meta:
            verbose_name = "Watch List"
            verbose_name_plural = "Watchlists"
```

```
    def __str__(self):
        return self.title

    @property
    def full_title(self):
        if(self.category=="MOVIE"):
            full_title = f"Movie Name: {self.title}"
        else:
            full_title = f"Series Name: {self.title}"
        return full_title

class Review(models.Model):
    review_user = models.ForeignKey(User, on_delete=models.
                  CASCADE)
    rating = models.PositiveIntegerField(validators=[MinValu
             eValidator(1), MaxValueValidator(5)])
    description = models.CharField(max_length=200,
                  null=True)
    watchlist = models.ForeignKey(WatchList,
                on_delete=models.CASCADE,
                related_name="reviews")
    active = models.BooleanField(default=True)
    created = models.DateTimeField(auto_now_add=True)
    update = models.DateTimeField(auto_now=True)
    review_date = models.DateField()

    class Meta:
        verbose_name = "Review"
        verbose_name_plural = "Reviews"

    def __str__(self):
        return str(self.rating) + " | " + self.watchlist.
        title + " | " + str(self.review_user)
```

10. Go to chapter3_project_setup/admin.py, and register all the created models into the admin:

```
from django.contrib import admin
from .models import WatchList, StreamPlatform, Review

# Register your models here.
admin.site.register(WatchList, WatchListAdmin)
admin.site.register(StreamPlatform)
admin.site.register(Review)
```

11. Do migrations again since we created new models:

```
python manage.py makemigrations
python manage.py migrate
```

12. Now run the Django server using the below command in the local environment:

```
python manage.py runserver
```

In the above example, we have created Django models to work on with our project. For more information on Django models, you can refer to the link: `https://docs.djangoproject.com/en/5.1/topics/db/models/`.

`In the above example, we have created 3 models such as` **`Watchlist, StreamPlatform`** `and` **`Review.`**

Now we have set up a project for our Django journey. Until now, it is all related to Django concepts. Now we are entering the Django REST Framework world. So, what is Django REST Framework and why it is used and how? Let's discuss all these details in the coming chapters.

CHAPTER 4

Django REST Framework

Django REST Framework (DRF) is a powerful and flexible framework for building web APIs (Application Programming Interfaces) using Django, a popular Python web framework. DRF provides a set of tools and libraries that make it easier to build, test, and consume RESTful APIs in Django-based applications.

Some key features and components of Django REST Framework are as follows.

Serialization and Deserialization

Serialization is a process of converting complex data types, like a queryset, to native data types like a dictionary. DRF provides a robust serialization framework that allows you to convert complex data models and querysets into Python data types (such as dictionaries or JSON) and vice versa. It simplifies the process of transforming data to be easily consumed by API clients.

Deserialization is the process of converting Python native data types to complex data types. So both actions are accomplished with the same serializer. Basically, when we call a serializer with parameter data (like serializer=Serializer(data=data_dict)), it returns a complex object. And when we call it with a complex object, it gives a dictionary.

Viewsets and Serializers

DRF offers viewsets and serializers as higher-level abstractions for building API views. Viewsets provide reusable logic for common CRUD (Create, Retrieve, Update, Delete) operations, while serializers handle the serialization and deserialization of data. They provide a clean and concise way to define API endpoints and data representation.

G. Patil, *Django REST APIs Demystified*, https://doi.org/10.1007/979-8-8688-1850-9_4

Authentication and Permissions

DRF includes various authentication methods such as token-based authentication, session-based authentication, and OAuth support. It also provides fine-grained permissions to control access to API endpoints based on user roles, groups, or other custom logic.

URL Routing and View Dispatching

DRF integrates with Django's URL routing system to define API URLs and map them to corresponding viewsets. It supports nested routing, custom URL patterns, and automatic generation of URL patterns based on the viewsets and routers.

Request/Response Handling

DRF handles incoming requests and outgoing responses in a standardized way. It provides request parsers and response renderers that handle content negotiation and support multiple data formats like JSON, XML, or HTML. It also includes features for handling file uploads.

Pagination and Filtering

DRF supports pagination and provides flexible options to paginate large result sets in API responses. It also includes filtering capabilities to allow clients to filter and search data based on specific criteria.

Content Negotiation

DRF supports content negotiation, allowing the API to respond with different data formats based on the client's requested format. It can automatically render responses as JSON, XML, HTML, or other formats based on the request's content negotiation headers.

Testing and Documentation

DRF includes extensive testing tools and utilities to help you write test cases for your APIs. It also integrates with popular API documentation tools like Swagger and provides its own web-browsable API interface for exploring and interacting with APIs.

Why Django REST Framework

DRF is built on top of Django, which is a mature and widely adopted web framework in the Python ecosystem. DRF leverages many of Django's features and components, such as the ORM (Object-Relational Mapping) for database access, an authentication system, and URL routing. This tight integration with Django makes it seamless to incorporate DRF into existing Django projects and leverage the rich ecosystem of Django packages.

It provides a comprehensive set of features and tools to simplify the development of RESTful APIs. It offers powerful serialization, viewsets, and serializers that enable rapid API development with minimal code. DRF also includes features like authentication, permissions, pagination, filtering, content negotiation, and more. These built-in functionalities save development time and effort, allowing developers to focus on building the core API logic.

DRF is designed to be highly flexible and customizable. It provides various extension points and hooks to override and customize its behavior to suit specific project requirements. Developers can define custom authentication schemes, permissions, serializers, and other components to tailor the API behavior according to their needs. This flexibility makes DRF suitable for a wide range of use cases and project complexities.

DRF has extensive and well-structured documentation, making it easy to learn and use. The documentation covers everything from getting started guides to advanced topics and best practices. DRF also has an active and supportive community, with a large user base and contributors. The community provides assistance, shares knowledge, and contributes to the continuous improvement of DRF.

DRF has gained significant traction in the industry and is widely adopted by organizations of all sizes, from startups to large enterprises. It has been battle-tested in numerous production environments, making it a reliable choice for building robust and scalable APIs. The stability and maturity of DRF make it a dependable framework for long-term projects.

DRF plays well with popular front-end JavaScript frameworks like React, Vue.js, and Angular. It supports various authentication mechanisms, such as token-based authentication or JWT (JSON Web Tokens), which are commonly used for securing API endpoints in front-end applications. The compatibility between DRF and front-end frameworks facilitates the development of full-stack applications.

While there are other frameworks available for building web APIs in Python, Django REST Framework stands out due to its integration with Django, comprehensive feature set, flexibility, extensive documentation, strong community support, industry adoption, and seamless integration with front-end frameworks. Ultimately, the choice of a web API framework depends on the specific project requirements, familiarity with the ecosystem, and the development team's preferences and expertise.

CHAPTER 5

Postman

Postman is an Application Programming Interface (API) testing tool. API acts like an interface between a couple of applications and establishes a connection between them.

Thus, an API is a collection of agreements, functions, and tools that an application can provide to its users for successful communication with another application. We require an API whenever we access an application like checking news over the phone, Facebook, and so on.

Postman was designed in the year 2012 by software developer and entrepreneur Abhinav Asthana to make API development and testing straightforward. It is a tool for testing the software of an API. It can be used to design, document, verify, create, and change APIs.

Postman has the feature of sending and observing the Hypertext Transfer Protocol (HTTP) requests and responses. It has a graphical user interface (GUI) and can be used on platforms like Linux, Windows, and Mac. It can build multiple HTTP requests—POST, PUT, GET, and PATCH—and translate them to code.

Why Use Postman?

- **Ease of Use**: Its intuitive interface allows users to make API calls without writing code.
- **API Testing**: Developers can test the functionality, performance, and security of APIs.
- **Automation**: Test collections can be automated using Postman's built-in scripting tools and Newman, its command-line companion.
- **Collaboration**: Postman enables teams to share APIs, test cases, and documentation easily.

G. Patil, *Django REST APIs Demystified*, https://doi.org/10.1007/979-8-8688-1850-9_5

- **Integration**: It supports integrations with CI/CD pipelines, version control systems, and other tools.
- **Dynamic Environments**: Postman allows the use of variables, making it easier to manage multiple environments (e.g., development, staging, production).

Since this book is concentrating on DRF, it only provides brief information about Postman. But you can refer to the link `https://learning.postman.com/docs/introduction/overview/` for complete details on using the Postman tool for API testing. In our project, we are going to use Postman to make API calls. Before going further with the remaining chapters, please go through the Postman reference link.

CHAPTER 6

Serializers and Views

A serializer in DRF is a class that defines the transformation between complex data structures and simpler representations. It provides a set of rules for converting complex data types into a format suitable for transmitting over the network, usually as JSON. The serializer determines how the data is represented when it is rendered as a response, as well as how it is deserialized when it is received as a request.

Serializers define the structure and format of the response data. They specify which fields to include, how they should be represented, and any transformations or formatting applied to the data. They can enforce validation rules on the incoming data during deserialization. They define fields, field types, and validation constraints, ensuring that the received data adheres to the specified format and requirements. Serializers support representing nested relationships between objects. They can handle relationships such as one-to-one, one-to-many, and many-to-many, allowing for easy serialization and deserialization of related data.

Using Serializer Fields

Like standard model field classes in Django, DRF also provides a number of serializer field classes that are available to use. The following table can be used as a reference when writing serializers:

G. Patil, *Django REST APIs Demystified*, https://doi.org/10.1007/979-8-8688-1850-9_6

BooleanField	CharField	ChoiceField
DateField	DateTimeField	DecimalField
DictField	DurationField	EmailField
Field	FileField	FilePathField
FloatField	HiddenField	HStoreField
IPAddressField	ImageField	IntegerField
JSONField	ListField	ModelField
MultipleChoiceField	ReadOnlyField	RegexField
SerializerMethodField	SlugField	TimeField
URLField	UUIDField	

For detailed information on core arguments and each field-related argument, please refer to `https://www.django-rest-framework.org/api-guide/fields/#custom-fields`.

Preparing for This Chapter

Create a new app with the name **chapter6_serializers_views** with steps specified in the **Project Setup** section in Chapter 3.

Go to drfproject/settings.py and add the following lines of code:

```
INSTALLED_APPS = [
    ...
    "chapter6_serializers_views",
]
```

Create chapter6_serializers_views/api/serializers.py and add the following lines of code:

```
from rest_framework import serializers
from django.contrib.auth import get_user_model
from chapter3_project_setup.models import WatchList, StreamPlatform, Review

User = get_user_model()
```

Go to chapter6_serializers_views/api/views.py and add the following lines of code:

```
from rest_framework.views import APIView
from rest_framework.response import Response
from rest_framework import status
from rest_framework import generics
from chapter3_project_setup.models import WatchList, Review, StreamPlatform
from chapter6_serializers_views.api import serializers
```

Create chapter6_serializers_views/api/urls.py and add the following lines of code:

```
from django.urls import path
from chapter6_serializers_views.api import views

urlpatterns = [

]
```

Go to drfproject/urls.py and add the following lines of code:

```
urlpatterns = [
    ...
    path('api/chapter6_serializers_views/', include('chapter6_serializers_
    views.api.urls')),
]
```

We are adding this URL redirection to route all the requests related to this application to the application's urls.py file created within the application's api folder.

Create a Serializer

Now let's try to understand a simple scenario, where the business wants only the title, storyline, and whether it is active—like whether it is broadcasted. For this, we need to send a response with these three fields from the database even though there are many fields on the Watchlist model.

Let's go one by one to understand the underlying concepts to achieve this.

Create a serializer in chapter6_serializers_views/api/serializers.py and add the following lines of code:

```
class WatchlistSerializer(serializers.Serializer):
    title = serializers.CharField(max_length=30)
    storyline = serializers.CharField(max_length=200)
    active = serializers.BooleanField()
```

The above serializer defines the structure and format of the response data. Now we need to use this serializer in views to make it use to create an API. Let's understand about Django REST Framework Views.

Views

Django REST Framework provides two types of views, just like Django:

1. Class-based views
2. Function-based views

Class-Based Views

Class-based views (CBVs) provide a powerful and flexible way to define API views. Class-based views offer reusable and organized code through inheritance and mixins, allowing for better code structure and separation of concerns. REST Framework provides an APIView class, which subclasses Django's View class.

APIView classes are different from regular View classes in the following ways:

- Requests passed to the handler methods will be REST Framework's **Request** instances, not Django's **HttpRequest** instances.
- Handler methods may return REST Framework's **Response**, instead of Django's **HttpResponse**. The view will manage content negotiation and setting the correct renderer on the response.
- Any **APIException** exceptions will be caught and mediated into appropriate responses.
- Incoming requests will be authenticated, and appropriate permission and/or throttle checks will be run before dispatching the request to the handler method.

Using the **APIView** class is pretty much the same as using a regular Django **View** class. As usual, the incoming request is dispatched to an appropriate handler method, such as **.get()** or **.post()**. Additionally, a number of attributes may be set on the class that control various aspects of the API policy.

In addition to the basic APIView, DRF provides various mixins and generic views that can be used in combination with class-based views to achieve common functionalities and handle common use cases. These mixins and generic views provide additional features such as authentication, permission handling, filtering, pagination, and more.

Class-based views in DRF offer a structured and reusable way to define API views. They are particularly useful for complex views that require more advanced functionality and can provide a clean and organized code base for building APIs.

Function-Based Views

Function-based views (FBVs) provide a way to define API views using regular Python functions. Function-based views are an alternative to class-based views and offer simplicity and flexibility in defining API endpoints. REST Framework also allows you to work with regular function-based views. It provides a set of simple decorators that wrap your function-based views to ensure they receive an instance of Request (rather than the usual Django **HttpRequest**) and allows them to return a Response (instead of a Django HttpResponse) and allows you to configure how the request is processed. The **@api_view** decorator is used to indicate that the function-based view should be treated as an API view. The decorator also specifies the HTTP methods that the view can handle, such as **"GET"** and **"POST"** in this case.

We can discuss in detail about function-based views in later sections of this chapter.

Implement Class-Based View for the Project

Let's use class-based view to implement the above business logic we discussed.

Go to chapter6_serializers_views/api/views.py and add the following lines of code:

```
#=====================Views Using Basic Serializer======================
class WatchlistBasicSerializerView(APIView):
    """
    View to list all Movies in the system.
    """
```

```
    def get(self, request, format=None):
        """
        Return a list of all watchlist.
        """
        watchlist = WatchList.objects.all()
        serializer = serializers.WatchlistSerializer(watchlist, many =
        True, context={'request': request})
        return Response(serializer.data)
```

In the above example, the **WatchlistBasicSerializerView** class is derived from the **APIView** class provided by DRF. Each HTTP method that the view should handle is defined as a separate method within the class, such as **get()** and **post()**. These methods correspond to the respective HTTP methods for handling GET and POST requests. Inside each method, you can implement the custom logic for the specific request method. The request object is accessible as the first argument of each method, allowing you to access information about the request and process the data accordingly. The response can be generated using the Response class provided by DRF.

Don't forget to import all the required modules on top of the file. In this view, when the request method is GET, then the above view function retrieves all the objects from the Watchlist model and sends them to WatchlistSerializer to convert complex queryset data into simple JSON format. We are specifying **many=True** here, since it is serializing a queryset. We should specify **many=False**, if it is a single object. JSON-formatted data is stored in a serializer.data variable which is returned using Response.

Now go to chapter6_serializers_views/api/urls.py and add the following lines of code:

```
urlpatterns = [
    # Using Basic Serializer for the views
    path('watchlist-basic-serializer/', views.WatchlistBasicSerializerView.
    as_view(), name="watchlist-basic-serializer"),
```

There are no objects in the database now. To create some data, log in to admin and create some objects on the Watchlist and Platform models.

Now all project setups are ready to test the business logic. To access the API endpoint on Postman, the request shall be in the format:

```
GET {{domain}}/api/chapter6_serializers_views/watchlist-basic-serializer/
```

where {{domain}} is **http://127.0.0.1:8000** if you are running on the local environment.

Its response will be in the below format:

```
[
    {
        "title": "Movie1",
        "storyline": "Movie1-Story",
        "active": true
    },
    ...
]
```

Now we understand how the API development flow works with simple business logic.

Serializer Advanced Concepts

Now let us go deeper into understanding the serializer.

Nested Serializer

A nested serializer in Django REST Framework (DRF) allows you to represent and handle relationships between different models or data structures within a single serializer. It provides a way to serialize and deserialize related objects, enabling you to work with hierarchical or nested data structures. Nested serializers are useful when dealing with complex data relationships and when you want to include related data in the serialization process.

Let us implement a serializer for the StreamPlatform model in our project. Go to chapter6_serializers_views/api/serializers.py and add the following lines of code:

```
class StreamPlatformSerializer(serializers.Serializer):
    name = serializers.CharField(max_length=30)
    about = serializers.CharField(max_length=150)
    website = serializers.URLField(max_length=100)
```

Now update **WatchlistSerializer** to include all the fields of the Watchlist model as below:

```
class WatchlistSerializer(serializers.Serializer):
    title = serializers.CharField(max_length=30)
    storyline = serializers.CharField(max_length=200)
    active = serializers.BooleanField()
    platform = StreamPlatformSerializer()
    imdb_rating = serializers.FloatField(default=0)
    created = serializers.DateTimeField()
    episodes = serializers.IntegerField(default=0)
    category = serializers.CharField(max_length=30)
```

If you notice in the above WatchlistSerializer, the platform field is assigned with StreamPlatformSerializer. This means that we are instructing DRF to provide StreamPlatform information in the Watchlist data. This approach is called a nested serializer.

In the above example, **StreamPlatformSerializer** represents the serialization and deserialization logic for the **StreamPlatform** model or data structure. The **WatchlistSerializer** includes the platform field as an instance of the **StreamPlatformSerializer**. This allows you to handle the parent-child relationship and serialize/deserialize the related child objects as nested data within the parent serializer.

Relational Fields

In Django REST Framework (DRF), relation fields are serializer fields that represent relationships between different models or data structures. They allow you to handle related objects and their relationships in your serializers. DRF provides several relation fields to handle different types of relationships. You can refer to `https://www.django-rest-framework.org/api-guide/relations/` to understand arguments and fields on relational fields.

PrimaryKeyRelatedField

This field represents a relationship by using the primary key of the related object. It can be used for relationships like ForeignKey or OneToOneField. By default, it renders as an integer representing the related object's primary key.

Now let us create a ReviewSerializer. Go to chapter6_serializers_views/api/serializers.py and add the following lines of code:

```
class ReviewSerializer(serializers.Serializer):
    review_user = serializers.PrimaryKeyRelatedField(
        queryset=User.objects.all()
    )
    rating = serializers.IntegerField()
    description = serializers.CharField(max_length=200)
    watchlist = WatchlistSerializer()
    active = serializers.BooleanField()
    created = serializers.DateTimeField()
    update = serializers.DateTimeField()
```

In the above example, the review_user field is formatted with type PrimarykeyRelatedField(). In the serializer output, this field is always assigned the primary key of the user.

Go to chapter6_serializers_views/api/views.py and add the following lines of code:

```
class ReviewlistBasicSerializerView(APIView):
    """
    View to list all Reviews in the system.
    """
    def get(self, request, format=None):
        """
        Return a list of all watchlist.
        """
        reviews = Review.objects.all()
        serializer = serializers.ReviewSerializer(reviews, many = True)
        return Response(serializer.data)
```

Go to chapter6_serializers_views/api/urls.py and add the following lines of code:

```
urlpatterns = [
    ...
    path('reviewlist-basic-serializer/', views.ReviewlistBasicSerializer
    View.as_view(), name="reviewlist-basic-serializer"),
    ...
]
```

To access the API endpoint on Postman, the request shall be in the format:

```
GET {{domain}}/api/chapter6_serializers_views/reviewlist-basic-serializer/
```

Its response will be in the below format:


```
[
    {
        "review_user": 9,
        "rating": 3,
        "description": "good movie",
        "watchlist": {
            "title": "Movie1",
            "storyline": "Movie1-Story",
            "active": true,
            "platform": {
                "name": "Netflix",
                "about": "Netflix About",
                "website": "https://www.netflix.com"
            },
            "imdb_rating": 2.0,
            "created": "2024-10-26T20:06:27.406145Z",
            "episodes": 0,
            "category": "MOVIE"
        },
        "active": true,
        "created": "2024-11-16T22:16:10.772881Z",
        "update": "2024-11-16T22:16:10.772903Z"
    },
    ...
]
```

StringRelatedField

This field represents a relationship by using the string representation of the related object instead of its primary key or other fields. It can be used for relationships like **ForeignKey** or **OneToOneField**. It renders the string representation of the related object. The StringRelatedField is read-only, meaning it is used for serialization but not for deserialization.

The StringRelatedField is particularly useful when you want to represent relationships in a human-readable form or when the related model has a meaningful string representation that you want to include in the serialized output.

For demo purposes, we can change the platform field of WatchlistSerializer in the file chapter6_serializers_views/api/serializers.py as below:

```
class WatchlistSerializer(serializers.Serializer):
    title = serializers.CharField(max_length=30)
    storyline = serializers.CharField(max_length=200)
    active = serializers.BooleanField()
    # platform = StreamPlatformSerializer()
    platform = serializers.StringRelatedField()
    imdb_rating = serializers.FloatField(default=0)
    created = serializers.DateTimeField()
    episodes = serializers.IntegerField(default=0)
    category = serializers.CharField(max_length=30)
```

To access the API endpoint on Postman, the request shall be in the format:

```
GET {{domain}}/api/chapter6_serializers_views/watchlist-basic-serializer/
```

Its response will be in the below format:

```
[
    {
        "title": "Movie1",
        "storyline": "Movie1-Story",
        "active": true,
        "platform": "Netflix",
        "imdb_rating": 2.0,
        "created": "2024-10-26T20:06:27.406145Z",
```

```
        "episodes": 0,
        "category": "MOVIE"
    },
]
```

HyperlinkedRelatedField

This field represents a relationship by using a hyperlink to the related object. It can be used for relationships like **ForeignKey** or **OneToOneField**. It allows you to include hyperlinks to related resources instead of using the related object's primary key or other fields.

The HyperlinkedRelatedField is primarily used to enhance the navigability and discoverability of your API. By including hyperlinks to related resources, clients can easily navigate to associated resources by following the provided links.

For demo purposes, we can change the platform field of WatchlistSerializer in the file chapter6_serializers_views/api/serializers.py as below:

```
class WatchlistSerializer(serializers.Serializer):
    title = serializers.CharField(max_length=30)
    storyline = serializers.CharField(max_length=200)
    active = serializers.BooleanField()
    # platform = StreamPlatformSerializer()
    # platform = serializers.StringRelatedField()
    platform = serializers.HyperlinkedRelatedField(view_name='stream
    platform-detail-basic-serializer', read_only=True)
    imdb_rating = serializers.FloatField(default=0)
    created = serializers.DateTimeField()
    episodes = serializers.IntegerField(default=0)
    category = serializers.CharField(max_length=30)
```

To make **HyperlinkedRelatedField** work for this project, we also need to create a detailed view for the **StreamPlatform** model.

Go to chapter6_serializers_views/api/views.py and add the following lines of code:

```
class StreamPlatformBasicSerializerView(APIView):
    """
    Stream Platform Using Basic Serializer View
```

```
    """

    def get(self, request, pk):
        try:
            platform = StreamPlatform.objects.get(pk=pk)
        except StreamPlatform.DoesNotExist:
            return Response({'error': 'Not found'}, status=status
            .HTTP_404_NOT_FOUND)

        serializer = serializers.StreamPlatformSerializer(platform)
        return Response(serializer.data)
```

Add the corresponding URL to access the endpoint in chapter6_serializers_views/api/urls.py as below:

```
urlpatterns = [
    ...
    path('streamplatform-detail-basic-serializer/<int:pk>/',
    views.StreamPlatformBasicSerializerView.as_view(),
    name="streamplatform-detail-
    basic-serializer"),
    ...
]
```

To access the watchlist API endpoint on Postman, the request shall be in the format:

```
GET {{domain}}/api/chapter6_serializers_views/watchlist-basic-serializer/
```

Its response will be in the below format:

```
[
     {
        "title": "Movie1",
        "storyline": "Movie1-Story",
        "active": true,
        "platform": "http://127.0.0.1:8000/api/chapter6_serializers_views/
        streamplatform-detail-basic-serializer/1/",
        "imdb_rating": 2.0,
        "created": "2024-10-26T20:06:27.406145Z",
```

```
        "episodes": 0,
        "category": "MOVIE"
    },
    ...
]
```

HyperlinkedIdentityField

This is a special type of field in Django REST Framework (DRF) that is used to generate **hyperlinks** for individual model instances in API responses. It's typically used in serializers to provide a URL for accessing the detailed representation of an object. It automatically generates hyperlinks to object details based on the view and URL patterns. Instead of just returning the primary key (e.g., id), it provides a hyperlink that allows clients to fetch more detailed information.

For demo purposes, we can change the platform field of WatchlistSerializer in the file chapter6_serializers_views/api/serializers.py as below:

```
class WatchlistSerializer(serializers.Serializer):
    title = serializers.CharField(max_length=30)
    storyline = serializers.CharField(max_length=200)
    active = serializers.BooleanField()
    # platform = StreamPlatformSerializer()
    # platform = serializers.StringRelatedField()
    # platform = serializers.HyperlinkedRelatedField(view_
      name='streamplatform-detail-basic-serializer', read_only=True)
    platform = serializers.HyperlinkedIdentityField(view_
    name='streamplatform-detail-basic-serializer', read_only=True)
    imdb_rating = serializers.FloatField(default=0)
    created = serializers.DateTimeField()
    episodes = serializers.IntegerField(default=0)
    category = serializers.CharField(max_length=30)
```

To access the watchlist API endpoint on Postman, the request shall be in the format:

```
GET {{domain}}/api/chapter6_serializers_views/watchlist-basic-serializer/
```

Its response will be in the below format:

```
[
    {
        "title": "Movie1",
        "storyline": "Movie1-Story",
        "active": true,
        "platform": "http://127.0.0.1:8000/api/chapter6_serializers_views
        /streamplatform-detail-basic-serializer/49/",
        "imdb_rating": 2.0,
        "created": "2024-10-26T20:06:27.406145Z",
        "episodes": 0,
        "category": "MOVIE"
    },
    ...
]
```

If we compare the above results, they seem to be the same. We shall use these fields based on the use cases and behavior.

Difference Between HyperlinkedRelatedField and Hyperlinked IdentityField

HyperlinkedRelatedField	HyperlinkedIdentityField
Represents a relationship by using a hyperlink to the related object	Represents the identity of an object by using a hyperlink
Used for representing relationships between objects, such as ForeignKey or OneToOneField relationships	Typically used for self-referential relationships, where the object itself has a URL endpoint for detailed information
Generates hyperlinks to related objects based on the view name and the related object's primary key	Generates a hyperlink to the object itself (e.g., its detail view) based on the view name and the object's primary key
Read-only field used for serialization	Read-only field used for serialization
Enhances navigability and discoverability by providing links to related resources	Useful for including hyperlinks to individual objects in the serialized output

In summary, the HyperlinkedIdentityField is used when you want to include a hyperlink to the object itself, typically for self-referential relationships. On the other hand, the HyperlinkedRelatedField is used to represent relationships between objects and generate hyperlinks to related resources. Both fields are read-only and provide a way to include hyperlinks in the serialized output, but their use cases and behaviors differ based on the type of relationship being represented.

SlugRelatedField

This serializer field represents a relationship using a slug field on the related object. It allows you to represent and handle relationships using the slug value of the related object instead of its primary key or other fields.

The SlugRelatedField is particularly useful when the related object has a slug field, which is typically a URL-friendly representation of the object. It allows you to easily include the slug value in the serialized output and handle relationships based on the slug field. You can specify any of the model fields as a slug or define a slug field to use it as a slug.

For demo purposes, we can change the platform field of WatchlistSerializer in the file chapter6_serializers_views/api/serializers.py as below:

```
class WatchlistSerializer(serializers.Serializer):
    title = serializers.CharField(max_length=30)
    storyline = serializers.CharField(max_length=200)
    active = serializers.BooleanField()
    # platform = StreamPlatformSerializer()
    # platform = serializers.StringRelatedField()
    # platform = serializers.HyperlinkedRelatedField(view_name='stream
      platform-detail-basic-serializer', read_only=True)
    # platform = serializers.HyperlinkedIdentityField(view_
      name='streamplatform-detail-basic-serializer', read_only=True)
    platform = serializers.SlugRelatedField(slug_field="name",
               queryset=StreamPlatform.objects.all())
    imdb_rating = serializers.FloatField(default=0)
    created = serializers.DateTimeField()
    episodes = serializers.IntegerField(default=0)
    category = serializers.CharField(max_length=30)
```

In the above code, we are mentioning the platform field as **SlugRelatedField** to consider the name of StreamingPlatform as a slug.

To access the watchlist API endpoint on Postman, the request shall be in the format: **GET** `{{domain}}/api/chapter6_serializers_views/watchlist-basic-serializer/`.

Its response will be in the below format:

```
[
    {
        "title": "Movie1",
        "storyline": "Movie1-Story",
        "active": true,
        "platform": "Netflix",
        "imdb_rating": 2.0,
        "created": "2024-10-26T20:06:27.406145Z",
        "episodes": 0,
        "category": "MOVIE"
    },
    ...
]
```

Create a New Object

Till now, we have worked on getting stored Watchlist information from the database. That is, we worked on only the GET request to get all list of Watchlists. Let's work on creating new objects in the database using the REST API. It means we are using a POST request to create new objects in the database.

Now go to chapter6_serializers_views/api/views.py and add a post method with the following lines of code to the class **WatchlistBasicSerializerView**:

```
class WatchlistBasicSerializerView(APIView):
    ...
    def post(self, request, format=None):
        """
        Create a new watchlist.
        """
        serializer = serializers.WatchlistSerializer(data=request.data)
```

```
        if serializer.is_valid():
            serializer.save()
            return Response(serializer.data, status=status.HTTP_201_CREATED)
        else:
            return Response(serializer.errors, status=status.HTTP_400_BAD_
            REQUEST)
```

In the above **post** method, we are sending post data to the serializer to serialize it. Then we are checking for validation. We run through validation in the next sections of this chapter. If all validation is successful, then we are saving data into the database by calling the serializer's save method.

For the serializer to save Watchlist data, we need to create a method called **create().**

Go to chapter6_serializers_views/api/serializers.py and add the following lines of code to the class **WatchlistSerializer** as below:

```
class WatchlistSerializer(serializers.Serializer):
    ...
    def create(self, validated_data):
        return WatchList.objects.create(**validated_data)
```

The **create** method defined above saves the created object to the database with validated data.

Let us test the above functionality with a POST request along with the below data on Postman: **POST** `{{domain}}/api/chapter6_serializers_views/watchlist-basic-serializer/`

Body:

```
{
    "title": "Movie3",
    "storyline": "Movie3 Story",
    "active": true,
    "platform": "Disneyplus",
    "imdb_rating": 2.0,
    "created": "2022-07-15T10:08:42.690612Z",
    "episodes": 0,
    "category": "MOVIE"
}
```

The above request returns a response with the created object details as below, with **201 Created** status:

```
{
    "title": "Movie3",
    "storyline": "Movie3 Story",
    "active": true,
    "platform": "Disneyplus",
    "imdb_rating": 2.0,
    "created": "2024-12-28T06:55:45.898257Z",
    "episodes": 0,
    "category": "MOVIE"
}
```

Now go to the admin page and see that the new Watchlist object with the above data has been created. You can also see the created object by using the above-specified URL with a GET request.

Before creating an object in the database, DRF provides methods to validate POST request data. Now let us discuss what this is all about: validation in the serializer.

Serializer Validation

Serializer validation in Django REST Framework (DRF) refers to the process of validating data that is being deserialized by a serializer. It ensures that the data meets certain criteria or constraints defined by the serializer's fields, validators, or custom validation methods. Serializer validation plays a crucial role in maintaining data integrity and ensuring that the received or transformed data is valid and consistent.

During the validation process, the serializer checks the data against the defined validation rules. If any validation rule fails, a **ValidationError** is raised, which contains detailed information about the validation error. The ValidationError can be caught and handled appropriately, such as returning error responses to the client.

Serializer validation ensures that the data being processed by the serializer adheres to the defined constraints, improving data integrity and preventing invalid or inconsistent data from being processed further. It helps to maintain data quality and provides a mechanism to ensure that the API only receives or produces valid data. Let's discuss different approaches available on DRF.

Field-Level Validation

You can specify custom field-level validation by adding **.validate_<field_name>** methods to your Serializer subclass. These are similar to the **.clean_<field_name>** methods on Django forms.

These methods take a single argument, which is the field value that requires validation. Your validate_**<field_name>** methods should return the validated value or raise a serializers.ValidationError.

Let's implement field-level validation for WatchlistSerializer. Go to chapter6_serializers_views/api/serializers.py and add the following lines of code:

```
class WatchlistSerializer(serializers.Serializer):
    ...
    def validate_title(self, value):
        if "@" in value:
            serializers.ValidationError("Invalid Title")
        return value

    def validate_storyline(self, value):
        if "@" in value:
            serializers.ValidationError("Invalid Storyline")
        return value

    def validate_category(self, value):
        if value not in ["MOVIE", "SERIES"]:
            serializers.ValidationError("Not a valid category")
        return value
```

The **validate_title()** function is called to check the value of the title, whether it contains the special character @ and raises a validation error if so. A similar check is also performed for storyline and category fields.

The above methods are invoked when the **.is_valid()** function is called during deserialization of the objects.

Object-Level Validation

Object-level validation refers to the validation of the entire object or the relationship between multiple fields within a serializer. Object-level validation allows you to perform validation logic that involves multiple fields and requires access to the complete set of serialized data.

To implement object-level validation in DRF, you can define a **validate()** method in your serializer class. This method is called after the individual field-level validation is performed and before the serializer saves or updates the object.

Now go to chapter6_serializers_views/api/serializers.py and add the following lines of code:

```
class WatchlistSerializer(serializers.Serializer):
    ...
    def validate(self, data):
        title = data.get("title", None)
        storyline = data.get("storyline", None)
        if (title and storyline) and (len(title) > len(storyline)):
            raise serializers.ValidationError("Length of title is bigger
            than storyline")
        return super().validate(data)
```

In the above code, the **validate()** function fetches the title and storyline and checks each length and raises a validation error if the title is longer than the storyline.

Until now we learned about getting a list of objects using a **GET** request and creating a new object using a **POST** request. Now let's discuss getting the individual object.

Get a Single Object

To get a specific object from the database, we need to provide the primary key value in the requested URL, and we need to create a view to get a specific object from the database. For that, we need to create a new view.

Let's go to chapter6_serializers_views/api/views.py and add the following lines of code:

```
class WatchlistDetailBasicSerializerView(APIView):
    """
```

```
    View in detail individual Watchlist in the system.
    """
    def get(self, request, pk, format=None):
        try:
            watchlist = WatchList.objects.get(pk=pk)
            serializer = serializers.WatchlistSerializer(watchlist)
            return Response(serializer.data)
        except WatchList.DoesNotExist:
            raise Http404
```

Add the corresponding URL in chapter6_serializers_views/api/urls.py as below:

```
urlpatterns = [
    ...
    path('watchlist-detail-basic-serializer/<int:pk>/', views.Watchlist
    DetailBasicSerializerView.as_view(), name="watchlist-detail-basic-
    serializer"),
]
```

To access the watchlist API endpoint on Postman, the request shall be in the format: **GET** `{{domain}}/api/chapter6_serializers_views/watchlist-detail-basic-serializer/64/`.

Its response will be in the below format:

```
{
    "title": "Movie1",
    "storyline": "Movie1 Storyline",
    "active": true,
    "platform": "Netflix",
    "imdb_rating": 4.0,
    "created": "2023-07-12T10:08:42.690612Z",
    "episodes": 0,
    "category": "MOVIE"
}
```

Update an Object

A single object can be updated using **PUT** or **PATCH** requests. The PUT request is used to update an entire resource with the new representation provided in the request. When making a PUT request, you need to send the complete representation of the resource, including both the existing and updated fields.

If the resource already exists, the entire resource will be replaced with the new representation sent in the request. If the resource does not exist, a new resource will be created with the provided representation. In practice, a PUT request should be idempotent, meaning that making the same request multiple times should have the same effect as making it once.

Example: Updating a user's profile with all the profile details provided in the request payload.

In contrast, the PATCH request is used to update part of a resource, rather than the entire resource. Unlike the PUT request, the PATCH request allows for a partial update of the resource. When making a PATCH request, you only need to send the specific fields that you want to update. The server applies the updates to the resource without affecting the other fields. In practice, a PATCH request is not necessarily idempotent, as subsequent requests might result in different updates.

Example: Updating the status field of a task without modifying other fields.

Now go to chapter6_serializers_views/api/views.py and create put and patch methods in class **WatchlistDetailBasicSerializerView** as below:

```
class WatchlistDetailBasicSerializerView(APIView):
    ...
    def put(self, request, pk):
        try:
            watchlist = WatchList.objects.get(pk=pk)
            serializer = serializers.WatchlistSerializer(watchlist,
                         data=request.data)
            if serializer.is_valid():
                serializer.save()
                return Response(serializer.data)
            else:
                return Response(serializer.errors, status=status
                .HTTP_400_BAD_REQUEST)
```

```
        except WatchList.DoesNotExist:
            raise Http404

    def patch(self, request, pk):
        try:
            watchlist = WatchList.objects.get(pk=pk)
            serializer = serializers.WatchlistSerializer(watchlist,
                         data=request.data, partial=True)
            serializer.is_valid(raise_exception=True)
            serializer.save()
            return Response(serializer.data)
        except WatchList.DoesNotExist:
            raise Http404
```

In the above code, both look similar except that, in the patch request, we are instructing the serializer to consider partial updates by setting **partial=True**.

For the serializer to work for updating a single object, we need to add an update method in **WatchlistSerializer**.

Go to chapter6_serializers_views/api/serializers.py and add the following lines of code:

```
class WatchlistSerializer(serializers.Serializer):
    ...
    def update(self, instance, validated_data):
        """
        Update and return an existing `Watchlist` instance, given the
        validated data.
        """
        instance.title = validated_data.get('title', instance.title)
        instance.storyline = validated_data.get('storyline', instance.
                             storyline)
        instance.active = validated_data.get('active', instance.active)
        instance.platform = validated_data.get('platform', instance.
                            platform)
        instance.imdb_rating = validated_data.get('imdb_rating', instance.
                               imdb_rating)
        instance.created = validated_data.get('created', instance.created)
```

```
        instance.episodes = validated_data.get('episodes', instance.
                            episodes)
        instance.category = validated_data.get('category', instance.
                            category)
        instance.save()
        return instance
```

To access the watchlist API endpoint on Postman, the request shall be in the format: **PUT** `{{domain}}/api/chapter6_serializers_views/watchlist-detail-basic-serializer/64/`.

Body:

```
{
    "title": "Movie3 Updated",
    "storyline": "Movie3 Story Updated",
    "active": true,
    "platform": "Disneyplus",
    "imdb_rating": 2.0,
    "created": "2022-07-15T10:08:42.690612Z",
    "episodes": 0,
    "category": "MOVIE"
}
```

Its response will be as below:

```
{
    "title": "Movie3 Updated",
    "storyline": "Movie3 Story Updated",
    "active": true,
    "platform": "Disneyplus",
    "imdb_rating": 2.0,
    "created": "2022-07-15T10:08:42.690612Z",
    "episodes": 0,
    "category": "MOVIE"
}
```

Now send a PATCH request using the same URL with the below data:

Body:

```
{
    "storyline": "Movie1 Storyline updated for patch request",
    "active": false
}
```

You should be able to see the updated result Response as below:

```
{
    "title": "Movie3 Updated",
    "storyline": "Movie1 Storyline updated for patch request",
    "active": false,
    "platform": "Disneyplus",
    "imdb_rating": 2.0,
    "created": "2022-07-15T10:08:42.690612Z",
    "episodes": 0,
    "category": "MOVIE"
}
```

In the above response from the patch request, you could be able to update only two parameters from all the remaining ones.

Delete an Object

To delete an object in DRF, we need to add a delete method to handle a delete request. For this view, we don't need to do anything with the serializer.

Now go to chapter6_serializers_views/api/views.py and add the following lines of code to the **WatchlistDetailBasicSerializerView** class:

```
class WatchlistDetailBasicSerializerView(APIView):
    ...
    def delete(self, request, pk):
        try:
            watchlist = WatchList.objects.get(pk=pk)
```

```
        watchlist.delete()
        return Response(status=status.HTTP_204_NO_CONTENT)
    except Exception as err:
        raise Http404
```

To access the watchlist API endpoint on Postman, the request shall be in the format:

DELETE `{{domain}}/api/chapter6_serializers_views/watchlist-detail-basic-serializer/64/`.

You will get a **"204 No Content"** response for the above request.

Now if you send a GET request to list all the watchlists, you don't see the deleted object in the response list.

Until now, we have learned about serializers and views concepts. In the code, we used many status codes when sending a response. Let's discuss the list of status codes available in the DRF.

Status Code

Status codes are HTTP status codes returned in the HTTP response to indicate the outcome of an API request. DRF provides a set of commonly used status codes as constants in the **rest_framework.status** module. DRF provides these status codes as constants to make it easier to use them consistently in your API views or viewsets. You can import these status codes from **rest_framework.status** and return them along with your API responses to provide meaningful information about the result of the request.

HTTP status codes are part of the HTTP protocol and are universally understood by clients and servers. By using standard status codes, DRF ensures consistency and interoperability across different systems. Status codes, especially the ones in the 4xx and 5xx range, help in error handling and troubleshooting. They allow clients and developers to identify the nature of the error, such as authentication issues (401 Unauthorized), validation errors (400 Bad Request), or server errors (500 Internal Server Error). Many libraries, frameworks, and tools rely on standard status codes to handle API responses effectively. By using the appropriate status codes, DRF ensures compatibility with these libraries and facilitates integration with various systems and technologies. All these status codes are sent from the server to the client in Response.

Let us go through the list of status codes and where they shall be used in server responses. There are some examples provided for some typical status codes.

HTTP_100_CONTINUE

This is used as an informational response from the server to indicate that it has received the initial part of the request and is willing to continue processing. It is typically used in scenarios where the client needs to send a large request body and wants to check if the server is willing to accept it before sending the entire request.

The **HTTP_100_CONTINUE** status code, along with the Expect request header, allows the client to send the request headers first and wait for the server's acknowledgement before sending the request body. If the server responds with HTTP_100_CONTINUE, the client proceeds to send the request body. If the server responds with a different status code, the client may choose to modify or cancel the request.

HTTP_101_SWITCHING_PROTOCOLS

This is used as a response from the server to indicate that it is switching to a different protocol, as requested by the client. It is typically used in scenarios where a client wants to initiate a protocol upgrade, such as switching from HTTP to WebSocket or from HTTP to a secure protocol like HTTPS.

The **HTTP_101_SWITCHING_PROTOCOLS** status code indicates that the server has acknowledged the client's request to switch protocols and is ready to establish the new protocol connection. It is followed by an **Upgrade** response header specifying the protocol being switched to.

HTTP_200_OK

This indicates a successful request.

The **HTTP_200_OK** status code is the most common status code used for successful responses. It signifies that the request has been successfully processed and the server is returning the requested resource or action. It indicates that the server understood the request and the response contains the requested information.

HTTP_201_CREATED

This code indicates that a new resource has been successfully created as a result of the request.

The **HTTP_201_CREATED** status code is typically used after a successful POST request to indicate that the requested resource has been created on the server. It is accompanied by a response body that contains the representation of the newly created resource or a reference to it.

HTTP_202_ACCEPTED

This code indicates that the server has accepted the request for processing but has not yet completed the processing.

The **HTTP_202_ACCEPTED** status code is typically used when the requested operation is asynchronous or long-running. It acknowledges that the server has received the request, will process it in the future, and may provide status updates or notifications about the progress of the operation.

HTTP_203_NON_AUTHORITATIVE_INFORMATION

This code indicates that the returned response is a representation of the requested resource, but it may be from a third-party source or a cache.

The **HTTP_203_NON_AUTHORITATIVE_INFORMATION** status code is typically used when a response is served from a cache or a different origin server, rather than the authoritative source. It signifies that the server providing the response is not the authoritative source for the requested resource. This can occur when a server acts as a gateway or proxy and obtains the response from a different server or cache.

Here's an example of using **HTTP_203_NON_AUTHORITATIVE_INFORMATION** in a view:

```
from rest_framework import status
from rest_framework.response import Response

def my_view(request):
    if some_condition:
        return Response(status=status.HTTP_203_NON_AUTHORITATIVE_
        INFORMATION)
    else:
        return Response(status=status.HTTP_200_OK)
```

HTTP_204_NO_CONTENT

This code indicates that the server has successfully processed the request but does not have any content to return in the response body.

The **HTTP_204_NO_CONTENT** status code is typically used when a request is successfully processed and there is no need to return any additional content in the response body. It is commonly used for successful DELETE requests or for requests where the server performs an action that does not require a response body.

HTTP_205_RESET_CONTENT

This code indicates that the server has successfully fulfilled the request and the user agent (e.g., a web browser) should reset the current document view.

The **HTTP_205_RESET_CONTENT** status code is typically used to instruct the user agent to clear the form or reset the current view after a form submission or data processing. It is useful when you want to prevent the user agent from displaying a success message or rendering the response body.

HTTP_206_PARTIAL_CONTENT

This code indicates the successful delivery of a partial content range in response to a request for a specific range of a resource.

The **HTTP_206_PARTIAL_CONTENT** status code is typically used when a client requests a specific range of data from a resource using the Range header in the request. The server then responds with a partial content range that corresponds to the requested range. This allows clients to retrieve specific portions of a resource without needing to download the entire content.

Here's an example of using HTTP_206_PARTIAL_CONTENT in a view:

```
from rest_framework import status
from rest_framework.response import Response

def get_partial_content(request):
    # Determine the requested range
    range_start = 100
    range_end = 199

    # Retrieve the partial content data based on the range
```

```
    partial_content = get_partial_content_data(range_start, range_end)

    # Build the response
    response = Response(partial_content, status=status.HTTP_206_PARTIAL_
               CONTENT)
    response['Content-Range'] = f'bytes {range_start}-{range_end}/*'
    response['Content-Length'] = len(partial_content)

    return response
```

HTTP_300_MULTIPLE_CHOICES

This code indicates that the server has multiple representations of the requested resource available, and the client should choose one of them.

The **HTTP_300_MULTIPLE_CHOICES** status code is typically used in scenarios where the requested resource has multiple representations, such as different formats or variants, and the server cannot determine the most suitable representation for the client. The server provides a list of choices, and the client can select one by following the provided links or by specifying the desired representation in the request.

Here's an example of using HTTP_300_MULTIPLE_CHOICES in a view:

```
from rest_framework import status
from rest_framework.response import Response

def choose_representation(request):
    choices = [
        {'name': 'Representation A', 'url': 'https://example.com/
                                             representation/a'},
        {'name': 'Representation B', 'url': 'https://example.com/
                                             representation/b'},
        {'name': 'Representation C', 'url': 'https://example.com/
                                             representation/c'},
    ]

    return Response(choices, status=status.HTTP_300_MULTIPLE_CHOICES)
```

HTTP_301_MOVED_PERMANENTLY

This code indicates that the requested resource has been permanently moved to a new URL.

The **HTTP_301_MOVED_PERMANENTLY** status code is used when a resource has been moved to a new location permanently and all future requests should be directed to the new URL. The client should update its bookmarks or references to the old URL and use the new URL for any future requests.

Here's an example of using HTTP_301_MOVED_PERMANENTLY in a view:

```
from rest_framework import status
from rest_framework.response import Response

def redirect_to_new_url(request):
    new_url = "https://example.com/new-url"
    return Response(status=status.HTTP_301_MOVED_PERMANENTLY,
    headers={'Location': new_url})
```

HTTP_302_FOUND

This code indicates a temporary redirect to a different URL.

The **HTTP_302_FOUND** status code is typically used when a resource has temporarily moved to a different location, and the client should temporarily redirect its requests to the new URL. It is commonly used for scenarios such as temporary site maintenance, load balancing, or when a resource is temporarily unavailable.

Here's an example of using HTTP_302_FOUND in a view:

```
from rest_framework import status
from rest_framework.response import Response

def temporary_redirect(request):
    new_url = "https://example.com/redirected-url"
    return Response(status=status.HTTP_302_FOUND, headers={'Location':
    new_url})
```

HTTP_303_SEE_OTHER

This code indicates that the client should redirect to a different URL to retrieve the requested resource.

The **HTTP_303_SEE_OTHER** status code is typically used when a client makes a request that should result in a different resource being served, rather than directly returning the requested resource. It is commonly used after a successful POST request to redirect the client to a different URL where the result or the next step of the operation can be obtained.

Here's an example of using **HTTP_303_SEE_OTHER** in a view:

```
from rest_framework import status
from rest_framework.response import Response

def perform_post_operation(request):
    # Perform the post operation
    # ...

    redirect_url = "https://example.com/redirect-url"
    return Response(status=status.HTTP_303_SEE_OTHER, headers={'Location':
    redirect_url})
```

HTTP_304_NOT_MODIFIED

This code indicates that the requested resource has not been modified since the last time it was requested. It is part of the HTTP/1.1 protocol.

The **HTTP_304_NOT_MODIFIED** status code is used as a response to a conditional GET request, where the client includes an **If-Modified-Since** or **If-None-Match** header to determine if the resource has been modified. If the server determines that the resource has not been modified, it returns a "**304 Not Modified"** response to inform the client that the cached version of the resource can be used, reducing unnecessary data transfer.

Here's an example of using HTTP_304_NOT_MODIFIED in a view:

```
from rest_framework import status
from rest_framework.response import Response

def get_resource(request):
    # Check if the resource has been modified
    if not resource_has_been_modified(request):
        return Response(status=status.HTTP_304_NOT_MODIFIED)

    # Retrieve and return the resource
```

```
    resource_data = retrieve_resource_data()
    return Response(resource_data)
```

HTTP_305_USE_PROXY

This code indicates that the client should use a proxy server to access the requested resource. It is part of the HTTP/1.1 protocol.

The **HTTP_305_USE_PROXY** status code is not commonly used in modern web applications and is considered deprecated. It was originally defined in the HTTP/1.1 specification to indicate that the requested resource can only be accessed through a proxy server specified in the Location header of the response.

However, due to security concerns and issues with the implementation of proxy servers, the **HTTP_305_USE_PROXY** status code has been deprecated and is no longer widely supported by modern browsers and servers. Clients are now expected to automatically follow the redirect specified by a **"307 Temporary Redirect"** status code instead.

If you encounter a situation where you believe a proxy server should be used to access a resource, it is recommended to use the **"307 Temporary Redirect"** status code instead. This will instruct the client to temporarily redirect the request to a different URL, including any necessary proxy information if applicable.

HTTP_306_RESERVED

This code is reserved for future use in the HTTP/1.1 protocol. However, it has been deprecated and is no longer used. The specification reserved the **"306 (Unused)"** status code for potential future use, but no specific purpose or semantics were assigned to it.

HTTP_307_TEMPORARY_REDIRECT

This code indicates a temporary redirect to a different URL.

The HTTP_307_TEMPORARY_REDIRECT status code is similar to the **"302 Found"** status code. It is used when a resource has temporarily moved to a different location, and the client should temporarily redirect its requests to the new URL. The client should continue to use the original HTTP method (GET, POST, etc.) when making subsequent requests to the new URL.

The main difference between **"307 Temporary Redirect"** and **"302 Found"** is that the 307 status code instructs the client to preserve the original HTTP method when making subsequent requests, while **"302"** allows the client to switch to a different HTTP method if necessary.

Here's an example of using HTTP_307_TEMPORARY_REDIRECT in a view:

```
from rest_framework import status
from rest_framework.response import Response

def temporary_redirect(request):
    new_url = "https://example.com/redirected-url"
    return Response(status=status.HTTP_307_TEMPORARY_REDIRECT,
    headers={'Location': new_url})
```

HTTP_308_PERMANENT_REDIRECT

This code indicates a permanent redirect to a different URL.

The **HTTP_308_PERMANENT_REDIRECT** status code is similar to the **"301 Moved Permanently"** status code. It is used when a resource has permanently moved to a different location and the client should permanently redirect its requests to the new URL. The client should update its bookmarks, references, or caches to use the new URL for any future requests.

The main difference between **"308 Permanent Redirect"** and **"301 Moved Permanently"** is that the **"308"** status code instructs the client to preserve the original HTTP method when making subsequent requests, while **"301"** allows the client to switch to a different HTTP method if necessary.

Here's an example of using **HTTP_308_PERMANENT_REDIRECT** in a view:

```
from rest_framework import status
from rest_framework.response import Response

def permanent_redirect(request):
    new_url = "https://example.com/new-url"
    return Response(status=status.HTTP_308_PERMANENT_REDIRECT,
    headers={'Location': new_url})
```

HTTP_400_BAD_REQUEST

This code indicates that the server cannot process the client's request due to a client error or invalid request syntax.

The **HTTP_400_BAD_REQUEST** status code is commonly used when the server cannot understand or process the client's request due to malformed syntax, missing or invalid parameters, or other client-side errors. It indicates that the client's request cannot be fulfilled as it is and the client needs to modify or correct the request before resubmitting it.

HTTP_401_UNAUTHORIZED

This code indicates that the client's request requires authentication and the client either failed to provide valid authentication credentials or lacks valid authentication for the requested resource.

The **HTTP_401_UNAUTHORIZED** status code is commonly used when the server requires authentication for the requested resource and the client fails to provide valid credentials or fails to authenticate properly. It indicates that the client needs to authenticate itself before accessing the requested resource.

HTTP_402_PAYMENT_REQUIRED

This code indicates that the client's request requires payment to access the requested resource.

The **HTTP_402_PAYMENT_REQUIRED** status code is reserved for future use, and its intended purpose is to indicate that a payment is required to access the requested resource. However, it is not currently in common use on the web, and its semantics and behavior are not defined in the HTTP specification.

While the **HTTP_402_PAYMENT_REQUIRED** status code exists in the HTTP specification, it is not supported by most web servers and clients. In practice, if you encounter a situation where payment is required to access a resource, it is more common to handle payment-related functionality and authorization outside of the HTTP protocol, using payment gateways, authentication mechanisms, or custom business logic.

HTTP_403_FORBIDDEN

This code indicates that the client's request is understood by the server, but the server refuses to fulfill the request due to access restrictions.

The **HTTP_403_FORBIDDEN** status code is commonly used when the server recognizes the client's request and authentication credentials (if applicable), but the client is not granted access to the requested resource. It indicates that the server understands the client's request, but for some reason, the server is prohibiting the client from accessing the resource.

Some common reasons for returning a 403 Forbidden response include

- The client lacks the necessary permissions to access the resource.
- The client is authenticated, but the requested resource is forbidden for the authenticated user.
- The client is authenticated, but the requested resource is forbidden based on other access restrictions or business rules.

HTTP_404_NOT_FOUND

This code indicates that the requested resource could not be found on the server.

The **HTTP_404_NOT_FOUND** status code is commonly used when the server is unable to locate the requested resource. It indicates that the server has searched for the resource at the specified URI but could not find it. This can occur due to various reasons, such as a nonexistent URL, a deleted or moved resource, or a resource that is not accessible to the client.

HTTP_405_METHOD_NOT_ALLOWED

This code indicates that the requested HTTP method is not allowed for the given resource.

The **HTTP_405_METHOD_NOT_ALLOWED** status code is commonly used when the server receives a request with an HTTP method that is not supported or allowed for the requested resource. It indicates that the server recognizes the resource but does not support the requested method. This can happen when a client tries to perform an operation that is not permitted or supported by the server.

HTTP_406_NOT_ACCEPTABLE

This code indicates that the server cannot produce a response that is acceptable to the client based on the requested content types or characteristics.

The **HTTP_406_NOT_ACCEPTABLE** status code is commonly used when the server receives a request with a specific content type or characteristics in the Accept header, but it cannot provide a response that matches the requested criteria. It indicates that the server cannot produce content that satisfies the client's requested content type or other requirements.

Here's an example of using HTTP_406_NOT_ACCEPTABLE in a view:

```
from rest_framework import status
from rest_framework.response import Response

def get_resource(request):
    if not request.accepted_renderer:
        return Response(status=status.HTTP_406_NOT_ACCEPTABLE)

    # Generate and return the appropriate response
    # ...

    return Response(data={'resource': resource})
```

HTTP_407_PROXY_AUTHENTICATION_REQUIRED

This code indicates that the client must authenticate itself with the proxy server before accessing the requested resource.

The **HTTP_407_PROXY_AUTHENTICATION_REQUIRED** status code is similar to the **"401 Unauthorized"** status code. However, it specifically indicates that the client needs to provide authentication credentials to the proxy server in order to access the requested resource. This typically occurs when a client is behind a proxy server that requires authentication before forwarding the request to the destination server. It is not commonly used in typical DRF applications, as the handling of proxy authentication is usually handled by infrastructure or web server configurations.

HTTP_408_REQUEST_TIMEOUT

This code indicates that the client's request took too long to complete, and the server timed out waiting for the entire request to be received.

The **HTTP_408_REQUEST_TIMEOUT** status code is commonly used when a server sets a time limit for how long it will wait for the client to complete the request. If the server does not receive the complete request within the specified time limit, it will return a **"408 Request Timeout"** response to indicate that the client's request has timed out. It is typically handled by the web server or infrastructure layer rather than being handled explicitly in DRF views or viewsets.

There can be various reasons for a request to timeout, such as slow network connections, excessive load on the server, or client-side issues that prevent the timely completion of the request.

Clients receiving a **"408 Request Timeout"** response should handle it by considering the reasons for the timeout and taking appropriate actions. This may involve retrying the request, optimizing the client's network connection, or investigating and resolving any issues that may have caused the request to take longer than expected.

HTTP_409_CONFLICT

This code indicates that the client's request conflicts with the current state of the server or a resource.

The **HTTP_409_CONFLICT** status code is commonly used when the server detects a conflict between the client's request and the current state of a resource. It indicates that the server cannot fulfil the request due to a conflict, such as a violation of business rules, data integrity constraints, or concurrent modifications.

Some common scenarios where a **"409 Conflict"** response may be returned include

- **Concurrent Updates**: When multiple clients attempt to modify the same resource simultaneously, and the server detects conflicting changes.
- **Data Integrity Violations**: When the client's request would result in a violation of data integrity rules or constraints defined by the server, such as duplicate entries or inconsistent data.
- **Business Rule Conflicts**: When the client's request conflicts with specific business rules or requirements defined by the server.

Here's an example of using HTTP_409_CONFLICT in a view:

```
from rest_framework import status
from rest_framework.response import Response
```

```
def update_resource(request, resource_id):
    try:
        resource = MyModel.objects.get(id=resource_id)
    except MyModel.DoesNotExist:
        return Response(status=status.HTTP_404_NOT_FOUND)

    if resource.is_locked():
        return Response(status=status.HTTP_409_CONFLICT, data={'message':
        'Resource is locked'})

    # Perform the resource update
    # ...

    return Response(data={'message': 'Resource updated successfully'})
```

HTTP_410_GONE

This code indicates that the requested resource is no longer available on the server and will not be available again in the future.

The HTTP_410_GONE status code is similar to the **"404 Not Found"** status code. However, it specifically indicates that the resource was previously available but has been intentionally removed and will not be restored. It is used when the server knows that the resource has been permanently deleted or discontinued.

Typically, a **"410 Gone"** response is returned for resources that have been deliberately removed, and there is no expectation that they will be available again in the future. This could be due to a variety of reasons, such as the expiration of a temporary resource, the closure of a service, or the permanent removal of a resource.

HTTP_411_LENGTH_REQUIRED

This code indicates that the server requires the Content-Length header to be included in the client's request.

The **HTTP_411_LENGTH_REQUIRED** status code is used when the server expects the client to include the **"Content-Length"** header in the request. The **"Content-Length"** header specifies the length of the request body in bytes. This header is typically required for requests that include a request body, such as **"POST"** or **"PUT"** requests.

If the server receives a request without the **"Content-Length"** header when it expects it, it can return a **"411 Length Required"** response to indicate that the client needs to include the **"Content-Length"** header.

However, this status code is not commonly used in typical DRF applications. The handling of the **"Content-Length"** header is typically handled automatically by the underlying web server or the HTTP client library being used.

HTTP_412_PRECONDITION_FAILED

This code indicates that the server is unable to meet the preconditions specified in the client's request headers.

The **HTTP_412_PRECONDITION_FAILED** status code is commonly used when the server receives a request with certain preconditions specified in the request headers, but the server determines that these preconditions are not satisfied or cannot be fulfilled. Preconditions can include conditions related to caching, conditional requests, or resource states.

Some common scenarios where a **"412 Precondition Failed"** response may be returned include

- **If-Match Header**: The client included an **"If-Match"** header in the request, indicating that the request should only be processed if the specified entity tag (ETag) matches the current representation of the resource on the server. If the ETag does not match, the server may return a **"412 Precondition Failed"** response.
- **If-None-Match Header**: The client included an **"If-None-Match"** header in the request, indicating that the request should only be processed if the specified entity tag (ETag) does not match the current representation of the resource on the server. If the ETag does match, indicating that the resource has not changed, the server may return a **"412 Precondition Failed"** response.
- **If-Unmodified-Since Header**: The client included an **"If-Unmodified-Since"** header in the request, indicating that the request should only be processed if the resource has not been modified since the specified date/time. If the resource has been modified, the server may return a **"412 Precondition Failed"** response.

Here's an example of using HTTP_412_PRECONDITION_FAILED in a view:

```
from rest_framework import status
from rest_framework.response import Response

def update_resource(request, resource_id):
    if request.META.get('HTTP_IF_MATCH') != 'desired_etag':
        return Response(status=status.HTTP_412_PRECONDITION_FAILED,
        data={'message': 'Precondition failed'})

    # Process the resource update
    # ...

    return Response(data={'message': 'Resource updated successfully'})
```

HTTP_413_REQUEST_ENTITY_TOO_LARGE

This code indicates that the server is refusing to process the client's request because the request entity (such as the request body) is too large.

The **HTTP_413_REQUEST_ENTITY_TOO_LARGE** status code is commonly used when the server receives a request with a request entity that exceeds its configured or allowed size limit. This limit can be imposed by the server configuration, infrastructure, or specific business requirements. However, the handling of this status code is typically done at the web server or infrastructure level rather than explicitly within DRF views or serializers.

If you encounter a situation where the server returns a **"413 Request Entity Too Large"** response, you should consider reducing the size of the request entity. This could involve compressing data, removing unnecessary content, or adjusting the client's request parameters to fit within the server's size limitations.

HTTP_414_REQUEST_URI_TOO_LONG

This code indicates that the server is refusing to process the client's request because the requested URI (Uniform Resource Identifier) is too long.

The **HTTP_414_REQUEST_URI_TOO_LONG** status code is commonly used when the server receives a request with a URI that exceeds its configured or allowed length limit. The URI includes the full URL path along with any query parameters.

When a server returns a **"414 Request-URI Too Long"** response, it indicates that the client needs to reduce the length of the requested URI and resubmit the request. However, the handling of this status code is typically done at the web server or infrastructure level rather than explicitly within DRF views or serializers.

If you encounter a situation where the server returns a **"414 Request-URI Too Long"** response, you should consider reducing the length of the requested URI. This could involve shortening the URL path, removing unnecessary query parameters, or using alternative methods to transmit the information needed by the server.

HTTP_415_UNSUPPORTED_MEDIA_TYPE

This code indicates that the server refuses to accept the client's request because the media type or content type of the request entity is not supported or not acceptable.

The **HTTP_415_UNSUPPORTED_MEDIA_TYPE** status code is commonly used when the server receives a request with a content type that it does not support or cannot process. This can happen when the server expects a specific content type for the request body, such as JSON or XML, but the client sends a different content type or an unsupported media type.

When a server returns a **"415 Unsupported Media Type"** response, it indicates that the client should use a different content type or media type that is supported by the server for the requested operation.

HTTP_416_REQUESTED_RANGE_NOT_SATISFIABLE

This code indicates that the server cannot fulfil the client's request for a specific range of a resource because the requested range is invalid or not satisfiable.

The **HTTP_416_REQUESTED_RANGE_NOT_SATISFIABLE** status code is commonly used when the client requests a specific range of a resource using the Range header, but the server is unable to provide that range. This can happen when the requested range falls outside the valid range of the resource or when the server cannot support partial content retrieval.

When a server returns a **"416 Requested Range Not Satisfiable"** response, it indicates that the requested range cannot be provided and the client should either modify the request range or request the entire resource. However, the handling of this status code is typically done automatically by the web server or infrastructure layer rather than explicitly within DRF views or serializers.

HTTP_417_EXPECTATION_FAILED

This code indicates that the server cannot meet the expectations specified by the client in the Expect request header.

The **HTTP_417_EXPECTATION_FAILED** status code is commonly used when the client includes an Expect header in the request, indicating certain expectations for the server's behavior or response, but the server cannot fulfill those expectations.

The Expect header allows the client to indicate expectations related to request processing, such as requiring certain headers, specific handling of the request, or applying certain behaviors. If the server cannot meet those expectations, it can return a **"417 Expectation Failed"** response to indicate the failure to meet the client's expectations. However, this status code is not commonly used in typical DRF applications. The handling of the Expect header and the **"417 Expectation Failed"** response is typically done at the web server or infrastructure level.

If you encounter a situation where the server returns a **"417 Expectation Failed"** response, you should review the server's documentation or error message to understand the specific expectations that were not met. Clients should adjust their expectations or modify the request accordingly.

HTTP_422_UNPROCESSABLE_ENTITY

This status code is an HTTP response code that is not part of the official HTTP/1.1 protocol, but it is widely used in APIs, including those built with Django REST Framework (DRF). It indicates that the server understands the client's request syntax, but the request cannot be processed due to semantic errors or failed validations.

The **HTTP_422_UNPROCESSABLE_ENTITY** status code is commonly used to indicate that the request entity (such as the request body) is syntactically valid but contains semantic errors that prevent it from being processed. It is often used when performing input validation or when encountering business rule violations.

HTTP_423_LOCKED

This code indicates that the requested resource is locked and currently unavailable for access. It is part of the WebDAV (Web Distributed Authoring and Versioning) extension to the HTTP/1.1 protocol.

The **HTTP_423_LOCKED** status code is commonly used when a client attempts to access a resource that is currently locked by another user or process. It indicates that the requested resource is temporarily unavailable due to being locked for editing, preventing concurrent modifications or conflicts.

In the context of WebDAV, the **HTTP_423_LOCKED** status code is used to indicate that a resource has been locked using a lock token, typically through the LOCK method. This lock token ensures exclusive access to the resource until it is released or expired.

While the HTTP_423_LOCKED status code is primarily associated with WebDAV, it can also be used in other scenarios where resource locking is implemented, such as in custom API designs. However, handling resource locking and returning a 423 Locked response typically requires a custom implementation based on the specific locking mechanism being used.

Clients receiving a **"423 Locked"** response should handle it by respecting the lock and avoiding any further modifications to the locked resource until it becomes available. The client may need to wait until the lock is released or expired before attempting to access or modify the resource again.

HTTP_424_FAILED_DEPENDENCY

This code indicates that the requested operation failed due to a failed dependency or a failed precondition. It is not part of the standard HTTP/1.1 protocol but is defined in the WebDAV (Web Distributed Authoring and Versioning) extension.

The **HTTP_424_FAILED_DEPENDENCY** status code is commonly used to indicate that the server encountered a failure in processing the request because it depends on another operation or resource that has failed. It is typically used in scenarios where the server is relying on external dependencies or has preconditions that need to be met for the requested operation to succeed.

The specific meaning and usage of **HTTP_424_FAILED_DEPENDENCY** can vary depending on the context and application. It is not as widely used as some of the more common HTTP status codes.

Clients receiving a **"424 Failed Dependency"** response should handle it by examining the response body or any additional error messages provided by the server. The client should review the server's documentation or error message to understand the specific dependency or precondition failure that caused the request to fail.

HTTP_426_UPGRADE_REQUIRED

This code indicates that the client needs to switch to a different protocol in order to fulfill the requested resource. It is part of the HTTP/1.1 protocol and is typically used in scenarios where the server requires the client to upgrade its protocol for further communication.

The **HTTP_426_UPGRADE_REQUIRED** status code is commonly used when the server determines that the current protocol version being used by the client is outdated or no longer supported. It is a way for the server to prompt the client to upgrade to a newer version of the protocol.

When a server returns a **"426 Upgrade Required"** response, it typically includes an Upgrade header in the response indicating the protocol(s) to which the client should switch. The client can then use this information to upgrade its protocol and continue the communication with the server. However, it is not commonly used in typical DRF applications. The handling of this status code, including the negotiation and implementation of protocol upgrades, is generally done at the web server or infrastructure level.

HTTP_428_PRECONDITION_REQUIRED

This code indicates that the server requires the client to include specific preconditions in the request headers for the requested resource.

The **HTTP_428_PRECONDITION_REQUIRED** status code is commonly used when the server expects the client to provide certain conditions or preconditions in the request headers for the resource to be accessed. These preconditions could include conditions related to caching, conditional requests, or other requirements specified by the server. The server typically includes additional information or instructions in the response headers to guide the client on the specific preconditions that need to be satisfied. However, the handling of this status code and the inclusion of specific preconditions in the request headers are typically implemented based on the requirements and logic of your application.

HTTP_429_TOO_MANY_REQUESTS

This code indicates that the client has sent too many requests to the server within a given timeframe. It is part of the HTTP/1.1 protocol and is commonly used to implement rate limiting or throttling mechanisms.

The **HTTP_429_TOO_MANY_REQUESTS** status code is typically used to limit the number of requests a client can make within a specified time period. It is often employed to prevent abuse, protect server resources, or ensure fair usage across clients. The server may include additional information in the response headers, such as the number of requests remaining or the time when the limit will reset, to inform the client about the rate-limiting conditions.

HTTP_431_REQUEST_HEADER_FIELDS_TOO_LARGE

This code indicates that the server is refusing to process the client's request because the headers included in the request are too large.

The **HTTP_431_REQUEST_HEADER_FIELDS_TOO_LARGE** status code is commonly used when the server receives a request with headers that exceed its configured or allowed size limit. This limit is set to prevent excessively large headers that may cause issues with server performance or security.

When a server returns a **"431 Request Header Fields Too Large"** response, it indicates that the client should reduce the size of the request headers and resubmit the request. The server may include additional information in the response headers or body to provide guidance on how to adjust the headers appropriately. However, the handling of this status code is typically done at the web server or infrastructure level rather than explicitly within DRF views or serializers.

HTTP_451_UNAVAILABLE_FOR_LEGAL_REASONS

This code indicates that the requested resource is unavailable due to legal restrictions or legal censorship. It is part of the HTTP/1.1 protocol and was introduced as a result of internet censorship and content blocking concerns.

The **HTTP_451_UNAVAILABLE_FOR_LEGAL_REASONS** status code is commonly used when a server is required to block access to a resource because of legal obligations or court orders. It is intended to provide transparency and inform users that the resource is unavailable due to legal reasons.

The name "451" is a reference to Ray Bradbury's novel *Fahrenheit 451*, which depicts a dystopian future where books are burned and information is censored. The server may include additional information in the response body or headers to provide details about the legal reasons or instructions for further action.

HTTP_500_INTERNAL_SERVER_ERROR

This code indicates that the server encountered an unexpected condition or error that prevented it from fulfilling the client's request. It is part of the HTTP/1.1 protocol and is a generic code used to indicate internal server errors.

The **HTTP_500_INTERNAL_SERVER_ERROR** status code is commonly used when the server encounters an error that was not anticipated or handled properly. This could be due to various reasons, such as a software bug, a database connectivity issue, a configuration problem, or any other unforeseen error within the server. The server may include additional information in the response body or headers to provide details about the error, although the level of detail can vary depending on the server configuration and error handling.

HTTP_501_NOT_IMPLEMENTED

This code indicates that the server does not support or has not implemented the functionality required to fulfill the client's request.

The **HTTP_501_NOT_IMPLEMENTED** status code is commonly used when the server receives a request for a feature or method that it does not support or has not implemented. It indicates that the server understands the request but is unable to fulfil it due to the lack of implementation.

When a server returns a **"501 Not Implemented"** response, it indicates that the requested functionality or method is not available. The server may include additional information in the response body or headers to provide details about the unsupported feature or method.

HTTP_502_BAD_GATEWAY

This code indicates that a server acting as a gateway or proxy received an invalid response from an upstream server while attempting to fulfill the client's request.

The **HTTP_502_BAD_GATEWAY** status code is commonly used when there is a problem with the intermediary server, such as a gateway or proxy server, while trying to establish a connection or retrieve a response from an upstream server. This can happen if the upstream server is temporarily unavailable, experiencing connectivity issues, or returns an invalid or unexpected response.

Clients receiving a **"502 Bad Gateway"** response should handle it by considering it as a temporary error caused by a problem with the intermediary server. The client can retry the request after a brief delay, or they may choose to report the error to the server administrators or technical support for further investigation and resolution.

HTTP_503_SERVICE_UNAVAILABLE

This code indicates that the server is temporarily unable to handle the request because it is overloaded or undergoing maintenance.

The **HTTP_503_SERVICE_UNAVAILABLE** status code is commonly used to inform clients that the server is currently unable to handle the request due to high traffic, maintenance activities, or other temporary conditions. It is a way for the server to indicate that the service is temporarily unavailable but may become available again in the future.

HTTP_504_GATEWAY_TIMEOUT

This code indicates that a server acting as a gateway or proxy did not receive a timely response from an upstream server while attempting to fulfill the client's request.

The **HTTP_504_GATEWAY_TIMEOUT** status code is commonly used when there is a timeout or delay in communication between the intermediary server, such as a gateway or proxy server, and the upstream server. This can occur if the upstream server is taking too long to respond, is overloaded, or is experiencing connectivity issues.

HTTP_505_HTTP_VERSION_NOT_SUPPORTED

This code indicates that the server does not support the HTTP protocol version used in the client's request.

The **HTTP_505_HTTP_VERSION_NOT_SUPPORTED** status code is commonly used when the server receives a request with an HTTP version that it does not support or recognize. It indicates that the server cannot fulfil the request because the HTTP version specified by the client is not supported.

When a server returns a **"505 HTTP Version Not Supported"** response, it indicates that the requested HTTP version is not compatible with the server's capabilities. The server may include additional information in the response body or headers to provide details about the supported HTTP versions or instructions for the client to use a different version.

HTTP_506_VARIANT_ALSO_NEGOTIATES

This code indicates that the server has an internal configuration issue with content negotiation and multiple representations of the requested resource. It is not part of the standard HTTP/1.1 protocol but is defined in the Transparent Content Negotiation in HTTP extension.

The **HTTP_506_VARIANT_ALSO_NEGOTIATES** status code is typically used when the server encounters a situation where it cannot confidently select the best representation of the requested resource based on the client's preferences. It indicates that the server has multiple options available and further negotiation is required to determine the appropriate representation. The server may include additional information in the response body or headers to provide details about the available variants and instructions for the client to proceed with the negotiation.

HTTP_507_INSUFFICIENT_STORAGE

This code indicates that the server is unable to store or fulfil the request due to insufficient storage space. It is not part of the standard HTTP/1.1 protocol but is defined in the WebDAV (Web Distributed Authoring and Versioning) extension.

The HTTP_507_INSUFFICIENT_STORAGE status code is commonly used when the server is unable to complete the requested operation because it has reached its storage capacity or there is insufficient space to store the requested resource. This can occur in scenarios where the server has limited disk space, database capacity, or other storage constraints. The server may include additional information in the response body or headers to provide details about the storage limitations or any instructions for freeing up space or reducing the storage requirements.

HTTP_508_LOOP_DETECTED

This code indicates that the server has detected an infinite loop or cyclic redirection in the processing of the client's request. It is not part of the standard HTTP/1.1 protocol but is defined in the WebDAV (Web Distributed Authoring and Versioning) extension.

The **HTTP_508_LOOP_DETECTED** status code is typically used when there is a redirection or routing configuration issue that causes an endless loop in the request processing. This can occur when the server receives a redirection instruction that leads to another redirection, and the process continues indefinitely. The server may include additional information in the response body or headers to provide details about the specific redirections or routing configuration that caused the loop.

HTTP_510_NOT_EXTENDED

This code indicates that the client's request requires further extensions or features that are not supported by the server. It is not part of the standard HTTP/1.1 protocol but is defined in the HTTP Extension Framework.

The HTTP_510_NOT_EXTENDED status code is typically used when a client sends a request that includes additional requirements or expectations beyond the capabilities of the server. It indicates that the server cannot fulfil the request without implementing further extensions or features. The server may include additional information in the response body or headers to provide details about the required extensions or any instructions for the client to proceed.

HTTP_511_NETWORK_AUTHENTICATION_REQUIRED

This code indicates that the client must authenticate itself with a network proxy in order to access the requested resource. It is not part of the standard HTTP/1.1 protocol but is defined in the Network Authentication Required extension.

The **HTTP_511_NETWORK_AUTHENTICATION_REQUIRED** status code is typically used when a network proxy requires authentication from the client before allowing access to the requested resource. This can occur in situations where the network administrator has implemented access control policies that require authentication for certain resources or network activities. The server may include additional information in the response body or headers to provide details about the authentication requirements or instructions for the client to provide the necessary credentials.

We discussed all the status codes available in DRF. Now let's continue our discussion on endpoints.

ModelSerializer

As the name suggests, it maps model fields to serializer fields automatically. This class is an extension of DRF's **Serializer** class, which provides the basic functionality for serializing and deserializing data. The **ModelSerializer** takes care of the fields mapping between Django model fields and the serializer fields, handling validation, and saving the data back to the database. It is used to simplify the process of serializing and deserializing Django model instances when building RESTful APIs. It's a specialized serializer that automatically generates the serializer fields based on the underlying model's fields, reducing the amount of boilerplate code needed to perform these tasks. It is a powerful tool that automates much of the serialization process, making it easier to work with Django models in RESTful APIs.

When you define a **ModelSerializer** for a Django model, you don't need to explicitly define each serializer field for every model field. The **ModelSerializer** will automatically generate the serializer fields for all the model fields, including their data types and validation rules. The **ModelSerializer** performs data validation by default. It ensures that the data being serialized or deserialized adheres to the model's field constraints, such as required fields, max length, data type, etc. If the input data doesn't meet the validation criteria, DRF will raise validation errors. It also handles both creating new model instances and updating existing ones. When deserializing data during object creation or update, the serializer will automatically handle saving the data to the database with the appropriate **create()** or **update()** methods. When your model has related fields, such as foreign keys or many-to-many relationships, the ModelSerializer can automatically handle the serialization and deserialization of these relationships. It provides nested representations of related models in the serialized output and can also handle deserializing nested data into related model instances.

While **ModelSerializer** provides automatic field generation, it also allows you to customize and override the default behavior easily. You can add additional fields, modify serialization logic, or include custom validation methods as needed.

Using **ModelSerializer** significantly speeds up the development process by reducing the amount of repetitive serialization and deserialization code. It ensures consistency between the API data representation and the database models, making it easier to maintain and evolve the API over time.

Let's understand how to apply this concept to our existing project. Go to chapter6_serializers_views/api/serializers.py and add the following lines of code:

```
class WatchListModelSerializer(serializers.ModelSerializer):
    class Meta:
        model = WatchList
        fields = "__all__"
        ref_name = 'C6WatchListModelSerializer'
    def validate_title(self, value):
        if "@" in value:
            serializers.ValidationError("Invalid Title")
        return value

    def validate_storyline(self, value):
        if "@" in value:
            serializers.ValidationError("Invalid Storyline")
        return value

    def validate_category(self, value):
        if value not in ["MOVIE", "SERIES"]:
            serializers.ValidationError("Not a valid category")
        return value

    def validate_platform(self, value):
        return value

    def validate(self, data):
        title = data.get("title", None)
        storyline = data.get("storyline", None)
        if (title and storyline) and (len(title) > len(storyline)):
            raise serializers.ValidationError("Length of title is bigger
            than storyline")
        return super().validate(data)
```

As mentioned above, we don't need to define create() or update() methods for serializers. Also, by default, serializer validates each serializer field against model fields. But if you need any additional validation, you can define it as defined in the above code.

Now go to chapter6_serializers_views/api/views.py and add the following lines of code:

```
class WatchlistModelSerializerView(APIView):
    """
```

```
    View to list all Movies in the system.
    """

    def get(self, request, format=None):
        """
        Return a list of all watchlist.
        """
        watchlist = WatchList.objects.all()
        serializer = serializers.WatchListModelSerializer(watchlist, many =
                     True, context={'request': request})
        return Response(serializer.data)

    def post(self, request, format=None):
        """
        Create a new watchlist.
        """
        serializer = serializers.WatchListModelSerializer(data=request.
                     data, context={'request': request})
        if serializer.is_valid():
            serializer.save()
            return Response(serializer.data, status=status.HTTP_201_
            CREATED)
        else:
            return Response(serializer.errors, status=status.HTTP_400_BAD_
            REQUEST)
```

To access the watchlist API endpoint on Postman, the request shall be in the format:

GET `{{domain}}/api/chapter6_serializers_views/watchlist-model-serializer/`.

Its response will be in the below format:

```
[
    {
        "id": 49,
        "title": "Movie1",
        "storyline": "Movie1-Story",
        "active": true,
        "imdb_rating": 2.0,
```

```
        "created": "2024-10-26T20:06:27.406145Z",
        "episodes": 0,
        "category": "MOVIE",
        "platform": 1
    },
    ...
]
```

Let us test the same endpoint to create a Watchlist object with the below data:

```
POST {{domain}}/api/chapter6_serializers_views/watchlist-model-serializer/
```

Body:

```
{
    "title": "Movie4",
    "storyline": "Movie4 Storyline",
    "active": true,
    "platform": 1,
    "imdb_rating": 2.0,
    "episodes": 0,
    "category": "MOVIE"
}
```

You should be able to see the below response format:

```
{
    "id": 66,
    "title": "Movie4",
    "storyline": "Movie4 Storyline",
    "active": true,
    "imdb_rating": 2.0,
    "created": "2024-12-28T08:14:47.409001Z",
    "episodes": 0,
    "category": "MOVIE",
    "platform": 1
}
```

Specifying Which Fields to Include

If we want to get any specific fields of Watchlist from endpoints, we can specify them using the **fields** attribute.

Go to chapter6_serializers_views/api/serializers.py and add the following lines of code to **WatchListModelSerializer:**

```
class WatchListModelSerializer(serializers.ModelSerializer):
    class Meta:
        model = WatchList
        # fields = "__all__"
        fields = ["title", "storyline", "platform"]
```

Let us test the same endpoint to get the Watchlist objects:

```
GET {{domain}}/api/chapter6_serializers_views/watchlist-model-serializer/
```

Its response will be in the below format:

```
[
    {
        "title": "Movie1",
        "storyline": "Movie1-Story",
        "platform": 1
    },
    ...
]
```

Now you should be able to see a list of movies with only the title, storyline, and platform fields.

Specifying Nested Serialization

You can use the depth attribute in your serializer to specify nested serialization without explicitly defining a nested serializer for related models. The depth attribute allows you to control how many levels of nested objects are included in the serialized representation. It's used to automatically include related objects in the serialized representation without explicitly defining separate serializers for them. While depth can be convenient in some scenarios, it also has its limitations and should be used with caution.

Let's suppose we have three models—**ModelA**, **ModelB**, and **ModelC**. **ModelA** depends on **ModelB**, while **ModelB** depends on **ModelC**. They are defined like so:

```
from django.db import models

class ModelC(models.Model):
    content = models.CharField(max_length=128)

class ModelB(models.Model):
    model_c = models.ForeignKey(to=ModelC, on_delete=models.CASCADE)
    content = models.CharField(max_length=128)

class ModelA(models.Model):
    model_b = models.ForeignKey(to=ModelB, on_delete=models.CASCADE)
    content = models.CharField(max_length=128)
```

Our **ModelA** serializer, which is the top-level object, looks like this:

```
from rest_framework import serializers


class ModelASerializer(serializers.ModelSerializer):
    class Meta:
        model = ModelA
        fields = '__all__'
```

If we serialize an example object, we'll get the following output:

```
{
    "id": 1,
    "content": "A content",
    "model_b": 1
}
```

Now let's say we also want to include **ModelB's** content when serializing **ModelA**. We could add the explicit definition to our **ModelASerializer** or use the depth field.

When we change depth to 1 in our serializer, like so:

```
from rest_framework import serializers

class ModelASerializer(serializers.ModelSerializer):
    class Meta:
```

```
        model = ModelA
        fields = '__all__'
        depth = 1
```

The output changes to the following:

```
{
    "id": 1,
    "content": "A content",
    "model_b": {
        "id": 1,
        "content": "B content",
        "model_c": 1
    }
}
```

If we change it to 2, our serializer will serialize a level deeper:

```
{
    "id": 1,
    "content": "A content",
    "model_b": {
        "id": 1,
        "content": "B content",
        "model_c": {
            "id": 1,
            "content": "C content"
        }
    }
}
```

Here are some reasons why you might consider using the depth attribute in DRF serialization:

- **Simplified Serialization**: When you have deeply nested relationships between models, using depth can simplify the serialization process. Instead of defining separate serializers for each related model, you can set depth to the desired level, and DRF will automatically include related objects up to that depth in the serialized output.

- **Reduced Boilerplate**: Defining nested serializers manually can lead to more code, especially when you have multiple nested relationships. By using depth, you can reduce the amount of boilerplate code needed to create serializers for related models.
- **Quick Exploration of Related Data**: During development or debugging, setting depth can be helpful for quickly exploring related data. It allows you to see a complete representation of the object and its related objects without explicitly specifying the nested serializers.

However, there are some considerations and potential drawbacks to keep in mind:

- **Lack of Customization**: The depth attribute provides limited control over the serialization of related objects. If you need more fine-grained control or want to customize the representation of related models, manually defining nested serializers is a better approach.
- **Over-serialization**: Using a high depth value or not setting it at all can lead to over-serialization, where large amounts of data are included in the response. This can result in slower API responses and unnecessarily bloated payloads.
- **Circular Dependencies**: If you have circular dependencies between models, using depth can lead to infinite recursion or errors in serialization. In such cases, manually defining nested serializers with depth=1 or using custom serializers to handle circular dependencies is necessary.
- **Security Considerations**: When exposing APIs to external clients, you should be cautious about overexposing sensitive data. Using depth without proper consideration can inadvertently reveal more information than intended.

The **"depth"** attribute can be useful for quick serialization of related models during development or when dealing with moderately nested relationships. However, for more complex scenarios, it's often better to define nested serializers manually, as it provides greater control and customization options over the serialization process. Always consider the specific requirements of your project and the potential performance and security implications before deciding whether to use **"depth"** or not.

Go to chapter6_serializers_views/api/serializers.py and add the following lines of code:

```
class StreamPlatformModelSerializer(serializers.ModelSerializer):
    class Meta:
        model = StreamPlatform
        fields = "__all__"
        depth = 1
        ref_name = 'C6StreamPlatformModelSerializer'
```

Specifying Fields Explicitly

You can add extra fields to a **ModelSerializer** or override the default fields by declaring fields on the class, just as you would for a **Serializer** class.

Go to chapter6_serializers_views/api/serializers.py and add the following lines of code:

```
class StreamPlatformModelSerializer(serializers.ModelSerializer):
    watchlist = WatchListModelSerializer(many=True, read_only=True)
    ...
```

Specifying Read-Only Fields

You may wish to specify multiple fields as read-only. Instead of adding each field explicitly with the **read_only=True** attribute, you may use the shortcut Meta option, **read_only_fields**.

This option should be a list or tuple of field names. Go to chapter6_serializers_views/api/serializers.py and add the following lines of code:

```
class WatchListModelSerializer(serializers.ModelSerializer):
    full_title = serializers.SerializerMethodField()

    class Meta:
        model = WatchList
        fields = "__all__"
        # fields = ["title", "storyline", "platform"]
```

```
        read_only_fields = ['full_title']

    def get_full_title(self, obj):
        return obj.full_title
```

Model fields that have **editable=False** set and **AutoField** fields will be set to read-only by default and do not need to be added to the **read_only_fields** option.

There is a special case where a read-only field is part of a **unique_together** constraint at the model level. In this case, the field is required by the serializer class in order to validate the constraint but should also not be editable by the user.

The right way to deal with this is to specify the field explicitly on the serializer, providing both the **read_only=True** and **default=...** keyword arguments.

One example of this is a read-only relation to the currently authenticated **User** which is **unique_together** with another identifier. In this case, you would declare the user field like so:

```
class WatchListModelSerializer(serializers.ModelSerializer):
    full_title = serializers.SerializerMethodField()
    user = serializers.PrimaryKeyRelatedField(read_only=True,
default=serializers.CurrentUserDefault())
    ...
```

Additional Keyword Arguments

The serializers allow you to provide additional configuration options for individual fields in the serializer. It provides a way to customize the behavior of serializer fields beyond the default settings derived from the model.

The **extra_kwargs** attribute is a dictionary where the keys are the field names and the values are dictionaries containing field-level options. These options can include various attributes that modify how the field behaves during serialization and deserialization.

Here are some common use cases for **extra_kwargs** in DRF serializers:

1. **Customizing Field-Level Attributes**

   You can use **extra_kwargs** to override field-level attributes such as **required**, **allow_null**, **default**, etc., for specific fields.
   For example: Go to chapter6_serializers_views/api/serializers.py and add the following lines of code:

```
class StreamPlatformModelSerializer(serializers.ModelSerializer):
    ...
    class Meta:
        ...
        extra_kwargs = {
            'about':{'allow_null':True, 'default':""},
            'website':{'required': False}
        }
```

In the above serializer, we are changing the **"about"** field to take null values and can set it to an empty string. Also, changing the **"website"** field attribute to a non-required field.

2. **Overriding Field-Level Validators**

   You can add or override field-level validators by using the validators attribute within **extra_kwargs.**
   For example: Go to chapter6_serializers_views/api/serializers.py and add the following lines of code:

```
class WatchListModelSerializer(serializers.ModelSerializer):
    ...
    class Meta:
        ...
        extra_kwargs = {
            'imdb_rating': {'validators':[MinValueValidator(1.0),
            MaxValueValidator(10.0)]}
        }
```

   In the above serializer, we have added **MinValueValidator** and **MaxValueValidator** for validating the **"imdb_rating"** field.

Customizing Field Mappings

The **ModelSerializer** class also exposes an API that you can override to alter how serializer fields are automatically determined when instantiating the serializer.

Normally, if a **ModelSerializer** does not generate the fields you need by default, then you should either add them to the class explicitly or simply use a regular **Serializer** class instead. However, in some cases, you may want to create a new base class that defines how the serializer fields are created for any given model.

1. **.serializer_field_mapping**

   This is a class attribute in Django Rest Framework's (DRF) serializers that allows you to define custom mappings between model fields and serializer fields. It provides a way to customize how specific fields in your model are represented in the serializer.

   By default, DRF automatically maps model fields to serializer fields based on the field types. However, in some cases, you may want to customize the serialization behavior for specific fields. This is where the **serializer_field_mapping** comes in handy.

2. **.serializer_related_field**

   This attribute is used to customize the representation of related fields in serializers. It allows you to specify a custom serializer field to be used for representing the related model instances, giving you fine-grained control over how related objects are displayed in API responses.

   When defining a serializer for a model, related fields, such as foreign keys, many-to-many relationships, or reverse relationships, are represented by default using serializers that match the type of the related model. However, in some cases, you might want to customize how related objects are serialized, such as displaying only specific fields, applying filtering, or performing additional operations on the related data.

   By using the **serializer_related_field** attribute, you can create custom serializers for related fields, which can provide more control over the representation of the related data. This is particularly useful when you want to display nested representations of related models, apply transformations, or filter the related data.

Create a chapter6_serializers_views/api/fields.py and add the following lines of code:

```
from rest_framework import serializers

class CustomPrimaryKeyRelatedField(serializers.
PrimaryKeyRelatedField):

    def to_representation(self, value):
        if self.pk_field is not None:
            return self.pk_field.to_representation(value.pk)
        return {"id": value.pk}
```

Go to chapter6_serializers_views/api/serializers.py and add the following lines of code:

```
from chapter6_serializers_views.api import fields


class WatchListModelSerializer(serializers.ModelSerializer):
    ...
    serializer_related_field = fields.CustomPrimaryKeyRelatedField
    ...
```

In the above code, we have made all related fields to map to **CustomPrimaryKeyRelatedField** which always points to the primary key of the related object.

3. **.serializer_url_field**

   This attribute is used to customize the representation of a URL field in serializers. It allows you to specify a custom serializer field to be used for representing URL fields, giving you control over how URLs are displayed in API responses.

   URL fields are commonly used in serializers to represent hyperlinks to related resources or external links. By default, DRF uses the **HyperlinkedIdentityField** or **HyperlinkedRelatedField** serializers to represent URL fields. These serializers generate hyperlinks based on the view names and lookup values of related objects. However, in some cases, you may want to customize how URLs are represented, for example, by including additional parameters or modifying the URL structure.

By using the **serializer_url_field** attribute, you can create custom serializers for URL fields, which allows you to define your own URL representation logic. This is useful when you need to customize the URL generation or include additional data in the URL based on the context.

4. **.serializer_choice_field**
   This attribute is used to customize the representation of a model's choice field in serializers. It allows you to specify a custom serializer field to be used for representing choice fields, providing you control over how choices are displayed in API responses.

   Choice fields in Django models are fields that limit the possible values to a predefined set of choices. For example, using the choices attribute on a model field, you can define the available choices for that field.

   By default, DRF uses the **ChoiceField** serializer to represent choice fields in serializers, which serializes the choices as they are defined in the model. However, in some cases, you may want to customize how the choices are represented, for example, by providing a different label or value for the choices.

   By using the **serializer_choice_field** attribute, you can create custom serializers for choice fields, allowing you to define your own representation logic for the choices.
   Go to chapter6_serializers_views/api/fields.py and add the following lines of code:

```
class CustomChoiceField(serializers.ChoiceField):
    def to_representation(self, value):
        # Custom representation of the choice field value
        # Here, we convert the value to lowercase
        return value.lower()
```

Go to chapter6_serializers_views/api/fields.py and add the following lines of code:

```
class WatchListModelSerializer(serializers.ModelSerializer):
    ...
    serializer_choice_field = fields.CustomChoiceField
```

In the above code, we are defining the custom field **CustomChoiceField** and assigning it to the attribute **serializer_choice_field** to apply to all choice fields related to this serializer.

The field_class and field_kwargs API

These attributes are part of the **serializer_field_mapping** API, which allows you to customize how model fields are represented in serializers.

The "**field_class**" is used to specify a custom serializer field class for a particular model field. When you define a serializer, DRF automatically maps each model field to an appropriate serializer field based on the field's type. However, you may want to use a custom serializer field for certain model fields to provide specific behavior or formatting in the API responses. By using the field_class attribute, you can override the default serializer field with your custom serializer field.

"field_kwargs" is used to pass additional keyword arguments to the custom serializer field defined with field_class. When using a custom serializer field, you may need to provide specific options or configurations for that field. The field_kwargs attribute allows you to pass any extra arguments required for the custom serializer field.

The following methods are called to determine the class and keyword arguments for each field that should be automatically included on the serializer. Each of these methods should return a two-tuple of **(field_class, field_kwargs)**. These methods are internal methods, and in most cases, you won't need to directly call or override it. Instead, you can rely on DRF's automatic serializer field generation to handle related model fields. However, understanding its functionality can be helpful when you need to customize how relational serializer fields are created for specific related model fields.

We can see the implementation of the below methods at the link: django-rest-framework/rest_framework/serializers.py at master · encode/django-rest-framework · GitHub.

1. **.build_standard_field(self, field_name, model_field)**

   This method is an internal method used within Django Rest Framework (DRF) to create a standard serializer field for a model field. This method is part of the serializer field creation process and is called when DRF automatically generates serializer fields for the model fields.

   This method takes the following two arguments:

   - **field_name**: The name of the model field for which the serializer field is being created
   - **model_field**: The actual model field object from the associated model

   When you define a serializer and include a model field in the fields or exclude list, DRF automatically generates the corresponding serializer field for that model field. The **build_standard_field** method is responsible for creating this default serializer field based on the given model field. The default implementation returns a serializer class based on the **serializer_field_mapping** attribute.

2. **.build_relational_field(self, field_name, relation_info)**

   This method is an internal method used within Django Rest Framework (DRF) to create relational serializer fields for related model fields. This method is called during the process of automatically generating serializer fields for model fields with relationships, such as ForeignKey, OneToOneField, or ManyToManyField.

   This method takes the following two arguments:

   - **field_name**: The name of the related model field for which the serializer field is being created.
   - **relation_info**: Information about the relationship between the current model and the related model. This information includes details such as the type of the relationship (ForeignKey,

OneToOneField, or ManyToManyField), the related model's serializer class, and other relevant metadata. This is a named tuple that contains model_field, related_model, to_many, and has_through_model properties.

When you define a serializer for a model that includes related model fields, DRF automatically generates serializer fields for those related fields. The **build_relational_field** method is responsible for creating these relational serializer fields based on the information about the relationship.

The **build_relational_field** method is defined within the **BaseSerializer** class in DRF. Subclasses, such as serializers. ModelSerializer, use this method to create relational serializer fields automatically based on the model's related fields.

DRF will use **build_relational_field** to automatically create relational serializer fields for each related model field specified in the fields or exclude. The method chooses an appropriate serializer field class based on the type of the related model field (e.g., PrimaryKeyRelatedField, HyperlinkedRelatedField, etc.).

3. **.build_nested_field(self, field_name, relation_info, nested_depth)**

   This method is called to generate a serializer field that maps to a relational model field, when the **depth** option has been set. It creates nested fields for forward and reverse relationships.

   The default implementation dynamically creates a nested serializer class based on either **ModelSerializer** or **HyperlinkedModelSerializer**.
   This method takes the following three arguments:

   - **field_name**: The name of the related model field for which the serializer field is being created.

- **relation_info**: Information about the relationship between the current model and the related model. This information includes details such as the type of the relationship (ForeignKey, OneToOneField, or ManyToManyField), the related model's serializer class, and other relevant metadata. It is a named tuple that contains model_field, related_model, to_many, and has_through_model properties.
- **nested_depth:** This is a value of the depth option, minus one.

4. **build_property_field(self, field_name, model_class)**

   This method is called to generate a serializer field that maps to a property or zero-argument method on the model class. It creates a read-only field for model methods and properties. The default implementation returns a **ReadOnlyField** class.
   This method takes the following two arguments:

   - **field_name**: The name of the model field for which the serializer field is being created
   - **model_class**: Class of the model

   This method implementation is still in progress. Even though this method takes the above two arguments, it does not use them. For now, by default, this method is used to assign **field_class** to the **ReadOnlyField** class.

5. **build_url_field(self, field_name, model_class)**

   This method is called to generate a serializer field for the serializer's own URL field. The default implementation returns a **HyperlinkedIdentityField** class. It is used to create a field representing the object's own URL.
   This method takes the following two arguments:

   - **field_name**: The name of the model field for which the serializer field is being created
   - **model_class**: Class of the model

6. **build_unknown_field(self, field_name, model_class)**
   This method is called when the field name does not map to any model field or model property. The default implementation raises an error, although subclasses may customize this behavior.
   This method takes the following two arguments:

   - **field_name**: The name of the model field for which the serializer field is being created
   - **model_class**: Class of the model

HyperlinkedModelSerializer

This is a subclass of Django Rest Framework's (DRF) **ModelSerializer**, specifically designed for representing related model fields as hyperlinks in the API responses rather than primary keys. It provides a convenient way to handle related models and create hyperlinks between different resources. When you use **HyperlinkedModelSerializer**, the related model fields are represented as hyperlinks to their detail views, allowing clients to easily navigate between resources using the provided hyperlinks.

In this serializer, by default, the serializer will include a URL field instead of a primary key field. The URL field will be represented using a **HyperlinkedIdentityField** serializer field, and any relationships on the model will be represented using a **HyperlinkedRelatedField** serializer field.

When instantiating a **HyperlinkedModelSerializer**, you must include the current request in the serializer context. Let's implement this concept in our Watchlist model.

Go to chapter6_serializers_views/api/serializers.py and add the following lines of code:

```
class WatchListHMSerializer(serializers.HyperlinkedModelSerializer):

    class Meta:
        model = WatchList
        fields = "__all__"
        read_only_fields = ['full_title']
        extra_kwargs = {
            'imdb_rating': {'validators':[MinValueValidator(1.0),
            MaxValueValidator(10.0)]},
```

```
            'platform': {'view_name':'streamplatform-detail-hm-
            serializer'},
            'url': {'view_name': 'streamplatform-detail-hm-serializer',
            'lookup_field': 'pk'},
        }

class StreamPlatformHMSerializer(serializers.HyperlinkedModelSerializer):
    watchlist = WatchListHMSerializer(many=True, read_only=True)

    class Meta:
        model = StreamPlatform
        fields = "__all__"
        depth = 1
        extra_kwargs = {
            'about':{'allow_null':True, 'default':""},
            'website':{'required': False},
            'url':{'view_name':'streamplatform-detail-hm-serializer',
            'lookup_field':'pk'}
        }
```

Go to chapter6_serializers_views/api/views.py and add the following lines of code:

```
class WatchlistHMSerializerView(APIView):
    """
    View to list all Movies in the system.
    """
    def get(self, request, format=None):
        """
        Return a list of all watchlist.
        """
        watchlist = WatchList.objects.all()
        serializer = serializers.WatchListHMSerializer(watchlist,
                     many = True, context={'request': request})
        return Response(serializer.data)

    def post(self, request, format=None):
```

```
        """
        Create a new watchlist.
        """
        serializer = serializers.WatchListHMSerializer(data=request.data,
                     context={'request': request})
        if serializer.is_valid():
            serializer.save()
            return Response(serializer.data, status=status.HTTP_201_CREATED)
        else:
            return Response(serializer.errors, status=status.HTTP_400_BAD_
            REQUEST)

class WatchlistDetailHMSerializerView(APIView):
    """
    View in detail individual Watchlist in the system.
    """
    def get(self, request, pk, format=None):
        try:
            watchlist = WatchList.objects.get(pk=pk)
            serializer = serializers.WatchListHMSerializer(watchlist,
            context={'request': request})
            return Response(serializer.data)
        except WatchList.DoesNotExist:
            raise Http404

class StreamPlatformDetailHMSerializerView(APIView):
    """
    Stream Platform Detail View
    """

    def get(self, request, pk):
        try:
            platform = StreamPlatform.objects.get(pk=pk)
        except StreamPlatform.DoesNotExist:
            return Response({'error': 'Not found'}, status=status.
            HTTP_404_NOT_FOUND)
```

```
        serializer = serializers.StreamPlatformHMSerializer(platform,
        context={'request': request})
        return Response(serializer.data)
```

In the above views, when instantiating **WatchListHMSerializer**, we have included the current request in the context. Doing so will ensure that the hyperlinks can include an appropriate hostname, so that the resulting representation uses fully qualified URLs.

Add the corresponding URL in chapter6_serializers_views/api/urls.py as below:

```
urlpatterns = [
    ...
    # Using HyperlinkedModelSerializer for the views
    path('watchlist-hm-serializer/', views.WatchlistHMSerializerView.as_
    view(), name="watchlist-hm-serializer"),
    path('watchlist-detail-hm-serializer/<int:pk>/', views.
    WatchlistDetailHMSerializerView.as_view(), name="watchlist-detail-hm-
    serializer"),
    path('streamplatform-detail-hm-serializer/<int:pk>/', views.
    StreamPlatformDetailHMSerializerView.as_view(), name="streamplatform-
    detail-hm-serializer"),
]
```

The following are examples of requests and their response for the above endpoints:

Request:

```
GET {{domain}}/api/chapter6_serializers_views/watchlist-hm-serializer
```

Response:

```
[
    {
        "url": "http://127.0.0.1:8000/api/chapter6_serializers_views/
        streamplatform-detail-hm-serializer/49/",
        "title": "Movie1",
        "storyline": "Movie1-Story",
        "active": true,
        "imdb_rating": 2.0,
        "created": "2024-10-26T20:06:27.406145Z",
```

```
        "episodes": 0,
        "category": "MOVIE",
        "platform": "http://127.0.0.1:8000/api/chapter6_serializers_views
        /streamplatform-detail-hm-serializer/1/"
    },
    ...
]
```


Request:

GET {{domain}}/api/chapter6_serializers_views/watchlist-detail-hm-serializer/63/

Response:


```
{
    "url": "http://127.0.0.1:8000/api/chapter6_serializers_views/
    streamplatform-detail-hm-serializer/63/",
    "title": "Scientist.",
    "storyline": "Show project board charge. Answer maintain seat prevent
    oil accept although.",
    "active": true,
    "imdb_rating": 3.1,
    "created": "2024-12-22T09:07:50.938324Z",
    "episodes": 83,
    "category": "SERIES",
    "platform": "http://127.0.0.1:8000/api/chapter6_serializers_views/
    streamplatform-detail-hm-serializer/13/"
}
```


Request:

GET {{domain}}/api/chapter6_serializers_views/streamplatform-detail-hm-serializer/1/

Response:


```
{
```

```
    "url": "http://127.0.0.1:8000/api/chapter6_serializers_views/
           streamplatform-detail-hm-serializer/1/",
    "watchlist": [
        {
            "url": "http://127.0.0.1:8000/api/chapter6_serializers_views/
                   streamplatform-detail-hm-serializer/49/",
            "title": "Movie1",
            "storyline": "Movie1-Story",
            "active": true,
            "imdb_rating": 2.0,
            "created": "2024-10-26T20:06:27.406145Z",
            "episodes": 0,
            "category": "MOVIE",
           "platform": "http://127.0.0.1:8000/api/chapter6_serializers_views/
                      streamplatform-detail-hm-serializer/1/"
        },
        ...
    ],
    "name": "Netflix",
    "about": "Netflix About",
    "website": "https://www.netflix.com"
}
```

How Hyperlinked Views Are Determined

There needs to be a way of determining which views should be used for hyperlinking to model instances. By default, hyperlinks are expected to correspond to a view name that matches the style "**{model_name}-detail"** and looks up the instance by a **pk** keyword argument.

You can override a URL field view name and lookup field by using either or both of the **view_name** and **lookup_field** options in the **extra_kwargs** setting in **WatchListHMSerializer** and **StreamPlatformHMSerializer**.

Properly matching together hyperlinked representations and your URL conf can sometimes be a bit fiddly. Printing the **repr** of a **HyperlinkedModelSerializer** instance is a particularly useful way to inspect exactly which view names and lookup fields the relationships are expected to map to.

Changing the URL Field Name

The name of the URL field defaults to "url". You can override this globally, by using the **URL_FIELD_NAME** setting.

ListSerializer

This is a specialized serializer used to handle multiple objects when serializing or deserializing lists of data. The **ListSerializer** class provides the behavior for serializing and validating multiple objects at once. You won't *typically* need to use **ListSerializer** directly but should instead simply pass **many=True** when instantiating a serializer. When a serializer is instantiated and many=True is passed, a **ListSerializer** instance will be created. The serializer class then becomes a child of the parent ListSerializer.

By default, when you use a regular serializer for a model or data, it handles single instances of that model or data. However, when you need to work with lists of instances, DRF uses **ListSerializer** to manage the serialization and deserialization of multiple objects.

The following argument can also be passed to a **ListSerializer** field or a serializer that is passed **many=True**:

allow_empty

This is **True** by default but can be set to **False** if you want to disallow empty lists as valid input.

max_length

This is **None** by default but can be set to a positive integer if you want to validate that the list contains no more than this number of elements.

min_length

This is **None** by default but can be set to a positive integer if you want to validate that the list contains no fewer than this number of elements.

Customizing ListSerializer Behavior

Customizing the behavior of a **ListSerializer** in Django Rest Framework (DRF) allows you to control how lists of objects are serialized and deserialized. You can apply custom transformations, validations, and handling specific to lists of instances for your model or data.

To customize the behavior of a **ListSerializer**, you need to create a custom ListSerializer subclass and override its methods or provide custom logic as needed. You can do this by defining a child attribute that refers to a regular serializer that will be used for individual items in the list.

There are a few use cases when you might want to customize the **ListSerializer** behavior. For example:

- You want to provide particular validation of the lists, such as checking that one element does not conflict with another element in a list.
- You want to customize the create or update behavior of multiple objects.

For these cases, you can modify the class that is used when **many=True** is passed, by using the **list_serializer_class** option on the serializer Meta class.

We can implement this concept in our project.

Customizing Multiple Create

Customizing the behavior of a **ListSerializer** in Django Rest Framework (DRF) allows you to control how lists of objects are serialized and deserialized. You can apply custom transformations, validations, and handling specific to lists of instances for your model or data.

To customize the behavior of a **ListSerializer**, you need to create a custom **ListSerializer** subclass and override its methods or provide custom logic as needed. You can do this by defining a child attribute that refers to a regular serializer that will be used for individual items in the list.

The default implementation for multiple object creation is to simply call **.create()** for each item in the list. If you want to customize this behavior, you'll need to customize the **.create()** method on the **ListSerializer** class that is used when **many=True** is passed.

Let's go to chapter6_serializers_views/api/serializers.py and add the following lines of code:

```
class CustomWatchlistListSerializer(serializers.ListSerializer):
    update_data=[]

    def create(self, validated_data):
        # You can do some validation here before making bulk create
        watchlist = [WatchList(**item) for item in validated_data]
        result = WatchList.objects.bulk_create(watchlist)
```

```
        return result

class WatchlistDemoListSerializer(serializers.ModelSerializer):

    class Meta:
        model = WatchList
        fields = "__all__"
        extra_kwargs = {
            'imdb_rating': {'validators':[MinValueValidator(1.0),
                            MaxValueValidator(10.0)]}
        }

        list_serializer_class = CustomWatchlistListSerializer


    def create(self, validated_data):
        instance = WatchList(**validated_data)

        if(isinstance(self._kwargs["data"], dict)):
            instance.save()

        return instance
```

In the above code, we are creating the **CustomWatchlistListSerializer** class to handle a list of objects.

Go to chapter6_serializers_views/api/views.py and add the following lines of code:

```
class WatchlistListSerializerView(APIView):
    """

    View to list all Movies in the system.
    """

    def get(self, request, format=None):
        """

        Return a list of all watchlist.
        """

        watchlist = WatchList.objects.all()
        serializer = serializers.WatchlistDemoListSerializer(watchlist,
                    many = True, context={'request': request})
        return Response(serializer.data)
```

```
    def post(self, request, format=None):
        """
        Create a new watchlist.
        """
        if type(request.data) is dict:
            serializer = serializers.WatchlistDemoListSerializer(data=reque
                         st.data, many=False)
        else:
            serializer = serializers.WatchlistDemoListSerializer(data=reque
                         st.data, many=True)
        serializer.is_valid(raise_exception=True)
        serializer.save()
        return Response(serializer.data, status=status.HTTP_201_CREATED)
```

Add the corresponding URL in chapter6_serializers_views/api/urls.py as below:

```
urlpatterns = [
    ...
    # Using ListSerializer for the views
    path('watchlist-list-serializer/', views.WatchlistListSerializerView.
    as_view(), name="watchlist-list-serializer"),
]
```

The following are examples of requests and their response for the above endpoints:

Request:

```
GET {{domain}}/api/chapter6_serializers_views/watchlist-list-serializer/
```

Response:


```
[
    {
        "id": 49,
        "title": "Movie1",
        "storyline": "Movie1-Story",
        "active": true,
        "imdb_rating": 2.0,
        "created": "2024-10-26T20:06:27.406145Z",
```

```
        "episodes": 0,
        "category": "MOVIE",
        "platform": 1
    },
    ...
]
```

Request:

```
POST {{domain}}/api/chapter6_serializers_views/watchlist-list-serializer/
```

Body:

```
[
    {
        "title": "Movie10",
        "storyline": "Movie10 Story",
        "active": true,
        "platform": "2",
        "imdb_rating": 4.0,
        "episodes": 0,
        "category": "MOVIE"
    },
    {
        "title": "Series10",
        "storyline": "Series10 Story",
        "active": true,
        "platform": "2",
        "imdb_rating": 4.0,
        "episodes": 0,
        "category": "SERIES"
    }
]
```

Response:

```
[
    {
        "id": 88,
```

```
        "title": "Movie10",
        "storyline": "Movie10 Story",
        "active": true,
        "imdb_rating": 4.0,
        "created": "2024-12-28T16:26:49.877404Z",
        "episodes": 0,
        "category": "MOVIE",
        "platform": 2
    },
    {
        "id": 89,
        "title": "Series10",
        "storyline": "Series10 Story",
        "active": true,
        "imdb_rating": 4.0,
        "created": "2024-12-28T16:26:49.877512Z",
        "episodes": 0,
        "category": "SERIES",
        "platform": 2
    }
]
```


BaseSerializer

BaseSerializer class that can be used to easily support alternative serialization and deserialization styles.

This class implements the same basic API as the Serializer class:

- **.data**: Returns the outgoing primitive representation
- **.is_valid()**: Deserializes and validates incoming data
- **.validated_data**: Returns the validated incoming data
- **.errors**: Returns any errors during validation
- **.save()**: Persists the validated data into an object instance

There are four methods that can be overridden, depending on what functionality you want the serializer class to support:

- **.to_representation()**: Override this to support serialization, for read operations.
- **.to_internal_value()**: Override this to support deserialization, for write operations.
- **.create()** and **.update()**: Override either or both of these to support saving instances.

Because this class provides the same interface as the Serializer class, you can use it with the existing generic class-based views exactly as you would for a regular Serializer or **ModelSerializer**.

The only difference you'll notice when doing so is that the **BaseSerializer** classes will not generate HTML forms in the browsable API. This is because the data they return does not include all the field information that would allow each field to be rendered into a suitable HTML input.

Two of the most useful functions inside the **BaseSerializer** class that we can override are **to_representation()** and **to_internal_value()**. By overriding them, we can change the serialization and deserialization behavior, respectively, to append additional data, extract data, and handle relationships.

- to_representation() allows us to change the serialization output.
- to_internal_value() allows us to change the deserialization output.

Read-Only BaseSerializer Classes

To implement a read-only serializer using the **BaseSerializer** class, we just need to override the **.to_representation()** method.

Assume that we have business requirements stating that, same required parameters which are defined in different models, we need only the data from each model. In this case, we can extract only the required parameters from the model using a serializer as in the below approach.

Go to chapter6_serializers_views/api/serializers.py and add the following lines of code:

```
class WatchlistBaseSerializer(serializers.BaseSerializer):
    def to_representation(self, instance):
```

```
        return {
            'title': instance.title,
            'platform': instance.platform.name,
            'category': instance.category,
        }
```

Go to chapter6_serializers_views/api/views.py and add the following lines of code:

```
class WatchlistBaseSerializerView(APIView):
    """
    View to list all Movies in the system.
    """
    def get(self, request, format=None):
        """
        Return a list of all watchlist.
        """
        watchlist = WatchList.objects.all()
        serializer = serializers.WatchlistBaseSerializer(watchlist, many = True)
        return Response(serializer.data)
```

Add the corresponding URL in chapter6_serializers_views/api/urls.py as below:

```
urlpatterns = [
    ...
    # Using BaseSerializer for the views
    path('watchlist-base-serializer/', views.WatchlistBaseSerializerView.
    as_view(), name="watchlist-base-serializer"),
]
```

Now you can access the endpoint as below:

Request:

```
GET {{domain}}/api/chapter6_serializers_views/watchlist-list-serializer/
```

Response:

```
[
    {
        "title": "Movie1",
```

```
        "platform": "Netflix",
        "category": "MOVIE"
    },
    ...
]
```

Read-Write BaseSerializer Classes

To create a read-write serializer, we first need to implement a **.to_internal_value()** method. This method returns the validated values that will be used to construct the object instance and may raise a **serializers.ValidationError** if the supplied data is in an incorrect format.

Once you've implemented **.to_internal_value()**, the basic validation API will be available on the serializer, and you will be able to use **.is_valid()**, **.validated_data**, and **.errors**.

If you want to also support **.save()**, you'll need to also implement either or both of the **.create()** and **.update()** methods.

Also, suppose the services that use our API appends unnecessary data to the endpoint when creating resources as below:

```
{
   "info": {
       "extra": "data"
   },
   "resource": {
    "title": "Movie6",
    "storyline": "Movie6 Story",
    "active": true,
    "platform": "Netflix",
    "imdb_rating": 2.0,
    "created": "2022-07-15T10:08:42.690612Z",
    "episodes": 0,
    "category": "MOVIE"
    }
}
```

If we try to serialize this data, our serializer will fail because it will be unable to extract the resource. In this case, we can override **to_internal_value()** to extract the resource data.

Now go to chapter6_serializers_views/api/serializers.py and add the following lines of code to the serializer **WatchlistBaseSerializer** as below:

```
class WatchlistBaseSerializer(serializers.BaseSerializer):
    ...
    def to_internal_value(self, data):
        instance_data = data["resource"]
        title = instance_data.get('title')
        storyline = instance_data.get('storyline')
        category = instance_data.get('category')
        imdb_rating = instance_data.get("imdb_rating")
        created = instance_data.get("created")
        platform = instance_data.get('platform')
        platform = StreamPlatform.objects.filter(name=platform).first()

        # Perform the data validation.
        if not title:
            raise serializers.ValidationError({
                'title': 'This field is required.'
            })
        if not category:
            raise serializers.ValidationError({
                'category': 'This field is required.'
            })
        if len(title) > 50:
            raise serializers.ValidationError({
                'title': 'May not be more than 50 characters.'
            })

        if not platform:
            raise serializers.ValidationError({
                'platform': 'Valid platform name is required.'
            })

        # Return the validated values. This will be available as
```

```
        # the `.validated_data` property.
        return {
            'title': title,
            'category': category,
            'platform': platform,
            'storyline': storyline,
            'imdb_rating': imdb_rating,
            'created': created
        }

    def create(self, validated_data):
        return WatchList.objects.create(**validated_data)
```

In the above-defined **to_internal_value** method, we are extracting model data from received data and performing validation on some of the fields and returning model-related data in a valid format.

Now, if you send a POST request with the below URL and data:

Request:

```
POST {{domain}}/api/chapter6_serializers_views/watchlist-base-serializer/
```

Body:

```
{
   "info": {
       "extra": "data"
   },
   "resource": {
    "title": "Movie71",
    "storyline": "Movie7 Story",
    "active": true,
    "platform": "Netflix",
    "imdb_rating": 2.0,
    "created": "2022-07-15T10:08:42.690612Z",
    "episodes": 0,
    "category": "MOVIE"
    }
}
```

Response:

```
{
    "title": "Movie71",
    "platform": "Netflix",
    "category": "MOVIE"
}
```

Now you are able to see the created movie when you do a GET request.

Creating New Base Classes

The **BaseSerializer** class is also useful if you want to implement new generic serializer classes for dealing with particular serialization styles or for integrating with alternative storage back ends.

The following class is an example of a generic serializer that can handle coercing arbitrary complex objects into primitive representations.

```
class ObjectSerializer(serializers.BaseSerializer):
    """
    A read-only serializer that coerces arbitrary complex objects
    into primitive representations.
    """
    def to_representation(self, instance):
        output = {}
        for attribute_name in dir(instance):
            attribute = getattr(instance, attribute_name)
            if attribute_name.startswith('_'):
                # Ignore private attributes.
                pass
            elif hasattr(attribute, '__call__'):
                # Ignore methods and other callables.
                pass
            elif isinstance(attribute, (str, int, bool, float, type(None))):
                # Primitive types can be passed through unmodified.
                output[attribute_name] = attribute
            elif isinstance(attribute, list):
                # Recursively deal with items in lists.
                output[attribute_name] = [
```

```
                self.to_representation(item) for item in attribute
            ]
        elif isinstance(attribute, dict):
            # Recursively deal with items in dictionaries.
            output[attribute_name] = {
                str(key): self.to_representation(value)
                for key, value in attribute.items()
            }
        else:
            # Force anything else to its string representation.
            output[attribute_name] = str(attribute)
    return output
```

Advanced Serializer Usage

Serializer Context

There are some cases when you need to pass additional data to your serializers. You can do that by using the serializer context property. You can then use this data inside the serializer such as **to_representation** or when validating data.

You pass the data as a dictionary via the **context** keyword:

```
from rest_framework import serializers
from examples.models import Resource

resource = Resource.objects.get(id=1)
serializer = ResourceSerializer(resource, context={'key': 'value'})
```

Then you can fetch it inside the serializer class from the **self.context** dictionary like so:

```
from rest_framework import serializers
from examples.models import Resource

class ResourceSerializer(serializers.ModelSerializer):
    class Meta:
        model = Resource
        fields = '__all__'
```

```
    def to_representation(self, instance):
        representation = super().to_representation(instance)
        representation['key'] = self.context['key']

        return representation
```

Source Keyword

The DRF serializer comes with the **source** keyword, which is extremely powerful and can be used in multiple case scenarios. We can use it to

1. Rename serializer output fields.
2. Attach serializer function response to data.
3. Fetch data from one-to-one models.

Let's say you're building a social network and every user has their own **UserProfile**, which has a one-to-one relationship with the **User** model:

```
from django.contrib.auth.models import User
from django.db import models

class UserProfile(models.Model):
    user = models.OneToOneField(to=User, on_delete=models.CASCADE)
    bio = models.TextField()
    birth_date = models.DateField()

    def __str__(self):
        return f'{self.user.username} profile'
```

We're using a **ModelSerializer** for serializing our users:

```
class UserSerializer(serializers.ModelSerializer):
    class Meta:
        model = User
        fields = ['id', 'username', 'email', 'is_staff', 'is_active']
```

Let's serialize the user:

```
{
  "id": 1,
  "username": "admin",
  "email": "admin@admin.com",
  "is_staff": true,
  "is_active": true
}
```

To rename a serializer output field, we need to add a new field to our serializer and pass it to the **fields** property.

```
class UserSerializer(serializers.ModelSerializer):
    active = serializers.BooleanField(source='is_active')

    class Meta:
        model = User
        fields = ['id', 'username', 'email', 'is_staff', 'active']
```

Our active field is now going to be named **active** instead of **is_active.** We can also use a **source** to add a field which equals to the function's return.

```
class UserSerializer(serializers.ModelSerializer):
    full_name = serializers.CharField(source='get_full_name')

    class Meta:
        model = User
        fields = ['id', 'username', 'full_name', 'email', 'is_staff',
        'active']
```

get_full_name() is a method from the Django user model that concatenates **user.first_name** and **user.last_name**. Our response will now contain **full_name**.

Now let's suppose we also wanted to include our user's **bio** and **birth_date** in **UserSerializer**. We can do that by adding extra fields to our serializer with the source keyword.

Let's modify our serializer class:

```
class UserSerializer(serializers.ModelSerializer):
    bio = serializers.CharField(source='userprofile.bio')
```

```
    birth_date = serializers.DateField(source='userprofile.birth_date')

    class Meta:
        model = User
        fields = [
            'id', 'username', 'email', 'is_staff',
            'is_active', 'bio', 'birth_date'
        ]  # note we also added the new fields here
```

We can access **userprofile.<field_name>**, because it is a **one-to-one relationship** with our user.

This is our final JSON response:

```
{
    "id": 1,
    "username": "admin",
    "email": "",
    "is_staff": true,
    "is_active": true,
    "bio": "This is my bio.",
    "birth_date": "1995-04-27"
}
```

Serializers Initial Data

Sometimes you may need to access a serializer's raw input. It's either because data has been already modified by running **serializer.is_valid()** or it's needed to compare the value of another field in a validation method when **validated_data** is not yet available. It can be achieved by accessing **serializer.initial_data**, which stores raw input as a **Dict**, as shown in this example:

```
from rest_framework import serializers

class SignupSerializer(serializers.ModelSerializer):
    password1 = serializers.CharField()
    password2 = serializers.CharField()
```

```
def validate_password1(self, password1):
    if password1 != self.initial_data["password2"]:
        raise serializers.ValidationError("Passwords do not match")
```

Till now, we have gone through basic class-based views and some of the advanced concepts of serializer usage. Now let's understand various ways of class-based views usage.

Generic Views

Generic views are pre-built views provided by the framework that simplify common CRUD (**Create, Retrieve, Update, Delete**) operations for Django models and querysets. Generic views help in reducing boilerplate code and speeding up the development process, as you can quickly create API views for standard operations without writing custom view logic. These were developed as a shortcut for common usage patterns. They take certain common idioms and patterns found in view development and abstract them so that you can quickly write common views of data without having to repeat yourself.

One of the key benefits of class-based views is the way they allow you to compose bits of reusable behavior. REST Framework takes advantage of this by providing a number of pre-built views that provide for commonly used patterns.

The generic views provided by REST Framework allow you to quickly build API views that map closely to your database models. If the generic views don't suit the needs of your API, you can drop down to using the regular **APIView** class or reuse the **mixins** and base classes used by the generic views to compose your own set of reusable generic views.

DRF provides various generic views, and they are typically used in conjunction with generic view mixins and viewsets. Here are some commonly used generic views in DRF:

- **GenericAPIView**: This is the base class for all generic views. It combines functionality from Django's View class with DRF's serializer handling.
- **ListAPIView**: A generic view that provides a read-only list of objects. It's commonly used for listing all instances of a model.
- **CreateAPIView**: A generic view that provides the ability to create a new object instance.

- **RetrieveAPIView**: A generic view that retrieves a single object instance.
- **UpdateAPIView**: A generic view that updates a single object instance.
- **DestroyAPIView**: A generic view that deletes a single object instance.
- **ListCreateAPIView**: A generic view that combines list and create functionality. It allows listing all instances and creating new instances in a single view.
- **RetrieveUpdateAPIView**: A generic view that combines retrieve and update functionality. It allows retrieving a single instance and updating it in a single view.
- **RetrieveDestroyAPIView**: A generic view that combines retrieve and delete functionality. It allows retrieving a single instance and deleting it in a single view.
- **RetrieveUpdateDestroyAPIView**: A generic view that combines retrieve, update, and delete functionality. It allows retrieving a single instance, updating it, and deleting it in a single view.

GenericAPIView

This is a class-based view that provides a generic implementation for common CRUD (Create, Retrieve, Update, Delete) operations and other HTTP methods on a single object or a collection of objects. It serves as a base class for creating custom views that need to perform standard operations on a Django model or a queryset.

GenericAPIView combines functionality from Django's View class with DRF's serializer handling, queryset filtering, and pagination support. By using GenericAPIView, you can create views with less boilerplate code and take advantage of DRF's powerful features. This class extends REST Framework's **APIView** class, adding commonly required behavior for standard list and detail views. Each of the concrete generic views provided is built by combining **GenericAPIView**, with one or more **mixin** classes.

Attributes

Basic Settings

The following attributes control the basic view behavior.

- **queryset**: The queryset that should be used for returning objects from this view. Typically, you must either set this attribute or override the **get_queryset()** method. If you are overriding a view method, it is important that you call **get_queryset()** instead of accessing this property directly, as queryset will get evaluated once and those results will be cached for all subsequent requests.
- **serializer_class**: The serializer class that should be used for validating and deserializing input and for serializing output. Typically, you must either set this attribute or override the **get_serializer_class()** method.
- **lookup_field**: The model field that should be used for performing object lookup of individual model instances. Defaults to "**pk**". Note that when using hyperlinked APIs, you'll need to ensure that *both* the API views *and* the serializer classes set the lookup fields if you need to use a custom value.
- **lookup_url_kwarg**: The URL keyword argument that should be used for object lookup. The URL conf should include a keyword argument corresponding to this value. If unset, this defaults to using the same value as lookup_field.

Pagination

The following attributes are used to control pagination when used with list views.

- **pagination_class**: The pagination class that should be used when paginating list results. Defaults to the same value as the **DEFAULT_PAGINATION_CLASS** setting, which is "**rest_framework.pagination.PageNumberPagination**". Setting **pagination_class=None** will disable pagination on this view.

Filtering

- **filter_backends**: A list of filter back-end classes that should be used for filtering the queryset. Defaults to the same value as the **DEFAULT_FILTER_BACKENDS** setting.

Methods

Base Methods

- **get_queryset(self)**

  This method returns the queryset that should be used for list views and that should be used as the base for lookups in detail views. Defaults to returning the **queryset** specified by the **queryset** attribute.

  This method should always be used rather than accessing **self.queryset** directly, as **self.queryset** gets evaluated only once and those results are cached for all subsequent requests.

  May be overridden to provide dynamic behavior, such as returning a **queryset**, that is specific to the user making the request.

  For example:

```
def get_queryset(self):
    user = self.request.user
    return user.accounts.all()
```

- **get_object(self)**

  This method returns an object instance that should be used for detail views. Defaults to using the **lookup_field** parameter to filter the base **queryset**.

  May be overridden to provide more complex behavior, such as object lookups based on more than one URL **kwarg**.

  For example:

```
def get_object(self):
    queryset = self.get_queryset()
```

```
    filter = {}
    for field in self.multiple_lookup_fields:
        filter[field] = self.kwargs[field]

    obj = get_object_or_404(queryset, **filter)
    self.check_object_permissions(self.request, obj)
    return obj
```

Note that if your API doesn't include any object-level permissions, you may optionally exclude the **self.check_object_permissions** and simply return the object from the **get_object_or_404** lookup.

- **filter_queryset(self, queryset)**

  This method is a built-in method that is used in views to perform additional filtering on the queryset based on the request parameters. When you define a custom view or a viewset, DRF automatically calls the **filter_queryset()** method before retrieving data from the database.

  Given a **queryset**, filter it with whichever filter back ends are in use, returning a new **queryset**.

  For example:

```
def filter_queryset(self, queryset):
    filter_backends = [CategoryFilter]

    if 'geo_route' in self.request.query_params:
        filter_backends = [GeoRouteFilter, CategoryFilter]
    elif 'geo_point' in self.request.query_params:
        filter_backends = [GeoPointFilter, CategoryFilter]

    for backend in list(filter_backends):
        queryset = backend().filter_queryset(self.request,
        queryset, view=self)

    return queryset
```

- **get_serializer_class(self)**

  This method is a built-in method used to determine the serializer class to use for data serialization based on the request. Defaults to returning the **serializer_class** attribute.

  When you define a custom view or viewset, you can override the **get_serializer_class(self)** method to dynamically select the appropriate serializer class to use for data serialization, depending on the request or other factors.

  For example:

  ```
  def get_serializer_class(self):

          # Determine which serializer class to use based on the request method
          if self.request.method == 'POST':
              return YourAlternateSerializer
          else:
              return YourModelSerializer
  ```

- Let's understand the above concepts in action with the project we are working on.

Go to chapter6_serializers_views/api/serializers.py and add the following lines of code:

```
class WatchlistModelBasicSerializer(serializers.ModelSerializer):
    platform = serializers.StringRelatedField()

    class Meta:
        model=WatchList
        fields = ["title", "platform", "imdb_rating", "created"]
```

In the above code, we are defining a basic serializer, where only the required fields are specified. This serializer is created to demonstrate how different serializers can be selected in views based on the request method in later sections.

Now go to chapter6_serializers_views/api/views.py and copy the following lines of code:

```
from rest_framework import filters
```

```
from rest_framework.pagination import PageNumberPagination

class WatchlistGAPIView(generics.GenericAPIView):
    queryset = WatchList.objects.all()
    serializer_class = serializers.WatchListModelSerializer
    pagination_class = PageNumberPagination
    filter_backends = [filters.SearchFilter, filters.OrderingFilter]  # Set
                      the filter backends

    # Specify the fields that can be used for search and ordering
    search_fields = ['title','imdb_rating']
    ordering_fields = ['title', 'imdb_rating', 'created']

    def get_queryset(self):
        # Custom queryset logic, e.g., applying filters or ordering
        return WatchList.objects.filter(active=True).order_by('title')

    def get_serializer_class(self):
        # Determine the serializer class based on the request method
        if self.request.method == 'POST':
            return serializers.WatchListModelSerializer
        elif self.request.method == 'GET':
            return serializers.WatchlistModelBasicSerializer

    def get(self, request, *args, **kwargs):
        """
        Return a list of all watchlist.
        """
        watchlist = self.filter_queryset(self.get_queryset())  # Apply
                    search filter
        serializer_class = self.get_serializer_class()
        page = self.paginate_queryset(watchlist)
        if page is not None:
            serializer = serializer_class(watchlist, many=True,
                         context=self.get_serializer_context())
            return self.get_paginated_response(serializer.data)

        serializer = self.get_serializer(watchlist, many=True)
```

```
        return Response(serializer.data)

    def post(self, request, *args, **kwargs):
        """
        Create a new watchlist.
        """
        serializer_class = self.get_serializer_class(data=request.data)
        serializer = serializer_class(data=request.data)
        if serializer.is_valid():
            serializer.save()
            return Response(serializer.data, status=status.HTTP_201_CREATED)
        else:
            return Response(serializer.errors, status=status.HTTP_400_BAD_
            REQUEST)

    def get_serializer_context(self):
        context = super().get_serializer_context()
        # You can add more context data here
        context["name"] = "TEST"
        return context

class WatchlistDetailGAPIView(generics.GenericAPIView):
    queryset = WatchList.objects.all()
    serializer_class = serializers.WatchListModelSerializer
    lookup_field = "title" # Set the lookup field to 'title' or any other
                  field you prefer
    lookup_url_kwarg = 'title'

    # Specify the fields that can be used for search and ordering
    search_fields = ['title','imdb_rating']
    ordering_fields = ['title', 'imdb_rating', 'created']

    def get_queryset(self):
        return WatchList.objects.filter(active=True)

    def filter_queryset(self, queryset):
        # Apply filters based on the lookup field (e.g., title)
        filter_kwargs = {self.lookup_field: self.kwargs[self.lookup_field]}
```

```
        queryset = queryset.filter(**filter_kwargs)
        return queryset

    def get_object(self):
        queryset = self.filter_queryset(self.get_queryset())
        filter_kwargs = {self.lookup_field: self.kwargs[self.lookup_field]}
        # Assuming URL pattern captures 'title'
        obj = generics.get_object_or_404(queryset, **filter_kwargs)
        return obj

    def get(self, request, *args, **kwargs):
        instance = self.get_object()  # Retrieve the instance using
                   get_object
        serializer = self.get_serializer(instance)
        return Response(serializer.data)
```

Add the corresponding URL in chapter6_serializers_views/api/urls.py as below:

```
urlpatterns = [
    ...
    # Using GenericAPIView for the views
    path('watchlist-generic-api/', views.WatchlistGAPIView.as_view(),
    name="watchlist-generic-api"),
    path('watchlist-detail-generic-api/<str:title>/', views.
WatchlistDetailGAPIView.as_view(), name="watchlist-detail-generic-api"),
]
```

In the above lines of code, we are defining **WatchlistGAPIView** and **WatchlistDetail GAPIView** for getting a list of objects and an individual object, respectively. In the above code, **get_serializer_class** is used to get **WatchListModelSerializer** if the request is of type POST and get **WatchlistModelBasicSerializer** if the request is of type GET. The attribute **serializer_class** is assigned to **WatchListModelSerializer**, which means, by default, it uses **WatchListModelSerializer**.

The attribute **pagination_class** is assigned with REST Framework-provided class **PageNumberPagination**. PageNumberPagination is a pagination class provided by Django REST Framework (DRF) that paginates the queryset's results into a series of pages. Each page will contain a specific number of items, and users can navigate through the pages using page number query parameters.

With **PageNumberPagination**, the response will include information about the current page, the total number of pages, and links to the next and previous pages if applicable. Users can navigate through the pages by appending **?page=<page_number>** to the URL.

The attribute **filter_backends** is assigned with two filters, **SearchFilter** and **OrderingFilter**.

SearchFilter is a filtering back end provided by Django REST Framework (DRF) that allows you to perform full-text searches on a queryset based on the provided search terms. It's used to enable search functionality in your API views. We also need to assign fields to be searched using the **search_fields** attribute. When you use the **SearchFilter**, users can pass a search query parameter in the URL to perform searches on specific fields of the data. The filter will then apply a search operation to the queryset and return results that match the search terms. Users can include a search query parameter in the URL to perform searches. For example: **api/chapter6_serializers_views/watchlist-generic-api/?search=Inception.**

OrderingFilter is a filtering back end provided by Django REST Framework (DRF) that allows you to control the ordering of querysets based on specified ordering fields. It's used to enable sorting functionality in your API views. We also need to assign fields to be used for ordering using the **ordering_fields** attribute. When you use the **OrderingFilter**, users can pass an ordering query parameter in the URL to specify the fields by which they want to order the results. The filter will then apply the specified ordering to the queryset and return the results in the desired order. Users can include an ordering query parameter in the URL to perform ordering. For example: **api/chapter6_serializers_views/watchlist-generic-api/?ordering=imdb_rating**.

The attribute **lookup_field** is assigned with "**title**" to look for a specific object. This attribute specifies the field to use when looking up instances of a model. It determines which field's value in the URL is used to retrieve a specific instance. By default, DRF uses the primary key ("pk") to look up instances. When you specify "title" as a field value, the user can access a specific object by specifying that specific field value. For example: **api/chapter6_serializers_views/watchlist-detail-generic-api/Movie3** where **Movie3** is the title of the Watchlist on one of the Watchlist model objects.

The attribute **lookup_url_kwarg** defines the name of the URL keyword argument used to extract the value for the lookup field when retrieving individual instances of a model. When you're using class-based views like **RetrieveAPIView** or **RetrieveUpdateAPIView**, the view needs to know which part of the URL contains the value to look up a specific instance. The **lookup_url_kwarg** attribute specifies the name of the URL parameter where this value can be found. Since we have set this attribute to "title", we can access this value in the view as **self.kwargs["title"]**.

We have defined **get_queryset** in **WatchlistGAPIView** to filter all Watchlists which are active and ordered by title.

We have defined **get_object** in **WatchlistDetailGAPIView** to get an individual object based on the title from the URL.

We have defined **filter_queryset** to filter the queryset based on the lookup_field entry values. It mainly filters the queryset based on the title value received from the URL.

Other Methods

You won't typically need to override the following methods, although you might need to call into them if you're writing custom views using **GenericAPIView**.

- **get_serializer_context(self)**

  This method allows you to customize the context data that is passed to serializer instances during serialization. It's often used to provide additional information to the serializers that might be needed for making serialization decisions or including context-specific data in the output.

  When a serializer instance is created within a view, the context data is passed to that serializer. This context includes information about the current request, user, and other relevant metadata. The **get_serializer_context** method is a hook provided by DRF views that you can override in your views to customize this context before it's passed to the serializer. By overriding **get_serializer_context**, you can add or modify data in the context that will be used during the serialization process. For example, in the above code, we have added context["name"]="TEST" as additional information, which is sent to the serializer.

- **get_serializer(self, instance=None, data=None, many=False, partial=False)**

  Returns a serializer instance. This method is a utility method provided by view classes to obtain an instance of the serializer associated with the view. This method is used to create a serializer instance that can be used for serializing or deserializing data.

The **get_serializer** method can be called within DRF view methods to obtain a serializer instance based on the view's configuration, including the serializer class defined for the view, the request data, and any additional context.

- **get_paginated_response(self, data)**

  This method is used to create a paginated response for a list of items. This method is often used in views that handle list-based requests (like **ListAPIView** or **GenericAPIView**) and include pagination.

  When a list of items is paginated, the **get_paginated_response** method takes care of formatting the response to include information about the current page, the total number of pages, and links to navigate to previous and next pages.

- **paginate_queryset(self, queryset)**

  This method is a built-in method available in views that support pagination, such as **ListAPIView**. This method is used to apply pagination to a queryset of items based on the current request. It will paginate a queryset if required, either returning a page object or None if pagination is not configured for this view.

  When a view is configured with pagination, the **paginate_queryset** method is responsible for retrieving the subset of items that correspond to the current page of results. It takes into account the pagination settings specified in the view's **pagination_class**.

- **filter_queryset(self, queryset)**

  This method is a utility method available in views that support filtering, such as **ListAPIView**. This method is used to apply filtering to a queryset of items based on the query parameters provided in the request. For a given queryset, filter it with whichever filter back ends are in use, returning a new queryset.

  When a view is configured to support filtering, the **filter_queryset** method is responsible for modifying the **queryset** to include only the items that match the filter criteria specified in the request.

Mixins

We have gone through the GenericAPIView class which extends the REST Framework's APIView class, adding commonly required behavior for standard list and detail views.

APIView is the base class for all views in Django REST Framework. It provides the basic implementation for handling requests and responses and can be used to create views for simple, one-off cases.

GenericAPIView, on the other hand, is a subclass of **APIView** that provides a more generic implementation for handling requests and responses. It includes additional functionality for working with model-based views, such as support for pagination and filtering, and provides a more reusable and configurable approach for creating views for common use cases.

In summary, **APIView** is more simple and is more suited for views that handle a single task, and **GenericAPIView** has more functionality and is more suited for views that handle common use cases with models.

The **Mixins** class provides the actions that are used to provide the basic view behavior. The mixin classes provide the actions that are used to provide the basic view behavior. Note that the mixin classes provide action methods rather than defining the handler methods, such as **.get()** and **.post()**, directly. This allows for more flexible composition of behavior. The mixin classes can be imported from **rest_framework.mixins**.

Use of Mixins

Mixins are a way of reusing view logic in Django REST Framework. They are classes that provide a specific functionality, such as authentication or pagination, that can be easily added to any view by including them as a base class. Mixins are typically used with the **APIView** or **GenericAPIView** classes to create views with specific functionality.

In summary, **Mixins** are used to add specific functionality to views and can be used with **APIView** and **GenericAPIView** to create more complex views, whereas APIView is the basic class for handling requests and responses for views and can be used for simple views.

DRF provides several built-in mixins that you can use to extend your views. Some of the commonly used mixins are as below.

ListModelMixin

ListModelMixin is a **mixin** class for Django's generic views that provides list-related actions, such as pagination and ordering. It is typically used in conjunction with the generic views provided by Django's views module, such as **ListView**. It provides a **.list(request, *args, **kwargs)** method that implements listing a queryset.

If the queryset is populated, this returns a **200 OK** response, with a serialized representation of the **queryset** as the body of the response. The response data may optionally be paginated.

To demonstrate this, let's go to watchlist_app/api/views.py and add the following lines of code:

```
from rest_framework import mixins

class WatchlistListModelMixinView(generics.GenericAPIView, mixins.
ListModelMixin):
    queryset = WatchList.objects.all()
    serializer_class = serializers.WatchListModelSerializer
    def get(self, request, *args, **kwargs):
        return self.list(request, *args, **kwargs)
```

Add the corresponding URL in chapter6_serializers_views/api/urls.py as below:

```
urlpatterns = [
    ...
    #Using ListModelMixin and GenericAPIView for views
    path('watchlist-list-model-mixin/', views.WatchlistListModelMixinView.
    as_view(), name="watchlist-list-model-mixin"),
]
```

You can access the endpoint using the below request:

```
GET {{domain}}/api/chapter6_serializers_views/watchlist-list-model-mixin/
```

CreateModelMixin

This mixin is provided by Django REST Framework (DRF) that is used to add the functionality of creating new model instances to a class-based view. This **mixin** simplifies the process of handling POST requests to create objects in your API.

It provides a **.create(request, *args, **kwargs)** method that implements creating and saving a new model instance. If an object is created, this returns a **201 Created** response, with a serialized representation of the object as the body of the response. If the representation contains a key named **url**, then the Location header of the response will be populated with that value.

If the request data provided for creating the object was invalid, a **400 Bad Request** response will be returned, with the error details as the body of the response.

To demonstrate this, let's go to chapter6_serializers_views/api/views.py and add the following lines of code:

```
class WatchlistCreateModelMixinView(generics.GenericAPIView, mixins.
CreateModelMixin):
    queryset = WatchList.objects.all()
    serializer_class = serializers.WatchListModelSerializer

    def perform_create(self, serializer):
        # Customize the creation process here, e.g., setting
        additional fields
        # before saving the object to the database.
        serializer.save()

    def post(self,request,*args,  **kwargs):
        return self.create(request, *args, **kwargs)
```

Add the corresponding URL in chapter6_serializers_views/api/urls.py as below:

```
urlpatterns = [
    ...
    #Using CreateModelMixin and GenericAPIView for views
    path('watchlist-create-model-mixin/', views.WatchlistCreate
ModelMixinView.as_view(), name="watchlist-create-model-mixin"),
]
```

You can create a new Watchlist using a **POST** request as below:

Request:

```
POST {{domain}}/api/chapter6_serializers_views/watchlist-create-
model-mixin/
```

Body:

```
{
    "title": "Movie2",
    "storyline": "Movie2 Story",
    "active": true,
    "platform": "1",
    "imdb_rating": 2.0,
    "created": "2022-07-15T10:08:42.690612Z",
    "episodes": 0,
    "category": "MOVIE"
}
```

Response:

```
{
    "id": 92,
    "full_title": "Movie Name: Movie2",
    "user": 1,
    "title": "Movie2",
    "storyline": "Movie2 Story",
    "active": true,
    "imdb_rating": 2.0,
    "created": "2024-12-28T19:20:40.386527Z",
    "episodes": 0,
    "category": "movie",
    "platform": {
        "id": 1
    }
}
```

RetrieveModelMixin

A RetrieveModelMixin is a mixin class that is often used in conjunction with Django's generic views to handle the retrieval of a single model instance. It provides a **.retrieve(request, *args, **kwargs)** method that handles fetching the model instance from the database.

It also provides a queryset attribute that specifies the **queryset** to use for fetching the model instance and a **lookup_field** attribute that specifies the field on the model to use as the lookup key when fetching the instance. If an object can be retrieved, this returns a **200 OK** response, with a serialized representation of the object as the body of the response. Otherwise, it will return a **404 Not Found**.

To demonstrate this, let's go to watchlist_app/api/views.py and add the following lines of code:

```
class WatchlistRetrieveModelMixinView(generics.GenericAPIView, mixins.
RetrieveModelMixin):
    queryset = WatchList.objects.all()
    serializer_class = serializers.WatchListModelSerializer
    def get(self, request, *args, **kwargs):
        return self.retrieve(request, *args, **kwargs)
```

Add the corresponding URL in chapter6_serializers_views/api/urls.py as below:

```
urlpatterns = [
    ...
    #Using RetrieveModelMixin and GenericAPIView for views
    path('watchlist-retrieve-model-mixin/<int:pk>/', views.
    WatchlistRetrieveModelMixinView.as_view(), name="watchlist-retrieve-
    model-mixin"),
]
```

You can access the endpoint using a GET request:

```
GET {{domain}}/api/chapter6_serializers_views/watchlist-retrieve-
model-mixin/63
```

UpdateModelMixin

This mixin class is often used in conjunction with Django's generic views to handle the update of a single model instance. It provides a **.update(request, *args, **kwargs)** method that handles updating the model instance and saving it to the database. It also provides a **.partial_update(request, *args, **kwargs)** method, which is similar to the **update** method, except that all fields for the update will be optional. This allows support for **HTTP PATCH** requests.

If an object is updated, this returns a 200 OK response, with a serialized representation of the object as the body of the response. If the request data provided for updating the object was invalid, a **400 Bad Request** response will be returned, with the error details as the body of the response.

To demonstrate this, let's go to chapter6_serializers_views/api/views.py and add the following lines of code:

```
class WatchlistUpdateModelMixinView(generics.GenericAPIView, mixins.
UpdateModelMixin):
    queryset = WatchList.objects.all()
    serializer_class = serializers.WatchListModelSerializer

    def perform_update(self, serializer):
        # Customize the update process here, e.g., perform additional
        # actions before saving the updated object.
        serializer.save()  # Saving the updated object

    def put(self,request, *args , **kwargs):
        # Use the update method provided by UpdateModelMixin
        return self.update(request, *args, **kwargs)
```

Add the corresponding URL in chapter6_serializers_views/api/urls.py as below:

```
urlpatterns = [
    ...
    #Using UpdateModelMixin and GenericAPIView for views
    path('watchlist-update-model-mixin/<int:pk>/', views.
    WatchlistUpdateModelMixinView.as_view(), name="watchlist-update-
    model-mixin"),
]
```

You can update the new Watchlist using a **PUT** request as below:

Request:

```
GET {{domain}}/api/chapter6_serializers_views/watchlist-update-model-
mixin/63/
```

Body:

```
{
```

```
    "title": "Movie1 updated",
    "storyline": "Movie1 Updated Story",
    "active": true,
    "platform": "1",
    "imdb_rating": 2.0,
    "created": "2022-07-15T10:08:42.690612Z",
    "episodes": 0,
    "category": "MOVIE"
}
```

Response:

```
{
    "id": 63,
    "full_title": "Movie Name: Movie1 updated",
    "user": 1,
    "title": "Movie1 updated",
    "storyline": "Movie1 Updated Story",
    "active": true,
    "imdb_rating": 2.0,
    "created": "2024-12-22T09:07:50.938324Z",
    "episodes": 0,
    "category": "movie",
    "platform": {
        "id": 1
    }
}
```

DestroyModelMixin

This **mixin** class is often used in conjunction with Django's generic views to handle the deletion of a single model instance. It provides a **.destroy(request, *args, **kwargs)** method that handles the deletion of the model instance from the database. This **mixin** simplifies the process of handling **DELETE** requests to remove objects in your API. If an object is deleted, this returns a **204 No Content** response; otherwise, it will return a **404 Not Found**.

To demonstrate this, let's go to watchlist_app/api/views.py and add the following lines of code:

```
class WatchlistDestroyModelMixinView(generics.GenericAPIView, mixins.
DestroyModelMixin):
    queryset = WatchList.objects.all()
    serializer_class = serializers.WatchListModelSerializer

    def perform_destroy(self, instance):
        # Customize the destruction process here, e.g., perform additional
        # actions before deleting the object.
        instance.delete()  # Delete the object

    def delete(self,request, *args , **kwargs):
        return self.destroy(request, *args, **kwargs)
```

Add the corresponding URL in chapter6_serializers_views/api/urls.py as below:

```
urlpatterns = [
    ...
    #Using DestroyModelMixin and GenericAPIView for views
    path('watchlist-destroy-model-mixin/<int:pk>/', views.
    WatchlistDestroyModelMixinView.as_view(), name="watchlist-destroy-
    model-mixin"),
]
```

You can access the endpoint using a request as below:

```
DELETE {{domain}}/api/chapter6_serializers_views/watchlist-destroy-model-
mixin/67/
```

Save and Deletion Hooks

The following methods are provided by the **mixin** classes and provide easy overriding of the object's save or deletion behavior.

- **perform_create(self, serializer)**: Called by **CreateModelMixin** when saving a new object instance
- **perform_update(self, serializer)**: Called by **UpdateModelMixin** when saving an existing object instance

- **perform_destroy(self, instance)**: Called by **DestroyModelMixin** when deleting an object instance

These hooks are particularly useful for setting attributes that are implicit in the request but are not part of the request data. For instance, you might set an attribute on the object based on the request user or based on a URL keyword argument.

For example:

```
def perform_create(self, serializer):
    serializer.save(user=self.request.user)
```

These override points are also particularly useful for adding behavior that occurs before or after saving an object, such as emailing a confirmation or logging the update.

For example:

```
def perform_update(self, serializer):
    instance = serializer.save()
    send_email_confirmation(user=self.request.user, modified=instance)
```

You can also use these hooks to provide additional validation by raising a **ValidationError**(). This can be useful if you need some validation logic to apply at the point of database save.

For example:

```
def perform_create(self, serializer):
    queryset = SignupRequest.objects.filter(user=self.request.user)
    if queryset.exists():
        raise ValidationError('You have already signed up')
    serializer.save(user=self.request.user)
```

Concrete View Classes

Concrete view classes in Django REST Framework (DRF) are pre-built, ready-to-use view classes that provide common functionalities out of the box. These concrete views are designed to simplify the process of building RESTful APIs in Django by handling common tasks such as creating, retrieving, updating, and deleting objects. They encourage code reusability and adhere to RESTful conventions.

In the previous section, we used **mixins** along with **GenericAPI**. But when using a specific mixin, we added corresponding methods, like **get** or **post** methods, to use the **mixin**-provided methods. But now, by using concrete view classes, we don't need to define these methods like **get** or **post.** These methods are provided by concrete view classes. These classes extend **mixins** and **GenericAPI** classes.

Concrete view classes eliminate the need to write repetitive code for common operations like listing objects, creating new objects, updating existing objects, and deleting objects. This can significantly reduce development time. They also come with built-in validation for HTTP methods, such as checking request data for correctness, validating request headers, and ensuring that requests conform to RESTful standards. These concrete views handle serialization of data for both request data (deserialization) and response data (serialization) automatically. This simplifies the process of converting data between Python objects and JSON or other formats. While concrete views provide default behavior for common operations, they are also highly customizable. You can override methods like **perform_create**, **perform_update**, and **perform_destroy** to add custom logic when needed.

The following classes are the concrete generic views. If you're using generic views, this is normally the level you'll be working at unless you need heavily customized behavior. The view classes can be imported from **rest_framework.generics**.

CreateAPIView

This concrete view class simplifies the creation of new objects in your API. It is specifically designed for handling **HTTP POST** requests to create instances of a model. It integrates seamlessly with DRF serializers. You specify a serializer class, and the view handles the deserialization of incoming data (request data) and serialization of the created object for the response. It automatically validates the incoming data based on the serializer's field definitions, ensuring that the data conforms to the expected format and data types. This view extends **GenericAPIView** and **CreateModelMixin**.

After successfully creating the object, the view returns an HTTP response with status code **201 (Created)** and includes the serialized representation of the newly created object in the response body. This follows RESTful conventions. While CreateAPIView provides sensible default behavior, you can customize its behavior by overriding methods such as **perform_create** to add custom logic or validations during the object creation process. You can control who is allowed to create objects using **permissions** and **authentication** classes. By using CreateAPIView, you can reduce the amount of boilerplate code required to handle object creation in your API views.

To demonstrate this, let's go to chapter6_serializers_views/api/views.py and add the following lines of code:

```
class WatchlistCreateAPIView(generics.CreateAPIView):
    queryset = WatchList.objects.all()
    serializer_class = serializers.WatchListModelSerializer

    def perform_create(self, serializer):
        # Customize the creation process here, e.g., setting
        additional fields
        # before saving the object to the database.
        serializer.save()
```

Add the corresponding URL in chapter6_serializers_views/api/urls.py as below:

```
urlpatterns = [
    ...
    #Using CreateAPIView for views
    path('watchlist-create-api/', views.WatchlistCreateAPIView.as_view(),
    name="watchlist-create-api"),
]
```

You can access the endpoint to create a Watchlist as below:

Request:

```
POST {{domain}}/api/chapter6_serializers_views/watchlist-create-api/
```

Body:

```
{
    "title": "The Godfather",
    "storyline": "The Godfather Story",
    "active": true,
    "platform": "2",
    "imdb_rating": 9.2,
    "episodes": 0,
    "category": "MOVIE"
}
```

Response:


```
{
    "id": 93,
    "full_title": "Movie Name: The Godfather",
    "user": 1,
    "title": "The Godfather",
    "storyline": "The Godfather Story",
    "active": true,
    "imdb_rating": 9.2,
    "created": "2024-12-28T20:01:34.781329Z",
    "episodes": 0,
    "category": "movie",
    "platform": {
        "id": 2
    }
}
```


ListAPIView

This concrete view class simplifies the process of listing and retrieving a collection of objects from your database in a RESTful API. It is specifically designed for handling **HTTP GET** requests to retrieve a list of instances of a model. This is used for read-only endpoints to represent a collection of model instances. It provides a get method handler. It extends the **GenericAPIView** and **ListModelMixin** classes.

It integrates seamlessly with DRF serializers. You specify a serializer class, and the view handles the serialization of objects for the response. You specify the queryset of objects that should be included in the response. This allows you to control which objects are retrieved and listed. **ListAPIView** includes built-in support for pagination. You can configure the pagination settings to control how many objects are included in each page of results. After successfully retrieving the objects, the view returns an HTTP response with a status code of **200 (OK)** and includes the serialized representation of the objects in the response body.

While ListAPIView provides sensible default behavior, you can customize its behavior by overriding methods such as **get_queryset** to define custom query logic or list to add custom logic to the listing process. The view works seamlessly with DRF's authentication and authorization mechanisms. You can control who is allowed to access the list of objects using **permissions** and **authentication** classes.

To demonstrate this, let's go to chapter6_serializers_views/api/views.py and add the following lines of code:

```
class WatchlistListAPIView(generics.ListAPIView):
    queryset = WatchList.objects.all()
    serializer_class = serializers.WatchListModelSerializer

    def get_queryset(self):
        # Customize the queryset here, e.g., apply filters or annotations
        return WatchList.objects.filter(active=True)
```

Add the corresponding URL in chapter6_serializers_views/api/urls.py as below:

```
urlpatterns = [
    ...
    #Using ListAPIView for views
    path('watchlist-list-api/', views.WatchlistListAPIView.as_view(),
    name="watchlist-list-api"),
]
```

You can see the list of Watchlist using a **GET** request on the URL:

```
GET {{domain}}/api/chapter6_serializers_views/watchlist-list-api/
```

RetrieveAPIView

This concrete view class simplifies the process of retrieving a single object from your database in a RESTful API. It is specifically designed for handling HTTP GET requests to retrieve a single instance of a model. It is used for **read-only** endpoints to represent a **single model instance**. It provides a **get** method handler, and it extends **GenericAPIView** and **RetrieveModelMixin.**

It integrates seamlessly with DRF serializers. You specify a serializer class, and the view handles the serialization of the object for the response. You specify the **queryset** of objects from which the single object should be retrieved. This allows you to control which object is retrieved. After successfully retrieving the object, the view returns an HTTP response with a status code of **200 (OK)** and includes the serialized representation of the object in the response body.

While RetrieveAPIView provides sensible default behavior, you can customize its behavior by overriding methods such as **get_object** to define custom lookup logic or retrieve to add custom logic to the retrieval process. The view works seamlessly with DRF's **authentication** and **authorization** mechanisms. You can control who is allowed to access the object using permissions and authentication classes.

To demonstrate this, let's go to chapter6_serializers_views/api/views.py and add the following lines of code:

```
class WatchlistRetrieveAPIView(generics.RetrieveAPIView):
    queryset = WatchList.objects.all()
    serializer_class = serializers.WatchListModelSerializer
    lookup_field = "title" # Set the lookup field to 'title' or any other
                  field you prefer

    def get_object(self):
        queryset = self.filter_queryset(self.get_queryset())
        filter_kwargs = {self.lookup_field: self.kwargs[self.lookup_
                        field]}  # Assuming URL pattern captures 'title'
        obj = generics.get_object_or_404(queryset, **filter_kwargs)
        return obj
```

Add the corresponding URL in chapter6_serializers_views/api/urls.py as below:

```
urlpatterns = [
    ...
    #Using RetrieveAPIView for views
    path('watchlist-retrieve-api/<str:title>/', views.WatchlistRetrieve
    APIView.as_view(), name="watchlist-retrieve-api"),
]
```

You can get the same below specific Watchlist response using the following request:

Request:

```
GET {{domain}}/api/chapter6_serializers_views/watchlist-retrieve-api/
Series1/
```

Response:


```
{
    "id": 2,
    "full_title": "Series Name: Series1",
    "user": null,
    "title": "Series1",
    "storyline": "Series1 Storyline",
    "active": true,
    "imdb_rating": 5.0,
    "created": "2023-07-12T15:43:57.024333Z",
    "episodes": 3,
    "category": "series",
    "platform": {
        "id": 2
    }
}
```


In the above code, we have defined a **get_object** function to customize it to get an object based on the title of the watchlist. To achieve this, we also set **lookup_field** to **title**. In the above object, the title is "Series1".

DestroyAPIView

This concrete view class simplifies the process of deleting a single object from your database in a RESTful API. It is specifically designed for handling **HTTP DELETE** requests to delete an instance of a model. It is used for delete-only endpoints for a single model instance. It provides a delete method handler. It extends **GenericAPIView** and **DestroyModelMixin**.

In this case, you specify the **queryset** of objects from which the single object should be deleted. This allows you to control which object is deleted. After successfully deleting the object, the view returns an HTTP response with a status code of **204 (No Content)** to indicate that the object has been deleted. While DestroyAPIView provides sensible default behavior, you can customize its behavior by overriding methods such as **get_object** to define custom lookup logic or **destroy** to add custom logic to the deletion process. The view works with DRF's **authentication** and **authorization** mechanisms. You can control who is allowed to delete the object using permissions and authentication classes.

To demonstrate this, let's go to chapter6_serializers_views/api/views.py and add the following lines of code:

```
class WatchlistDestroyAPIView(generics.DestroyAPIView):
    queryset = WatchList.objects.all()
    serializer_class = serializers.WatchListModelSerializer
    lookup_field = "title" # Set the lookup field to 'title' or any other
    field you prefer

    def get_object(self):
        queryset = self.filter_queryset(self.get_queryset())
        filter_kwargs = {self.lookup_field: self.kwargs[self.lookup_
                        field]}  # Assuming URL pattern captures 'title'
        obj = generics.get_object_or_404(queryset, **filter_kwargs)
        return obj

    def delete(self, request, *args, **kwargs):
        instance = self.get_object()
        instance.delete()
        return Response({"detail": "WatchList object deleted
        successfully."}, status=status.HTTP_204_NO_CONTENT)
```

Add the corresponding URL in chapter6_serializers_views/api/urls.py as below:

```
urlpatterns = [
    ...
    #Using DestroyAPIView for views
    path('watchlist-destroy-api/<str:title>/', views.WatchlistDestroy
    APIView.as_view(), name="watchlist-destroy-api"),
]
```

You can delete the Watchlist with the title "Movie5" as below:

Request:

```
DELETE {{domain}}/api/chapter6_serializers_views/watchlist-destroy-
api/Movie5/
```

Response:

Gives the below response with status code **204 No Content:**

```
{
    "detail": "WatchList object deleted successfully."
}
```

UpdateAPIView

This concrete view class simplifies the process of updating a single object in your database in a RESTful API. It is specifically designed for handling **HTTP PUT** and **PATCH** requests to update an instance of a model. It is used for update-only endpoints for a single model instance. It provides put and patch method handlers. It extends **GenericAPIView** and **UpdateModelMixin**.

UpdateAPIView is designed to handle HTTP PUT and PATCH requests, which are typically used to update a single object in a RESTful API. PUT requests are used to update the entire object, while PATCH requests are used to update specific fields of the object. It integrates with DRF serializers. You specify a serializer class, and the view handles the deserialization of incoming data (request data) and serialization of the updated object for the response. You specify the **queryset** of objects from which the single object should be retrieved and updated. This allows you to control which object is updated. After successfully updating the object, the view returns an HTTP response with a status code of **200 (OK)** and includes the serialized representation of the updated object in the response body.

While UpdateAPIView provides sensible default behavior, you can customize its behavior by overriding methods such as **get_object** to define custom lookup logic or update to add custom logic to the update process. The view works with DRF's authentication and authorization mechanisms. You can control who is allowed to update the object using permissions and authentication classes.

To demonstrate this, let's go to chapter6_serializers_views/api/views.py and add the following lines of code:

```
class WatchlistUpdateAPIView(generics.UpdateAPIView):
    queryset = WatchList.objects.all()
    serializer_class = serializers.WatchListModelSerializer
```

Add the corresponding URL in chapter6_serializers_views/api/views.py as below:

```
urlpatterns = [
    ...
    #Using UpdateAPIView
    path('watchlist-update-api/<int:pk>/', views.WatchlistUpdateAPIView.
    as_view(), name="watchlist-update-api"),
]
```

You can access the endpoint as below:

Request:

```
PUT {{domain}}/api/chapter6_serializers_views/watchlist-update-api/80/
```

Body:

```
{
    "title": "Movie2-updated",
    "storyline": "Movie2-updated Story",
    "active": true,
    "platform": "1",
    "imdb_rating": 2.0,
    "episodes": 0,
    "category": "MOVIE"
}
```

Response:

```
{
    "id": 80,
    "full_title": "Movie Name: Movie2-updated",
    "user": 1,
    "title": "Movie2-updated",
    "storyline": "Movie2-updated Story",
    "active": true,
    "imdb_rating": 2.0,
    "created": "2024-12-28T15:56:58.625793Z",
    "episodes": 0,
    "category": "movie",
```

```
    "platform": {
        "id": 1
    }
}
```

ListCreateAPIView

This concrete view class combines the functionalities of both listing a collection of objects and creating new objects in a RESTful API. It's a versatile view class that is specifically designed for handling **HTTP GET (list)** and **POST (create)** requests for a model. It is used for read-write endpoints to represent a collection of model instances. It provides **get** and **post** method handlers. It extends **GenericAPIView**, **ListModelMixin**, and **CreateModelMixin**.

The features provided by this concrete class are the same as the combination of **CreateAPIView** and **ListAPIView** features.

To demonstrate this, let's go to watchlist_app/api/views.py and add the following lines of code:

```
class WatchlistListCreateAPIView(generics.ListCreateAPIView):
    queryset = WatchList.objects.all()
    serializer_class = serializers.WatchListModelSerializer
```

Add the corresponding URL in chapter6_serializers_views/api/urls.py as below:

```
urlpatterns = [
    ...
    #Using ListCreateAPIView for views
    path('watchlist-list-create-api/', views.WatchlistListCreateAPIView.
    as_view(), name="watchlist-list-create-api"),
]
```

You can get a list of the Watchlist using a **GET** request on the URL: `{{domain}}/api/chapter6_serializers_views/watchlist-list-create-api/` or create an object using the same URL with data using a POST request.

RetrieveUpdateAPIView

This concrete view class combines the functionalities of both retrieving a single object and updating that object in a RESTful API. It's a versatile view class that is specifically designed for handling **HTTP GET (retrieve)** and **PUT/PATCH (update)** requests for a model. It is used for read or update endpoints to represent a single model instance. It provides **get**, **put**, and **patch** method handlers. It extends **GenericAPIView**, **RetrieveModelMixin**, and **UpdateModelMixin**.

The features provided by this concrete class are the same as the combination of **RetrieveAPIView** and **UpdateAPIView** features.

To demonstrate this, let's go to watchlist_app/api/views.py and add the following lines of code:

```
class WatchlistRetrieveUpdateAPIView(generics.RetrieveUpdateAPIView):
    queryset = WatchList.objects.all()
    serializer_class = serializers.WatchListModelSerializer
```

Add the corresponding URL in chapter6_serializers_views/api/urls.py as below:

```
urlpatterns = [
    ...
    #Using RetrieveUpdateAPIView
    path('watchlist-retrieve-update-api/<int:pk>/', views.
    WatchlistRetrieveUpdateAPIView.as_view(), name="watchlist-retrieve-
    update-api"),
]
```

You can use the below URL to perform GET and PUT/PATCH operations for a specific object:

For example, if you are working on an object with ID 68:

```
{{domain}}/api/chapter6_serializers_views/watchlist-retrieve-update-api/68/
```

RetrieveDestroyAPIView

This concrete view class combines the functionalities of both retrieving a single object and deleting that object in a RESTful API. It's a versatile view class designed to handle **HTTP GET (retrieve)** and **DELETE (destroy)** requests for a model. It is used for read or delete endpoints to represent a single model instance. It provides get and delete method handlers. It extends **GenericAPIView**, **RetrieveModelMixin**, and **DestroyModelMixin**.

The features provided by this concrete class are the same as the combination of **RetrieveAPIView** and **DestroyAPIView** features.

To demonstrate this, let's go to chapter6_serializers_views/api/views.py and add the following lines of code:

```
class WatchlistRetrieveDestroyAPIView(generics.RetrieveDestroyAPIView):
    queryset = WatchList.objects.all()
    serializer_class = serializers.WatchListModelSerializer
```

Add the corresponding URL in chapter6_serializers_views/api/urls.py as below:

```
urlpatterns = [
    ...
    #Using RetrieveDestroyAPIView
    path('watchlist-retrieve-destroy-api/<int:pk>/', views.
    WatchlistRetrieveDestroyAPIView.as_view(), name="watchlist-retrieve-
    destroy-api"),
]
```

You can use the below endpoint to perform GET and DELETE operations for a specific object:

For example: if you are working on an object with ID 68:

```
{{domain}}/api/chapter6_serializers_views/watchlist-retrieve-
destroy-api/68/
```

RetrieveUpdateDestroyAPIView

This concrete view class combines the functionalities of retrieving, updating, and deleting a single object in a RESTful API. It's a versatile view class designed to handle **HTTP GET (retrieve)**, **PUT/PATCH (update)**, **and DELETE (destroy)** requests for a model. It is used for read-write-delete endpoints to represent a single model instance. It provides **get**, **put**, **patch,** and **delete** method handlers. It extends **GenericAPIView**, **RetrieveModelMixin**, **UpdateModelMixin,** and **DestroyModelMixin**.

The features provided by this concrete class are the same as a combination of **RetrieveAPIView, UpdateAPIView, and DestroyAPIView** features.

To demonstrate this, let's go to watchlist_app/api/views.py and add the following lines of code:

```
class WatchlistRudAPIView(generics.RetrieveUpdateDestroyAPIView):
    queryset = WatchList.objects.all()
    serializer_class = serializers.WatchListModelSerializer
```

Add the corresponding URL in chapter6_serializers_views/api/urls.py as below:

```
urlpatterns = [
    ...
    #Using RetrieveUpdateDestroyAPIView
    path('watchlist-rud-api/<int:pk>/', views.WatchlistRudAPIView.as_
    view(), name="watchlist-rud-api"),
]
```

You can use the below URL to perform GET, UPDATE, and DELETE operations for a specific object:

For example: if you are working on an object with ID 68:

```
{{domain}}/api/chapter6_serializers_views/watchlist-rud-api/68/
```

Customizing the Generic Views

Customizing generic views in Django REST Framework (DRF) is a common practice because it allows developers to adapt the default behavior of these views to meet the specific requirements of their API. But often, you want to use the existing generic views but use some slightly customized behavior. If you find yourself reusing some bit of customized behavior in multiple places, you might want to refactor the behavior into a common class that you can then just apply to any view or viewset as needed. Generic views provide a lot of built-in functionality, but they are designed to cover a wide range of use cases. Customizing them allows you to fine-tune the behavior of these views to match the specific needs of your API. APIs often involve complex business logic that goes beyond simple CRUD (Create, Read, Update, Delete) operations. Customizing views lets you incorporate your application's unique business logic into the API endpoints. You may need to implement custom validation logic or transform data before it's saved or serialized. Customizing views allows you to insert this logic at the appropriate points in the request-response cycle.

You might want to format responses in a particular way, such as adding custom fields to the JSON response or changing the response status codes. Customizing views lets you control the response format. Sometimes, you need to add custom endpoints to your API that don't fit the standard CRUD operations. Customizing views allows you to define these additional endpoints by adding custom methods to your view classes. Customizing views allows you to include logging for debugging purposes and to handle errors in a way that's consistent with your application's error-handling strategy. If your API interacts with third-party services or external systems, customizing views can help you integrate with these services effectively. In some cases, you may need to optimize performance by customizing the way data is fetched from the database or cached.

If you have different versions of your API, you can use custom views to implement version-specific behavior while maintaining backward compatibility. Customizing views can simplify unit testing by allowing you to isolate specific pieces of logic in your views for testing. Customizing views can improve the user experience by providing more informative error messages or handling edge cases gracefully.

We have come across some of the custom functions such as **get_queryset**, **perform_create**, **to_representation,** and **update** methods**.** These methods customize functionality based on the business logic. If some part of the functionality is common and can be used across views, then we can turn that into a custom mixin, so that you can easily add it to the views. Let's understand creating custom mixins to achieve this.

Creating Custom Mixins

Creating custom mixins is a powerful way to encapsulate and reuse specific pieces of functionality across multiple views or viewsets. Mixins allow you to define and reuse common functionality across different views. Instead of duplicating code in multiple views, you can create a mixin and include it wherever needed. Mixins promote a modular and organized code structure. You can break down complex views into smaller, reusable components, making your code base easier to manage and maintain.

The **Don't Repeat Yourself (DRY)** principle is a fundamental concept in software development. Mixins help you avoid duplicating code and promote a more maintainable code base. Mixins can help keep your view classes clean and focused on their primary responsibilities. You can move common or secondary logic into mixins, leaving your views with a clear and concise purpose.

Mixins allow you to mix and match functionality. You can combine multiple mixins to create views with a combination of features. This makes it easy to adapt your views to different requirements. Mixins help organize your code base by keeping related functionality together. This can improve code readability and maintainability. You can create mixins to integrate third-party libraries or services. This allows you to abstract the integration logic, making it easier to switch or update external dependencies.

Mixins enable you to add custom behavior to views that can't be achieved with DRF's built-in generic views. You have the flexibility to tailor views to your specific needs. Mixins can enforce consistent behavior and conventions across your views. For example, you can create mixins that standardize error responses or pagination logic. You can use mixins to implement security-related features, such as authentication checks or permission handling, and ensure that these checks are consistent across views.

To demonstrate this, let's create chapter6_serializers_views/api/mixins.py and copy the following lines of code:

```
from chapter3_project_setup.models import WatchList
from rest_framework import generics

class MultipleFieldLookupMixin:
    """
    Apply this mixin to any view or viewset to get multiple field filtering
    based on a `lookup_fields` attribute, instead of the default single
    field filtering.
    """
    def get_object(self):
        queryset = self.get_queryset()             # Get the base queryset
        queryset = self.filter_queryset(queryset)  # Apply any filter
                   backends
        filter = {}
        for field in self.lookup_fields:
            if self.kwargs.get(field): # Ignore empty fields.
                filter[field] = self.kwargs[field]
```

```
        obj = generics.get_object_or_404(queryset, **filter)
              # Lookup the object
        self.check_object_permissions(self.request, obj)
        return obj
```

Go to chapter6_serializers_views/api/views.py and add the following lines of code:

```
class WatchlistMFLMixinView(MultipleFieldLookupMixin, generics.
RetrieveAPIView):
    """
    Retrieve a WatchList object using multiple field lookup.
    """
    queryset = WatchList.objects.all()
    serializer_class = serializers.WatchListModelSerializer

    # Define the fields to use for multiple field lookup
    lookup_fields = ['title']  # Customize this based on your needs

    # Optionally, you can override other methods or add custom behavior
    as needed.
```

Add the corresponding URL in chapter6_serializers_views/api/urls.py as below:

```
urlpatterns = [
    ...
    #Using MultipleFieldLookupMixin
    path('watchlist-mfl-mixin/<str:title>/', views.WatchlistMFLMixinView.
    as_view(), name='watchlist-mfl-mixin'),
]
```

In the above code, we've created a view class called **WatchlistMFLMixinView** that also inherits from both **MultipleFieldLookupMixin** and **generics.RetrieveAPIView**. We specify the **queryset**, **serializer class**, and **lookup_fields** attribute. In this case, we use ['title'] as the lookup field. This allows you to retrieve a **WatchList** object by providing values for both the title and category fields in the URL.

You can customize the **lookup_fields** list to include the fields you want to use for multiple field lookup based on your specific requirements.

As with the previous example, you can optionally override other methods or add custom behavior to the view as needed.

Now, you can retrieve a WatchList object using a title in the URL, such as `{{domain}}/api/chapter6_serializers_views/watchlist-mfl-mixin/Series1`, to retrieve a specific WatchList object with the title "Series1"

Creating Custom Base Classes

Creating custom base classes helps you define a set of shared behaviors, configurations, or utility methods that can be inherited by various **views**, **viewsets**, or **serializers** in your project. These base classes can serve as a foundation for specific **views** or **viewsets**, promoting code reusability and maintainability.

In order to create custom base class, first identify the common functionality, behaviors, or methods that you want to encapsulate in your custom base class. This could include authentication logic, permission checks, common serializer fields, or utility methods. Create a Python class that serves as your custom base class. This class should inherit from the appropriate DRF class or mixin that you want to extend or enhance. In your base class, define the methods and attributes that provide the shared functionality. These methods can include **get()**, **post()**, or any other **HTTP method handlers**, as well as utility methods. You can also set class-level properties and attributes, such as **authentication classes**, **permission classes**, **serializer classes**, or any other configuration options relevant to your views. Once the base class is created, in your **views** or **viewsets** where you want to reuse the common functionality, inherit from your custom base class.

To demonstrate this, let's go to chapter6_serializers_views/api/views.py and add the following lines of code:

```
class WatchListBaseView():
    """
    Custom base view class for WatchList.
    """
    queryset = WatchList.objects.all()
    serializer_class = serializers.WatchListModelSerializer

class WatchlistIListAPIView(WatchListBaseView, generics.ListAPIView):
    """
    View to list Watchlist or to create a new watchlist
    """
    pass
```

```
    # Add view-specific logic here

class WatchlistICreateAPIView(WatchListBaseView, generics.CreateAPIView):
    """
    View to list Watchlist or to create a new watchlist
    """
    pass
    # Add view-specific logic here
```

Add the corresponding URL in chapter6_serializers_views/api/urls.py as below:

```
urlpatterns = [
    ...
    #Using Custom Base class for views
    path('watchlist-inherited-list-api/', views.WatchlistIListAPIView.as_
    view(), name="watchlist-inherited-list-api"),
    path('watchlist-inherited-create-api/', views.WatchlistICreateAPIView.
    as_view(), name="watchlist-inherited-create-api"),
]
```

In the above code, **WatchListBaseView** is a custom base class that defines the common **queryset** and **serializer class** for all views that inherit from it.

WatchlistIListAPIView and **WatchlistICreateAPIView** are views that inherit from **WatchListBaseView**. They have access to the common functionality defined in the base class, along with view-specific functionality like listing or creating an object.

Now you can get a list of Watchlist using a GET request using the URL: `{{domain}}/api/chapter6_serializers_views/watchlist-inherited-list-api/`.

You can create a new Watchlist using a POST request with the URL: `{{domain}}/api/chapter6_serializers_views/watchlist-inherited-create-api/`.

We have covered implementing class-based views. Similarly, let's implement function-based views for the Watchlist model.

Go to chapter6_serializers_views/api/views.py and add the following lines of code:

```
from rest_framework.decorators import api_view

...
@api_view(['GET', 'POST'])
def watchlist_list(request):
```

```
    # Handle GET requests
    if request.method == 'GET':
        watchlists = WatchList.objects.all()
        serializer = serializers.WatchListModelSerializer(watchlists,
                     many=True, context={'request': request})
        return Response(serializer.data, status=status.HTTP_200_OK)

    # Handle POST requests
    elif request.method == 'POST':
        serializer = serializers.WatchListModelSerializer(data=request.
                     data, context={'request': request})
        if serializer.is_valid():
            serializer.save()
            return Response(serializer.data, status=status.HTTP_201_CREATED)
        return Response(serializer.errors, status=status.HTTP_400_BAD_REQUEST)

@api_view(['GET', 'PUT', 'DELETE'])
def watchlist_detail(request, pk):
    try:
        watchlist = WatchList.objects.get(pk=pk)
    except WatchList.DoesNotExist:
        return Response({"error": "Watchlist not found."}, status=status.
        HTTP_404_NOT_FOUND)

    # Handle GET request
    if request.method == 'GET':
        serializer = serializers.WatchListModelSerializer(watchlist,
        context={'request': request})
        return Response(serializer.data)

    # Handle PUT request
    elif request.method == 'PUT':
        serializer = serializers.WatchListModelSerializer(watchlist,
                     data=request.data, context={'request': request})
        if serializer.is_valid():
            serializer.save()
            return Response(serializer.data)
```

```
        return Response(serializer.errors, status=status.HTTP_400_BAD_REQUEST)

    # Handle DELETE request
    elif request.method == 'DELETE':
        watchlist.delete()
        return Response({"message": "Watchlist deleted successfully."},
        status=status.HTTP_204_NO_CONTENT)
```

DRF provides a decorator **@api_view,** which takes a list of HTTP methods that your view should respond to.

Add the corresponding URLs for the above FBVs in chapter6_serializers_views/api/urls.py as below:

```
urlpatterns = [
    ...
    #Function Based Views
    path('watchlists/', views.watchlist_list, name="watchlist-list"),
    path('watchlists/<int:pk>/', views.watchlist_detail, name="watchlist-
    detail"),
]
```

You can access the endpoint as below:

> **Get Watchlist List**: **GET** `{{domain}}/api/chapter6_serializers_views/watchlists/`
>
> **Create Watchlist**: **POST** `{{domain}}/api/chapter6_serializers_views/watchlists/`
>
> **Get Single Watchlist**: **GET** `{{domain}}/api/chapter6_serializers_views/watchlists/<pk>`
>
> **Update Single Watchlist**: **PUT** `{{domain}}/api/chapter6_serializers_views/watchlists/<pk>`
>
> **Delete Single Watchlist**: **DELETE** `{{domain}}/api/chapter6_serializers_views/watchlists/<pk>`
>
> where **<pk>** is the primary key of the object.

CHAPTER 7

ViewsSets and Routers

In the previous chapters, we went through different types of views to develop APIs using DRF. These traditional views offer fine-grained control over each HTTP method (GET, POST, PUT, DELETE, etc.). This level of control is beneficial when you need to implement complex and custom logic for specific actions. They allow you to define custom URL patterns and endpoints, giving you the flexibility to create API routes that match your project's requirements precisely. When your API needs to perform actions that don't fit the standard CRUD operations, traditional views are a better choice. You can define custom actions with descriptive names.

Basically, traditional views offer greater flexibility and control, making them advantageous when your API has custom behavior, non-standard endpoints, or complex logic. Traditional views are a valuable tool for handling unique or complex API requirements.

But when a project requires API endpoints to follow the CRUD pattern, then the best way to choose is **viewsets** over the traditional **views**.

ViewSets provide a structured way to organize your API code. They group together related API views into a single class, making it easier to manage and maintain your code base. ViewSets work seamlessly with routers (e.g., **DefaultRouter**), which automatically generate URL patterns for your API views. This eliminates the need to manually define URL patterns for each view. ViewSets encourage a consistent API design by providing a standard set of actions (list, retrieve, create, update, delete) for each resource. This consistency makes your API predictable and user-friendly. While ViewSets offer a standard set of actions, they are highly customizable. You can add custom actions to perform specific tasks, and you have full control over how each action is implemented. ViewSets work with serializers in DRF, simplifying the process of converting data between Python objects and JSON/XML representations.

ViewSets can be configured with authentication classes and permission classes to enforce access control and security policies consistently across your API. ViewSets make it easier to write unit tests for your API views. You can test each action in isolation,

G. Patil, *Django REST APIs Demystified*, https://doi.org/10.1007/979-8-8688-1850-9_7

ensuring that your API behaves as expected. ViewSets can speed up API development by providing a higher-level abstraction. You can focus on defining the high-level behavior of your resources rather than writing boilerplate code for each view.

REST Framework includes an abstraction for dealing with ViewSets that allows the developer to concentrate on modeling the state and interactions of the API and leave the URL construction to be handled automatically, based on common conventions. ViewSet classes are almost the same thing as **View** classes, except that they provide operations such as **retrieve**, or **update**, and not method handlers such as **get** or **put**. The method handlers for a ViewSet are only bound to the corresponding actions at the point of finalizing the view, using the **.as_view()** method. Typically, rather than explicitly registering the views in a viewset in the **urlconf**, you'll register the viewset with a **router** class that automatically determines the **urlconf** for you.

Using viewsets can be a really useful abstraction. It helps ensure that URL conventions will be consistent across your API, minimizes the amount of code you need to write, and allows you to concentrate on the interactions and representations your API provides rather than the specifics of the URL conf.

That doesn't mean it's always the right approach to take. There's a similar set of trade-offs to consider when using class-based views instead of function-based views. Using viewsets is less explicit than building your views individually.

There are four types of ViewSets, from the most basic to the most powerful:

- ViewSet
- GenericViewSet
- ModelViewSet
- ReadOnlyModelViewSet

The relation between each of the above types is as below:

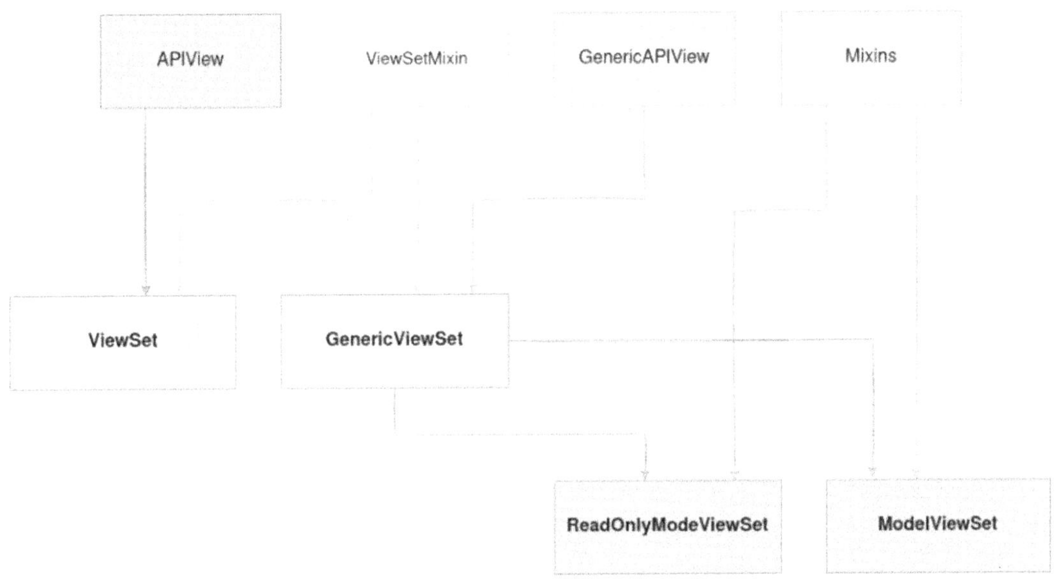

ViewSetMixin is a class where all the "magic happens." It's the only class that all four of the **ViewSets** share. It overrides the **as_view** method and combines the method with the proper action.

Preparing for This Chapter

Create a new app with the name **chapter7_viewsets_routers** with the steps specified in the **Project Setup** section in Chapter 3.

Go to drfproject/settings.py and add the following lines of code:

```
INSTALLED_APPS = [
    ...
    "chapter7_viewsets_routers",
]
```

Go to chapter7_viewsets_routers/api/serializers.py and add the following lines of code:

```
from rest_framework import serializers
from django.contrib.auth import get_user_model
from chapter3_project_setup.models import WatchList, StreamPlatform, Review
```

```
#############################ModelSerializer#########################

class WatchlistModelBasicSerializer(serializers.ModelSerializer):
    platform = serializers.StringRelatedField()

    class Meta:
        model=WatchList
        fields = ["title", "platform", "imdb_rating", "created"]

class WatchListModelSerializer(serializers.ModelSerializer):
    class Meta:
        model = WatchList
        fields = "__all__"
        ref_name = 'C7WatchListModelSerializer'

class StreamPlatformModelSerializer(serializers.ModelSerializer):

    class Meta:
        model = StreamPlatform
        fields = "__all__"
        ref_name = 'C7StreamPlatformModelSerializer'

class ReviewModelSerializer(serializers.ModelSerializer):
    review_user = serializers.StringRelatedField(read_only=True)

    class Meta:
        model = Review
        fields = "__all__"
        ref_name = 'C7ReviewModelSerializer'
```

Go to chapter7_viewsets_routers/api/views.py and add the following lines of code:

```
from rest_framework.decorators import api_view
from rest_framework.response import Response
from rest_framework import status, viewsets
from rest_framework import generics
from rest_framework import mixins
```

```
from rest_framework.decorators import action
from django.db import transaction
from chapter3_project_setup.models import WatchList, Review, StreamPlatform
from . import serializers
```

Go to chapter7_viewsets_routers/api/urls.py and add the following lines of code:

```
from django.urls import path, include
from rest_framework.routers import DefaultRouter
from chapter7_viewsets_routers.api import views

router = DefaultRouter()

urlpatterns = [
    # Using ViewSet
    path("", include(router.urls)),
]
```

Go to drfproject/urls.py and add the following lines of code:

```
urlpatterns = [
    ...
    path('api/chapter7_viewsets_routers/', include('chapter7_viewsets_
    routers.api.urls')),
]
```

ViewSet

ViewSet is a base class in DRF for creating custom views. It provides a way to define your own custom actions and views that don't necessarily map directly to a model. You should use **ViewSet** when you need a high level of customization for your views and actions and when the views are not tied to a specific model. You have full control over the methods you define in a **ViewSet**, making it suitable for building non-standard or highly customized API views. For example, implementing a view that performs complex business logic that doesn't fit the standard CRUD operations.

The **ViewSet** class inherits from **APIView**. You can use any of the standard attributes such as **permission_classes** and **authentication_classes** in order to control the API policy on the viewset. The **ViewSet** class does not provide any implementations of actions. In order to use a ViewSet class, you'll override the class and define the action implementations explicitly. Basically, use **ViewSet** for maximum customization and when views are not tied to a model.

Let us create an endpoint using a **viewset** for **Watchlist** model operations.

Let's go to chapter7_viewsets_routers/api/views.py and add the following lines of code:

```
class WatchListViewSet(viewsets.ViewSet):
    queryset = WatchList.objects.all()
    def list(self, request):
        serializer = serializers.WatchListModelSerializer(self.queryset,
                     many=True, context={"request":request})
        return Response(serializer.data)

    def create(self, request):
        serializer = serializers.WatchListModelSerializer(data=req
                     uest.data)
        if serializer.is_valid():
            serializer.save()
            return Response(serializer.data, status=status.HTTP_201_CREATED)
        return Response(serializer.errors, status=status.HTTP_400_BAD_REQUEST)

    def retrieve(self, request, pk=None):
        watchlist = generics.get_object_or_404(self.queryset, pk=pk)
        serializer = serializers.WatchListModelSerializer(watchlist,
        context={"request":request})
        return Response(serializer.data)

    def update(self, request, pk=None):
        watchlist = generics.get_object_or_404(self.queryset, pk=pk)
        serializer = serializers.WatchListModelSerializer(watchlist,
        data=request.data, context={"request":request})
        if serializer.is_valid():
            serializer.save()
```

```
            return Response(serializer.data)
        return Response(serializer.errors, status=status.HTTP_400_BAD_REQUEST)

    def partial_update(self, request, pk=None):
        watchlist = generics.get_object_or_404(self.queryset, pk=pk)
        serializer = serializers.WatchListModelSerializer(watchlist,
                     data=request.data, partial=True,
                     context={"request":request})
        if serializer.is_valid():
            serializer.save()
            return Response(serializer.data)
        return Response(serializer.errors, status=status.HTTP_400_BAD_REQUEST)

    def destroy(self, request, pk=None):
        watchlist = generics.get_object_or_404(self.queryset, pk=pk)
        watchlist.delete()
        return Response(status=status.HTTP_204_NO_CONTENT)

    @action(detail=False, methods=['get'])
    def watchlist_count(self, request):
        movies = WatchList.objects.filter(category="MOVIE").count()
        series = WatchList.objects.filter(category="SERIES").count()
        return Response({"movies":movies, "series":series})
```

Add the corresponding URL in chapter7_viewsets_routers/api/urls.py as below:

```
router = DefaultRouter()

# Using ViewSet
router.register(r"watchlist-viewset", views.WatchListViewSet, basename=
"c7-watchlist-viewset")
```

In the above code, we have inherited the DRF-provided **viewsets.ViewSet** to create a custom view **WatchListViewSet** for creating an endpoint. Each methods defined in **WatchListViewSet** are the actions for each CRUD operation:

- **list**: List all WatchList items.

  Endpoint: `{{domain}}/api/chapter7_viewsets_routers/watchlist-viewset/`

- **create**: Create a new WatchList item.

  Endpoint: `{{domain}}/api/chapter7_viewsets_routers/watchlist-viewset/`

- **retrieve**: Retrieve a specific WatchList item by its primary key(pk).

  Endpoint: `{{domain}}/api/chapter7_viewsets_routers/watchlist-viewset/{pk}/`

- **update**: Update a specific WatchList item by its primary key(pk).

  Endpoint: `{{domain}}/api/chapter7_viewsets_routers/watchlist-viewset/{pk}/`

- **partial_update**: Partially update a specific WatchList item by its primary key(pk).

  Endpoint: `{{domain}}/api/chapter7_viewsets_routers/watchlist-viewset/{pk}/`

- **destroy**: Delete a specific WatchList item by its primary key(pk).

  Endpoint: `{{domain}}/api/chapter7_viewsets_routers/watchlist-viewset/{pk}/`

- **watchlist_count**: This is a custom action created to count the number of Movies and Series in the Watchlist. This action is created with the **@action** decorator. This action allows only the HTTP GET method. The method parameter is optional, whereas the detail parameter is not. The detail parameter should be set as True if the action is meant for a single object or False if it's meant for all objects.

  Endpoint: `{{domain}}/api/chapter7_viewsets_routers/watchlist-viewset/watchlist_count`

  If you want to change this URL by setting the **url_path** parameter in the decorator.

If you notice all the above endpoints are created using only one URL path: **path ("", include(router.urls)).** DRF provided a **router that** takes care the part of creating different endpoints for each CRUD operation/action.

Now let's understand more about routers.

GenericViewSet

This is a subclass of ViewSet that is designed to work with DRF's generic views and mixins. It provides a way to use DRF's generic views and mixins with custom actions. You should use GenericViewSet when you want to mix DRF's generic views and mixins with custom actions and views.

The GenericViewSet class inherits from **GenericAPIView** and provides the default set of **get_object**, **get_queryset** methods, and other generic view base behavior but does not include any actions by default. In order to use a GenericViewSet class, you'll override the class and either mix in the required mixin classes or define the action implementations explicitly.

The GenericViewSet class allows you to reuse common behavior provided by DRF, such as **list** and **retrieve**, while also defining custom actions. For example, combining standard list and retrieve actions with custom actions like "approve" or "reject." Basically, use GenericViewSet when you want to mix DRF's generic views and mixins with custom actions.

Let's create an endpoint using GenericViewSet for **Watchlist** model operations.

Let's go to chapter7_viewsets_routers/api/views.py and add the following lines of code:

```
class WatchListGenericViewSet(
    mixins.ListModelMixin,
    mixins.CreateModelMixin,
    mixins.RetrieveModelMixin,
    mixins.UpdateModelMixin,
    mixins.DestroyModelMixin,
    viewsets.GenericViewSet
):
    queryset = WatchList.objects.all()
    serializer_class = serializers.WatchListModelSerializer

    def get_queryset(self):
        # Custom queryset logic, e.g., applying filters or ordering
        return WatchList.objects.filter(active=True).order_by('title')

    # Custom action to mark a watchlist item as 'inactive'
    @action(detail=False, methods=['get'])
```

```
    def watchlist_count(self, request):
        movies = WatchList.objects.filter(category="MOVIE").count()
        series = WatchList.objects.filter(category="SERIES").count()
        return Response({"movies":movies, "series":series})
```

Add the corresponding URL in chapter7_viewsets_routers/api/urls.py as below:

```
router = DefaultRouter()
...
# Using GenericViewSet
router.register(r"watchlist-generic-viewset", views.
WatchListGenericViewSet, basename="watchlist-generic-viewset")
```

The above code defines a **WatchListGenericViewSet** class that inherits from **viewsets.GenericViewSet** and includes several **mixins** for standard CRUD (Create, Read, Update, Delete) operations. When using mixins, we don't have to explicitly define standard actions such as list, create, etc. Mixins provide all the action methods required by the view. The @action decorator is used to define a custom action named **watchlist_count**. This action is associated with the URL path /**watchlist_count**/ and accepts GET requests.

The following endpoints can be used for the CRUD operations:

- **list**: List all WatchList items.

  Endpoint: `{{domain}}/api/chapter7_viewsets_routers/watchlist-generic-viewset/`

- **create**: Create a new WatchList item.

  Endpoint: `{{domain}}/api/chapter7_viewsets_routers/watchlist-generic-viewset/`

- **retrieve**: Retrieve a specific WatchList item by its primary key(pk).

  Endpoint: `{{domain}}/api/chapter7_viewsets_routers/watchlist-generic-viewset/{pk}/`

- **update**: Update a specific WatchList item by its primary key(pk).

  Endpoint: `{{domain}}/api/chapter7_viewsets_routers/watchlist-generic-viewset/{pk}/`

- **partial_update**: Partially update a specific WatchList item by its primary key(pk).

  Endpoint: `{{domain}}/api/chapter7_viewsets_routers/watchlist-generic-viewset/{pk}/`

- **destroy**: Delete a specific WatchList item by its primary key(pk).

  Endpoint: `{{domain}}/api/chapter7_viewsets_routers/watchlist-generic-viewset/{pk}/`

- **watchlist_count**: This is a custom action created to count the number of Movies and Series in the Watchlist.

  Endpoint: `{{domain}}/api/chapter7_viewsets_routers/watchlist-generic-viewset/watchlist_count`

ModelViewSet

This view class combines the functionalities of all CRUD operations (list, create, retrieve, update, delete) for a model. It's commonly used with DRF's router for automatic URL routing. This is the most commonly used **ViewSet** and is designed to work with Django models. It automatically generates views for listing, creating, retrieving, updating, and deleting model instances. You can use it when you want full CRUD functionality for your models. It is a subclass of **GenericViewSet** and provides default implementations for standard CRUD operations (**list, retrieve, create, update, destroy**). The ModelViewSet class inherits from **GenericAPIView** and includes implementations for various actions, by mixing in the behavior of the various mixin classes. Because ModelViewSet extends GenericAPIView, you'll normally need to provide at least the **queryset** and **serializer_class** attributes.

You should use ModelViewSet when you want to create a standard RESTful API for a Django model with minimal customization. It simplifies the process of creating views for CRUD operations on a model by providing default implementations. You can also customize it by adding your own actions.

Let's create an endpoint using ModelViewSet for **Watchlist** model operations.

Let's go to chapter7_viewsets_routers/api/views.py and add the following lines of code:

```
class WatchListModelViewSet(viewsets.ModelViewSet):
    queryset = WatchList.objects.all()
    serializer_class = serializers.WatchListModelSerializer

    def get_queryset(self):
        # Custom queryset logic, e.g., applying filters or ordering
        return WatchList.objects.filter(active=True).order_by('title')

    # Custom action to get summary information
    @action(detail=False, methods=['get'])
    def watchlist_count(self, request):
        movies = WatchList.objects.filter(category="MOVIE").count()
        series = WatchList.objects.filter(category="SERIES").count()
        return Response({"movies":movies, "series":series})
```

Add the corresponding URL in chapter7_viewsets_routers/api/urls.py as below:

```
router = DefaultRouter()
...
# Using ModelViewSet
router.register(r"watchlist-model-viewset", views.WatchListModelViewSet,
basename="watchlist-model-viewset")
```

The functionality of the above view is the same as WatchListGenericViewSet, except the endpoints are going to change as below:

- **list**: List all WatchList items.

  Endpoint: {{domain}}/api/chapter7_viewsets_routers/watchlist-model-viewset/

- **create**: Create a new WatchList item.

  Endpoint: {{domain}}/api/chapter7_viewsets_routers/watchlist-model-viewset/

- **retrieve**: Retrieve a specific WatchList item by its primary key(pk).

  Endpoint: {{domain}}/api/chapter7_viewsets_routers/watchlist-model-viewset/{pk}/

- **update**: Update a specific WatchList item by its primary key(pk).

Endpoint: {{domain}}/api/chapter7_viewsets_routers/watchlist-model-viewset/{pk}/

- **partial_update**: Partially update a specific WatchList item by its primary key(pk).

  Endpoint: {{domain}}/api/chapter7_viewsets_routers/watchlist-model-viewset/{pk}/

- **destroy**: Delete a specific WatchList item by its primary key(pk).

  Endpoint: {{domain}}/api/chapter7_viewsets_routers/watchlist-model-viewset/{pk}/

- **watchlist_count**: This is a custom action created to count the number of Movies and Series in the Watchlist.

  Endpoint: {{domain}}/api/chapter7_viewsets_routers/watchlist-model-viewset/watchlist_count

ReadOnlyModelViewSet

This is a viewset class that provides read-only operations (i.e., GET requests) on a model. It is a specialized viewset designed for scenarios where you want to expose read-only endpoints for a model without allowing any modification operations like creating, updating, or deleting objects.

ReadOnlyModelViewSet inherits from **mixins.RetrieveModelMixin** and **mixins.ListModelMixin**, which provide the standard actions for retrieving single objects and listing multiple objects. These mixins are combined to create a viewset that supports only the read operations. As with ModelViewSet, it also includes implementations for various actions but unlike ModelVicwSet only provides the "read-only" actions, **.list()** and **.retrieve()**.

However, ReadOnlyModelViewSet does not support creating, updating, or deleting objects. This makes it suitable for scenarios where you want to expose a read-only API for a model, such as providing a list of articles or details of a user profile. Creating endpoints using ReadOnlyModelViewSet explicitly communicates the intent that the viewset is intended for read-only operations. When other developers work with your code base, they can quickly understand that this viewset should not be used for creating, updating, or deleting objects. By using ReadOnlyModelViewSet, you can ensure that the viewset does not accidentally expose modification operations. This helps in securing your API, especially in situations where certain users or clients should have read-only access to your data. As with ModelViewSet, you'll normally need to provide at least the **queryset** and **serializer_class** attributes.

Let's create an endpoint using ReadOnlyModelViewSet for **Watchlist** model operations.

Let's go to watchlist_app/api/views.py and add the following lines of code:

```
class WatchListReadOnlyModelViewSet(viewsets.ReadOnlyModelViewSet):
    queryset = WatchList.objects.all()
    serializer_class = serializers.WatchListModelSerializer
```

Add the corresponding URL in chapter7_viewsets_routers/api/urls.py as below:

```
router = DefaultRouter()
...
# Using ReadOnlyModelViewSet
router.register(r"watchlist-readonly-model-viewset", views.
WatchListReadOnlyModelViewSet, basename="watchlist-readonly-model-viewset")
```

The functionality of the above view is the same as WatchListViewSet2, except the endpoints are going to change as below:

- **list**: List all WatchList items.

  Endpoint: {{domain}}/api/chapter7_viewsets_routers/watchlist-readonly-model-viewset/

- **retrieve**: Retrieve a specific WatchList item by its primary key(pk).

  Endpoint: {{domain}}/api/chapter7_viewsets_routers/watchlist-readonly-model-viewset/{pk}/

This endpoint does not allow any write operations such as post, put, patch, or delete operations. It restricts only to the get or list methods.

Routers

Routers are a powerful feature that simplifies the process of defining URL patterns for your API views. Routers automatically generate URL patterns for your API views based on the registered viewsets. This eliminates the need to manually define and maintain URL patterns for each view. It reduces the chances of URL configuration errors and keeps your code DRY (Don't Repeat Yourself). Routers enforce consistent URL patterns following RESTful conventions. This consistency makes your API more intuitive and easier to understand for both developers and clients. As your API grows and you add more views and viewsets, routers help you maintain a clean and organized URL structure. You can simply register new viewsets with the router, and the corresponding URLs are automatically generated. While routers provide standard CRUD actions (list, create, retrieve, update, destroy), they also support custom actions defined in your viewsets using the **@action** decorator. This means you can easily add additional actions to your API without complex URL configuration.

DRF comes with two routers out of the box:

1. SimpleRouter
2. DefaultRouter

The main difference between them is that **DefaultRouter** includes a default API root view.

For example, in our project, entering the root URL `{{domain}}/api/chapter7_viewsets_routers/` returns the below response:

```
{
    "watchlist-viewset": "http://127.0.0.1:8000/api/chapter7_viewsets_
    routers/watchlist-viewset/",
    "watchlist-generic-viewset": "http://127.0.0.1:8000/api/chapter7_
    viewsets_routers/watchlist-generic-viewset/",
    "watchlist-model-viewset": "http://127.0.0.1:8000/api/chapter7_
    viewsets_routers/watchlist-model-viewset/",
    "streamplatform-model-viewset": "http://127.0.0.1:8000/api/chapter7_
    viewsets_routers/streamplatform-model-viewset/",
    "watchlist-readonly-model-viewset": "http://127.0.0.1:8000/api/
    chapter7_viewsets_routers/watchlist-readonly-model-viewset/"
}
```

The default API root view lists hyperlinked list views, which makes navigating through your application easier. Other than this additional feature, **SimpleRouter** and **DefaultRouter** have the same functionality.

Let's understand the router concept in detail. If you refer to the following lines of code in chapter7_viewsets_routers/api/urls.py:

```
router = DefaultRouter()

# Using ViewSet
router.register(r"watchlist-viewset", views.WatchListViewSet, basename="c7-
watchlist-viewset")

# Using GenericViewSet
router.register(r"watchlist-generic-viewset", views.
WatchListGenericViewSet, basename="watchlist-generic-viewset")

# Using ModelViewSet
router.register(r"watchlist-model-viewset", views.WatchListModelViewSet,
basename="watchlist-model-viewset")
router.register(r"streamplatform-model-viewset", views.
StreamPlatformModelViewSet, basename="streamplatform-model-viewset")

# Using ReadOnlyModelViewSet
router.register(r"watchlist-readonly-model-viewset", views.
WatchListReadOnlyModelViewSet, basename="watchlist-readonly-model-viewset")
```

In the above lines of code, we have registered each viewset to the router using the **register()** method. There are two mandatory fields for this method:

- **prefix**: The URL prefix to use for this set of routes
- **viewset**: The viewset class

We can provide optional arguments to the register method:

- **basename:** The base to use for the URL names that are created. If unset, the basename will be automatically generated based on the **queryset** attribute of the viewset if it has one. Note that if the viewset does not include a **queryset** attribute, then you must set basename when registering the viewset.

Referring to the above URLs would generate the following URL patterns:

- **URL Pattern**: {{domain}}/api/chapter7_viewsets_routers/watchlist-viewset/$ **Name**: 'c7-watchlist-viewset-list'
- **URL Pattern**: {{domain}}/api/chapter7_viewsets_routers/watchlist-viewset/{pk}/$ **Name**: ' c7-watchlist-viewset-detail'
- **URL Pattern**: {{domain}}/api/chapter7_viewsets_routers/watchlist-generic-viewset/$ **Name**: 'watchlist-generic-viewset-list'
- **URL Pattern**: {{domain}}/api/chapter7_viewsets_routers/watchlist-generic-viewset/{pk}/$ **Name**: ' watchlist-generic-viewset-detail'
- **URL Pattern**: {{domain}}/api/chapter7_viewsets_routers/watchlist-model-viewset/$ **Name**: ' watchlist-model-viewset-list'
- **URL Pattern**: {{domain}}/api/chapter7_viewsets_routers/watchlist-model-viewset/{pk}/$ **Name**: 'watchlist-model-viewset-detail'
- **URL Pattern**: {{domain}}/api/chapter7_viewsets_routers/watchlist-readonly-model-viewset/$ **Name**: 'watchlist-readonly-model-viewset-list'
- **URL Pattern**: {{domain}}/api/chapter7_viewsets_routers/watchlist-readonly-model-viewset/{pk}/$ **Name**: 'watchlist-readonly-model-viewset-detail'

The **basename** argument is used to specify the initial part of the view name pattern. In the example above, that's the **c7-watchlist-viewset** or **watchlist-readonly-model-viewset** part.

Typically, you won't need to specify the **basename** argument, but if you have a viewset where you've defined a custom **get_queryset** method, then the viewset may not have a **queryset** attribute set. If you try to register that viewset, you'll see an error like this:

> *'basename' argument not specified, and could not automatically determine the name from the viewset, as it does not have a '.queryset' attribute.*

This means you'll need to explicitly set the **basename** argument when registering the viewset, as it could not be automatically determined from the model name.

It is important to note that when routers are created using the register method, you should include router URLs with the existing **urlpatterns** list. The following are ways to include router URLs with existing urlpatterns:

1. Append to existing urlpatterns like below:

    ```
    urlpatterns += router.urls
    ```

2. Using the Django include function like below:

    ```
    from django.urls import path, include
    urlpatterns = [
        path("", include(router.urls))

    ]
    ```

3. Using the Django include function with application namespace:

    ```
    from django.urls import path, include
    urlpatterns = [
        path("", include(router.urls, "app_name"))

    ]
    ```

4. Using the Django include function with the application and instance namespace:

    ```
    from django.urls import path, include
    urlpatterns = [
        path("", include(router.urls, "app_name"),
        namespace="instance_name")

    ]
    ```

If using namespacing with hyperlinked serializers, you'll also need to ensure that any **view_name** parameters on the serializers correctly reflect the namespace. In the examples above, you'd need to include a parameter such as **view_name='app_name: c7-watchlist-viewset-detail'** for serializer fields hyperlinked to the **c7-watchlist-viewset-detail** view.

The automatic **view_name** generation uses a pattern like **%(model_name)-detail**. Unless your model names actually clash, you may be better off **not** namespacing your Django REST Framework views when using hyperlinked serializers.

To demonstrate the above concept, let's go to chapter7_viewsets_routers/api/serializers.py and add the following lines of code:

```
class WatchListHyperlinkedModelSerializer(serializers.
HyperlinkedModelSerializer):

    class Meta:
        model = WatchList
        fields = "__all__"
        read_only_fields = ['full_title']
        extra_kwargs = {
            'platform': {'view_name':'instance_name:streamplatform-hlms-
            viewset-detail'},
            'url': {'view_name': 'instance_name:watchlist-hlms-viewset-
            detail', 'lookup_field': 'pk'},
        }

class StreamPlatformHyperlinkedModelSerializer(serializers.
HyperlinkedModelSerializer):
    watchlist = WatchListHyperlinkedModelSerializer(many=True, read_
    only=True)

    class Meta:
        model = StreamPlatform
        fields = "__all__"
        extra_kwargs = {
            'url':{'view_name':'instance_name:streamplatform-hlms-viewset-
            detail', 'lookup_field':'pk'}
        }
```

Go to chapter7_viewsets_routers/api/views.py and add the following lines of code:

```
class WatchListHLMSViewset(viewsets.ModelViewSet):
    queryset = WatchList.objects.all()
    serializer_class = serializers.WatchListHyperlinkedModelSerializer

class StreamPlatformHLMSViewset(viewsets.ModelViewSet):
    queryset = StreamPlatform.objects.all()
    serializer_class = serializers.StreamPlatformHyperlinkedModelSerializer
```

Go to chapter7_viewsets_routers/api/urls.py and add the following lines of code:

```
router = DefaultRouter()
...

# Using HyperLinkedModelSerializer
router1 = DefaultRouter()
router1.register(r"watchlist-hlms-viewset", views.WatchListHLMSViewset,
basename="watchlist-hlms-viewset")
router1.register(r"streamplatform-hlms-viewset", views.
StreamPlatformHLMSViewset, basename="streamplatform-hlms-viewset")

urlpatterns = [
    ...
    #Using HyperlinkedModelSerializer
    path('', include((router1.urls, 'app_name'), namespace='instance_
    name')),
]
```

In the above code, we have defined a serializer inherited from **HyperlinkedModelSerializer** and created views to use them for **Watch** and **StreamPlatform** models. When setting the **view_name** attribute, we can specify either **'view_name': 'instance_name: watchlist-hlms-viewset-detail'** or **'view_name': 'app_name: watchlist-hlms-viewset-detail'** for the Watchlist model. A similar approach applies to the **StreamPlatform** model also.

Note that the trailing slashes on the URL routes can be removed by setting the **trailing_slash** argument to **False** when instantiating the router.

```
router = DefaultRouter(trailing_slash=False)
```

Trailing slashes are conventional in Django but are not used by default in some other frameworks such as Rails. Which style you choose to use is largely a matter of preference, although some JavaScript frameworks may expect a particular routing style.

Routing for Extra Actions

Routing with customized actions is essential because it allows you to define and expose custom functionality in your API beyond the standard CRUD (Create, Read, Update, Delete) operations. This is particularly useful when you need to implement specific, non-standard behavior in your API that doesn't fit neatly into the standard RESTful actions. Like regular actions, extra actions may be intended for either a single object or an entire collection. To indicate this, set the **detail** argument to **True** or **False**. The router will configure its URL patterns accordingly. For example, the **DefaultRouter** will configure detailed actions to contain **pk** in their URL patterns. A **viewset** may mark extra actions for routing by decorating a method with the **@action** decorator. These extra actions will be included in the generated routes.

We have defined one custom action **watchlist_count** for the viewset watchlist_count. Let's define a viewset for the **StreamPlatform** model with custom actions to understand them better.

Let's go to chapter7_viewsets_routers/api/views.py and add the following lines of code:

```
class StreamPlatformModelViewSet(viewsets.ModelViewSet):
    queryset = StreamPlatform.objects.all()
    serializer_class = serializers.StreamPlatformModelSerializer

    @action(detail=True, url_path="watchlist", url_name="watchlist")
    def get_watchlist(self, request, pk=None):
        try:
            stream_platform = self.get_object()
            serializer = serializers.WatchListModelSerializer(stream_
            platform.watchlist, many=True, context={"request":request})
            return Response(serializer.data, status=status.HTTP_200_OK)
            except Exception as e:
            return Response({'error': str(e)}, status=status.HTTP_400_BAD_
            REQUEST)
```

```
@action(detail=False, methods=['post', 'put'], url_path="bulk-update",
url_name="bulk_update")
def bulk_update(self, request):
    # Implement the logic for bulk updates here
    data = request.data

    # Extract a list of IDs and corresponding updates
    ids_to_update = [item['id'] for item in data]
    updates = {item['id']: item for item in data}

    # Perform bulk updates
    try:
        with transaction.atomic():
            for streamplatform_item in StreamPlatform.objects.
            filter(id__in=ids_to_update):
                update_data = updates.get(streamplatform_item.id)
                if update_data:
                    streamplatform_item.name = update_data.get('name',
                    streamplatform_item.name)
                    streamplatform_item.about = update_data.
                    get('about', streamplatform_item.about)
                    streamplatform_item.website = update_data.
                    get('website', streamplatform_item.website)
                    # Add more fields to update as needed
                    streamplatform_item.save()
    except Exception as e:
        return Response({'error': str(e)}, status=status.HTTP_400_BAD_
        REQUEST)

    return Response({'message': 'Bulk update successful'})

@action(detail=False, methods=['delete'], url_path="bulk-delete",
url_name="bulk_delete")
def bulk_delete(self, request):
    # Implement the logic for bulk deletes here
    data = request.data

    # Extract a list of IDs to delete
```

```
        ids_to_delete = [item['id'] for item in data]

        # Perform bulk deletes
        try:
            StreamPlatform.objects.filter(id__in=ids_to_delete).delete()
        except Exception as e:
            return Response({'error': str(e)}, status=status.HTTP_400_BAD_
            REQUEST)

        return Response({'message': 'Bulk delete successful'})
```

We have defined three custom actions. The `get_watchlist` action to get watchlists for a specific platform. The action decorator will route **GET** requests by default but may also accept other HTTP methods by setting the methods argument. Since we have not mentioned any methods, by default, it accepts a GET request. The @action decorator also allows you to override any viewset-level configuration, such as **permission_classes**, **serializer_class,** and **filter_backends**. We will cover these in later sections of this book. We have used the **url_path** and **url_name** parameters to change the URL segment and the reverse URL name of the action. To view all extra actions, call the **.get_extra_actions()** method.

We don't need to add additional URLs for the above-defined custom actions. You can get a watchlist for the platform with ID 1 using the URL: `{{domain}}/api/chapter7_viewsets_routers/streamplatform-model-viewset/1/watchlist/`.

Similarly, we have defined a custom action **bulk_update** to accept a **PUT** request. This action retrieves the list of updated items from the request data, fetches the corresponding **StreamPlatform** objects to be updated, and then updates the specified fields. To perform the bulk update, you can make a **PUT** request to the `{{domain}}/api/chapter7_viewsets_routers/streamplatform-model-viewset/bulk-update/` URL with the updated data in the request body.

For example:

```
[
    {
        "id": 1,
        "name": "Netflix",
        "about": "Netflix-updated",
        "website": "http://www.netflix.com"
```

```
    },
    {
        "id": 2,
        "name": "Disneyplus",
        "about": "Disnyplus About updated",
        "website": "http://www.disneyplus.com"
    }
]
```

We have also defined the action **bulk_delete** to accept the DELETE request. The request data should include a list of objects, where each object contains an ID field to identify the **StreamPlatform** items to delete. To perform the bulk delete, you can make a DELETE request to the `{{domain}}/api/chapter7_viewsets_routers/streamplatform-model-viewset/bulk-delete/` URL with an array of objects containing the ID to identify the **StreamPlatform** items to delete.

For example:

```
[
    {
        "id": 7
    },
    {
        "id": 8
    }
]
```

Routing Additional HTTP Methods for Extra Actions

If you want to use the same endpoint, but a different functionality with a different HTTP method, then you can use the mapping approach on actions. Extra actions can map additional HTTP methods to separate **ViewSet** methods. Note that additional mappings do not accept arguments.

For example, let's create a new action **update_streamplatform** which can be used with the same endpoint used for **get_watchlist** but with the **HTTP PUT** method.

Let's go to watchlist_app/api/views.py and add the following function to class **StreamPlatformModelViewSet** as follows:

```
@get_watchlist.mapping.put
def update_streamplatform(self, request, pk=None, *args, **kwargs):
    try:
        partial = kwargs.pop('partial', False)
        instance = self.get_object()
        serializer = self.get_serializer(instance, data=request.data,
        partial=partial)
        serializer.is_valid(raise_exception=True)
        self.perform_update(serializer)

        if getattr(instance, '_prefetched_objects_cache', None):
            # If 'prefetch_related' has been applied to a queryset,
            we need to
            # forcibly invalidate the prefetch cache on the instance.
            instance._prefetched_objects_cache = {}

        return Response(serializer.data)
    except Exception as e:
        return Response({'error': str(e)}, status=status.HTTP_400_BAD_
        REQUEST)
```

In the above code, we have decorated **update_streamplatform** with **@get_watchlist.mapping.put** instead of the **@action** decorator. This makes the function use the same endpoint but with the **HTTP PUT** method.

You can update the individual **StreamPlatform** instance with the **PUT** method using the URL: `{{domain}}/api/chapter7_viewsets_routers/streamplatform-model-viewset/{pk}/watchlist/`

where {pk} is the primary key of the **StreamPlatform** instance.

Custom Routers

Custom routers in Django REST Framework (DRF) are used to define and customize the URL routing for your API views. While DRF provides default routers like **DefaultRouter** for standard viewsets, you might need custom routers for various reasons.

- **Granular Control**: Custom routers allow you to have granular control over your API's URL structure. You can define specific URL patterns, including custom actions and endpoints, to match your application's needs.
- **Complex URL Structures**: Some APIs have complex URL structures that can't be easily handled by the default routers. Custom routers give you the flexibility to design URLs that align with your API's requirements.
- **Custom Actions**: If your viewsets have custom actions beyond the standard CRUD operations (e.g., custom methods like list_active or search), you can create custom routes for these actions.
- **Versioning**: Custom routers are often used for versioning APIs. You can create version-specific routers to ensure backward compatibility while introducing new API versions.
- **Nested Resources**: In APIs with nested resources (e.g., /parent/child/), custom routers help you define the correct URL patterns to access nested resources.
- **Complex Query Parameters**: For APIs that rely heavily on query parameters, custom routers can help you define URL patterns that include query parameters as part of the route.

Implementing a custom router isn't something you'd need to do very often, but it can be useful if you have specific requirements about how the URLs for your API are structured. Doing so allows you to encapsulate the URL structure in a reusable way that ensures you don't have to write your URL patterns explicitly for each new view.

The simplest way to implement a custom router is to subclass one of the existing router classes. The **.routes** attribute is used to template the URL patterns that will be mapped to each viewset. The **.routes** attribute is a list of **Route** named tuples.

The arguments to the **Route** named tuple are

1. **url:** A string representing the URL to be routed. May include the following format strings:
    - **{prefix}**: The URL prefix to use for this set of routes
    - **{lookup}**: The lookup field used to match against a single instance
    - **{trailing_slash}**: Either a '/' or an empty string, depending on the trailing_slash argument
2. **mapping:** A mapping of HTTP method names to the view methods.
3. **name:** The name of the URL as used in reverse calls. May include the following format string:
    - **{basename}**: The base to use for the URL names that are created
4. **initkwargs:** A dictionary of any additional arguments that should be passed when instantiating the view. Note that the detail, basename, and suffix arguments are reserved for viewset introspection and are also used by the browsable API to generate the view name and breadcrumb links.

You can also customize how the **@action** decorator is routed. Include the **DynamicRoute** named tuple in the **.routes** list, setting the detail argument as appropriate for the list-based and detail-based routes. In addition to the details, the arguments to **DynamicRoute** are

1. **url:** A string representing the URL to be routed. May include the same format strings as Route and additionally accepts the **{url_path}** format string.
2. **name:** The name of the URL as used in reverse calls. May include the following format strings:
    - **{basename}**: The base to use for the URL names that are created
    - **{url_name}**: The **url_name** provided to the **@action**
3. **initkwargs:** A dictionary of any additional arguments that should be passed when instantiating the view.

To demonstrate the above concept, let's create a custom router. Let's create a file chapter7_viewsets_routers/api/custom_routers.py and add the following lines of code:

```
from rest_framework.routers import Route, DynamicRoute, DefaultRouter

class CustomRouter(DefaultRouter):
    """
    A router for read-only APIs, which doesn't use trailing slashes.
    """
    routes = [
        # List route.
        Route(
            url=r'^{prefix}/test1{trailing_slash}$',
            mapping={
                'get': 'list',
                'post': 'create'
            },
            name='{basename}-list',
            detail=False,
            initkwargs={'suffix': 'List'}
        ),
        # Detail route.
        Route(
            url=r'^{prefix}/test1/{lookup}{trailing_slash}$',
            mapping={
                'get': 'retrieve',
                'put': 'update',
                'patch': 'partial_update',
                'delete': 'destroy'
            },
            name='{basename}-detail',
            detail=True,
            initkwargs={'suffix': 'Instance'}
        ),
```

```
        # Dynamically generated list routes. Generated using
        # @action(detail=False) decorator on methods of the viewset.
        DynamicRoute(
            url=r'^{prefix}/test2/{url_path}{trailing_slash}$',
            name='{basename}-{url_name}',
            detail=False,
            initkwargs={}
        ),

        # Dynamically generated detail routes. Generated using
        # @action(detail=True) decorator on methods of the viewset.
        DynamicRoute(
            url=r'^{prefix}/test3/{lookup}/{url_path}{trailing_slash}$',
            name='{basename}-{url_name}',
            detail=True,
            initkwargs={}
        )
    ]
```

Go to chapter7_viewsets_routers/api/urls.py and add the following lines of code:

```
router = DefaultRouter()
...

router2 = CustomRouter()
router2.register(r"streamplatform-custom-viewset", views.
StreamPlatformModelViewSet, basename="streamplatform-custom-viewset")

urlpatterns = [
    ...
    # Using CustomRouter
    path("", include(router2.urls)),

]
```

In the above code, we have inherited **DefaultRouter** when creating a custom Router **CustomRouter** and customized the list, detail, and extra actions.

We can use the following URLs for accessing the list, detail, and extra actions:

- To get the all **StreamPlatform** list:

  {{domain}}/api/chapter7_viewsets_routers/streamplatform-custom-viewset/test1/

- To get the individual **StreamPlatform**:

  {{domain}}/api/chapter7_viewsets_routers/streamplatform-custom-viewset/test1/{pk}

  where **{pk}** is the primary key of the **StreamPlatform** object

- To get a watch for a specific object, which is calling an extra action endpoint:

  {{domain}}/api/chapter7_viewsets_routers/streamplatform-custom-viewset/test3/{pk}/watchlist/

  where **{pk}** is the primary key of the **StreamPlatform** object

- To make a call to extra action to perform a bulk update:

  {{domain}}/api/chapter7_viewsets_routers/streamplatform-custom-viewset/test2/bulk-update/

  Example request data:

```
[
    {
        "id": 9,
        "name": "Netflix",
        "about": "Netflix-updated2",
        "website": "http://www.netflix.com"
    },
    {
        "id": 2,
        "name": "Disneyplus",
        "about": "Disnyplus About updated2",
        "website": "http://www.disneyplus.com"
    }
]
```

CHAPTER 8

Validators

In Django REST Framework (DRF), validators are components used to perform data validation on incoming or outgoing data in your API views and serializers. Validators are essential for ensuring that the data your API receives or sends adheres to certain rules, constraints, or requirements. They help maintain data integrity, prevent errors, and enforce business logic. These are essential parts of software development for several reasons, including data integrity, error prevention, security, and adherence to business logic. In the context of web development and APIs, validators are crucial for ensuring that data transmitted over the network is in the expected format and complies with API specifications. They help protect against both accidental data issues and malicious attacks, making your applications more robust and secure.

Here's why validators are crucial:

1. **Data Integrity**: Validators help maintain data integrity by ensuring that data conforms to expected formats, constraints, and rules. They prevent the entry of invalid or inconsistent data into a system or database.

2. **Error Prevention**: Validators help prevent common data-related errors, such as type mismatches, out-of-range values, and missing required fields. By catching errors early, validators save development and debugging time.

3. **Security**: Validators play a critical role in security by protecting against data vulnerabilities and attacks. For example, input validation prevents SQL injection, cross-site scripting (XSS), and other security risks.

4. **Business Logic Enforcement**: Validators enforce business rules and logic by verifying that data adheres to specific requirements. For example, you can ensure that a user's age is within a certain range or that an email address is unique.

G. Patil, *Django REST APIs Demystified*, https://doi.org/10.1007/979-8-8688-1850-9_8

5. **Consistency**: Validators promote data consistency across an application or system. They ensure that data is consistently formatted and structured, making it easier to work with and maintain.

6. **User Experience**: Validating data on the client side (front end) and server side (back end) improves the user experience by providing immediate feedback to users when they enter invalid data. This reduces frustration and errors during data entry.

7. **Compliance**: Validators help applications comply with data standards and regulations. For instance, they can enforce data privacy regulations like GDPR by ensuring that sensitive data is handled securely.

8. **Debugging**: Validators assist in identifying and diagnosing data-related issues during development and testing. They provide clear error messages that pinpoint the cause of validation failures.

9. **Performance Optimization**: Validating data before processing it can optimize performance by avoiding unnecessary computation and database queries. For example, if you know a value is invalid, you can skip expensive database queries.

10. **Documentation and Self-Documentation**: Validators serve as documentation for expected data formats and rules. They make it clear to developers and maintainers what data is valid and how it should be structured.

11. **Preventing Code Smells**: Proper validation reduces the likelihood of code smells and anti-patterns in your code base. It promotes clean, maintainable, and reliable code.

Most of the time you're dealing with validation in REST Framework, you'll simply be relying on the default field validation or writing explicit validation methods on serializer or field classes.

However, sometimes, you'll want to place your validation logic into reusable components so that it can easily be reused throughout your code base. This can be achieved by using validator functions and validator classes.

Validation in REST Framework

In Django REST Framework (DRF), data validation plays a crucial role in ensuring that incoming data meets certain criteria, adheres to business rules, and is in the expected format. Data validation helps prevent errors, improve data integrity, enhance security, and maintain the consistency of your API. DRF provides several mechanisms for data validation:

- **Serializer Validation:** Serializers in DRF are responsible for data validation when deserializing input data (e.g., request data) and serializing output data (e.g., response data). You can define validation rules within serializer classes using various validators and custom methods.

- **Built-In Validators:** DRF provides a set of built-in validators for common cases, such as **validators.LengthValidator**, **validators.EmailValidator**, and **validators.MinValueValidator**. You can use these validators in serializer fields.

  For example:

  ```
  from rest_framework import serializers
  class MySerializer(serializers.Serializer):
      name = serializers.CharField(max_length=100)
      email = serializers.EmailField()
  ```

- **Custom Validation Methods**: You can define custom validation methods within your serializer class by creating methods with names like **validate_<field_name>.**

  For example:

  ```
  class MySerializer(serializers.Serializer):

      def validate_email(self, value):
          if "example.com" in value:
              raise serializers.ValidationError("Emails from
              example.com are not allowed.")

          return value
  ```

- **View-Level Validation**: You can perform validation at the view level by overriding the validate method of your view class. This allows you to validate data as a whole before processing it. You can raise **serializers.ValidationError** to indicate validation failures.

  For example:

```
from rest_framework.views import APIView

from rest_framework.response import Response
class MyView(APIView):
    def validate(self, data):
        if "username" not in data:
            raise serializers.ValidationError("Username is
            required.")
        return data
    def post(self, request):
        validated_data = self.validate(request.data)
        # Process the validated data
        return Response({'message': 'Data is valid.'})
```

- **Model Validation**: When working with Django models, you can define custom validation logic within your model classes. These validations can enforce data integrity and business rules at the database level.

  For example:

```
from django.db import models
from rest_framework.exceptions import ValidationError

class MyModel(models.Model):
    name = models.CharField(max_length=100)

    def clean(self):
        if "example.com" in self.name:
            raise ValidationError("Name containing 'example.com'
            is not allowed.")
```

- **Custom Validators**: You can create custom validation functions or classes to validate data in various parts of your DRF application. Custom validators are reusable and can be applied to multiple serializers or views.

  For example:

```
from rest_framework import serializers, validators

def validate_positive(value):
    if value < 0:
        raise serializers.ValidationError("Value must be
        positive.")

class MySerializer(serializers.Serializer):
    age = serializers.IntegerField(validators=[validate_positive])
```

- **Middleware Validation**: You can also perform validation at the middleware level, where you can inspect and validate incoming requests before they reach the view.

  For example:

```
class MyMiddleware:
    def __init__(self, get_response):
        self.get_response = get_response
    def __call__(self, request):
        if not request.user.is_authenticated:
            return Response({"detail": "Authentication
            required."}, status=401)
        return self.get_response(request)
```

Validation in Django REST Framework serializers is handled a little differently from how validation works in Django's **ModelForm** class.

With **ModelForm**, the validation is performed partially on the form and partially on the model instance. With REST Framework, the validation is performed entirely on the **serializer** class. This is advantageous for the following reasons:

- It introduces a proper separation of concerns, making your code behavior more obvious.

- It is easy to switch between using shortcut **ModelSerializer** classes and using explicit **Serializer** classes. Any validation behavior being used for **ModelSerializer** is simple to replicate.
- Printing the **repr** of a serializer instance will show you exactly what validation rules it applies. There's no extra hidden validation behavior being called on the model instance.

When you're using **ModelSerializer**, all of this is handled automatically for you. If you want to drop down to using Serializer classes instead, then you need to define the validation rules explicitly.

Because of this more explicit style, REST Framework includes a few validator classes that are not available in core Django. These classes are detailed below.

UniqueValidator

This is a built-in validator provided by Django REST Framework (DRF) that you can use to enforce uniqueness constraints on a field within a serializer. This validator is commonly used to ensure that a field's value is unique among the existing records in a database table. This validator enforces the **unique=True** constraint on model fields. It takes a single required argument and an optional messages argument:

- **queryset required**: This is the queryset against which uniqueness should be enforced.
- **message**: The error message that should be used when validation fails.
- **lookup**: The lookup used to find an existing instance with the value being validated. Defaults to "exact".

For example:

```
from rest_framework.validators import UniqueValidator
from django.core.validators import MaxValueValidator, MinValueValidator

class WatchListModelSerializer(serializers.ModelSerializer):
    title = serializers.CharField(max_length=50, validators=[UniqueValidato
r(queryset=WatchList.objects.all()),])
```

```
    class Meta:
        model = WatchList
        fields = "__all__"
        extra_kwargs = {
            'imdb_rating': {'validators':[MinValueValidator(1.0),
            MaxValueValidator(10.0)]}
        }
```

UniqueTogetherValidator

This is another built-in validator provided by Django REST Framework (DRF) that enforces uniqueness constraints on multiple fields in a serializer. This validator ensures that the combination of values across several fields is unique within a **queryset** of records. It's useful when you want to prevent duplicate combinations of field values in your database table. This validator enforces **unique_together** constraints on model instances.

It has two required arguments and a single optional messages argument:

- **queryset required:** This is the **queryset** against which uniqueness should be enforced.
- **fields required:** A list or tuple of field names which should make a unique set. These must exist as fields on the serializer class.
- **message:** The error message that should be used when validation fails.

For example:

```
from rest_framework.validators import UniqueTogetherValidator

class StreamPlatformModelSerializer(serializers.ModelSerializer):

    class Meta:
        model = StreamPlatform
        fields = "__all__"
        validators = [
```

```
            UniqueTogetherValidator(
                queryset=StreamPlatform.objects.all(),
                fields=['name', 'website']
            )
        ]
```

Note that the **UniqueTogetherValidator** class always imposes an implicit constraint that all the fields it applies to are always treated as required. Fields with default values are an exception to this, as they always supply a value even when omitted from user input.

Unique Date/Month/Year Validator

Django REST Framework (DRF) provides the following built-in validators to validate uniqueness for a date or month or year:

- UniqueForDateValidator
- UniqueForMonthValidator
- UniqueForYearValidator

These validators can be used to enforce the **unique_for_date**, **unique_for_month**, and **unique_for_year** constraints on model instances. They take the following arguments:

- **queryset required:** This is the queryset against which uniqueness should be enforced.
- **field required:** A field name against which uniqueness in the given date range will be validated. This must exist as a field on the serializer class.
- **date_field required:** A field name which will be used to determine the date range for the uniqueness constraint. This must exist as a field on the serializer class.
- **message:** The error message that should be used when validation fails.

For example:

```
from rest_framework.validators import UniqueForDateValidator

class ReviewModelSerializer(serializers.ModelSerializer):

    class Meta:
        model = Review
        fields = "__all__"
        validators = [
            UniqueForDateValidator(
                queryset=Review.objects.all(),
                field='rating',
                date_field='review_date'
            )
        ]
```

In the above **ReviewModelSerializer**, it allows users to give a unique rating for a day. Similarly, we can enforce **uniqueness** for a **rating** field for a month and year using the validators **UniqueForMonthValidator** and **UniqueForYearValidator**, respectively.

Writing Custom Validators

In Django REST Framework (DRF), you can write custom validators to add custom validation logic to your serializers. Custom validators allow you to enforce specific validation rules on fields in your serializers. You can either write function-based validators or class-based validators.

Preparing for This Chapter

Create a new app with the name **chapter8_validators** with the steps specified in the **Project Setup** section in Chapter 3.

Go to drfproject/settings.py and add the following lines of code:

```
INSTALLED_APPS = [
    ...
    "chapter8_validators",
]
```

Go to chapter8_validators/api/serializers.py and add the following lines of code:

```
from rest_framework import serializers
from django.core.validators import MaxValueValidator, MinValueValidator
from django.utils.translation import gettext_lazy as _
from django.contrib.auth import get_user_model
from chapter3_project_setup.models import WatchList, StreamPlatform, Review
from rest_framework.validators import ( UniqueValidator,
                                        UniqueTogetherValidator,
                                        UniqueForDateValidator,
                                      )
```

Go to chapter8_validators/api/views.py and add the following lines of code:

```
from rest_framework import viewsets
from chapter3_project_setup.models import WatchList, Review, StreamPlatform
from chapter8_validators.api import serializers
```

Go to chapter8_validators/api/urls.py and add the following lines of code:

```
from django.urls import path, include
from rest_framework.routers import DefaultRouter
from chapter8_validators.api import views

router = DefaultRouter()
urlpatterns = [
    # Using ViewSet
    path("", include(router.urls)),

]
```

Go to drfproject/urls.py and add the following lines of code:

```
urlpatterns = [
    ...
    path('api/chapter8_validators/', include('chapter8_validators.api.
    urls')),
]
```

Let's implement the validators concept discussed in this chapter for our project.

Go to chapter8_validators/api/validators.py and add the following lines of code:

```
from django.core.exceptions import ValidationError
from django.utils.translation import gettext_lazy as _
from django.db.models import Q

def validate_watchlist_title(value):
    if len(value)<5 or len(value)>30:
        raise ValidationError("Movie title shall be meaningful")

def validate_watchlist_type(attrs):
    try:
        if attrs["category"]=="MOVIE" and attrs["episodes"]>0:
            raise ValidationError("Movie cannot have episodes")

        if attrs["category"]=="SERIES" and attrs["episodes"]==0:
            raise ValidationError("Series shall have number of episodes")
    except Exception as e:
        raise ValidationError(f"{str(e)} field is missing.")

class RequiredTogetherValidator(object):

    message = _("The fields {field_names} are required together.")
    missing_message = _("This field is required.")
    requires_context = True

    def __init__(self, fields, message=None, missing_message=None):
        self.fields = fields
        self.message = message or self.message
        self.missing_message = missing_message or self.missing_message
```

```
    def enforce_required_fields(self, attrs):
        raise NotImplementedError

    def __call__(self, attrs, serializer):
        self.instance = getattr(serializer, "instance", None)
        self.enforce_required_fields(attrs)

class CreateRequiredTogetherValidator(RequiredTogetherValidator):
    def enforce_required_fields(self, attrs):
        filled = 0

        number_of_fields = len(self.fields)
        fields_filled = []
        if self.instance is not None:
            for field_name in self.fields:
                try:
                    if attrs[field_name]:
                        filled +=1
                        fields_filled.append(field_name)
                except:
                    pass

        missing_items = {
            field_name: self.missing_message
            for field_name in self.fields
            if filled > 0
            and filled > number_of_fields
            and field_name not in fields_filled
        }

        if missing_items:
            raise ValidationError(missing_items, code="required")
```

In the above code, we have defined the following two function-based validators:

- **validate_watchlist_title**: This validator function validates whether the title has a meaningful length of string value.

- **validate_watchlist_type:** This validator function validates multiple attributes to make sure that if the watchlist category is of type SERIES, then it should have a number of episodes value. If the watchlist is of type MOVIE, then it should not have a number of episodes value greater than zero. If there are any deviations, the validator function raises an error.

We have also implemented a class-based validator such as **CreateRequiredTogetherValidator** which inherits another validator **RequiredTogetherValidator** which is a base validator. We have inherited validators here to show how we can combine common functionalities even when creating validators. **CreateRequiredTogetherValidator** enforces the user to provide required fields with values. If the user misses to provide the required values, then the validator raises a validation error.

To write a class-based validator, use the **__call__** method. Class-based validators are useful as they allow you to parameterize and reuse behavior. In some advanced cases, you might want a validator to be passed the serializer field it is being used with as additional context. You can do so by setting a **requires_context** = **True** attribute on the validator. The **__call__** method will then be called with the **serializer_field** or serializer as an additional argument.

Now let's see how we can use these validators in serializers.

Go to chapter8_validators/api/serializers.py and add the following lines of code:

```
...
from chapter8_validators.api import validators
...

class WatchListModelSerializer(serializers.ModelSerializer):
    title = serializers.CharField(max_length=50, validators=[UniqueV
    alidator(queryset=WatchList.objects.all()), validators.validate_
    watchlist_title])

    class Meta:
        model = WatchList
        fields = "__all__"
        extra_kwargs = {
            'imdb_rating': {'validators':[MinValueValidator(1.0), MaxValue
            Validator(10.0)]}
```

```
        }
        validators = [validators.validate_watchlist_type,
                      validators.CreateRequiredTogetherValidator(
                          fields=("title", "category", "episodes"),
                          message= _("This field is required."),
                          missing_message=_("This field is required.")
                      )
                     ]
        ref_name = 'C8WatchListModelSerializer'

class StreamPlatformModelSerializer(serializers.ModelSerializer):
    name = serializers.CharField(max_length=30, validators=[UniqueValidator
(queryset=StreamPlatform.objects.all())])

    class Meta:
        model = StreamPlatform
        fields = "__all__"
        validators = [
            UniqueTogetherValidator(
                queryset=StreamPlatform.objects.all(),
                fields=['name', 'website']
            )
        ]
        ref_name = 'C8StreamPlatformModelSerializer'

class ReviewModelSerializer(serializers.ModelSerializer):
    user = serializers.HiddenField(
            default=serializers.CurrentUserDefault()
        )

    class Meta:
        model = Review
        fields = "__all__"
        validators = [
            UniqueTogetherValidator(
                queryset=Review.objects.all(),
                fields=['review_user', 'watchlist']
```

```
            ),
            UniqueForDateValidator(
                queryset=Review.objects.all(),
                field='rating',
                date_field='review_date'
            )
        ]
        ref_name = 'C8ReviewModelSerializer'
```

In the above code, we have used the **validate_watchlist_title** function for the watchlist model title field to validate the **title**. We just need to specify the function name for a specific field.

If validation is to be performed for multiple fields, then we need to specify validators as **Meta** options. So, we have specified **validate_watchlist_type** and **CreateRequiredTogetherValidator** in the Meta options. In a similar approach, we can use DRF's inbuilt validators such as **UniqueTogetherValidator** or **UniqueForDateValidator** in Meta options for a specific serializer.

Now let's implement the views for endpoints. Go to chapter8_validators/api/views.py and add the following lines of code:

```
class WatchListViewSet(viewsets.ModelViewSet):
    queryset = WatchList.objects.all()
    serializer_class = serializers.WatchListModelSerializer

class StreamPlatformViewSet(viewsets.ModelViewSet):
    queryset = StreamPlatform.objects.all()
    serializer_class = serializers.StreamPlatformModelSerializer

class ReviewViewSet(viewsets.ModelViewSet):
    queryset = Review.objects.all()
    serializer_class = serializers.ReviewModelSerializer
```

Add the corresponding URLs in chapter8_validators/api/urls.py as below:

```
router = DefaultRouter()
# Using ViewSet
router.register(r"watchlist-viewset", views.WatchListViewSet)
```

```
router.register(r"platform-viewset", views.StreamPlatformViewSet)
router.register(r"review-viewset", views.ReviewViewSet)
...
```

Now you can access endpoints using the below URLs:

For Watchlist: `{{domain}}/api/chapter8_validators/watchlist-viewset/`

For StreamPlatform: `{{domain}}/api/chapter8_validators/platform-viewset/`

For Reviews: `{{domain}}/api/chapter8_validators/review-viewset/`

CHAPTER 9

Authentication

Authentication helps identify and verify the identity of users or clients interacting with your API. This is essential for maintaining security and ensuring that only authorized users can access certain resources or perform specific actions. It is a mechanism of associating an incoming request with a set of identifying credentials, such as the user the request came from or the token that it was signed with. The **permission** and **throttling** policies can then use those credentials to determine if the request should be permitted. It also ensures that sensitive data and functionality are protected from unauthorized access. Without proper authentication, anyone could potentially access, modify, or delete data in your API, leading to data breaches or data corruption.

Authentication is often closely tied to authorization. Once a user is authenticated, authorization mechanisms can be used to control what actions that user is allowed to perform. This helps in enforcing fine-grained access control over your API resources. Authentication can be used in conjunction with session management to maintain a user's state across multiple requests. For example, Django's **SessionAuthentication** uses server-side sessions to keep track of authenticated users between requests. In addition to user authentication, APIs may also require authentication of other services or clients (e.g., mobile apps, third-party integrations). Token-based authentication or API keys are common methods to authenticate these clients. Authentication is a fundamental aspect of securing your API, and it is often a requirement for compliance with security standards and regulations such as GDPR, HIPAA, or PCI DSS.

Authentication helps in creating an audit trail by associating actions taken in your API with specific authenticated users or clients. This can be crucial for tracking and accountability purposes. Authentication can be used to implement rate-limiting and abuse prevention mechanisms. By identifying and tracking authenticated clients, you can enforce usage limits and prevent abuse of your API. Authenticated users can access personalized content and user-specific data, making it possible to deliver tailored

G. Patil, *Django REST APIs Demystified*, https://doi.org/10.1007/979-8-8688-1850-9_9

experiences in your application. If your API interacts with third-party services or applications, proper authentication is necessary to establish trust and ensure that only authorized external entities can access your API.

REST Framework provides several authentication schemes out of the box and also allows you to implement custom schemes. Authentication always runs at the very start of the view, before the permission and throttling checks occur, and before any other code is allowed to proceed.

The **request.user** property will typically be set to an instance of the **contrib.auth** package's **User** class.

The **request.auth** property is used for any additional authentication information; for example, it may be used to represent an authentication token that the request was signed with. Note that authentication by itself won't allow or disallow an incoming request; it simply identifies the credentials that the request was made with.

How Authentication Is Determined

Django REST Framework (DRF) determines authentication through a series of steps and classes. It follows a process to authenticate incoming requests based on the available authentication classes and settings. Here's how authentication is determined in DRF:

1. **Authentication Classes**

   DRF allows you to configure one or more authentication classes in your project's settings. These authentication classes are defined in the DEFAULT_AUTHENTICATION_CLASSES setting. Authentication classes are Python classes that implement the authentication logic.

```
REST_FRAMEWORK = {
    'DEFAULT_AUTHENTICATION_CLASSES': [
        'rest_framework.authentication.TokenAuthentication',
        'rest_framework.authentication.SessionAuthentication',
    ],
}
```

In the above example, two authentication classes are configured: **TokenAuthentication** and **SessionAuthentication**. These classes will be used to determine the authentication for incoming requests.

2. **Authentication Attempt**

   When a request is received by a view or viewset in your DRF API, DRF makes an authentication attempt by iterating through the authentication classes in the order they are defined in **DEFAULT_AUTHENTICATION_CLASSES**.

3. **Authentication Classes Order**

   DRF processes authentication classes in the order they are listed in **DEFAULT_AUTHENTICATION_CLASSES**. It tries each authentication class one by one until one of them successfully authenticates the request.

4. **Authenticate Method**

   Each authentication class defines an authenticate method that is called during the authentication attempt. The authenticate method takes the request object as its argument and returns a two-tuple: **(user, auth)**. If authentication fails, it returns **(None, None)**.

5. **Authentication Success**

   If one of the authentication classes successfully authenticates the request (i.e., it will set **request.user** and **request.auth** using the return value of the first class that successfully authenticates), the authentication process stops, and thc user is considered authenticated.

6. **Authentication Failure**

   If none of the authentication classes can authenticate the request, the request is considered unauthenticated, and **request.user** will be set to an instance of **django.contrib.auth.models.AnonymousUser**, and **request.auth** will be set to None. The value of **request.user** and **request.auth** for unauthenticated requests can be modified using the **UNAUTHENTICATED_USER** and **UNAUTHENTICATED_TOKEN** settings.

When authentication failed, the view or viewset will typically raise an **AuthenticationFailed** exception, and the user remains anonymous (unless you have a permissive permission class that allows unauthenticated access).

7. **User Object**

   Once authentication is successful, the authenticated user object is set on the **request.user** attribute. This user object represents the authenticated user and can be used by your views to make authorization decisions.

8. **Permission Classes**

   After authentication, DRF applies permission classes to determine whether the authenticated user has the necessary permissions to perform the requested action. If permission checks fail, a **PermissionDenied** exception is raised.

DRF determines authentication by iterating through the configured authentication classes, attempting to authenticate the request using each class in order. Once authentication is successful, the user object is set on the request, allowing views and viewsets to make authorization decisions based on permissions. If none of the authentication classes succeed, the request remains unauthenticated.

Setting the Authentication Scheme

To set the authentication scheme in Django REST Framework (DRF), you need to configure the **DEFAULT_AUTHENTICATION_CLASSES** setting in your Django project's settings file. This setting allows you to specify one or more authentication classes that DRF should use to authenticate incoming requests.

Here's how to set the authentication scheme in DRF:

```
REST_FRAMEWORK = {
    'DEFAULT_AUTHENTICATION_CLASSES': [
        'rest_framework.authentication.TokenAuthentication',
```

```
        'rest_framework.authentication.SessionAuthentication',
    ],
}
```

In this example, the **TokenAuthentication** and **SessionAuthentication** classes are used for authentication. Requests will be authenticated using these classes in the order they are listed.

You can also set the authentication scheme on a **per-view** or **per-viewset** basis, using the **APIView** class-based views. We will discuss this in later sections of this chapter.

Unauthorized and Forbidden Responses

When an unauthenticated request is denied permission, there are two different error codes that may be appropriate:

- HTTP 401 Unauthorized
- HTTP 403 Permission Denied

HTTP 401 responses must always include a WWW-Authenticate header that instructs the client how to authenticate. HTTP 403 responses do not include the WWW-Authenticate header.

The kind of response that will be used depends on the authentication scheme. Although multiple authentication schemes may be in use, only one scheme may be used to determine the type of response. **The first authentication class set on the view is used when determining the type of response**.

Note that when a request may successfully authenticate, but still be denied permission to perform the request, in which case a 403 Permission Denied response will always be used, regardless of the authentication scheme.

In Django REST Framework (DRF), you can also customize the responses for unauthorized (authentication failure) and forbidden (authorization failure) requests by defining custom views, serializers, or exception handlers. Here's how you can handle these responses:

1. **Unauthorized (Authentication Failure)**

   When a request fails to authenticate (e.g., due to missing or invalid credentials), you can customize the response message and status code. DRF provides the **AuthenticationFailed** exception that you can raise when authentication fails. To customize the response, you can override the **exception_handler** in your DRF settings. In your project's settings file (settings.py), define a custom exception handler:

```
REST_FRAMEWORK = {
    'EXCEPTION_HANDLER': 'myapp.exceptions.custom_exception_
    handler',
}
```

   Then, in your app, create a **custom_exception_handler** function:

```
from rest_framework.views import exception_handler
from rest_framework.exceptions import AuthenticationFailed
from rest_framework.response import Response

def custom_exception_handler(exc, context):
    if isinstance(exc, AuthenticationFailed):
        return Response({'detail': 'Authentication failed. Please
        provide valid credentials.'}, status=401)

    return exception_handler(exc, context)
```

   In this example, when an **AuthenticationFailed** exception is raised, it returns a custom response with a status code of 401 (Unauthorized). You can customize the message and status code to your needs.

2. **Forbidden (Authorization Failure)**

   When a request is authenticated but doesn't have the necessary permissions to access a resource, you can customize the response message and status code. You can do this by using DRF's built-in **PermissionDenied** exception and overriding the **permission_denied** method in your views.

In your views, override the **permission_denied** method:

```
from rest_framework.exceptions import PermissionDenied
from rest_framework.response import Response

class MyView(APIView):
    def get(self, request):
        if not user_has_permission(request.user):
            raise PermissionDenied('You do not have permission to
            access this resource.')

        # Your view logic here
        return Response({'message': 'Resource accessed
        successfully.'})
```

In this example, when **user_has_permission** returns False, it raises a **PermissionDenied** exception with a custom message. You can customize the message as needed.

By handling authentication and authorization exceptions and providing custom responses, you can provide clear and informative feedback to clients when unauthorized or forbidden requests are made to your DRF API. This helps improve the security and usability of your API.

Preparing for This Chapter

In this chapter, we are going to create two applications. The first application named **user_app** is to implement user-related functionalities like user registration, login, generating a token, and logout. The second one named **chapter9_authentication** is to use authentication for models defined for this project.

Create a new app with the name **user_app** with the steps specified in the **Project Setup** section in Chapter 3.

Go to drfproject/settings.py and add the following lines of code:

```
INSTALLED_APPS = [
    ...
    " user_app",
]
```

Go to user_app/api/serializers.py and add the following lines of code:

```
from django.contrib.auth import get_user_model
from rest_framework import serializers

User = get_user_model()
```

Go to user_app/api/views.py and add the following lines of code:

```
from rest_framework.response import Response
from rest_framework.authtoken.models import Token
from rest_framework import status
from rest_framework.views import APIView
from rest_framework.authtoken.views import ObtainAuthToken
from rest_framework.permissions import IsAuthenticated
```

Go to user_app/api/urls.py and add the following lines of code:

```
from django.urls import path
from rest_framework.authtoken.views import obtain_auth_token
from user_app.api import views

urlpatterns = [

]
```

Let's create another application with the name **chapter9_authentication** with the steps specified in the **Project Setup** section in Chapter 3.

Go to drfproject/settings.py and add the following lines of code:

```
INSTALLED_APPS = [
    ...
    "chapter9_authentication",
]
```

Go to chapter9_authentication/api/serializers.py and add the following lines of code:

```
from rest_framework import serializers
from chapter3_project_setup.models import WatchList, StreamPlatform, Review

class WatchListModelSerializer(serializers.ModelSerializer):
```

```
    class Meta:
        model = WatchList
        fields = "__all__"
        ref_name = 'C9WatchListModelSerializer'

class StreamPlatformModelSerializer(serializers.ModelSerializer):
    class Meta:
        model = StreamPlatform
        fields = "__all__"
        ref_name = 'C9StreamPlatformModelSerializer'

class ReviewModelSerializer(serializers.ModelSerializer):
    user = serializers.StringRelatedField()
    class Meta:
        model = Review
        fields = "__all__"
        ref_name = 'C9ReviewModelSerializer'
```

Go to chapter9_authentication/api/views.py and add the following lines of code:

```
from rest_framework import viewsets
from rest_framework.exceptions import ValidationError
from rest_framework.authentication import BasicAuthentication,
TokenAuthentication
from rest_framework.permissions import IsAuthenticated
from rest_framework.decorators import api_view, permission_classes,
authentication_classes
from rest_framework.response import Response
from chapter3_project_setup.models import WatchList, Review, StreamPlatform
from chapter9_authentication.api import serializers
```

Go to chapter9_authentication/api/urls.py and add the following lines of code:

```
from django.urls import path, include
from rest_framework.routers import DefaultRouter

from chapter9_authentication.api import views
router = DefaultRouter()
```

```
urlpatterns = [
    # Using ViewSet
    path("", include(router.urls)),
]
```

Go to drfproject/urls.py and add the following lines of code:

```
urlpatterns = [
    ...
    path('api/ chapter9_authentication/', include(chapter9_authentication.
    api.urls')),
]
```

API Reference

DRF comes with several built-in authentication classes that you can use out of the box. You can configure these authentication classes in your project's settings. Some commonly used authentication classes include

- **BasicAuthentication**: This authentication class uses HTTP Basic Authentication.
- **TokenAuthentication**: Token-based authentication, where clients send an API token with each request.
- **SessionAuthentication**: It uses Django's built-in session framework for authentication.
- **RemoteUserAuthentication:** This class authenticates users based on the **REMOTE_USER** environment variable provided by your web server, typically when using an external authentication system like Shibboleth or a reverse proxy.

You can choose the authentication classes that fit your project's requirements and add them to the **DEFAULT_AUTHENTICATION_CLASSES** setting in your Django settings. Let's discuss each of the authentication classes.

BasicAuthentication

This is a simple and widely supported authentication method that can be used in Django REST Framework (DRF) when you need a straightforward and easy-to-implement way to secure your API endpoints. It's called "basic" because it uses a basic, Base64-encoded **username** and **password** for authentication. While it is simple, it is not recommended for transmitting sensitive credentials over the internet without HTTPS because the credentials can be easily decoded if intercepted. Basic authentication is typically used when you need a quick and simple form of authentication and are already operating over a secure connection (HTTPS).

This authentication scheme uses **HTTP Basic Authentication**, signed against a user's **username** and **password**. Basic authentication is generally only appropriate for testing.

If successfully authenticated, **BasicAuthentication** provides the following credentials:

- **request.user** will be a Django User instance.
- **request.auth** will be None.

Unauthenticated responses that are denied permission will result in an **HTTP 401 Unauthorized** response with an appropriate WWW-Authenticate header. For example: WWW-Authenticate: Basic realm="api".

Here's how to implement **BasicAuthentication** in DRF:

1. Configure DEFAULT_AUTHENTICATION_CLASSES

   Go to drfproject/settings.py and add the following lines of code:

   ```
   REST_FRAMEWORK = {
       'DEFAULT_AUTHENTICATION_CLASSES': [
           'rest_framework.authentication.BasicAuthentication',
       ],
   }
   ```

   The above setting makes sure that all the API endpoints shall have at least basic authentication to be accessed by the user.

2. Secure Your API with HTTPS

   It's essential to secure your API with HTTPS to encrypt the data transferred between the client and server. Basic authentication sends the credentials in **Base64 encoding**, which is easily decodable if the communication is not encrypted. Using HTTPS ensures that the credentials are transmitted securely.

3. Create a View

   Go to chapter9_authentication/api/views.py and add the following lines of code:

```
class WatchListViewSet(viewsets.ModelViewSet):
    permission_classes = [IsAuthenticated]  # Ensure that the user
is authenticated
    queryset = WatchList.objects.all()
    serializer_class = serializers.WatchListModelSerializer
```

   In the above lines of code, we have defined **WatchListViewSet** for the Watchlist model. Here, we have not assigned any authentication classes. But since we specified default authentication classes as **BasicAuthentication**, this endpoint at least requires basic authentication from the user.

   In the above code, we have also mentioned permission_classes which is a must to specify the endpoints along with authentication. **authentication_classes** and **permission_classes** are two separate but closely related concepts used to control access to your API endpoints. They work together to determine whether a request is authenticated and whether the authenticated user has the necessary permissions to perform the requested action. Authentication classes are responsible for identifying and authenticating users or clients making requests to your API. They extract user credentials from the request, verify them, and determine the user's identity. In contrast, Permission classes determine whether the authenticated user (i.e., request.user) has the necessary permissions to access a particular view or perform a specific action within that view. The combination of these two mechanisms allows you to control access to your API endpoints effectively. By specifying appropriate authentication and permission classes for your views, you can implement fine-grained access control and ensure that only authorized users can perform specific actions.

4. Configure URLs

   Go to chapter9_authentication/api/urls.py and add the following lines of code:

```
from django.urls import path, include
from rest_framework.routers import DefaultRouter

from chapter9_authentication.api import views

router = DefaultRouter()
# Using ViewSet
router.register(r"watchlist-viewset", views.WatchListViewSet)

urlpatterns = [
    # Using ViewSet
    path("", include(router.urls)),
]
```

   Now you can access the endpoint at the URL: `{{domain}}/api/chapter9_authentication/watchlist-viewset/`

   But you need to provide the username and password to access the endpoint.

Note If you use **BasicAuthentication** in production, you must ensure that your API is only available over https. You should also ensure that your API clients will always re-request the username and password at login and will never store those details in persistent storage.

TokenAuthentication

This is a popular authentication method provided by Django REST Framework (DRF) for securing web APIs. It allows clients to authenticate themselves by presenting a unique token in their requests. This token-based authentication is commonly used in modern web and mobile applications to grant access to specific resources on an API.

TokenAuthentication in Django REST Framework (DRF) serves as a popular and effective method of authentication for a variety of reasons:

- **Stateless Authentication**: Token authentication is stateless, meaning the server doesn't need to maintain session data for each authenticated user. This is particularly useful in building scalable and distributed systems because it allows each API request to be self-contained.
- **Cross-Platform Compatibility**: Tokens can be easily used across different platforms, including web applications, mobile apps, and single-page applications. They are simple to transmit and store on the client side.
- **Security**: Tokens can be designed with strong security measures. They can include user-specific information and be cryptographically signed to prevent tampering. Token expiration can also be enforced, enhancing security by automatically invalidating tokens after a certain period.
- **Scalability**: Because token authentication doesn't rely on server-side sessions, it's well suited for APIs that need to handle high traffic and scale horizontally. It doesn't burden the server with session management.
- **Third-Party Integration**: Tokens are commonly used for third-party integrations. External applications can use tokens to access your API without needing to handle cookies or sessions.
- **Clear Separation of Authentication and Authorization**: Token authentication separates authentication (verifying the user's identity) from authorization (determining what actions the user is allowed to perform). This allows you to use different permission classes to control access to different parts of your API.

- **Flexibility**: DRF allows you to customize token authentication further if needed. For example, you can create custom token serializers or authentication classes to fit your project's requirements.
- **User Control**: Tokens can be revoked or regenerated, providing an additional layer of control over user access. If a token is compromised or a user logs out, you can revoke the token to prevent further access.
- **Single Sign-On (SSO)**: Token authentication can be used as part of a Single Sign-On (SSO) system where users can authenticate once and access multiple services or applications.

When a user logs in or registers for an account, a unique token is generated for that user. This token is associated with the user account in the back-end database. It typically includes user-specific information, such as the user's ID or username, and is cryptographically signed to prevent tampering. To access protected API endpoints, clients must include their token in the Authorization header of their HTTP requests.

The Authorization header typically takes the form:

"**Authorization: Token <token_key>**", where <token_key> is the user's unique token.

If you want to use a different keyword in the header, such as **Bearer**, simply subclass **TokenAuthentication** and set the keyword class variable.

If successfully authenticated, **TokenAuthentication** provides the following credentials:

- **request.user** will be a Django User instance.
- **request.auth** will be a **rest_framework.authtoken.models.Token** instance.

Unauthenticated responses that are denied permission will result in an HTTP 401 Unauthorized response with an appropriate WWW-Authenticate header. For example: **WWW-Authenticate: Token**.

When a request with a token is received by the API, the **TokenAuthentication** class extracts the token from the Authorization header. It then looks up the associated user in the database based on the token. If the token is valid and matches a user, the user is considered authenticated, and the request is allowed to proceed. Tokens can have expiration dates, which means they are valid for a certain period. After the token expires, clients must obtain a new one. Tokens can also be revoked by the user or administrator if needed. Revoked tokens will no longer grant access to the API.

In general, we can use the following steps to implement token authentication in DRF:

1. **Configure TokenAuthentication in Your Project's Settings**

   ```
   REST_FRAMEWORK = {
       'DEFAULT_AUTHENTICATION_CLASSES': [
           'rest_framework.authentication.TokenAuthentication',
       ],
   }
   ```

2. **Create Tokens for Users**

   When users register or log in, generate and provide them with a unique token.

3. **Secure Your API with HTTPS**

   Always use HTTPS to ensure that token-based authentication is secure.

4. **Require Authentication for Protected Views**

   Use the **IsAuthenticated** permission class or other custom permission classes to enforce authentication for specific **views** or **viewsets**.

5. **Include the Token in Your Requests**

   Clients should include their token in the Authorization header when making requests to protected endpoints.

Generating Tokens

DRF provides various ways to generate a token. Even DRF provides an inbuilt view to provide a token for the user.

By Using Signals

Let's understand how to implement token generation for our project.

Let's go to drfproject/settings.py and add the following lines of code to INSTALLED_APPS as below:

```
INSTALLED_APPS = [
```

```
    ...
    'rest_framework.authtoken',
    ...
]
```

Update REST_FRAMEWORK to include TokenAuthentication as below:

```
REST_FRAMEWORK = {
    ...
    'DEFAULT_AUTHENTICATION_CLASSES': [
        'rest_framework.authentication.TokenAuthentication',
  'rest_framework.authentication.BasicAuthentication',

    ],
}
```

Go to user_app/models.py and add the following lines of code:

```
from django.conf import settings
from django.db.models.signals import post_save
from django.dispatch import receiver
from rest_framework.authtoken.models import Token

@receiver(post_save, sender=settings.AUTH_USER_MODEL)
def create_auth_token(sender, instance=None, created=False, **kwargs):
    if created:
        Token.objects.create(user=instance)
```

In the above lines of code, we are creating a signal which triggers the **create_auth_token** function when any user is created or updated. When a user is created, the above function generates a token for that user in the database. Note that you'll want to ensure you place this code snippet in an installed **models.py** module or some other location that will be imported by Django on startup.

Let's implement user registration functionality to add a new user. Let's go to user_app/api/serializers.py and add the following lines of code:

```
class RegistrationSerializer(serializers.ModelSerializer):
    password2 = serializers.CharField(style={'input_type': 'password'},
    write_only=True)
```

```
    class Meta:
        model = User
        fields = ['username', 'email', 'password', 'password2']
        extra_kwargs = {
            'password' : {'write_only': True}
        }

    def save(self):
        password = self.validated_data['password']
        password2 = self.validated_data['password2']

        if password != password2:
            raise serializers.ValidationError({'error': 'P1 and P2 should
            be same!'})

        if User.objects.filter(email=self.validated_data['email']).
        exists():
            raise serializers.ValidationError({'error': 'Email already
            exists!'})

        account = User(email=self.validated_data['email'], username=self.
        validated_data['username'])
        account.set_password(password)
        account.save()

        return account
```

In the above lines of code, we are defining the **RegistrationSerializer** class. We have added one more attribute, password2, to verify passwords entered are correct. If the **password** and **password2** fields mismatch, then it raises a validation error. It also verifies the uniqueness of the user email to avoid duplication of the user email IDs. When all the fields are validated, the user gets saved at the line **account.save()**. This triggers the **post_save** signal, which calls **create_auth_token**, which in turn generates a token for the user.

Let's create a view for this user registration functionality. Let's go to user_app/api/views.py and add the following lines of code:

```
from rest_framework.response import Response
from rest_framework.authtoken.models import Token
```

```
from rest_framework import status
from rest_framework.views import APIView
from rest_framework.authtoken.views import ObtainAuthToken
from rest_framework.permissions import IsAuthenticated

from user_app.api.serializers import RegistrationSerializer

class RegistrationView(APIView):
    def post(self, request):
        serializer = RegistrationSerializer(data=request.data)

        data = {}
        if serializer.is_valid():
            account = serializer.save()

            data['response'] = "Registration Successful!"
            data['username'] = account.username
            data['email'] = account.email

            token = Token.objects.get(user=account).key
            data['token'] = token
        else:
            data = serializer.errors

        return Response(data, status=status.HTTP_201_CREATED)
```

In the above lines of code, we have defined **RegistrationView** which receives a post request with username, password, password2, and email as data and returns the created user information along with the generated token.

Let's go to user_app/api/urls.py and add the following lines of code:

```
from django.urls import path
from user_app.api import views
urlpatterns = [
    path('register/', views.RegistrationView.as_view(), name='register'),
]
```

Now you can create a new user using the below request:

Request:

POST `{{domain}}/api/user/register/`

Body:

```
{
    "username":"test_user1",
    "password": "test_password1",
    "password2": "test_password1",
    "email": "test_user1@email.com"
}
```

Response:

The token gets created for the user and returns a response as below:

```
{
    "response": "Registration Successful!",
    "username": "test_user1",
    "email": "test_user1@email.com",
    "token": "d148be531f24eb1eb1d55a9c38e010d6765304ed"
}
```

If you've already created some users, you can generate tokens for all existing users like this:

```
from django.contrib.auth.models import User
from rest_framework.authtoken.models import Token

for user in User.objects.all():
    Token.objects.get_or_create(user=user)
```

By Exposing an API Endpoint

When using **TokenAuthentication**, you may want to provide a mechanism for clients to obtain a token given the **username** and **password**. REST Framework provides a built-in view to provide this behavior. To use it, add the **obtain_auth_token** view to your **URLconf**.

Let's go to user_app/api/urls.py and add the following lines of code:

```
urlpatterns = [
    ...
    path('login/', obtain_auth_token, name='login'),
]
```

Note that the URL part of the pattern can be whatever you want to use. The **obtain_auth_token** view will return a JSON response when valid **username** and **password** fields are POSTed to the view using form data or JSON.

Now you can post user credentials with the URL `{{domain}}/api/user/login/` with the below data:

```
{
    "username": "test_user1",
    "password": "test_password1"
}
```

You will get a response in the below format:

```
{
    "token": "d148be531f24eb1eb1d55a9c38e010d6765304ed"
}
```

Note that the default **obtain_auth_token** view explicitly uses JSON requests and responses, rather than using the default renderer and parser classes in your settings.

By default, there are no permissions or throttling applied to the **obtain_auth_token** view. If you do wish to apply to throttle, you'll need to override the view class and include it using the **throttle_classes** attribute.

If you need a customized version of the **obtain_auth_token** view, you can do so by subclassing the **ObtainAuthToken** view class and using that in your URL conf instead.

For example, you may return additional user information beyond the token value.

Let's go to user_app/api/views.py and add the following lines of code:

```
from rest_framework.response import Response
from rest_framework.authtoken.models import Token
from rest_framework.authtoken.views import ObtainAuthToken

from user_app.api.serializers import RegistrationSerializer
from user_app.api.authentication import CustomBasicAuthentication

class CustomAuthTokenView(ObtainAuthToken):

    def post(self, request, *args, **kwargs):
        serializer = self.serializer_class(data=request.data,
                                           context={'request': request})
```

```
        serializer.is_valid(raise_exception=True)
        user = serializer.validated_data['user']
        token, created = Token.objects.get_or_create(user=user)
        return Response({
            'token': token.key,
            'user_id': user.pk,
            'email': user.email
        })
```

In the above lines of code, we have created a custom authentication view which extends the DRF's **ObtainAuthToken** view to modify the response format. By extending the built-in **ObtainAuthToken** view, you can override specific methods and customize the behavior.

Now go to user_app/api/urls.py and add the following lines of code:

```
from django.urls import path
from user_app.api import authentication

urlpatterns = [
    ...
    path('user-login/', views.CustomAuthTokenView.as_view(),
    name='user-login'),
]
```

Now you can post user credentials with the URL `{{domain}}/api/user/user-login/` with the below data:

```
{
    "username": "test_user1",
    "password": "test_password1"
}
```

You will get a response in the below format:

```
{
    "token": "d148be531f24eb1eb1d55a9c38e010d6765304ed",
    "user_id": 9,
    "email": "test_user1@email.com"
}
```

With Django Admin

It is also possible to create tokens manually through the admin interface. In case you are using a large user base, we recommend that you monkey patch the **TokenAdmin** class and customize it to your needs, more specifically by declaring the user field as **raw_field**.

Go to user_app/admin.py and add the following lines of code:

```
from django.contrib import admin
from rest_framework.authtoken.admin import TokenAdmin

TokenAdmin.raw_id_fields = ['user']
```

The above lines of code are using the **TokenAdmin** class from the rest_framework.authtoken.admin module to customize the way the Token model is displayed in the Django admin panel. The line **TokenAdmin.raw_id_fields = ['user']** configures the user field to be displayed as a raw ID field in the admin panel for the Token model.

By setting **raw_id_fields** to **['user']**, you make it more efficient to manage tokens in the admin panel when associating tokens with users. Instead of displaying a drop-down list with user choices, the user field will be displayed as a simple text input where you can enter the user's ID directly. This can be particularly helpful when you have a large number of users in your database.

Using the Django manage.py Command

Since version 3.6.4, it's possible to generate a user token using the following command:

```
python manage.py drf_create_token <username>
```

For example:

```
python manage.py drf_create_token test_user1
```

This command will return the API token for the given user, creating it if it doesn't exist:

```
Generated token 1ab5ed84e107537884ddb44089f24c1d40d11912 for user
test_user1
```

In case you want to regenerate the token (e.g., if it has been compromised or leaked), you can pass an additional parameter:

```
python manage.py drf_create_token -r <username>
```

All the above scenarios mentioned creating a token for new and existing users. User can use the token for authentication purposes. Once the user has completed accessing the required resources, the user can delete the token in an automated way.

Let's implement a logout functionality where user token can be deleted automatically when logged out.

Let's go to user_app/api/views.py and add the following lines of code:

```
class LogoutView(APIView):
    def post(self, request):
        request.user.auth_token.delete()
        return Response(status=status.HTTP_200_OK)
```

Go to user_app/api/urls.py and add the following lines of code:

```
urlpatterns = [
    ...
    path('logout/', views.LogoutView.as_view(), name='logout'),
    ...
]
```

Now you can send a post request with the URL `{{domain}}/api/user/logout/`.

Let's apply these authentication concepts to views for models in our project. Currently, the default authentication is set to **BasicAuthentication** as below:

```
REST_FRAMEWORK = {
    'DEFAULT_AUTHENTICATION_CLASSES': (
        'rest_framework.authentication.BasicAuthentication',
    ),
    'DEFAULT_PERMISSION_CLASSES': (
        # 'rest_framework.permissions.IsAuthenticated',
        # 'user_app.api.authentication.BearerAuthentication',
    ),
}
```

This means that if specific authentication is not mentioned in the views by default, it asks for basic authentication by providing the username and password.

Let's go to chapter9_authentication/api/views.py and add the following lines of code:

```
class WatchListViewSet(viewsets.ModelViewSet):
    permission_classes = [IsAuthenticated]  # Ensure that the user is
    authenticated
    queryset = WatchList.objects.all()
    serializer_class = serializers.WatchListModelSerializer
```

Add the corresponding URL in chapter9_authentication/api/urls.py as below:

```
router = DefaultRouter()
# Using ViewSet
router.register(r"watchlist-viewset", views.WatchListViewSet)
```

In the above view, there is no authentication class assigned. Hence, it always accepts the **BasicAuthentication** mechanism for accessing the endpoint.

The above endpoint can be accessed using the endpoint `{{domain}}/api/chapter9_authentication/watchlist-viewset/`, providing the username and password as authorization in the request.

We can assign authentication at the view level. Go to chapter9_authentication/api/views.py and add the following lines of code:

```
class ReviewViewSet(viewsets.ModelViewSet):
    queryset = Review.objects.all()
    serializer_class = serializers.ReviewModelSerializer
    authentication_classes = [TokenAuthentication,]
    permission_classes = [IsAuthenticated,]  # Ensure that the user is
    authenticated

    def perform_create(self, serializer):
        pk = self.kwargs.get('pk')
        watchlist = WatchList.objects.get(pk=pk)

        review_user = self.request.user
        review_queryset = Review.objects.filter(watchlist=watchlist,
        review_user=review_user)

        if review_queryset.exists():
```

```
            raise ValidationError("You have already reviewed this movie!")

        if watchlist.number_rating == 0:
            watchlist.imdb_rating = serializer.validated_data['rating']
        else:
            watchlist.imdb_rating = (watchlist.imdb_rating + serializer.
            validated_data['rating'])/2

        watchlist.number_rating = watchlist.number_rating + 1
        watchlist.save()

        serializer.save(watchlist=watchlist, review_user=review_user)
```

Add the corresponding URL in chapter9_authentication/api/urls.py as below:

```
router = DefaultRouter()
...
router.register(r"review-viewset", views.ReviewViewSet)
```

In the above view, the **TokenAuthentication** class is assigned to this specific view to access the endpoint. The function **perform_create** is used to handle the logic for creating a new review while also performing custom validation and updating related fields in the associated WatchList model. It ensures that a user cannot submit multiple reviews for the same WatchList and also updates the WatchList's IMDb rating and review count whenever a new review is created.

The above endpoint can be accessed using the endpoint `{{domain}}/api/chapter9_authentication/review-viewset/`, providing the token as authorization in the request.

DRF provides decorators to assign view-level permission and an authentication mechanism for function-based views. Let's apply the **TokenAuthentication** class to function-based views.

Go to chapter9_authentication/api/views.py and add the following lines of code:

```
@api_view(['GET', 'POST'])
@permission_classes([IsAuthenticated])  # Require authentication
@authentication_classes([TokenAuthentication])  # Token-based
authentication
def streamplatform_list(request):
    # Handle GET requests
    if request.method == 'GET':
```

```
        platforms = StreamPlatform.objects.all()
        serializer = serializers.StreamPlatformModelSerializer(platforms,
         many=True, context={'request': request})
        return Response(serializer.data, status=status.HTTP_200_OK)

    # Handle POST requests
    elif request.method == 'POST':
        serializer = serializers.StreamPlatformModelSerializer(data=reque
        st.data, context={'request': request})
        if serializer.is_valid():
            serializer.save()
            return Response(serializer.data, status=status.HTTP_201_
            CREATED)
        return Response(serializer.errors, status=status.HTTP_400_BAD_
        REQUEST)

@api_view(['GET', 'PUT', 'DELETE'])
@permission_classes([IsAuthenticated])  # Require authentication
@authentication_classes([TokenAuthentication])  # Token-based
authentication
def streamplatform_detail(request, pk):
    try:
        platform = StreamPlatform.objects.get(pk=pk)
    except StreamPlatform.DoesNotExist:
        return Response({"error": "StreamPlatform not found."},
        status=status.HTTP_404_NOT_FOUND)

    # Handle GET request
    if request.method == 'GET':
        serializer = serializers.StreamPlatformModelSerializer(platform,
        context={'request': request})
        return Response(serializer.data)

    # Handle PUT request
    elif request.method == 'PUT':
        serializer = serializers.StreamPlatformModelSerializer(platform,
        data=request.data, context={'request': request})
```

```
        if serializer.is_valid():
            serializer.save()
            return Response(serializer.data)
        return Response(serializer.errors, status=status.HTTP_400_BAD_
        REQUEST)

    # Handle DELETE request
    elif request.method == 'DELETE':
        platform.delete()
        return Response({"message": "StreamPlatform deleted
        successfully."}, status=status.HTTP_204_NO_CONTENT)
```

Add the corresponding URL in chapter9_authentication/api/urls.py as below:

```
urlpatterns = [
    path('streamplatforms/', views.streamplatform_list,
    name="streamplatform-list"),
    path('streamplatforms/<int:pk>/', views.streamplatform_detail,
    name="streamplatform-detail"),
    ...
]
```

The above endpoint can be accessed using the below endpoints by providing token in the request header.

List: **GET** `{{domain}}/api/chapter9_authentication/streamplatforms/`

Create: **POST** `{{domain}}/api/chapter9_authentication/streamplatforms/`

Get Single Object: **GET** `{{domain}}/api/chapter9_authentication/streamplatforms/<pk>`

Update: **PUT** `{{domain}}/api/chapter9_authentication/streamplatforms/<pk>`

Delete: **DELETE** `{{domain}}/api/chapter9_authentication/streamplatforms/<pk>`

where `<pk>` is the primary key of the object.

SessionAuthentication

It is an authentication class provided by Django REST Framework (DRF) for authenticating users based on their Django session. It is designed to work seamlessly with Django's built-in session management, making it suitable for web applications that use traditional server-side sessions. It uses Django's default session back end for authentication. Session authentication is appropriate for AJAX clients that are running in the same session context as your website.

If successfully authenticated, SessionAuthentication provides the following credentials.

- **request.user** will be a Django **User** instance.
- **request.auth** will be **None**.

Unauthenticated responses that are denied permission will result in an **HTTP 403 Forbidden** response.

If you're using an AJAX-style API with SessionAuthentication, you'll need to make sure you include a valid CSRF token for any "unsafe" HTTP method calls, such as **PUT, PATCH, POST,** or **DELETE** requests. Note that always use Django's standard login view when creating login pages. This will ensure your login views are properly protected.

CSRF validation in REST Framework works slightly differently from standard Django due to the need to support both session and non-session-based authentication to the same views. This means that only authenticated requests require CSRF tokens and anonymous requests may be sent without CSRF tokens. This behavior is not suitable for login views, which should always have CSRF validation applied.

The SessionAuthentication works as below:

1. **Session-Based Authentication**: When a user logs in to your web application, Django creates a session for that user. This session is associated with a unique session ID stored in a session cookie. The session data, which typically includes the user's authentication information, is stored on the server.

2. **Transmitting the Session ID**: When the user interacts with your API, the session ID is typically transmitted to the server as a cookie in the request headers. This is done automatically by the browser for requests originating from the same origin (i.e., same domain and protocol).

3. **Session Authentication in DRF**: DRF's SessionAuthentication class extracts the session ID from the request's cookies and uses it to authenticate the user.

4. **DRF Permissions**: Once a user is authenticated using SessionAuthentication, DRF's permission classes are used to determine whether the user has the necessary permissions to access the requested resource or perform the desired action.

SessionAuthentication is well suited for web applications that use server-side sessions to manage user authentication and authorization. It allows DRF to integrate seamlessly with Django's session management, ensuring that authenticated users have access to the API endpoints.

However, it's important to note that SessionAuthentication is typically used for web applications that serve HTML views alongside their APIs and require user interaction through web forms. For APIs that are intended for client-side applications (e.g., single-page applications or mobile apps) and do not rely on server-side sessions, token-based authentication methods like TokenAuthentication or JSON Web Tokens (JWT) are often more appropriate.

RemoteUserAuthentication

It is an authentication class in Django REST Framework (DRF) that allows you to authenticate users based on their "REMOTE_USER" environment variable, typically in scenarios where your Django application is integrated with a web server that handles user authentication and passes the authenticated user's information to your application. It allows you to delegate authentication to your web server, which sets the REMOTE_USER environment variable.

To use it, you must have **django.contrib.auth.backends.RemoteUserBackend** (or a subclass) in your **AUTHENTICATION_BACKENDS** setting. By default, RemoteUserBackend creates User objects for usernames that don't already exist.

If successfully authenticated, RemoteUserAuthentication provides the following credentials:

- **request.user** will be a Django **User** instance.
- **request.auth** will be **None**.

The RemoteUserAuthentication works as follows:

1. **Integration with Web Server**: In this setup, a web server, such as Apache or Nginx, is responsible for authenticating users. The web server authenticates users based on various mechanisms (e.g., HTTP Basic Authentication, LDAP, SSO, etc.), and upon successful authentication, it sets the "REMOTE_USER" environment variable in the request.

2. **Django Configuration**: Your Django application is configured to use the RemoteUserMiddleware middleware, which is included with Django. This middleware captures the "REMOTE_USER" environment variable and associates it with the request.

3. **RemoteUserAuthentication**: When a request is received by your DRF view, the RemoteUserAuthentication class extracts the "REMOTE_USER" value from the request and attempts to authenticate the user.

4. **DRF Permissions**: After authentication, DRF's permission classes are used to determine whether the authenticated user has the necessary permissions to access the requested resource or perform the desired action.

This authentication method is particularly useful in environments where a web server handles user authentication and passes the user identity to the Django application. It allows your Django application to trust the web server's authentication and focus on application-specific authorization and resource handling.

To use RemoteUserAuthentication in your DRF project, you need to configure your Django settings to enable the RemoteUserMiddleware and set the authentication classes in your DRF settings, like this:

```
# settings.py
MIDDLEWARE = [
    # ...
    'django.contrib.auth.middleware.RemoteUserMiddleware',
    # ...
]
```

```
REST_FRAMEWORK = {
    'DEFAULT_AUTHENTICATION_CLASSES': [
        'rest_framework.authentication.RemoteUserAuthentication',
    ],
}
```

It's important to note that the exact configuration and integration details may vary depending on your specific web server, authentication method, and application requirements.

Custom Authentication

Custom authentication in Django Rest Framework (DRF) refers to the process of implementing your own authentication mechanism instead of relying on DRF's built-in methods like **SessionAuthentication** or **TokenAuthentication**. This is useful when your application has unique authentication requirements that differ from the default methods. It allows you to design a specific way to validate and authenticate users based on your business or security needs. For example, you can authenticate users based on custom tokens, API keys, headers, or by integrating with external authentication services (like LDAP or OAuth).

To implement a custom authentication scheme, subclass **BaseAuthentication** and override the **.authenticate(self, request)** method. The method should return a two-tuple of **(user, auth)** if authentication succeeds or None otherwise.

In some circumstances, instead of returning **None**, you may want to raise an **AuthenticationFailed** exception from the **.authenticate()** method.

Typically, the approach you should take is

- If authentication is not attempted, return **None**. Any other authentication schemes also in use will still be checked.
- If authentication is attempted but fails, raise an **AuthenticationFailed** exception. An error response will be returned immediately, regardless of any permissions checks, and without checking any other authentication schemes.

You may also override the **.authenticate_header(self, request)** method. If implemented, it should return a string that will be used as the value of the **WWW-Authenticate** header in an **HTTP 401 Unauthorized** response.

If the **.authenticate_header()** method is not overridden, the authentication scheme will return HTTP 403 Forbidden responses when an unauthenticated request is denied access.

Let's implement custom authentication for our project:

Go to **drfproject/settings.py** and include the following for DEFAULT_AUTHENTICATION_CLASSES as below:

```
REST_FRAMEWORK = {
    'DEFAULT_AUTHENTICATION_CLASSES': (
        'user_app.api.authentication.CustomBasicAuthentication',
  'rest_framework.authentication.TokenAuthentication',
        'rest_framework.authentication.BasicAuthentication',
    ),
}
```

In the above code, we are adding **CustomBasicAuthentication** as the top authorization method to authorize the user.

Go to user_app/api/authentication.py and add the following lines of code:

```
from rest_framework.exceptions import AuthenticationFailed
from django.contrib.auth import get_user_model
User = get_user_model()

class CustomBasicAuthentication(authentication.BaseAuthentication):
    def authenticate(self, request):
        auth_header = request.headers.get('Authorization')

        if not auth_header:
            return None  # No header provided, return None for default
            behavior

        try:
            # Assuming the header format is "Custom <token>"
            auth_type, token = auth_header.split()
            if auth_type != 'Custom':
                return None  # Not the right type

            # Implement your token validation logic
            user = self.get_user_from_token(token)
```

```
            if user is None:
                raise AuthenticationFailed('Invalid token')

            return (user, None)  # Return user and None for the second
            parameter

        except ValueError:
            raise AuthenticationFailed('Invalid authorization header
            format')

    def get_user_from_token(self, token):
        # Your logic to get the user from the token
        try:
            user = User.objects.get(auth_token=token)  # Adjust according
            to your model
            return user
        except User.DoesNotExist:
            return None

    def authenticate_header(self, request):
        return 'Custom'  # Return the authentication type for the WWW-
        Authenticate header
```

In the above lines of code, a custom authentication class is defined to authenticate a custom user token for authentication

Now define a custom view class **CustomAuthenticationView**, and add an authorization class. Go to user_app/api/views.py and add the following lines of code:

```
class CustomAuthenticationView(APIView):
    authentication_classes = [CustomBasicAuthentication]  # Use your custom
    authentication
    permission_classes = [IsAuthenticated]  # Ensure the user is
    authenticated

    def get(self, request):
        return Response({"message": "Hello, you are authenticated!"})
```

Go to user_app/api/urls.py and add the following lines of code:

```
urlpatterns = [
    ...
    path('custom-auth/', views.CustomAuthenticationView.as_view(),
    name='custom-auth'),
]
```

Calling the endpoint `{{domain}}/api/user/custom-auth/` with Authorization as a bearer token prefixed with Custom will invoke the endpoint and return the response as below:

```
{
    "detail": "Invalid token"
}
```

When to Use Custom Authentication

- **Non-standard Authentication**: When your app needs something beyond DRF's default methods, like JWT, OAuth, or session-based auth.
- **External Systems**: Authenticating users through an external service like LDAP, a custom API, or a third-party service.
- **API Key or Token-Based Authentication**: When you need to authenticate via a custom header, a token, or an API key.
- **Additional Security Layers**: Implementing two-factor authentication, biometric login, or custom logic to check IP, location, or roles before authentication.

Benefits of Custom Authentication

- **Flexibility**: You can design the authentication flow according to your requirements.
- **Security**: Allows implementation of stronger or more specific security mechanisms.
- **Integration**: Easily integrate with external identity providers or legacy systems.

CHAPTER 10

Permissions

In Django Rest Framework (DRF), **permissions** are a way to control access to views or APIs based on specific rules. Permissions define **who is allowed** to perform certain actions (like viewing, editing, or deleting data) and are a key part of DRF's security system. Permissions are checked **after** authentication, so the request must already include valid credentials. Permissions are applied to a view or a viewset to determine if a particular user (or request) has the right to interact with the resource. If the user doesn't have the necessary permissions, DRF will return a **403 Forbidden** response. They are crucial for controlling access to your API and ensuring that only authorized users can perform specific actions on your resources. Together with authentication and throttling, permissions determine whether a request should be granted or denied access.

Key reasons why permissions are important in DRF:

1. **Security**

    - **Prevent Unauthorized Access**: Permissions prevent unauthorized users from accessing, modifying, or deleting sensitive data. By enforcing different permission levels, you ensure that only users with the right level of access can interact with the API.
    - **Granular Access Control**: Permissions allow for fine-grained control over different actions like viewing, editing, or deleting. You can specify which users can perform which operations on various endpoints or objects.
    - **Confidentiality**: In applications that handle sensitive or private data (e.g., user profiles, financial data, medical records), permissions ensure that only authorized individuals can access confidential information.

G. Patil, *Django REST APIs Demystified*, https://doi.org/10.1007/979-8-8688-1850-9_10

2. **Role-Based Access Control (RBAC)**

    - **Assign Roles**: With permissions, you can implement role-based access control, where different user roles (e.g., admin, editor, regular user) have different access rights. For example, an admin user may have full control over all resources, while regular users can only view or edit their own data.

    - **Different Permission Levels**: You can define custom permission classes to control access based on user roles or user attributes, ensuring that users can only interact with data in ways that align with their assigned roles.

      Example:

        - Admins can create, edit, and delete any resource.
        - Regular users can view public resources and edit only their own content.
        - Guests can only view public resources.

3. **Object-Level Access Control**

    - **Protect Ownership**: In many cases, users should only be allowed to modify or delete objects they own (e.g., a blog post, an uploaded file). Object-level permissions allow you to enforce rules based on the ownership of resources, ensuring that users can only interact with objects they own or have specific rights to.

    - **Fine-Grained Permissions**: DRF allows object-level permissions where you can define rules like "users can only edit their own profiles" or "users can only delete comments they created."

      ```
      from rest_framework.permissions import BasePermission
      class IsOwner(BasePermission):
          def has_object_permission(self, request, view, obj):
              return obj.owner == request.user
      ```

4. **Compliance and Data Protection**

    - **Legal and Regulatory Requirements**: In many industries (e.g., healthcare, finance, and education), you are required by law to restrict access to certain data. Permissions help you meet compliance standards (such as GDPR, HIPAA, etc.) by ensuring that only authorized users can access, update, or delete sensitive data.

    - **Auditability**: By enforcing strict permissions, you can track and audit who accessed what data, when, and under what circumstances. This helps with accountability and ensuring compliance with legal standards.

5. **Separation of Concerns**

    - **Separation Between Authentication and Authorization**: Permissions in DRF allow a clean separation between **authentication** (verifying the user's identity) and **authorization** (determining what actions a user can take). This separation makes your code more modular, easier to manage, and more secure.

    - **Modular Permission Classes**: DRF's permission system allows you to apply different permission classes to different views or APIs. This modularity makes it easier to define varying access rules for different endpoints in your project.

6. **Scalability**

    - **Customizable and Extendable**: DRF provides built-in permission classes (e.g., **IsAuthenticated**, **IsAdminUser**, etc.) but also allows developers to create custom permission classes tailored to specific application needs. This flexibility allows the permissions system to grow and adapt as your application becomes more complex.

    - **Easily Manageable in Large Applications**: As your application grows, managing who can access certain parts of the API becomes more complex. DRF's permission system provides a consistent and scalable way to handle authorization rules, reducing the risk of security loopholes or oversight.

7. **Flexible Control over API Access**

   - **Public vs. Private APIs**: Permissions allow you to make certain parts of your API public (accessible to anyone) and other parts private (restricted to authenticated users). This flexibility is essential when you need to expose some resources for public use (e.g., an open API) but restrict access to others (e.g., user management, admin-level APIs).

   - **Granular API Protection**: You can apply different permission classes to different views, ensuring that more sensitive operations (e.g., modifying a database) are protected, while less sensitive ones (e.g., reading public data) remain open.

     Example:

     ```
     class PublicView(APIView):
         permission_classes = [AllowAny]
         # Anyone can access this view

     class UserOnlyView(APIView):
         permission_classes = [IsAuthenticated]  # Only
         authenticated users can access this view
     ```

8. **Prevent Data Tampering and Abuse**

   - **Restricting Actions**: Permissions help in restricting specific actions such as modifying or deleting records to authorized users. For example, in a financial application, it's important to restrict who can perform transactions or make changes to sensitive records.

   - **Protecting Data Integrity**: By allowing only specific users to modify data, permissions help protect the integrity of your data and prevent unauthorized tampering or accidental changes by users who shouldn't have access.

9. **Custom Business Logic**

    - **Context-Specific Permissions**: You can create custom permission classes that include business logic specific to your application. For example, you can create permissions that check for specific conditions, such as whether a user has an active subscription or whether they belong to a specific group.

      Example:

      ```
      from rest_framework.permissions import BasePermission
      class IsPremiumUser(BasePermission):
          def has_permission(self, request, view):
              return request.user.is_premium_member
      ```

Permission checks are always run at the very start of the view, before any other code is allowed to proceed. Permission checks will typically use the authentication information in the **request.user** and **request.auth** properties to determine if the incoming request should be permitted.

Default User Permissions

When you create a Django model and run migrations, Django automatically generates a set of default permissions for that model. These default permissions are created for each model and can be viewed and managed in the Django admin panel.

For each model, Django automatically creates two sets of default permissions for each model (two sets of add, change, delete, view). One set with app_label and another set without app_label.

Each set will have the below types of permissions:

1. **add_<modelname>**: Permission to add a new object of the model (corresponds to POST requests in an API).

2. **change_<modelname>**: Permission to change an existing object of the model (corresponds to PUT or PATCH requests in an API).

3. **delete_<modelname>**: Permission to delete an object of the model (corresponds to DELETE requests in an API).

4. **view_<modelname>**: Permission to view an object of the model (corresponds to GET requests in an API). This permission has been automatically added since **Django 2.1**.

For example, if you have a model called Review, Django will create the following permissions:

- add_review: Can add Review
- change_ review: Can change Review
- delete_ review: Can delete Review
- view_ review: Can view Review

These permissions can be assigned to users or groups via the Django admin interface.

Permissions Without App Label (Global Permissions)

When you see the permissions **without the app label**, they are global permissions. These permissions are typically related to actions available on objects across **all models** and usually come from Django's built-in user model (**django.contrib.auth**), not from your specific models. These are general permissions that come from Django's authentication framework and give permission to manage user-related actions.

These global permissions exist to allow superusers and staff users to have broad permissions (e.g., to add, change, delete, and view objects across all models).

Permissions with App Label (Model-Specific Permissions)

The permissions with the app label (e.g., add_review, change_review, delete_review, view_review) are the model-specific permissions that Django creates for each model in your app when you run migrations. These are specific to your models, generated by Django when migrations are run, and control actions related to each model.

These permissions are applied specifically to actions on the particular model you define (e.g., Post model).

How Permissions Are Determined

Permissions in REST Framework are always defined as a list of permission classes. Before running the main body of the view, each permission in the list is checked. If any permission check fails, an **exceptions.PermissionDenied** or **exceptions.NotAuthenticated** exception will be raised, and the main body of the view will not run.

When the permission checks fail, either a "**403 Forbidden**" or a "**401 Unauthorized**" response will be returned, according to the following rules:

- The request was successfully authenticated, but permission was denied: Then an HTTP 403 Forbidden response will be returned.
- The request was not successfully authenticated, and the highest priority authentication class does not use **WWW-Authenticate** headers: Then an HTTP 403 Forbidden response will be returned.
- The request was not successfully authenticated, and the highest priority authentication class does use WWW-Authenticate headers: An HTTP 401 Unauthorized response, with an appropriate **WWW-Authenticate** header, will be returned.

In Django Rest Framework (DRF), **permissions** are determined at two levels: **view-level** and **object-level**. The process involves checking whether the user making a request has the necessary rights to access a particular API endpoint and, if needed, specific objects within the system.

Permissions in DRF are determined using the following steps.

View-Level Permission Checks

These checks determine whether the user has the right to access the view (the API endpoint) itself. The **has_permission** method is used for this level of permission check.

It follows the below process:

- When a request is made to an API endpoint (view), DRF first checks the view-level permissions.
- These permissions are applied globally (via settings) or per view/viewset (using the **permission_classes** attribute).

- DRF will loop through each permission in the **permission_classes** list, calling the **has_permission** method for each permission class.
- If any permission check fails (returns False), the request is denied with a **403 Forbidden** response.

Object-Level Permission Checks (Optional)

Object-level permission checks are more granular and verify whether the user has permission to perform an action on a specific object (e.g., whether a user can edit or delete a particular resource). The **has_object_permission** method is used for this level of check.

Object-level permissions are only applied after view-level permissions are satisfied. It follows the below process:

- After passing the view-level permissions, DRF checks object-level permissions (if implemented).
- The **has_object_permission** method is called for each object in the viewset or the object the view is operating on.
- Like view-level permissions, DRF loops through the **permission_classes** and checks **has_object_permission** for each class.
- If any object-level permission check fails, the request is denied with a **403 Forbidden** response.

In general, object-level permissions are run by REST Framework's generic views when **.get_object()** is called. As with view-level permissions, an **exceptions.PermissionDenied** exception will be raised if the user is not allowed to act on the given object.

If you're writing your own views and want to enforce object-level permissions or if you override the **get_object** method on a generic view, then you'll need to explicitly call the **.check_object_permissions(request, obj)** method on the view at the point at which you've retrieved the object.

This will either raise a **PermissionDenied** or **NotAuthenticated** exception or simply return if the view has the appropriate permissions.

For example:

```
def get_object(self):
    obj = get_object_or_404(self.get_queryset(), pk=self.kwargs["pk"])
    self.check_object_permissions(self.request, obj)
    return obj
```

Note that with the exception of **DjangoObjectPermissions**, the provided permission classes in **rest_framework.permissions** do not implement the methods necessary to check object permissions.

If you wish to use the provided permission classes in order to check object permissions, you must subclass them and implement the **has_object_permission()** method using custom permissions.

But there are limitations on using object-level permissions. For performance reasons, the generic views will not automatically apply object-level permissions to each instance in a **queryset** when returning a list of objects.

Often, when you're using object-level permissions, you'll also want to filter the queryset appropriately to ensure that users only have visibility onto instances that they are permitted to view.

Because the **get_object()** method is not called, object-level permissions from the **has_object_permission()** method **are not applied** when creating objects. In order to restrict object creation, you need to implement the permission check either in your Serializer class or override the **perform_create()** method of your ViewSet class.

Permission Evaluation Key Points

1. **Order of Evaluation**

    - DRF first evaluates **view-level permissions** using the **has_permission** method.

    - If the view-level permissions pass and the view operates on an object (e.g., a Retrieve, Update, or Destroy view), DRF evaluates **object-level permissions** using the **has_object_permission** method.

2. **Default Permissions**

   If no **permission_classes** are specified in the view or globally, DRF uses **AllowAny** by default, meaning that anyone can access the view or API.

3. **check_object_permissions Method**

   - DRF views and viewsets include a **check_object_permissions**(request, obj) method that triggers object-level permission checks.
   - This is especially important for views like **RetrieveUpdateDestroyAPIView** where a specific object is being modified.

4. **Short-Circuiting**

   As soon as any permission check fails (view-level or object-level), the request is immediately rejected with a **403 Forbidden**.

5. **Combination of Permissions**

   You can combine multiple permissions to apply different rules (e.g., **IsAuthenticatedOrReadOnly** and **IsOwnerOrReadOnly**). In such cases, the most restrictive rule applies.

Preparing for This Chapter

Create a new app with the name **chapter10_permissions** with the steps specified in the **Project Setup** section in Chapter 3.

Go to drfproject/settings.py and add the following lines of code:

```
INSTALLED_APPS = [
    ...
    "chapter10_permissions",
]
```

Go to chapter10_permissions/api/serializers.py and add the following lines of code:

```
from rest_framework import serializers
from chapter3_project_setup.models import WatchList, StreamPlatform, Review

class WatchListModelSerializer(serializers.ModelSerializer):
    class Meta:
        model = WatchList
        fields = "__all__"
        ref_name = 'C10WatchListModelSerializer'

class StreamPlatformModelSerializer(serializers.ModelSerializer):
    class Meta:
        model = StreamPlatform
        fields = "__all__"
        ref_name = 'C10StreamPlatformModelSerializer'

class ReviewModelSerializer(serializers.ModelSerializer):
    user = serializers.StringRelatedField()
    class Meta:
        model = Review
        fields = "__all__"
        ref_name = 'C10ReviewModelSerializer'
```

Go to chapter10_permissions/api/views.py and add the following lines of code:

```
from rest_framework import viewsets
from rest_framework.authentication import BasicAuthentication,
TokenAuthentication
from rest_framework.permissions import AllowAny, IsAuthenticated,
IsAuthenticatedOrReadOnly, DjangoModelPermissions, IsAdminUser
from rest_framework.decorators import api_view, permission_classes,
authentication_classes
from rest_framework.response import Response
from rest_framework import status
from rest_framework import generics
from rest_framework.views import APIView
from rest_framework.permissions import DjangoObjectPermissions
from django.contrib.auth import get_user_model
```

```
from guardian.shortcuts import assign_perm
from chapter3_project_setup.models import WatchList, Review, StreamPlatform
from chapter10_permissions.api import serializers
```

Go to chapter10_permissions/api/urls.py and add the following lines of code:

```
from django.urls import path, include
from rest_framework.routers import DefaultRouter
from . import views

urlpatterns = [

    # Using ViewSet
    path("", include(router.urls)),
]
```

Go to drfproject/urls.py and add the following lines of code:

```
urlpatterns = [
    ...
    path('api/chapter10_permissions/', include('chapter10_permissions.api.
    urls')),
]
```

Setting the Permission Policy

Now let's implement setting up permissions for our application.

You can configure permissions globally in your settings.py to apply to all views:

```
# settings.py
REST_FRAMEWORK = {
    'DEFAULT_PERMISSION_CLASSES': [
        'rest_framework.permissions.IsAuthenticated',
    ]
}
```

This means that every view will require the user to be authenticated unless you override it locally. You can apply permissions to specific views or viewsets by setting the **permission_classes** attribute.

Let's go to chapter10_permissions/api/views.py and add the following lines of code:

```
class WatchListIsAuthenticatedView(viewsets.ModelViewSet):
    authentication_classes = [TokenAuthentication,]
    permission_classes = [IsAuthenticated,]  # Ensure that the user is
    authenticated
    queryset = WatchList.objects.all()
    serializer_class = serializers.WatchListModelSerializer
```

In the above code, we are specifying **permission_classes** with the **IsAuthenticated** permission. This allows only authenticated users can access this view. The request needs to be authenticated with a token in the request header.

Add the corresponding URL in chapter10_permissions/api/urls.py as below:

```
router = DefaultRouter()
# Using ViewSet
router.register(r"watchlist-isauthenticated", views.
WatchListIsAuthenticatedView, basename="watchlist-isauthenticated")
```

The above endpoint can be accessed using endpoint: **GET** `{{domain}}/api/chapter10_permissions/watchlist-isauthenticated/` by providing the token in the request header.

You can also set permissions to function-based views as below:

```
# Function based view with basic authentication
@api_view(['GET', 'POST'])
@permission_classes([IsAuthenticated])
@authentication_classes([BasicAuthentication])
def stream_platform_isauthenticated_view(request):
    if request.method == 'GET':
        # Handle GET request
        watchlist = StreamPlatform.objects.all()
        serializer = serializers.StreamPlatformModelSerializer(watchlist,
        many=True)
        return Response(serializer.data)
    elif request.method == 'POST':
        # Handle POST request
```

```
        serializer = serializers.StreamPlatformModelSerializer(data=req
        uest.data)
        if serializer.is_valid():
            serializer.save()
            return Response(serializer.data, status=status.HTTP_201_CREATED)
        return Response(serializer.errors, status=status.HTTP_400_BAD_
        REQUEST)
```

Add the corresponding URL in chapter10_permissions/api/urls.py as below:

```
urlpatterns = [
    path(r"stream-platform", views.stream_platform_isauthenticated_view),
    ...
]
```

You can also use multiple permissions by passing a list as below:

```
#IsAdminUser
class WatchListIsAdminUserView(viewsets.ModelViewSet):
    authentication_classes = [TokenAuthentication,]
    permission_classes = [IsAuthenticated, IsAdminUser]
    queryset = WatchList.objects.all()
    serializer_class = serializers.WatchListModelSerializer
```

Built-In Classes

Although you can create your own permission classes, DRF comes with seven built-in classes intended to make your life easier:

- AllowAny
- IsAuthenticated
- IsAuthenticatedOrReadOnly
- IsAdminUser
- DjangoModelPermissions
- DjangoModelPermissionsOrAnonReadOnly
- DjangoObjectPermissions

Using them is as simple as including the class in the **permission_classes** list of a specific API view. They stretch from entirely open (AllowAny) to access granted only to admin users (IsAdminUser). With very little additional work, you can use them to implement fine-grained access control—either on a model or at the object level. You can also set permissions globally, for all API endpoints.

All of those classes, except the last one, **DjangoObjectPermissions**, override just the **has_permission** method and inherit the **has_object_permission** from the **BasePermission** class. **has_object_permission** in the **BasePermission** class always returns True, so it has no impact on object-level access restriction:

Permission Class	has_permission	has_object_permission
AllowAny	✓	✗
IsAuthenticated	✓	✗
IsAuthenticatedOrReadOnly	✓	✗
IsAdminUser	✓	✗
DjangoModelPermissions	✓	✗
DjangoModelPermissionsOrAnonReadOnly	✓	✗
DjangoObjectPermissions	by extending DjangoModelPermissions	✓

AllowAny

The most open permission of all is **AllowAny**. The **has_permission** and **has_object_permission** methods on AllowAny always return True without checking anything. Using it isn't necessary (by not setting the permission class, you implicitly set this one), but you still should, since it makes the intent explicit and helps to maintain consistency throughout the app. You specify it by including **permission_classes** in your view.

Go to chapter10_permissions/api/views.py and add the following lines of code:

```
#AllowAny
class WatchlistAllowAnyView(viewsets.ModelViewSet):
    authentication_classes = [TokenAuthentication,]
    permission_classes = [AllowAny]  # Ensure that the user is authenticated
    queryset = WatchList.objects.all()
    serializer_class = serializers.WatchListModelSerializer
```

Add the corresponding URL in chapter10_permissions/api/urls.py as below:

```
router = DefaultRouter()
# Using ViewSet
router.register(r"watchlist-allowany", views.WatchlistAllowAnyView,
basename="watchlist-allowany")
```

IsAuthenticated

This permission checks if the request has a user and if that user is authenticated. Setting **permission_classes** to **IsAuthenticated** means that **only authenticated** users will be able to access the API endpoint with any of the request methods. Refer to the **Setting the Permission Policy** section for an example of this permission.

IsAuthenticatedOrReadOnly

The **IsAuthenticatedOrReadOnly** will allow authenticated users to perform any request. Requests for unauthenticated users will only be permitted if the request method is one of the "safe" methods: GET, HEAD, or OPTIONS.

This permission is suitable if you want your API to allow read permissions to anonymous users and only allow write permissions to authenticated users.

Go to chapter10_permissions/api/views.py and add the following lines of code:

```
#IsAuthenticatedOrReadOnly
class WatchListIsAuthenticatedOrReadOnlyView(viewsets.ModelViewSet):
    authentication_classes = [TokenAuthentication,]
    permission_classes = [IsAuthenticatedOrReadOnly,]
    queryset = WatchList.objects.all()
    serializer_class = serializers.WatchListModelSerializer
```

Add the corresponding URL in chapter10_permissions/api/urls.py as below:

```
router = DefaultRouter()
...
router.register(r"watchlist-isauthenticatedorreadonly", views.
WatchListIsAuthenticatedOrReadOnlyView, basename="watchlist-
isauthenticatedorreadonly")
```

In the above endpoint, an unauthenticated user can view the watchlist that was created by an authenticated user, but they can't do anything with it or add their own.

IsAdminUser

Permissions set to **IsAdminUser** means that the request needs to have a user and that user must have **is_staff** set to True. This means that only admin users can **see, add, change, or delete** objects.

Go to chapter10_permissions/api/views.py and add the following lines of code:

```
#IsAdminUser
class WatchListIsAdminUserView(viewsets.ModelViewSet):
    authentication_classes = [TokenAuthentication,]
    permission_classes = [IsAuthenticated, IsAdminUser]  # Ensure that the
    user is authenticated
    queryset = WatchList.objects.all()
    serializer_class = serializers.WatchListModelSerializer
```

Add the corresponding URL in chapter10_permissions/api/urls.py as below:

```
router = DefaultRouter()
...
router.register(r"watchlist-adminuser", views.WatchListIsAdminUserView,
basename="watchlist-adminuser")
```

The interesting part here is that unauthenticated users and authenticated users without admin access will get different errors.

For unauthenticated users, a NotAuthenticated exception is raised as below:

```
{
    "detail": "Authentication credentials were not provided."
}
```

Meanwhile, for an authenticated user without admin access, a **PermissionDenied** exception is raised:

```
{
    "detail": "You do not have permission to perform this action."
}
```

DjangoModelPermissions

As we discussed in the section **Default User Permissions**, when models are migrated to the database, they generate four default permissions for each model. This permission class ties into Django's standard **django.contrib.auth** model permissions. This permission must only be applied to views that have a **.queryset** property or **get_queryset()** method. Authorization will only be granted if the user *is authenticated* and has the *relevant model permissions* assigned. The appropriate model is determined by checking **get_queryset().model** or **queryset.model**.

- POST requests require the user to have the add permission on the model.
- PUT and PATCH requests require the user to have the change permission on the model.
- DELETE requests require the user to have the delete permission on the model.

The default behavior can also be overridden to support custom model permissions. For example, you might want to include a view model permission for GET requests.

To use custom model permissions, override **DjangoModelPermissions** and set the **.perms_map** property.

By using **DjangoModelPermissions** permission, you can control model permissions for users as below:

Go to chapter10_permissions/api/views.py and add the following lines of code:

```
#DjangoModelPermissions
class WatchListModelPermView(viewsets.ModelViewSet):
    authentication_classes = [TokenAuthentication,]
    permission_classes = [DjangoModelPermissions]
    queryset = WatchList.objects.all()
    serializer_class = serializers.WatchListModelSerializer
```

The user shall be assigned with corresponding permissions as below on the admin page to access the above view:

- Chapter3_Project_Setup | Watch List | Can add watch list
- Chapter3_Project_Setup | Watch List | Can change watch list
- Chapter3_Project_Setup | Watch List | Can delete watch list
- Chapter3_Project_Setup | Watch List | Can view watch list

Add the corresponding URL in chapter10_permissions/api/urls.py as below:

```
router = DefaultRouter()
...
router.register(r"watchlist-modelperm", views.WatchListModelPermView,
basename="watchlist-modelperm")
```

To apply multiple permissions to different actions in a view, you can create a custom permission class that checks if the user has the required permissions based on the request method. This custom permission class will look at the permissions attribute in your view and validate if the user has the specified permissions for the action being performed. These multiple custom permissions are to be defined for the model.

Let's go to chapter3_project_setup/models.py and update the Watchlist model with the permissions attribute as below:

```
class WatchList(models.Model):
    ...

    class Meta:
        ...
        permissions = (
            ("can_view_watchlist", "User can view watchlist"),
```

```
            ("can_create_watchlist", "User can create watchlist"),
            ("can_update_watchlist", "User can update watchlist"),
            ("can_partially_update_watchlist", "User can partially update
            watchlist"),
            ("can_delete_watchlist", "User can delete watchlist"),
        )
```

Once the permissions attribute is added, run the migrate command to apply permissions changes to the database.

Let's create chapter10_permissions/api/permissions.py and add the following lines of code:

```
from rest_framework import permissions
from django.core.exceptions import ImproperlyConfigured

class MultiplePermissionsRequired(permissions.BasePermission):
    """
    allows authenticated users which have permissions listed in permissions
    dictionary
    """

    def has_permission(self, request, view):
        if not request.user or not request.user.is_authenticated:
            return False
        return self.check_permissions(request, view)

    def check_permissions(self, request, view):
        permissions = self.get_required_permissions(view)

        perms_all = permissions.get("all") or None
        perms_any = permissions.get("any") or None
        perms_get = permissions.get("get") or None
        perms_post = permissions.get("post") or None
        perms_put = permissions.get("put") or None
        perms_patch = permissions.get("patch") or None
        perms_delete = permissions.get("delete") or None

        #if all in permissions dict, check the user has all permissions in
        the tuple
```

```
        if perms_all:
            if not request.user.has_perms(perms_all):
                return False

        #if any in permissions dict, check the user has atleast one
        permissions in the tuple
        if perms_any:
            for perm in perms_any:
                if request.user.has_perm(perm):
                    return True

            return False

        if perms_get and request.method=="GET":
            return self._check_method_permission(request, perms_get)

        if perms_post and request.method=="POST":
            return self._check_method_permission(request, perms_post)

        if perms_put and request.method=="PUT":
            return self._check_method_permission(request, perms_put)

        if perms_patch and request.method=="PATCH":
            return self._check_method_permission(request, perms_patch)

        if perms_delete and request.method=="DELETE":
            return self._check_method_permission(request, perms_delete)

        return True

    def _check_method_permission(self, request, permissions):
        status=True
        for perm in permissions:
            if not request.user.has_perm(perm):
                status = False
        return status

    def get_required_permissions(self, view):
        self._check_permissions_attr(view)
        return view.permissions
```

```
    def _check_permissions_attr(self, view):
        """
        check whether permissions attribute is set and it is dict format
        """
        if not hasattr(view, "permissions") or not isinstance(view.
        permissions, dict):
            raise ImproperlyConfigured(f'{self.__class__.__name__} requires
            "permissions" attribute to be set as a dict.' )
```

The **MultiplePermissionsRequired** permission class will dynamically check the user's permissions based on the view's request method (e.g., GET, POST, PUT, etc.). It will validate the required permission specified in the view's permissions dictionary for each HTTP method.

In your viewset, use the **MultiplePermissionsRequired** class and define the permissions for each action (HTTP method) in the permissions attribute.

Let's go to chapter10_permissions/api/views.py and add the following lines of code:

```
class WatchListMultiplePermView(viewsets.ModelViewSet):
    authentication_classes = [TokenAuthentication,]
    permission_classes = [MultiplePermissionsRequired,]
    permissions = {
        "get": ("chapter3_project_setup.can_view_watchlist",),
        "post": ("chapter3_project_setup.can_create_watchlist",),
        "put": ("chapter3_project_setup.can_update_watchlist",),
        "patch": ("chapter3_project_setup.can_partially_update_
        watchlist",),
        "delete": ("chapter3_project_setup.can_delete_watchlist",),
    }
    queryset = WatchList.objects.all()
    serializer_class = serializers.WatchListModelSerializer
```

The **permissions** attribute in the view dictionary maps HTTP methods (get, post, put, etc.) to required permissions for that method. Each permission is checked dynamically based on the request's HTTP method.

The **MultiplePermissionsRequired** permission class retrieves the required permissions for the current method and ensures the user has each of them. If any permission is missing, it denies access.

Add the corresponding URL in chapter10_permissions/api/urls.py as below:

```
router = DefaultRouter()
...
router.register(r"watchlist-multiplepermview", views.
WatchListMultiplePermView, basename="watchlist-multiplepermview")
```

This configuration will enforce the following:

- Users with chapter3_project_setup.can_view_watchlist can access GET requests.
- Users with chapter3_project_setup.can_create_watchlist can perform POST requests.
- Users with chapter3_project_setup.can_update_watchlist can perform PUT requests, and so forth.

DjangoModelPermissionsOrAnonReadOnly

Similar to **DjangoModelPermissions** but also allows unauthenticated users to have read-only access to the API.

DjangoObjectPermissions

While **DjangoModelPermissions** limits the user's permission for interacting with a model (all the instances), **DjangoObjectPermissions** limits the interaction to a single instance of the model (an object). To use **DjangoObjectPermissions**, you'll need a permission back end that supports object-level permissions. We'll look at django-guardian.

As with DjangoModelPermissions, this permission must only be applied to views that have a .queryset property or .get_queryset() method; authorization will only be granted if the user *is authenticated* and has the *relevant per-object permissions* and *relevant model permissions* assigned.

- POST requests require the user to have the add permission on the model instance.

- PUT and PATCH requests require the user to have the change permission on the model instance.
- DELETE requests require the user to have the delete permission on the model instance.

While there are quite a few packages that cover Django permissions, DRF explicitly mentions django-guardian, which is why we're working with it in this article.

Other packages that deal with object-level permissions:

- drf-extensions
- django-oso
- django-rules
- django-role-permissions

Installing django-guardian

To use django-guardian, you first need to install it as below:

```
(venv)$ pip install django-guardian
```

If you want to see the permissions for a single object, you need to use GuardedModelAdmin instead of ModelAdmin.

Go to chapter3_project_setup/admin.py and add the following lines of code:

```
from guardian.admin import GuardedModelAdmin

class WatchListAdmin(GuardedModelAdmin):
    pass
...
```

Now, if you open a single object in the admin panel, on the top right, there's a new button called "OBJECT PERMISSIONS." Upon clicking it, the Object permissions panel opens:

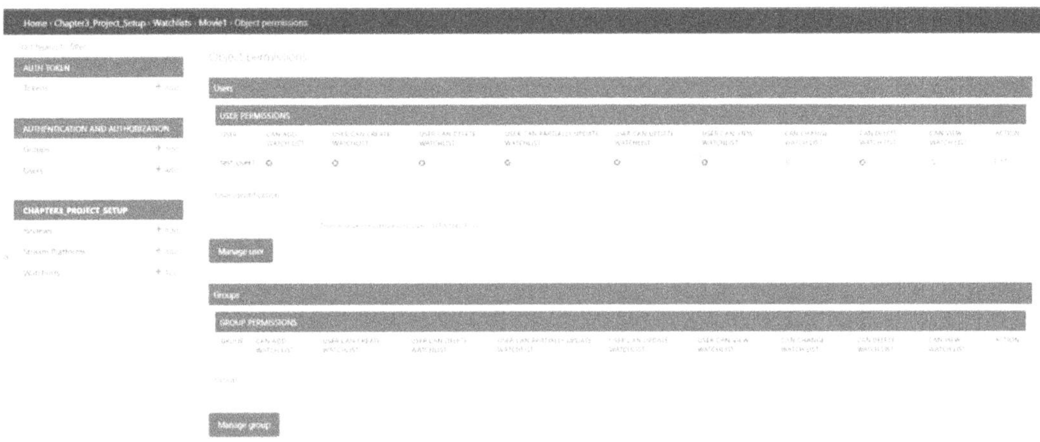

Using DjangoObjectPermissions

Now knowing the difference between **has_permission** and **has_object_permission** will come in handy. In short, DRF first checks if the request has permission to access the model. If it doesn't, DRF doesn't care about the object-level permissions.

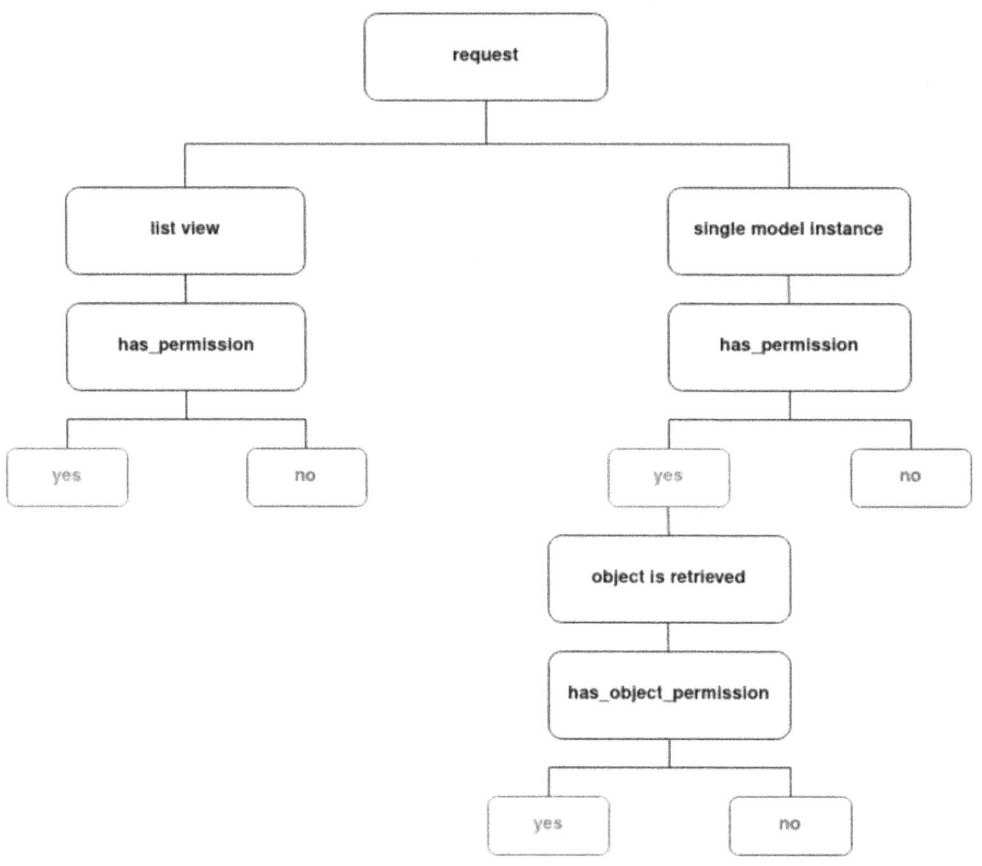

That means that the user **must have** model permission if you want the object-level permission to be checked. A good use case for object-level permissions is for only allowing the owner of an object to change or delete it. Here's a view that allows only the creator of the object to delete it.

Go to chapter10_permissions/api/views.py and add the following lines of code:

```
#DjangoObjectPermissions
class WatchListObjectPermissionsView(viewsets.ModelViewSet):
    queryset = WatchList.objects.all()
    serializer_class = serializers.WatchListModelSerializer
    authentication_classes = [TokenAuthentication]
    permission_classes = [DjangoObjectPermissions,]  # Use
    DjangoObjectPermissions
```

```
    def perform_create(self, serializer): # new function
        instance = serializer.save()
        assign_perm("delete_watchlist", self.request.user, instance)
        assign_perm("change_watchlist", self.request.user, instance)
```

Add the corresponding URL in chapter10_permissions/api/urls.py as below:

```
router = DefaultRouter()
...
router.register(r"watchlist-objectpermissionview", views.
WatchListObjectPermissionsView, basename="watchlist-objectpermissionview")
```

As you can see, there are two important changes:

1. First, the permission class is **DjangoObjectPermissions**.
2. Next, we tapped into the model instance creation. We can't assign permission to a non-existing object, so we first need to create the instance and, after that, assign object permission to it via the assign_perm shortcut from django-guardian.

assign_perm is a django-guardian function used for assigning permissions to certain users or groups. It takes three arguments:

1. permission: For example, delete_watchlist
2. user_or_group: self.request.user
3. object (defaults to None): Instance

Again, for the object permission to work, the user **must have** model-level permission for the corresponding model. Let's say you have two users with the same permissions on the model:

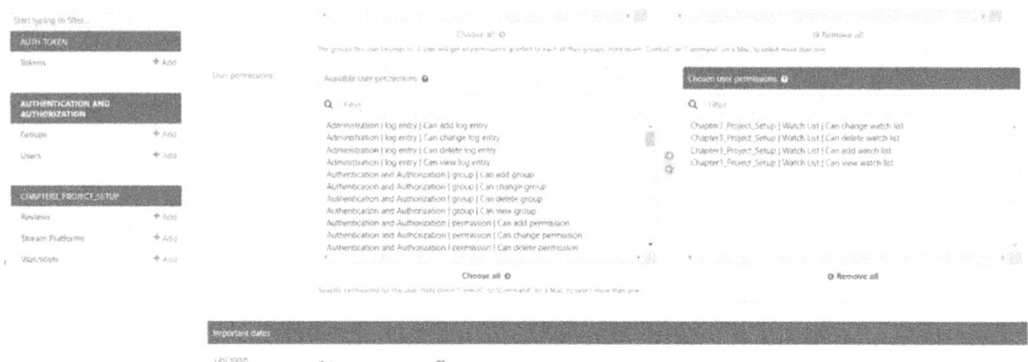

And you use the code above to assign permission only to the creator. test_user1 who is the creator of the object and can also delete it. But test_user2 can't delete it even though they have model-level permissions.

Note that **DjangoObjectPermissions** does not require the **django-guardian package** and should support other object-level back ends equally well. To use custom model permissions in Django REST Framework (DRF) with **DjangoObjectPermissions**, you can extend it and override its **perms_map** property. This allows you to define custom permissions that DRF will check against based on the action or HTTP method being used.

In our project, you have defined custom permissions in the WatchList model, so we'll use those permissions instead of the default (add, change, delete, view). By customizing **perms_map**, you can make **DjangoObjectPermissions** check for your defined permissions (can_view_watchlist, can_create_watchlist, etc.) based on the request method.

Go to chapter10_permissions/api/permissions.py and add the following lines of code:

```
from rest_framework.permissions import DjangoObjectPermissions

class CustomDjangoObjectPermissions(DjangoObjectPermissions):
    """
    Custom permissions class that uses custom permissions from the model's
    Meta class.
    Overrides the default `perms_map` to map custom permissions based on
    the request method.
    """
```

```
    # Override the perms_map with your custom permissions
    perms_map = {
        'GET': ['chapter3_project_setup.can_view_watchlist'],
        'POST': ['chapter3_project_setup.can_create_watchlist'],
        'PUT': ['chapter3_project_setup.can_update_watchlist'],
        'PATCH': ['chapter3_project_setup.can_partially_update_watchlist'],
        'DELETE': ['chapter3_project_setup.can_delete_watchlist'],
    }

    def has_object_permission(self, request, view, obj):
        # Bypass object-level checks for 'GET' requests, only use
        model-level
        if request.method == 'GET':
            return request.user.has_perm('chapter3_project_setup.can_view_
            watchlist')
        return super().has_object_permission(request, view, obj)
```

In the above code, the custom permission class is created by extending **DjangoObjectPermissions** and overriding the **perms_map** to define the custom permissions. The **perms_map** dictionary in **CustomDjangoObjectPermissions** maps HTTP methods to specific permission codenames that are checked against the user's permissions on the WatchList model. Here's how each key in perms_map works:

- **GET**: Maps to can_view_watchlist, allowing users to read/watch list items
- **POST**: Maps to can_create_watchlist, allowing users to create new items
- **PUT**: Maps to can_update_watchlist, allowing full updates of items
- **PATCH**: Maps to can_partially_update_watchlist, allowing partial updates
- **DELETE**: Maps to can_delete_watchlist, allowing deletion of items

Go to chapter10_permissions/api/views.py and add the following lines of code:

```
#DjangoObjectPermissions with perms_map
class WatchListObjectPermissionsMapView(viewsets.ModelViewSet):
    authentication_classes = [TokenAuthentication,]
```

```
    permission_classes = [CustomDjangoObjectPermissions]
    queryset = WatchList.objects.all()
    serializer_class = serializers.WatchListModelSerializer
```

Now, in your **WatchList** viewset, use the **CustomDjangoObjectPermissions** permission class. This will ensure that DRF checks for the correct permission according to the HTTP method.

Add the corresponding URL in chapter10_permissions/api/urls.py as below:

```
router = DefaultRouter()
...
router.register(r"watchlist-objectpermissionmapview", views.
WatchListObjectPermissionsMapView, basename="watchlist-
objectpermissionmapview")
```

By customizing **DjangoObjectPermissions** in this way, you can ensure that DRF enforces your model's custom permissions for each specific HTTP method, allowing for fine-grained access control on a per-object basis without needing external packages like **django-guardian**. This makes it both flexible and straightforward to manage custom permissions for models in DRF.

Custom Permissions

In Django REST Framework (DRF), **custom permissions** are a way to control access to views or viewsets based on criteria specific to your application, beyond the built-in permissions (**IsAuthenticated, IsAdminUser**, etc.). Custom permissions allow you to define specific conditions under which a user can access, modify, or delete data. This is especially useful when you need complex, granular control over permissions that don't fit the default patterns.

You may want custom permissions in cases like

- Restricting access to certain views only for specific user roles
- Limiting actions based on attributes of a model instance (e.g., only allowing access to an object if the user is the creator)
- Adding multiple permissions requirements to different actions within the same view (e.g., users can read only if they're in one group but edit only if they're in another)

Custom permissions let you define such object-level controls, which are essential for handling user-specific data securely. Many applications have rules specific to their business logic that go beyond the standard role-based permissions. Examples include

- Allowing premium users to access additional features
- Restricting API access based on the user's subscription level
- Implementing rate limits or throttling based on user roles or status

Custom permissions help integrate these rules into your API, ensuring that the system reflects the application's real-world requirements. Implementing custom permissions allows for more secure and restricted access to sensitive data. By clearly defining who can view, edit, or delete certain resources, you reduce the risk of unauthorized access, especially in applications with sensitive information.

To implement a custom permission, override **BasePermission** and implement either or both of the following methods:

- .has_permission(self, request, view)
- .has_object_permission(self, request, view, obj)

The methods should return True if the request should be granted access and False otherwise.

If you need to test if a request is a read operation or a write operation, you should check the request method against the constant SAFE_METHODS, which is a tuple containing "GET", "OPTIONS", and "HEAD".

Note that the instance-level **has_object_permission** method will only be called if the view-level **has_permission** checks have already passed. Also note that in order for the instance-level checks to run, the view code should explicitly call **.check_object_permissions(request, obj)**. If you are using the generic views, then this will be handled for you by default. (Function-based views will need to check object permissions explicitly, raising **PermissionDenied** on failure.)

Custom permissions will raise a **PermissionDenied** exception if the test fails. To change the error message associated with the exception, implement a message attribute directly on your custom permission. Otherwise, the **default_detail** attribute from **PermissionDenied** will be used. Similarly, to change the code identifier associated with the exception, implement a code attribute directly on your custom permission; otherwise, the **default_code** attribute from **PermissionDenied** will be used.

Let's implement custom permissions into our project.

Go to chapter10_permissions/api/permissions.py and add the following lines of code:

```
class IsAdminOrReadOnly(permissions.IsAdminUser):

    def has_permission(self, request, view):
        if request.method in permissions.SAFE_METHODS:
            return True
        else:
            return bool(request.user and request.user.is_staff)

class IsReviewUserOrReadOnly(permissions.BasePermission):

    def has_object_permission(self, request, view, obj):
        if request.method in permissions.SAFE_METHODS:
            #Check permission for read-only request
            return True
        else:
            # Check permission for write request
            return obj.review_user == request.user or request.user.is_staff
```

In the above code, the **IsAdminOrReadOnly** permission class customizes DRF's IsAdminUser permission to allow safe (read-only) methods for all users while restricting unsafe (write) methods to admin users only.

The **IsReviewUserOrReadOnly** permission class is designed to allow read-only access to all users but restrict write access (e.g., updating or deleting) to the user who created the review (review_user) and admin users (users with is_staff status).

Go to chapter10_permissions/api/views.py and add the following lines of code:

```
# This view allows only admin users to create a watchlist
#remaining users only can get the list of movies.
class WatchlistCustomPermissionView(APIView):
    permission_classes = [IsAdminOrReadOnly]

    def get(self, request):
        movies = WatchList.objects.all()
        serializer = serializers.WatchListModelSerializer(movies,
        many=True)
        return Response(serializer.data)
```

```
    def post(self, request):
        serializer = serializers.WatchListModelSerializer(
        data=request.data)
        if serializer.is_valid():
            serializer.save()
            return Response(serializer.data)
        else:
            return Response(serializer.errors)

# This view prevents user from update/delete operations
# for non review users
class ReviewDetailCustomPermissionView(generics.
RetrieveUpdateDestroyAPIView):
    queryset = Review.objects.all()
    serializer_class = serializers.ReviewModelSerializer
    permission_classes = [IsReviewUserOrReadOnly]
```

Add the corresponding URL in chapter10_permissions/api/urls.py as below:

```
urlpatterns = [
    ...
    path('reviews/<int:pk>/', views.ReviewDetailCustomPermissionView.as_
    view(), name='review-detail'),
    path('watchlist/', views.WatchlistCustomPermissionView.as_view(),
    name='watchlist'),

    # Using ViewSet
    path("", include(router.urls)),
]
```

In the above code, **IsAdminOrReadOnly** permission is applied by assigning it to **permission_classes**. Since GET is a safe method, any authenticated user can access it, and only admin users (users with the **is_staff** status) can access this endpoint to add a new WatchList item. So, this permission enforces read-only access for regular users while allowing admin users to create or modify content.

The permission **IsReviewUserOrReadOnly** is applied to **ReviewDetailCustom PermissionView** by assigning to **permission_classes**. By using this permission, any user, authenticated or not, can view individual reviews. But only the user who created the review or an admin user can edit or delete the review.

Using custom permissions like **IsAdminOrReadOnly** and **IsReviewUserOrReadOnly** provides fine-grained control over who can view, add, or modify resources in the application.

Note that the generic views will check the appropriate object-level permissions, but if you're writing your own custom views, you'll need to make sure you check the object-level permission checks yourself. You can do so by calling **self.check_object_permissions(request, obj)** from the view once you have the object instance. This call will raise an appropriate **APIException** if any object-level permission checks fail and will otherwise simply return.

Also note that the generic views will only check the object-level permissions for views that retrieve a single model instance. If you require object-level filtering of list views, you'll need to filter the queryset separately.

Access Restriction Methods

REST Framework offers three different methods to customize access restrictions on a case-by-case basis. These apply in different scenarios and have different effects and limitations:

- **queryset/get_queryset():** Limits the general visibility of existing objects from the database. The queryset limits which objects will be listed and which objects can be modified or deleted. The get_queryset() method can apply different querysets based on the current action.
- **permission_classes/get_permissions():** General permission checks based on the current action, request, and targeted object. Object-level permissions can only be applied to retrieve, modify, and deletion actions. Permission checks for list and create will be applied to the entire object type. (In case of list: subject to restrictions in the queryset.)

- **serializer_class/get_serializer():** Instance-level restrictions that apply to all objects on input and output. The serializer may have access to the request context. The get_serializer() method can apply different serializers based on the current action.

The following table lists the access restriction methods and the level of control they offer over which actions.

	queryset	**permission_classes**	**serializer_class**
Action: list	global	global	object-level*
Action: create	no	global	object-level
Action: retrieve	Global	Object-level	Object-level
Action: update	Global	Object-level	Object-level
Action: partial_update	Global	Object-level	Object-level
Action: destroy	Global	Object-level	No
Can reference action in decision	No**	Yes	No**
Can reference request in decision	No**	Yes	Yes

** A Serializer class should not raise PermissionDenied in a list action, or the entire list would not be returned.** The get_*() methods have access to the current view and can return different Serializer or QuerySet instances based on the request or action.*

CHAPTER 11

Caching

Caching is the process of storing data in memory, typically for a limited period, so that it can be quickly retrieved when needed instead of fetching it again from its original source. In Django REST Framework (DRF), **caching** is a technique used to store the results of expensive database queries, computations, or entire API responses temporarily, so subsequent requests for the same data can be served faster. By caching data, DRF reduces database load, improves response times, and enhances overall application performance, especially in read-heavy applications.

Preparing for This Chapter

Create a new app with the name **chapter11_caching** with the steps specified in the **Project Setup** section in Chapter 3.

Go to drfproject/settings.py and add the following lines of code:

```
INSTALLED_APPS = [
    ...
    "chapter11_caching",
]
```

Go to chapter11_caching/api/serializers.py and add the following lines of code:

```
from rest_framework import serializers
from chapter3_project_setup.models import WatchList

class WatchListModelSerializer(serializers.ModelSerializer):
    class Meta:
        model = WatchList
        fields = "__all__"
        ref_name = 'C11WatchListModelSerializer'
```


G. Patil, *Django REST APIs Demystified*, https://doi.org/10.1007/979-8-8688-1850-9_11

Go to chapter11_caching/api/views.py and add the following lines of code:

```
from rest_framework import viewsets
from rest_framework.authentication import TokenAuthentication
from rest_framework.permissions import IsAuthenticated
from rest_framework.throttling import UserRateThrottle, AnonRateThrottle,
ScopedRateThrottle
from chapter3_project_setup.models import WatchList, StreamPlatform, Review
from chapter12_throttling.api import serializers
```

Go to chapter11_caching/api/urls.py and add the following lines of code:

```
from django.urls import path, include
from rest_framework.routers import DefaultRouter
from . import views

urlpatterns = [

    # Using ViewSet
    path("", include(router.urls)),
]
```

Go to drfproject/urls.py and add the following lines of code:

```
urlpatterns = [
    ...
    path('api/chapter11_caching/', include('chapter11_caching.api.urls')),
]
```

To enable caching, configure Django's caching settings in your project's settings.py file. For instance, you can use in-memory caching for local development or a cache back end like Redis or Memcached for production.

Go to drfproject/settings.py and add the following lines of code:

```
CACHES = {
    'default': {
```

```
        'BACKEND': 'django.core.cache.backends.locmem.LocMemCache',
        # In-memory caching
        'LOCATION': 'unique-snowflake',
    }
}
```

This configures in-memory caching.

There are several types of caching available in DRF. Let's go through them.

View-Level Caching

View-level caching in Django REST Framework (DRF) is a method of caching the entire response of a view. When a view is cached, any request to that view with the same parameters retrieves the response from the cache rather than regenerating it by querying the database or performing other expensive operations. This is especially helpful for views that return frequently accessed data that does not change often, allowing faster response times and reduced server load.

How View-Level Caching Works

- **Entire Response Cache**: When a request is made to a cached view, the entire response (including HTTP headers and body) is saved in the cache.
- **Cache Duration**: The cached response is stored for a specified amount of time (known as the cache timeout). Once this time expires, the cache is cleared, and the next request regenerates the view response.
- **Keyed by URL and Parameters**: Each cached response is stored with a unique cache key based on the request's URL and any query parameters, ensuring that only identical requests retrieve the same cached response.

Applying the @cache_page Decorator

You can apply view-level caching to both function-based views and class-based views in DRF using Django's **@cache_page** decorator from django.views.decorators.cache

1) Class-Based View Example

With class-based views, you use Django's **method_decorator** to apply **@cache_page** to specific HTTP methods (like get or post) or to the entire view.

Go to chapter11_caching/api/views.py and add the following lines of code:

```
class WatchlistCachingView(viewsets.ModelViewSet):
    authentication_classes = [TokenAuthentication,]
    permission_classes = [IsAuthenticated]  # Ensure that the user is
    authenticated
    queryset = WatchList.objects.all()
    serializer_class = serializers.WatchListModelSerializer

    @method_decorator(cache_page(60 * 15))  # Cache for 15 minutes
    def list(self, request, *args, **kwargs):
        return super().list(request, *args, **kwargs)

    @method_decorator(cache_page(60 * 15))  # Cache for 15 minutes
    def retrieve(self, request, *args, **kwargs):
        return super().retrieve(request, *args, **kwargs)
```

Add the corresponding URL in chapter11_caching/api/urls.py as below:

```
router = DefaultRouter()
# Using ViewSet
router.register(r"watchlist-caching", views.WatchlistCachingView,
basename="watchlist-caching")
```

In this WatchlistCachingView example, view-level caching is applied to the list and retrieve methods of a ModelViewSet class-based view in Django REST Framework (DRF). The decorator @method_decorator(cache_page(60 * 15)) is applied to the list and retrieve methods, caching the responses for each of these methods for **15 minutes**. cache_page(60 * 15) tells Django to store the response for **15 minutes** (900 seconds). During this time, subsequent requests to these methods will return the cached response, skipping the usual query to the database and reducing response time.

By caching the list and retrieve views, this setup minimizes the frequency of database queries. Instead of fetching WatchList data on every request, Django serves the cached response for each cached URL. Caching is specific to the list and retrieve actions, allowing other actions (e.g., create, update, delete) to remain uncached and function without cache interference.

2) Function-Based View Example

A similar concept of caching can be applied to function-based views.

Go to chapter11_caching/api/views.py and add the following lines of code:

```
# List View for WatchList with 15 minutes caching
@api_view(['GET'])
@authentication_classes([TokenAuthentication])
@permission_classes([IsAuthenticated])
@cache_page(60 * 15)  # Cache for 15 minutes
def watchlist_list_view(request):
    queryset = WatchList.objects.all()
    serializer = serializers.WatchListModelSerializer(queryset, many=True)
    return Response(serializer.data)

# Retrieve View for WatchList with 15 minutes caching
@api_view(['GET'])
@authentication_classes([TokenAuthentication])
@permission_classes([IsAuthenticated])
@cache_page(60 * 15)  # Cache for 15 minutes
def watchlist_detail_view(request, pk):
    try:
        watchlist_item = WatchList.objects.get(pk=pk)
    except WatchList.DoesNotExist:
        return Response({"error": "WatchList item not found"},
        status=status.HTTP_404_NOT_FOUND)

    serializer = serializers.WatchListModelSerializer(watchlist_item)
    return Response(serializer.data)
```

Add the corresponding URL in chapter11_caching/api/urls.py as below:

```
urlpatterns = [
    path(r"watchlist-list", views.watchlist_list_view),
    path(r"watchlist-list/<int:pk>/", views.watchlist_detail_view),
    ...
]
```

In both function-based and class-based views, the cache will automatically expire 15 minutes after it is created. After expiry, the next request to that endpoint will generate a fresh cache. Since caching here does not automatically invalidate when data changes (like creating or updating WatchList entries), this setup is best for use cases where data is either infrequently modified or where slight staleness is acceptable.

Low-Level Caching (Custom Caching in Views or Functions)

Sometimes, caching an entire view isn't efficient. You might want to cache only specific data or computations within the view. Django's low-level cache API allows this. With low-level caching, you can selectively cache only specific parts of a view's data. You're not restricted to caching the entire view response, which allows for more efficient cache use, especially when only parts of the data are expensive to retrieve or process. You can also set custom expiration times for different types of data, depending on how frequently that data changes, giving you a better balance between data freshness and performance.

Low-level caching is ideal when

- You need control over individual data fragments rather than entire views.
- Specific data requires distinct expiration times or cache keys.
- Manual cache refresh or conditional cache usage is required based on certain events or triggers.

Let's implement low-level caching for our project.

Go to chapter11_caching/api/views.py and add the following lines of code:

```
from django.core.cache import cache

#low level caching
class WatchLowLevelCachingView(APIView):
```

```
    def get(self, request):
        cached_data = cache.get("watchlist_data")
        if not cached_data:
            # Expensive database query or operation
            queryset = WatchList.objects.all()
            serializer = serializers.WatchListModelSerializer(queryset,
            many=True)
            cached_data = serializer.data
            cache.set("watchlist_data", cached_data, timeout=60*15)
        return Response(cached_data)
```

Add the corresponding URL in chapter11_caching/api/urls.py as below:

```
urlpatterns = [
    ...
    path(r"watchlist-lowlevelcaching", views.WatchLowLevelCachingView.
    as_view()),
]
```

In the above code, the **cache.get("watchlist_data")** method tries to retrieve the cached watchlist_data from the cache store. If watchlist_data is **not in the cache** (meaning this is either the first request or the cache has expired), the code retrieves data from the database and stores it in the cache. After fetching the data from the database, the set method stores watchlist_data in the cache with a **15-minute expiration** (900 seconds) using **cache.set("watchlist_data", cached_data, timeout=60*15)**. This makes the data available in the cache for any subsequent requests within the next 15 minutes.

You can also apply a similar concept of low-level caching strategy at the object level as well. Go to chapter11_caching/api/views.py and add the following lines of code:

```
class WatchListObjectLevelCachingView(APIView):
    def get(self, request, pk):
        cache_key = f"watchlist_{pk}"
        cached_data = cache.get(cache_key)
        if not cached_data:
            try:
                watchlist_item = WatchList.objects.get(pk=pk)
```

```
                cached_data = serializers.WatchListModelSerializer(watchli
                st_item).data
                cache.set(cache_key, cached_data, timeout=60*15)
            except WatchList.DoesNotExist:
                return Response(status=status.HTTP_404_NOT_FOUND)
        return Response(cached_data)
```

Add the corresponding URL in the file chapter11_caching/api/urls.py as below:

```
urlpatterns = [
    ...
    path(r"watchlist-objectlevelcaching/<int:pk>/", views.
    WatchListObjectLevelCachingView.as_view()),
]
```

In the above code, the view creates a **unique cache key** for each WatchList item based on its primary key (pk) value. For instance, if the primary key is 5, the cache key will be "watchlist_5". This allows caching each item separately, enabling the cache to be applied specifically to each unique object. Each item's data is cached independently, meaning requests for frequently accessed objects are served directly from the cache rather than hitting the database.

Limitations and Considerations

- **Cache Staleness**: Since cached data does not automatically update when the database changes, the cache may serve outdated data. This setup is ideal when changes to WatchList data are infrequent or slight data staleness is acceptable.
- **Manual Invalidation**: If data updates frequently, consider adding a mechanism to invalidate the cache manually after changes (e.g., updating or deleting WatchList objects).

This caching strategy is useful for caching large or frequently accessed data at a low level, giving precise control over cache storage and expiration, especially when caching at the view level is too restrictive.

Cache Invalidation

Caching needs to be carefully managed to ensure data consistency. Invalidation refers to updating or deleting the cache when the underlying data changes.

- **Automatic Invalidation**: Set the cache timeout for each cached item, so it's automatically refreshed after a set period.
- **Manual Invalidation**: Use cache functions to delete or update cache entries when necessary.

Use the following approach to clear the cache:

```
cache.delete("watchlist_data")  # Deletes specific cache entry
cache.clear()  # Clears all cache entries
```

DRF Cache Mixins

In Django Rest Framework (DRF), cache mixins provide a way to easily add caching functionality to views without manually adding caching code in every method. They offer a streamlined approach to enable caching, particularly useful for list and detail views. Let's walk through how this works with an example using the WatchList model.

Let's create a file chapter11_caching/api/mixins.py and add the following lines of code:

```
from django.core.cache import cache

class CacheMixin:
    cache_timeout = 60 * 15  # 15 minutes timeout

    def get_cached_response(self, cache_key, queryset):
        cached_data = cache.get(cache_key)
        if not cached_data:
            cached_data = queryset
            cache.set(cache_key, cached_data, timeout=self.cache_timeout)
        return cached_data
```

Using the above CacheMixin, we can create a caching mechanism for views in Django and Django Rest Framework (DRF) by caching specific querysets. This mixin provides a simple way to check if a queryset is already cached and retrieve it from the cache or otherwise set it if it doesn't exist.

In a WatchList API view, we can use this CacheMixin to cache the list of all WatchList objects and an individual WatchList object by ID. Let's apply this to two views: a list view and a detail view.

Go to chapter11_caching/api/views.py and add the following lines of code:

```
from chapter11_caching.api.mixins import CacheMixin

class WatchListCacheMixinListView(CacheMixin, APIView):
    def get(self, request):
        cache_key = "watchlist_all"  # Define a unique cache key for the
        list view
        queryset = self.get_cached_response(cache_key, WatchList.
        objects.all())
        serializer = serializers.WatchListModelSerializer(queryset,
        many=True)
        return Response(serializer.data)

class WatchListCacheMixinDetailView(CacheMixin, APIView):
    def get(self, request, pk):
        cache_key = f"watchlist_{pk}"  # Define a unique cache key per
        watchlist object
        try:
            queryset = self.get_cached_response(
                cache_key, WatchList.objects.get(pk=pk)
            )
        except WatchList.DoesNotExist:
            return Response(
                {"error": "WatchList item not found"}, status=status.
                HTTP_404_NOT_FOUND
            )
        serializer = serializers.WatchListModelSerializer(queryset)
        return Response(serializer.data)
```

Create a corresponding URL in the file chapter11_caching/api/urls.py as below:

```
urlpatterns = [
    ...
    path(r"watchlist-cachemixinlist", views.WatchListCacheMixinListView.
    as_view()),
    path(r"watchlist-cachemixinlist/<int:pk>/", views.
    WatchListCacheMixinDetailView.as_view()),
    ...
]
```

The CacheMixin can be reused across different views, simplifying cache management. Each view can define its own cache keys, allowing for targeted caching and cache invalidation when needed.

vary_on_headers

In Django, **vary_on_headers** is used to cache different versions of a response based on specific request headers. This is particularly useful when you want to cache different responses for different users or based on custom request headers (e.g., Authorization headers in an API). In Django Rest Framework (DRF), this can help manage caching efficiently when responses vary based on user authentication or other criteria sent in headers.

Go to chapter11_caching/api/views.py and add the following lines of code:

```
from django.views.decorators.vary import vary_on_headers

class WatchListVaryOnHeaderCacheView(APIView):
    permission_classes = [IsAuthenticated]  # Only authenticated users
    can access

    # Apply caching for 15 minutes and vary based on Authorization header
    @method_decorator(cache_page(60 * 15))  # Cache response for 15 minutes
    @method_decorator(vary_on_headers("Authorization"))
    def get(self, request):
        # Cache key is created internally by cache_page; varying on
        Authorization
```

```
        watchlist_items = WatchList.objects.all()
        serializer = serializers.WatchListModelSerializer(watchlist_items,
        many=True)
        return Response(serializer.data)
```

Create a corresponding URL in the file chapter11_caching/api/urls.py as below:

```
urlpatterns = [
    ...
    path(r"watchlist-varyonheadercache", views.
    WatchListVaryOnHeaderCacheView.as_view()),

    # Using ViewSet
    path("", include(router.urls)),
]
```

In the above code, vary_on_headers("Authorization") tells Django to cache separate versions of the response based on the value of the Authorization header.

Additional Notes

- **Other Headers**: You can vary based on other headers as well, such as Accept-Language, User-Agent, etc.
- **Cache Storage and Size**: Make sure that your cache storage (e.g., Redis, Memcached) has sufficient memory, as varying by headers can increase the number of cache entries significantly.
- **Combining with Low-Level Cache**: For even more granular control, consider combining vary_on_headers with low-level cache management using Django's cache.get and cache.set functions if you need to manually define and manage cache keys.

vary_on_cookie

In Django, @vary_on_cookie is a decorator that allows caching to vary based on the presence or value of a cookie. This is useful when you want to cache different responses for users based on their authentication status or specific cookie values, allowing more personalized caching.

Go to chapter11_caching/api/views.py and add the following lines of code:

```
from django.views.decorators.vary import vary_on_cookie
class WatchListVaryOnCookieCacheView(APIView):
    # Apply caching for 15 minutes and vary based on the user's
    session cookie
    @method_decorator(cache_page(60 * 15))  # Cache response for 15 minutes
    @method_decorator(vary_on_cookie)
    def get(self, request):
        # This will cache separate responses for each unique cookie value
        watchlist_items = WatchList.objects.all()
        serializer = serializers.WatchListModelSerializer(watchlist_items,
        many=True)
        return Response(serializer.data)
```

Add the corresponding URL in the file chapter11_caching/api/urls.py as below:

```
urlpatterns = [
    ...
    path(r"watchlist-varyoncookiecache", views.
    WatchListVaryOnCookieCacheView.as_view()),

    # Using ViewSet
    path("", include(router.urls)),
]
```

By using vary_on_cookie, Django will cache separate versions of the response for each unique cookie value, such as a user's session cookie.

This is particularly useful for

- Differentiating between authenticated and anonymous users
- Providing user-specific data when cookies affect the view's output

In this case, each user session gets its own cached response, so personalized content (e.g., user-specific recommendations) remains consistent across requests from the same session but won't be shared with other users.

Additional Notes

- **Use Cases**: vary_on_cookie is most useful when the response changes based on the user's session or a specific cookie (e.g., for authentication or localization).
- **Performance Impact**: Like with vary_on_headers, using vary_on_cookie can increase the number of cached entries since each unique cookie value creates a separate cache entry. It's best used when you have sufficient cache memory available.
- **Testing**: If you're testing this locally, ensure your browser or client sends a session or custom cookie, or consider using Django's session middleware to set session cookies automatically.

CHAPTER 12

Throttling

In today's digital age, managing traffic to your API is crucial for maintaining its performance and security. Whether you're dealing with a high-traffic API or simply want to prevent abuse, throttling can be an effective way to control the flow of requests.

In Django Rest Framework (DRF), throttling is a mechanism to control the rate of requests that a client can make to an API. It helps prevent abuse by limiting the number of requests a user, IP address, or any client can make within a specified time period. Throttling is especially useful in APIs to mitigate issues like excessive traffic, DoS attacks, or overuse of resources.

Throttling is similar to permissions in that it determines if a request should be authorized. Throttles indicate a temporary state and are used to control the rate of requests that clients can make to an API.

As with permissions, multiple throttles may be used. Your API might have a restrictive throttle for unauthenticated requests and a less restrictive throttle for authenticated requests.

Another scenario where you might want to use multiple throttles would be if you need to impose different constraints on different parts of the API, due to some services being particularly resource intensive.

Multiple throttles can also be used if you want to impose both burst throttling rates and sustained throttling rates. For example, you might want to limit a user to a maximum of 60 requests per minute and 1000 requests per day.

Throttles do not necessarily only refer to rate-limiting requests. For example, a storage service might also need to throttle against bandwidth, and a paid data service might want to throttle against a certain number of records being accessed.

Throttling in DRF is not intended as a primary line of defense against malicious activities like **brute force attacks** or **denial-of-service (DoS) attacks**. While throttling helps control the number of requests, it isn't a foolproof security mechanism.

G. Patil, *Django REST APIs Demystified*, https://doi.org/10.1007/979-8-8688-1850-9_12

Determined attackers may bypass these restrictions by **spoofing IP addresses** or using other techniques to evade detection. Therefore, throttling should be complemented with other security measures such as firewalls, rate limiting at the infrastructure level, and more comprehensive security monitoring. DRF's throttling implementation relies on **Django's cache framework** to keep track of request counts for different clients. The use of caching means that throttling is **not atomic** (i.e., not transactional or fully consistent at every exact moment). As a result, there may be some **"fuzziness"** or slight inconsistencies in how throttling limits are enforced, especially in high-traffic situations. For example, a user might be able to slightly exceed the set limits before throttling kicks in due to nonatomic cache operations. The primary goal of DRF's built-in throttling is to enable the implementation of **business logic policies** for controlling API usage. For example, it can support features like **tiered rate limits** for different user plans or **basic protection** against overuse of an API. It is more suited to **controlling resource usage** and **ensuring fair access** rather than acting as a hardened security layer. This is very important because, if you are building a public-facing API, it's important to understand that DRF throttling is a **convenience and policy enforcement tool** rather than a security guarantee. Relying solely on DRF throttling could leave your application exposed to sophisticated attacks. This also required ensuring comprehensive protection and combining application-level throttling with **network-level controls** (like load balancers, IP whitelisting/blacklisting) and **rate-limiting strategies** at the API gateway or infrastructure level.

Why Use Throttling?

Throttling is helpful for

1. **Preventing Abuse**: Limiting the number of requests reduces the risk of overload and ensures the API is not overwhelmed by high-traffic users or bots.

2. **Improving Performance**: By managing request rates, throttling helps ensure a more stable response time and resource usage across the application.

3. **Fair Access**: Throttling ensures fair usage of resources by allowing all users to access the API within reasonable limits.

Types of Throttling in DRF

DRF provides several built-in throttling classes, each with different throttling strategies:

1. **AnonRateThrottle**: Limits requests from anonymous users
2. **UserRateThrottle**: Limits requests from authenticated users
3. **ScopedRateThrottle**: Allows throttling to be applied on a per-view or per-viewset basis

You can define custom throttling classes to implement more complex throttling strategies as well.

AnonRateThrottle

The AnonRateThrottle class in Django REST Framework (DRF) is used to throttle requests for unauthenticated users. This mechanism is useful when you want to limit access to your API for users who are not logged in or otherwise unidentified.

Key Features of AnonRateThrottle

1. **Applies to Unauthenticated Users Only**
   - The AnonRateThrottle is specifically designed to restrict the number of requests coming from unauthenticated sources. This helps prevent overuse or abuse of your API by unknown clients, such as bots or unregistered users.
   - If a user is authenticated (typically by using a token or session-based authentication), this throttle class does not apply.
2. **Throttling Mechanism Using IP Address**
   - For unauthenticated users, a unique key is generated based on the IP address of the incoming request. This key is used to track and count the number of requests made by that particular IP address within a given time window.

- If the number of requests from the IP exceeds the allowed limit within the specified time frame, further requests are blocked until the limit resets.

3. **Determining the Allowed Request Rate**

   The allowed rate of requests for AnonRateThrottle can be set in one of two ways:

   1. **By Overriding the Rate Property on the Class**

      You can create a custom throttling class by subclassing AnonRateThrottle and setting a custom rate property.

```
from rest_framework.throttling import AnonRateThrottle

class CustomAnonRateThrottle(AnonRateThrottle):
    rate = '10/minute'  # Set a custom rate limit
```

   2. **Through Global Settings**

      The DEFAULT_THROTTLE_RATES['anon'] setting in your DRF configuration can define a default rate limit for all uses of AnonRateThrottle. This setting is defined in the settings.py file of your project:

```
REST_FRAMEWORK = {
    'DEFAULT_THROTTLE_RATES': {
        'anon': '5/minute',  # Allow 5 requests per minute for
        unauthenticated users
    }
}
```

      The rate can be specified using a format like '5/minute', '100/hour', etc., where you can control the number of allowed requests and the time window.

4. **Use Case for AnonRateThrottle**

   If your API is publicly accessible, using AnonRateThrottle helps protect your endpoints from abuse by limiting how frequently unauthenticated users can make requests. This is particularly useful for preventing denial-of-service attacks, scraping, or excessive API calls from untrusted sources.

Example Scenario

Suppose you have an ecommerce API that provides product data, and you want to allow unauthenticated users to view up to ten product requests per minute. By applying AnonRateThrottle with a rate of '10/minute', any unauthenticated user exceeding that limit will receive a "429 Too Many Requests" response until their quota resets.

This helps maintain the availability and performance of your API for legitimate users while also protecting it from potential abuse or unexpected traffic spikes.

UserRateThrottle

The UserRateThrottle class in Django REST Framework (DRF) is used to limit the number of API requests that a single user can make over a specified time period. This throttle class is useful for implementing global rate limits on a per-user basis, thereby ensuring that individual users don't overwhelm the system with excessive requests.

Key Features of UserRateThrottle

1. **Per-User Request Limiting**

   - The UserRateThrottle uses the user's unique identifier (such as user.id or username) to generate a key for throttling purposes. This ensures that each authenticated user is subject to a separate rate limit.
   - For unauthenticated users, it falls back to using the incoming request's IP address as the key to identify and throttle requests.

2. **Customizing the Allowed Request Rate**

   You can configure the allowed request rate using either of the following methods:

   1. **Class-Level Rate Property**

      You can create a custom throttling class by subclassing UserRateThrottle and specifying the rate property.

      ```
      from rest_framework.throttling import UserRateThrottle

      class CustomUserRateThrottle(UserRateThrottle):
          rate = '5/hour'  # Limit to 5 requests per hour per user
      ```

   2. **Global Settings Using a Scope**

      You can define default throttle rates for users using the DEFAULT_THROTTLE_RATES setting in your project's configuration.

      For example:

      ```
      REST_FRAMEWORK = {
          'DEFAULT_THROTTLE_RATES': {
              'user': '10/minute'  # Allow 10 requests per minute for
              each user
          }
      }
      ```

      The rate is specified in the form of "requests/time_window", where you can define different rates for different scopes or specific use cases.

   3. **Multiple Throttle Classes**

      An API can have multiple instances of UserRateThrottle in use simultaneously. This is achieved by creating custom throttle classes with different scope attributes. Each scope represents a different rate limit, enabling finer control over request limits.

For example:

```
from rest_framework.throttling import UserRateThrottle

class BurstRateThrottle(UserRateThrottle):
    scope = 'burst'

class SustainedRateThrottle(UserRateThrottle):
    scope = 'sustained'
```

In this case, you would configure the rate limits for the different scopes in the settings file:

```
REST_FRAMEWORK = {
    'DEFAULT_THROTTLE_CLASSES': [
        'path.to.BurstRateThrottle',
        'path.to.SustainedRateThrottle',
    ],
    'DEFAULT_THROTTLE_RATES': {
        'burst': '60/min',     # Allow up to 60 requests per
        minute for burst requests
        'sustained': '1000/day'  # Allow up to 1000 requests per
        day for sustained usage
    }
}
```

This configuration enables you to enforce different limits for “bursty” behavior (like rapid interactions over a short period) versus “sustained” long-term interactions over a day.

Example Scenario

UserRateThrottle is effective in scenarios where you want to limit the overall API usage per user. This can be especially important for ensuring fair usage of your API, preventing abuse, and maintaining API availability for legitimate users.

For example, you might want to limit a free tier of users to a certain number of requests per day while allowing premium users to have a higher limit or no limit at all.

ScopedRateThrottle

The ScopedRateThrottle in Django REST Framework (DRF) is a throttling mechanism used to apply specific rate limits to different parts of an API based on a defined scope. This allows fine-grained control over which parts of the API should be throttled and how strictly they should be throttled. Here's how it works, with a breakdown of the example you've provided.

How ScopedRateThrottle Works

- **Throttle Scopes**: The ScopedRateThrottle applies rate limiting based on a throttle_scope property defined in the view classes. The throttle_scope serves as a unique identifier for the scope of requests being handled.
- **Throttle Keys**: The throttle key is formed by combining the throttle_scope with a unique identifier for the user (like the user ID) or the request's IP address for unauthenticated users.
- **Rate Configuration**: The request rate for each scope is configured using the DEFAULT_THROTTLE_RATES setting in your project's settings. Each scope can have its own rate limit, making it easy to create different levels of throttling across your API.

Example Explanation

```
# Consider the provided example:
class WatchlistListView (APIView):
    throttle_scope = 'watchlists'
    ...

class WatchlistDetailView (APIView):
    throttle_scope = 'watchlists'
    ...

class StreamPlatformView(APIView):
    throttle_scope = 'streamplatforms'
    ...
```

The **WatchlistListView and WatchlistDetailView** views are assigned the throttle_ scope = 'watchlists'. This means that requests made to either view will count toward the same throttling limit. This scope can be useful if you want to limit how frequently a user can access any "watchlist-related" functionality.

The **StreamPlatformView** view has its own scope: throttle_scope = 'streamplatforms'. Requests to this view will be throttled independently of the requests to the streamplatforms scope.

Configuration in Settings

```
REST_FRAMEWORK = {
    'DEFAULT_THROTTLE_CLASSES': [
        'rest_framework.throttling.ScopedRateThrottle',
    ],
    'DEFAULT_THROTTLE_RATES': {
        watchlists: '1000/day',
        'streamplatforms': '20/day'
    }
}
```

Throttle Rates

- watchlists: '1000/day'—Users are allowed up to 1000 requests per day to views using the watchlists scope.
- streamplatforms: '20/day'—Users are allowed up to 20 requests per day to views using the streamplatforms scope.

Use Cases

- **Fine-Grained Control**: ScopedRateThrottle is ideal for applying different rate limits to various API views or endpoints. This is useful for controlling API usage based on the function of the endpoint.
- **Shared Throttling Limits**: By using the same throttle_scope across multiple views (as shown with ContactListView and ContactDetailView), you can enforce a shared throttling policy. For example, it can prevent abuse of "contact-related" endpoints, even if multiple routes are exposed for accessing contact data.

- **Isolated Limits**: You can isolate specific functionality with separate throttling rules. For example, uploads have a much lower limit than contacts in the example, which may reflect a business rule where file uploads are more resource-intensive and require stricter control.

Practical Benefits

- **Protect Critical Resources**: Scoped throttling can prevent specific API endpoints from being overwhelmed, ensuring fair usage of critical resources.
- **Different Policies per Endpoint**: You can set stricter limits for sensitive or resource-intensive operations, such as file uploads, while applying more lenient policies to general data retrieval operations.
- **Flexible Rate Management**: Changing the rate limits is as simple as updating the DEFAULT_THROTTLE_RATES configuration, giving you flexibility to adapt your throttling strategy based on user demand, system resources, or business requirements.

Preparing for This Chapter

Create a new app with the name **chapter12_throttling** with the steps specified in the **Project Setup** section in Chapter 3.

Go to drfproject/settings.py and the following lines of code:

```
INSTALLED_APPS = [
    ...
    "chapter12_throttling",
]
```

Go to chapter12_throttling/api/serializers.py and add the following lines of code:

```
from rest_framework import serializers
from chapter3_project_setup.models import WatchList, StreamPlatform, Review

class WatchListModelSerializer(serializers.ModelSerializer):
```

```
    class Meta:
        model = WatchList
        fields = "__all__"
        ref_name = 'C13WatchListModelSerializer'

class StreamPlatformModelSerializer(serializers.ModelSerializer):
    class Meta:
        model = StreamPlatform
        fields = "__all__"
        ref_name = 'C13StreamPlatformModelSerializer'

class ReviewModelSerializer(serializers.ModelSerializer):
    user = serializers.StringRelatedField()
    class Meta:
        model = Review
        fields = "__all__"
        ref_name = 'C13ReviewModelSerializer'
```

Go to chapter12_throttling/api/views.py and add the following lines of code:

```
from rest_framework import viewsets
from rest_framework.authentication import TokenAuthentication
from rest_framework.permissions import IsAuthenticated
from rest_framework.throttling import UserRateThrottle, AnonRateThrottle,
ScopedRateThrottle
from chapter3_project_setup.models import WatchList, StreamPlatform, Review
from chapter12_throttling.api import serializers
```

Go to chapter12_throttling/api/urls.py and add the following lines of code:

```
from django.urls import path, include
from rest_framework.routers import DefaultRouter
from . import views

urlpatterns = [

    # Using ViewSet
    path("", include(router.urls)),
]
```

Go to drfproject/urls.py and add the following lines of code:

```
urlpatterns = [
    ...
    path('api/chapter12_throttling/', include('chapter12_throttling.api.
    urls')),
]
```

How Throttling Is Determined

As with permissions and authentication, throttling in REST Framework is always defined as a list of classes. Before running the main body of the view, each throttle in the list is checked. If any throttle check fails, an **exceptions.Throttled** exception will be raised, and the main body of the view will not run.

How Clients Are Identified

DRF uses the **X-Forwarded-For** HTTP header and REMOTE_ADDR WSGI variable to uniquely identify client IP addresses for applying throttling rules. If the X-Forwarded-For header is present in the incoming request, it will be preferred and used for identifying the client. If the X-Forwarded-For header is absent, DRF falls back to using the value of the REMOTE_ADDR variable from the WSGI environment, which contains the IP address of the client connecting to the server.

The X-Forwarded-For header is commonly added by proxies and load balancers to preserve the original client's IP address. It often contains a comma-separated list of IP addresses, where the first IP is typically the originating client's IP, followed by intermediate proxy IP addresses.

The NUM_PROXIES is a setting used to determine how many proxy layers are present between the client and the server. If NUM_PROXIES is set to a value greater than zero, the API will identify the client IP as the last IP in the X-Forwarded-For header, after excluding the IP addresses of the configured number of proxies. If NUM_PROXIES is set to zero, the REMOTE_ADDR variable is used as the identifying IP address without considering any proxies or X-Forwarded-For values. Setting the NUM_PROXIES correctly is important if your application is behind multiple layers of reverse proxies, as it ensures that you correctly identify and throttle unique client requests instead of treating all requests as coming from a shared proxy.

If NUM_PROXIES is configured and many clients connect from behind a Network Address Translation (NAT) gateway (e.g., an ISP, corporate network), then all those clients will be treated as a single client based on their shared IP in the X-Forwarded-For header. This behavior can lead to throttling applied at the network level rather than for individual clients, which may not be desirable for some use cases.

Correctly identifying the client IP address ensures accurate rate limiting, preventing scenarios where a shared IP (e.g., from a corporate network or ISP) is mistakenly throttled as a single client. Proper configuration is particularly important when your application is behind a reverse proxy or load balancer (e.g., AWS ELB, Cloudflare). For public APIs, this configuration can prevent abuse from individual users while not mistakenly throttling all users behind common gateways.

Suppose you have NUM_PROXIES set to 2, and the X-Forwarded-For header contains 192.0.2.1, 198.51.100.101, and 203.0.113.5:

- The first two IPs (192.0.2.1 and 198.51.100.101) represent the proxy layers.
- The actual client IP is 203.0.113.5, which will be used for throttling decisions.

This setting ensures that applications behind proxies can still apply fine-grained throttling and other policies without being impacted by the intermediate network infrastructure. Proper configuration is critical for ensuring that throttling logic behaves correctly in different deployment environments.

Setting Up the Cache

The throttle classes provided by Django REST Framework (DRF), such as **AnonRateThrottle** and **UserRateThrottle**, rely on Django's caching framework to track the number of requests made by each user or client over a given period. This cache is essential for storing the request counts and managing throttling efficiently.

Cache Back End in DRF

- **Default Cache Back End (LocMemCache)**

  By default, DRF uses Django's LocMemCache, which is a simple, in-memory cache. This back end works well for development and small-scale applications, where the cache doesn't need to be shared between different instances or servers.

  The LocMemCache is not persistent, meaning the cache data will be cleared when the application restarts, and it is not suitable for production in multi-server environments.

- **Custom Cache Back End**

  In production or for more complex use cases, you may want to use a distributed cache, such as Redis or Memcached. These caches can persist data across restarts and can be shared among multiple application instances, ensuring that throttling data remains consistent.

If you want to use a cache back end other than the default, you can configure your throttle classes to use a specific cache back end by specifying the cache attribute.

Example of Custom Throttle Class with Custom Cache

Here is an example where we define a custom throttle class that uses a different cache back end, specifically using a cache named 'alternate':

```
from rest_framework.throttling import AnonRateThrottle
from django.core.cache import caches

# Define a custom throttle class
class CustomAnonRateThrottle(AnonRateThrottle):
    # Set the cache attribute to use a specific cache backend ('alternate')
    cache = caches['alternate']  # Replace with your actual cache
    configuration
```

In the above example:

- The class CustomAnonRateThrottle inherits from AnonRateThrottle.
- The cache attribute is overridden to use the 'alternate' cache, which is defined in Django's cache settings.

Configuring the Cache in settings.py

To ensure that your custom cache back end works, you need to configure it in the settings.py file of your Django project. For example, you could configure a Redis cache back end as follows:

```
# settings.py

# Use Redis for caching
CACHES = {
    'default': {
        'BACKEND': 'django.core.cache.backends.locmem.LocMemCache',
        'TIMEOUT': 60 * 15,  # Cache timeout (15 minutes)
    },
    'alternate': {
        'BACKEND': 'django_redis.cache.RedisCache',
        'LOCATION': 'redis://127.0.0.1:6379/1',  # Redis server URL
        'OPTIONS': {
            'CLIENT_CLASS': 'django_redis.client.DefaultClient',
        },
    },
}
```

In this configuration:

- The default cache is still using LocMemCache.
- The alternate cache is configured to use Redis, with the connection URL specified (redis://127.0.0.1:6379/1).

You'll need to remember to also set your custom throttle class in the 'DEFAULT_THROTTLE_CLASSES' settings key or use the throttle_classes view attribute.

Setting Up Throttling in DRF

To enable throttling in DRF, you need to

- Set up the default throttling classes in your Django settings.
- Define the rate limit for each throttling class.

Go to drfproject/settings.py and add the following lines of code:

```
REST_FRAMEWORK = {
    ...
    'DEFAULT_THROTTLE_CLASSES': [
        'rest_framework.throttling.AnonRateThrottle',
        'rest_framework.throttling.UserRateThrottle',
    ],
    'DEFAULT_THROTTLE_RATES': {
        'anon': '5/day',       # 5 requests per day for anonymous users
        'user': '10/day',      # 10 requests per day for authenticated users
    },
}
```

Now we can apply throttling to views.

Go to chapter12_throttling/api/views.py and add the following lines of code:

```
class WatchlistThrottlingView(viewsets.ModelViewSet):
    authentication_classes = [TokenAuthentication,]
    permission_classes = [IsAuthenticated]  # Ensure that the user is
    authenticated
    queryset = WatchList.objects.all()
    serializer_class = serializers.WatchListModelSerializer
    throttle_classes = [UserRateThrottle, AnonRateThrottle]

class StreamPlatformThrottlingView(viewsets.ModelViewSet):
    queryset = StreamPlatform.objects.all()
    serializer_class = serializers.StreamPlatformModelSerializer
    throttle_classes = [UserRateThrottle, AnonRateThrottle]
```

Go to chapter12_throttling/api/urls.py and add the following lines of code:

```
router = DefaultRouter()
# Using ViewSet
router.register(r"watchlist-throttling", views.WatchlistThrottlingView,
basename="watchlist-throttling")
router.register(r"streamplatform-throttling", views.
StreamPlatformThrottlingView, basename="streamplatform-throttling")
```

The **WatchlistThrottlingView** allows only authenticated users to access it. Only authenticated users can access up to the throttling rate mentioned in the settings file. But unauthenticated users cannot access the view. When a user exceeds the limit, DRF raises a Throttled exception, which returns a **429 Too Many Requests** response. You can customize the response message or status code if needed by catching this exception in your views. By default, it returns a response as below:

```
{
    "detail": "Request was throttled. Expected available in 86386 seconds."
}
```

In the above cases, throttling is applied globally. But if you need a more granular level of throttling, you can use **ScopedRateThrottle**.

Let's apply this concept in our project.

Let's go to chapter12_throttling/api/views.py and add the following lines of code:

```
class WatchlistScopedRateThrottleView(viewsets.ModelViewSet):
    authentication_classes = [TokenAuthentication,]
    permission_classes = [IsAuthenticated]  # Ensure that the user is
    authenticated
    queryset = WatchList.objects.all()
    serializer_class = serializers.WatchListModelSerializer
    throttle_classes = [ScopedRateThrottle]
    throttle_scope = 'watchlist'  # Set a scope name for this view
```

Add the corresponding URL in chapter12_throttling/api/urls.py as below:

```
router = DefaultRouter()
# Using ViewSet
...
router.register(r"watchlist-scopedratethrottle", views.
WatchlistScopedRateThrottleView, basename="watchlist-scopedratethrottle")
```

Go to drfproject/settings.py and add the following lines of code:

```
REST_FRAMEWORK = {
    ...
    'DEFAULT_THROTTLE_CLASSES': [
        ...
        'rest_framework.throttling.ScopedRateThrottle',
    ],
    'DEFAULT_THROTTLE_RATES': {
        ...
        'watchlist': '3/hour',  # Example rate: 5 requests per hour for the
        'watchlist' scope
        # Add other scopes if needed
    },
}
```

In the above lines of code, **throttle_scope = 'watchlist'** links the WatchlistThrottlingView to the watchlist scope defined in settings.py, and **Throttling Rates**: '5/hour' limits users to five requests per hour for this specific view.

If you still want to apply UserRateThrottle and AnonRateThrottle alongside ScopedRateThrottle, you can combine them for different behavior, but make sure the throttle_classes list includes all applicable throttling types:

```
throttle_classes = [UserRateThrottle, AnonRateThrottle, ScopedRateThrottle]
```

This means that the general rate limits for users and anonymous requests are applied globally (or based on their respective settings). Additionally, more specific rate limits are enforced based on the scope defined for this particular view (watchlist scope). This helps achieve layered throttling control based on the scope, user types, or endpoint-specific needs.

Custom Throttling

Custom throttling in Django REST Framework (DRF) allows developers to create their own throttling logic to control the rate of requests based on specific rules or conditions that aren't covered by built-in throttling classes such as UserRateThrottle and AnonRateThrottle. Custom throttling is useful when you need more complex throttling behavior based on user attributes, request data, custom headers, etc.

To create a custom throttle in Django REST Framework, you override the BaseThrottle class and implement the allow_request() method. This method determines whether or not a request should be allowed. Optionally, you can also override the wait() method to indicate how long a user should wait before making the next request if throttling is applied.

Explanation of the Methods

1. **allow_request(self, request, view)**

   This method is used to define the logic for determining if a request should be allowed. It returns True if the request is allowed and False otherwise.

   You can implement custom logic here, such as tracking request counts over a specific period or using specific criteria for throttling.

2. **wait(self)**

   This method is optional and is called only if allow_request() returns False. It returns an integer representing the number of seconds the user should wait before they can make another request or None if you don't want to specify a wait time.

   If wait() returns a non-None value, the Retry-After header will be included in the response to notify the client how long to wait before retrying.

Let's implement the concept in our project.

Let's create a file chapter12_throttling/api/throttling.py and add the following lines of code:

```
from rest_framework.throttling import UserRateThrottle, BaseThrottle
from rest_framework.exceptions import Throttled
from django.core.cache import cache
import time

class CustomCacheRateThrottle(BaseThrottle):
    rate_limit = 5  # Maximum requests allowed
    window_duration = 60  # Time window in seconds (1 minute)

    def get_cache_key(self, request):
        # Identify user uniquely based on authentication status or
        IP address
        user_identifier = request.user.username if request.user.is_
        authenticated else request.META['REMOTE_ADDR']
        return f"throttle_{user_identifier}"

    def allow_request(self, request, view):
        cache_key = self.get_cache_key(request)
        current_time = time.time()

        # Get existing request timestamps list from cache
        request_history = cache.get(cache_key, [])

        # Filter out timestamps that are outside of the window duration
        request_history = [timestamp for timestamp in request_history if
        current_time - timestamp < self.window_duration]

        if len(request_history) >= self.rate_limit:
            # Deny request if rate limit is reached
            return False

        # Add current timestamp to request history
        request_history.append(current_time)
        # Save updated request history back to cache
        cache.set(cache_key, request_history, timeout=self.window_duration)
        return True
```

```
class ExceptionCustomMessageThrottle(UserRateThrottle):
    def throttle_failure(self):
        # Raise a Throttled exception with a custom detail message
        raise Throttled(detail="Custom message: You have exceeded your
        request limit. Please wait before retrying.")
```

Go to chapter12_throttling/api/views.py and add the following lines of code:

```
from chapter12_throttling.api.throttling import CustomCacheRateThrottle,
ExceptionCustomMessageThrottle
#----------------------Custom Throttle----------------------------------
class WatchlistCustomThrottleView(viewsets.ModelViewSet):
    authentication_classes = [TokenAuthentication,]
    permission_classes = [IsAuthenticated]  # Ensure that the user is
    authenticated
    queryset = WatchList.objects.all()
    serializer_class = serializers.WatchListModelSerializer
    throttle_classes = [CustomCacheRateThrottle,
    ExceptionCustomMessageThrottle]
```

Add the corresponding URL in chapter12_throttling/api/urls.py as below:

```
router = DefaultRouter()
# Using ViewSet
...
router.register(r"watchlist-customthrottle", views.
WatchlistCustomThrottleView, basename="watchlist-customthrottle")
```

In the above lines of code, we have implemented **CustomCacheRateThrottle** which implements a custom throttling mechanism.

Key Components

- **Attributes**
    - **rate_limit**: The maximum number of requests allowed within a specified time window (five requests in this example).
    - **window_duration**: The time window during which the request count is evaluated, specified in seconds (60 seconds or 1 minute here).

- **get_cache_key Method**
    - This method generates a unique cache key for each user. The key is based on
        - The username if the user is authenticated
        - The user's IP address (REMOTE_ADDR) if they are not authenticated
    - The generated cache key is used to track the request history for each unique user or IP address.
- **allow_request Method**

  This method determines if a request should be allowed or denied based on the throttling logic:

    - **Generate a Cache Key**: Calls get_cache_key to obtain a unique key for the current user
    - **Retrieve Request History**: Fetches the list of request timestamps from the cache using the generated cache key
    - **Filter Requests Within the Time Window**: Filters out timestamps that fall outside the defined window_duration. This ensures that only recent requests (within the last 60 seconds in this example) are counted.
    - **Check Rate Limit**: Compares the length of the filtered request history with the rate_limit. If the number of requests exceeds the limit, the request is denied.
    - **Update Request History**: If the request is allowed, the current timestamp is added to the history, and the updated list is stored in the cache with a timeout equal to window_duration.

The **ExceptionCustomMessageThrottle** custom subclass of UserRateThrottle that modifies the behavior when throttling fails. The method **throttle_failure** triggers when a request exceeds the rate limit. It raises a Throttled exception with a custom error message. Instead of the default "Request was throttled" message, this method allows you to provide a more descriptive or user-friendly error message, such as "Custom message: You have exceeded your request limit. Please wait before retrying."

A Note on Concurrency

In Django REST Framework (DRF), the built-in throttle implementations (like UserRateThrottle and AnonRateThrottle) work by maintaining a count of requests in a cache (such as LocMemCache, Redis, etc.) to track how many times a user or anonymous client has accessed an endpoint. Throttling is based on checking and updating this count whenever a request is made. But the built-in throttle implementations are open to race conditions, so under high concurrency, they may allow a few extra requests through.

In applications that receive a high volume of concurrent requests, the built-in throttling may allow some extra requests due to the above behavior. This might not be a problem for basic throttling needs, but for applications where strict request limits must be enforced (e.g., payment processing APIs, high-security APIs), this behavior can lead to potential issues.

Guaranteeing the Number of Requests

If your project requires **strict enforcement of throttling limits**, you may need to

1. **Implement a Custom Throttle Class**

   You can create your own throttle class using more robust synchronization methods to avoid race conditions.

   For example, you can use database-backed counters or distributed locks to ensure atomic updates.

2. **Use Synchronized or Atomic Operations**

   Consider using more advanced tools or back ends, like Redis scripts (Lua scripts) or atomic transactions, to update counts without race conditions.

Example of a More Robust Custom Throttle

Here's a simplified example demonstrating a concept that addresses race conditions with a more robust approach:

```
from rest_framework.throttling import BaseThrottle
from django.core.cache import caches
import redis  # Using Redis as an example for atomic increments
```

```
class RedisAtomicThrottle(BaseThrottle):
    cache = caches['default']  # Assuming default is set to Redis
    rate = 5  # Limit to 5 requests per minute
    window = 60  # Time window in seconds

    def get_cache_key(self, request):
        return f"throttle_{request.user.id}" if request.user.is_
        authenticated else f"throttle_{request.META['REMOTE_ADDR']}"

    def allow_request(self, request, view):
        cache_key = self.get_cache_key(request)
        redis_client = redis.Redis()  # Configure your Redis client here

        # Atomically increment counter in Redis
        count = redis_client.incr(cache_key)
        if count == 1:
            # Set expiration on first use
            redis_client.expire(cache_key, self.window)

        return count <= self.rate
```

In this example:

- A Redis client is used to **atomically increment** the request count using incr().
- This approach avoids race conditions inherent in using cache counts directly.

Built-in throttling works for basic use cases but may allow some extra requests during high concurrency due to nonatomic operations. Custom throttling is needed for strict enforcement of limits, especially under high load or critical business scenarios. Race conditions can be mitigated by using atomic operations and a more robust back end like Redis or implementing custom solutions.

CHAPTER 13

Filtering, Searching, and Ordering

Filtering data in Django and Django REST Framework (DRF) often involves selecting a subset of objects from the database based on certain criteria when accessing an API endpoint. As mentioned, the default behavior of DRF's generic list views is to return all objects in the queryset for a particular model. However, this is rarely practical for real-world APIs. Filtering allows you to narrow down the data returned, making it more relevant and performant. This is a crucial feature in API development, as it provides flexibility and enhances efficiency by returning only the requested subset of data. The simplest way to filter the queryset of any view that subclasses GenericAPIView is to override the .get_queryset() method. Overriding this method allows you to customize the queryset returned by the view in a number of different ways.

Preparing for This Chapter

Create a new app with the name **chapter13_filtering_searching_ordering** with the steps specified in the **Project Setup** section in Chapter 3.

Go to drfproject/settings.py and add the following lines of code:

```
INSTALLED_APPS = [
    ...
    "chapter13_filtering_searching_ordering",
]
```

Go to chapter13_filtering_searching_ordering/api/serializers.py and the following lines of code:

```
from rest_framework import serializers
```


G. Patil, *Django REST APIs Demystified*, https://doi.org/10.1007/979-8-8688-1850-9_13

```
from chapter3_project_setup.models import WatchList, StreamPlatform, Review

class WatchListModelSerializer(serializers.ModelSerializer):
    class Meta:
        model = WatchList
        fields = "__all__"
        ref_name = 'C13WatchListModelSerializer'

class StreamPlatformModelSerializer(serializers.ModelSerializer):
    class Meta:
        model = StreamPlatform
        fields = "__all__"
        ref_name = 'C13StreamPlatformModelSerializer'

class ReviewModelSerializer(serializers.ModelSerializer):
    user = serializers.StringRelatedField()
    class Meta:
        model = Review
        fields = "__all__"
        ref_name = 'C13ReviewModelSerializer'
```

Go to chapter13_filtering_searching_ordering/api/urls.py and add the following lines of code:

```
from django.urls import path, include
from rest_framework.routers import DefaultRouter

from . import views

router = DefaultRouter()

urlpatterns = [

    # Using ViewSet
    path("", include(router.urls)),
]
```

Go to chapter13_filtering_searching_ordering/api/views.py and add the following lines of code:

```
from django.shortcuts import get_object_or_404
from django_filters.rest_framework import DjangoFilterBackend
from rest_framework.filters import SearchFilter, OrderingFilter
from rest_framework.authentication import TokenAuthentication
from rest_framework.permissions import IsAuthenticated
from rest_framework.response import Response
from rest_framework import status
from rest_framework import generics
from chapter3_project_setup.models import WatchList, Review
from chapter13_filtering_searching_ordering.api import serializers
```

Go to drfproject/urls.py and add the following lines of code:

```
urlpatterns = [
    ...
    path('api/chapter13_filtering_searching_ordering/', include
    ('chapter13_filtering_searching_ordering.api.urls')),
]
```

Filtering Against the Current User

In Django REST Framework (DRF), filtering a queryset based on a request.user means modifying the set of results returned by a view to only include data that is relevant to the authenticated user making the request. This is a common approach when creating user-specific APIs, where each user should only have access to their own data.

Key Concepts

1. **request.user Attribute**

   request.user represents the currently authenticated user making the request. If the user is logged in, this will be a user instance; otherwise, it will typically be an anonymous user.

   By accessing this attribute in a view, you can tailor the returned data to only include results associated with that user.

2. **Filtering Based on request.user**

   When you filter a queryset using request.user, you restrict the data to ensure that the user can only see objects related to them. For example, if you have a Review model with a review_user foreign key that links reviews to their authors, you can filter the reviews so that a user only sees their own reviews.

Consider a scenario where you have a Review model that stores reviews created by different users. You might want an endpoint that returns only the reviews created by the currently authenticated user. Let's create a view for the Review model.

Go to chapter13_filtering_searching_ordering/api/views.py and add the following lines of code:

```
class ReviewsListCurrentUserFilterView(generics.ListAPIView):
    serializer_class = serializers.ReviewModelSerializer
    authentication_classes = [TokenAuthentication]
    permission_classes = [IsAuthenticated]

    def get_queryset(self):
        # Return reviews where `review_user` matches the current user
        return Review.objects.filter(review_user=self.request.user)
```

Add the corresponding URL in chapter13_filtering_searching_ordering/api/urls.py as below:

```
urlpatterns = [
    path('reviews/', views.ReviewsListCurrentUserFilterView.as_view(),
    name='reviews-current-user'),
]
```

By filtering data based on **request.user**, you ensure that each user can only access their own data. This is important for maintaining data privacy and security, especially in multiuser systems. This approach allows you to create fine-grained filters based on the logged-in user's attributes or relationships. For example, you can filter records based on the user's roles, permissions, or relationships with other objects. Filtering by **request.user** is a simple and efficient way to create user-specific views, making it a common practice in DRF applications.

Filtering Against the URL

Filtering against the URL involves modifying the queryset returned by a view based on parameters or values found directly within the URL path. This approach can help create more flexible and targeted API endpoints. By extracting values from the URL and applying them as filters on a queryset, you can dynamically change the data returned to clients based on their requests.

Go to chapter13_filtering_searching_ordering/api/views.py and add the following lines of code:

```
class ReviewListUrlFilterView(generics.ListAPIView):
    serializer_class = serializers.ReviewModelSerializer

    def get_queryset(self):
        # Extract 'watchlist_id' from the URL using 'self.kwargs'
        watchlist_id = self.kwargs['watchlist_id']
        # Filter reviews that are related to the specified watchlist
        return Review.objects.filter(watchlist_id=watchlist_id)
```

Add the corresponding URL in chapter13_filtering_searching_ordering/api/urls.py as below:

```
urlpatterns = [
    ...
    path('watchlist/<int:watchlist_id>/reviews/', views.
    ReviewListUrlFilterView.as_view(), name='reviews-url-filter'),

    # Using ViewSet
    path("", include(router.urls)),
]
```

In the URL pattern path(**'watchlist/<int:watchlist_id>/reviews/'**, ...), watchlist_id is a dynamic part of the URL that changes based on the request. In the view, **self.kwargs** contains all named URL parameters as a dictionary. This allows you to access watchlist_id by using self.kwargs['watchlist_id']. The queryset is filtered based on the watchlist_id provided in the URL. Only Review objects that are associated with the specified WatchList object will be included in the response.

Benefits of URL-Based Filtering

1. **Clean and RESTful URLs**: Filtering based on URL parameters follows the RESTful principles of structuring endpoints clearly and meaningfully.

2. **Dynamic Behavior**: You can create views that behave differently based on URL segments, providing more flexible API designs.

3. **Contextual Filtering**: Filtering data based on URL segments makes it easy to create endpoints for nested resources, such as "all reviews for a specific watchlist" in this example.

You can also ensure that any URL parameters used for filtering are properly validated. For example, handle cases where the value provided might not correspond to an existing object. Here's how you can achieve this with the above example, including appropriate error handling for cases where the watchlist_id may not correspond to an existing object.

Go to chapter13_filtering_searching_ordering/api/views.py and add the following lines of code:

```
class ReviewsUrlFilterWithValidationView(generics.ListAPIView):
    serializer_class = serializers.ReviewModelSerializer

    def get_queryset(self):
        # Extract 'watchlist_id' from the URL
        watchlist_id = self.kwargs['watchlist_id']

        # Ensure 'watchlist_id' corresponds to an existing WatchList
        watchlist = get_object_or_404(WatchList, id=watchlist_id)

        # If the WatchList exists, filter reviews by 'watchlist_id'
        return Review.objects.filter(watchlist=watchlist)

    def list(self, request, *args, **kwargs):
        # Custom response to handle the case where no reviews exist
        queryset = self.get_queryset()
        if not queryset.exists():
            return Response({"detail": "No reviews found for the specified
            watchlist."}, status=status.HTTP_404_NOT_FOUND)
```

```
        return super().list(request, *args, **kwargs)
```

Add the corresponding URL in chapter13_filtering_searching_ordering/api/urls.py as below:

```
urlpatterns = [
    ...
    path('watchlists/<int:watchlist_id>/reviews/', views.ReviewsUrlFilter
    WithValidationView.as_view(), name='reviews-url-filter-
    with-validation'),

    # Using ViewSet
    path("", include(router.urls)),
]
```

You can call the API using the below approach:

```
{{domain}}/api/chapter13_filtering_searching_ordering/watchlists/50/
reviews/
```

In the above code, the **get_object_or_404** function checks whether a WatchList object exists with the provided watchlist_id. If the watchlist_id does not match any existing WatchList, it raises a 404 Not Found error automatically. If the WatchList exists but no reviews are associated with it, the overridden list method provides a custom error response with a 404 status and a helpful message.

The use of **get_object_or_404** guarantees that only valid watchlist_id values are processed. It provides a graceful and informative response to the client if the resource does not exist. You can easily modify the response messages or add additional checks as needed. This approach ensures that the API remains robust and provides informative error messages, making it user-friendly and easier to debug.

Filtering Against Query Parameters

Filtering against query parameters in Django REST Framework (DRF) allows you to dynamically filter data based on the values of parameters passed in the URL's query string. This is a powerful and flexible approach to filtering data, providing an intuitive and customizable way for clients to narrow down results.

We'll modify a view for the Review model to demonstrate filtering against query parameters such as rating or date. Go to chapter13_filtering_searching_ordering/api/views.py and add the following lines of code:

```
class ReviewsFilterQueryParamsView(generics.ListAPIView):
    serializer_class = serializers.ReviewModelSerializer

    def get_queryset(self):
        # Start with the base queryset for all reviews
        queryset = Review.objects.all()

        # Get query parameters from the request
        rating = self.request.query_params.get('rating')
        start_date = self.request.query_params.get('start_date')
        end_date = self.request.query_params.get('end_date')

        # Apply filters based on query parameters if they are present
        if rating is not None:
            queryset = queryset.filter(rating=rating)

        if start_date is not None:
            queryset = queryset.filter(review_date__gte=start_date)

        if end_date is not None:
            queryset = queryset.filter(review_date__lte=end_date)

        return queryset
```

Add the corresponding URL in chapter13_filtering_searching_ordering/api/urls.py as below:

```
urlpatterns = [
    ...
    path('reviews-query-params/', views.ReviewsFilterQueryParamsView.as_
    view(), name='reviews-query-params'),

    # Using ViewSet
    path("", include(router.urls)),
]
```

You can call the API using the below approach:

```
{{domain}}/api/chapter13_filtering_searching_ordering/reviews-query-
params/?rating=5&start_date=2024-01-01&end_date=2024-11-17
```

In the above lines of code, the view starts by retrieving all objects from the Review model using queryset = Review.objects.all(). The self.request.query_params object allows you to access query parameters passed in the URL. These parameters are extracted using get(), which returns None if the parameter is not present.

Filters are conditionally applied to the queryset based on the presence of query parameters. For example, if the rating parameter is provided, the queryset is filtered using queryset = queryset.filter(rating=rating). Similarly, the start_date and end_date parameters are used to filter reviews based on a date range using __gte (greater than or equal) and __lte (less than or equal) lookups.

For more advanced filtering functionality, you can leverage the **django-filter** package, which integrates seamlessly with DRF and simplifies the filtering logic. We will discuss the Django-filter module in later sections of this chapter.

Generic Filtering

Generic filtering provides a flexible and reusable way to perform filtering and searching on API data. Rather than manually handling filtering logic for every view, generic filters can be applied at a higher level using DRF's built-in filtering back ends, or with custom back ends. These filters can also integrate seamlessly into the browsable API, presenting themselves as HTML controls for user-friendly interaction.

By adding filtering back ends to your views, you can control how data is filtered when accessed through an API endpoint. The filtering back ends are added to a viewset or view using the filter_backends attribute.

You can apply a generic filtering logic to your Review model using DRF's DjangoFilterBackend by setting the filter_backends either globally in the REST_FRAMEWORK settings or on a per-view basis. If you want to apply the default filter back ends globally for your entire API, you can configure it as follows in your settings.py file.

To proceed with implementation for this, we need to install Django-filter first using the below command on a virtual environment as below:

```
(venv)$ pip install django-filter
```

Now, let's go to drfproject/settings.py and add the following lines of code:

```
INSTALLED_APPS = [
    ...
    'django_filters',
    ...
]

REST_FRAMEWORK = {
    ...
    'DEFAULT_FILTER_BACKENDS': ['django_filters.rest_framework.Django
    FilterBackend'],
}
```

Go to chapter13_filtering_searching_ordering/api/views.py and add the following lines of code:

```
class ReviewsGenericFilteringView(generics.ListAPIView):
    queryset = Review.objects.all()
    serializer_class = serializers.ReviewModelSerializer
    filter_backends = [DjangoFilterBackend]
    filterset_fields = ['rating', 'review_user', 'active']  # Fields to
    filter on
```

Add the corresponding URL in chapter13_filtering_searching_ordering/api/urls.py as below:

```
urlpatterns = [
    ...
    path('reviews-generic-filter/', views.ReviewsGenericFilteringView.
    as_view(), name='reviews-generics-filter'),

    # Using ViewSet
    path("", include(router.urls)),
]
```

You can call the API using the below approach:

```
{{domain}}/api/chapter13_filtering_searching_ordering/reviews-generic-
filter/?rating=5&active=true
```

Note that if a filter back end is configured for a view, then, as well as being used to filter list views, it will also be used to filter the querysets used for returning a single object. In the above example, the **filter_backends** attribute allows you to specify a list of filter back ends that should be used for filtering the queryset. Here, we used DjangoFilterBackend, which is provided by the django-filter package. The **filterset_fields** is a list of fields on the Review model that you want to allow filtering on. In this example, we are allowing filtering by rating, review_user, and active.

This approach has many benefits. You can easily specify which fields you want to filter on without writing additional filtering logic. You can add more complex filters by creating custom filter classes if needed. The filters are exposed in the browsable API, making it easy for developers to interact with the API.

Overriding the Initial queryset

Note that you can use both an overridden .get_queryset() and generic filtering together, and everything will work as expected. To demonstrate how you can use both an overridden .get_queryset() method and generic filtering together in a view for the Review model, let's extend the above example. Suppose we want to filter Review objects such that only reviews related to the authenticated user are displayed while still allowing generic filtering for fields such as rating, active, etc.

Let's go to chapter13_filtering_searching_ordering/api/views.py and add the following lines of code:

```
class ReviewsOverridingQuerysetView(generics.ListAPIView):
    serializer_class = serializers.ReviewModelSerializer
    filter_backends = [DjangoFilterBackend]
    filterset_fields = ['rating', 'active']

    def get_queryset(self):
        """
        Optionally restricts the returned reviews to only those
        related to the
        currently authenticated user.
        """
        user = self.request.user
        if user.is_authenticated:
```

```
            # Filter reviews where the `review_user` is the currently
            authenticated user
            return Review.objects.filter(review_user=user)
        # For unauthenticated users, you can return an empty queryset or
        handle it differently
        return Review.objects.none()
```

Add the corresponding URL in chapter13_filtering_searching_ordering/api/urls.py as below:

```
urlpatterns = [
    ...
    path('reviews-overriding-queryset-filter/', views.
    ReviewsGenericFilteringView.as_view(), name='reviews-overriding-
    queryset-filter'),

    # Using ViewSet
    path("", include(router.urls)),
]
```

In the above code, get_queryset() customizes the initial queryset returned by the view based on the authenticated user making the request. If the user is authenticated, only reviews where review_user matches the currently authenticated user are returned. If the user is unauthenticated, an empty queryset is returned using Review.objects.none(). Alternatively, you could handle unauthenticated access differently depending on your needs. The filter_backends attribute uses DjangoFilterBackend, which enables generic filtering based on query parameters. The filterset_fields list allows filtering by rating and active fields in the URL query parameters.

You can call the API using the following approach:

- **Authenticated User Request (Filtering by Authenticated User's Reviews)**

  If a user is logged in and makes a request to this view, they will only see their own reviews.

  GET {{domain}}/api/chapter13_filtering_searching_ordering/reviews-overriding-queryset-filter/

  This request will return all reviews created by the authenticated user.

- **Filtering by Query Parameters**

  You can combine filtering based on fields like rating or active, along with the filtering done by get_queryset():

```
GET {{domain}}/api/chapter13_filtering_searching_ordering/reviews-overriding-queryset-filter/?rating=4
```

  This request will return all reviews with a rating of 4, but only those created by the authenticated user.

API Guide

DjangoFilterBackend

DjangoFilterBackend is a powerful and flexible filtering back end for Django REST Framework (DRF) that leverages the django-filter package. It allows you to filter querysets based on URL query parameters in an easy and customizable way, making it a popular choice for building complex, searchable APIs with minimal code.

How DjangoFilterBackend Works

When you use DjangoFilterBackend in a DRF view or viewset, it automatically applies filtering logic based on the fields specified in the filterset_fields attribute (or by using a custom filter class if you need more complex behavior). The filtering parameters are passed as query parameters in the URL.

Key Features

- **Automatic Filtering by Fields**: You can specify fields you want to filter by using filterset_fields.
- **Custom Filter Classes**: You can define custom filter classes to handle more complex filtering logic or apply additional validation to input.
- **Integration with the Browsable API**: When using DjangoFilterBackend, input controls for filters appear in the browsable API, making it easy to explore the available filters.

We have already covered the usage of this API in the above examples.

SearchFilter

The SearchFilter class in Django REST Framework (DRF) provides a simple way to perform text-based searches over a set of fields in your model. It enables a "search" capability on APIs using a single query parameter (commonly ?search=) and is inspired by the search behavior found in the Django admin interface.

The **SearchFilter** performs searches on a single query parameter. By default, it looks for the search query parameter (e.g., ?search=keyword). It supports partial matches, case-insensitive matches, and searching across multiple fields. You can control which fields are searched using the search_fields attribute in the view.

Let's set up searchFilter for our project. Let's go to drfproject/settings.py and add the following lines of code:

```
REST_FRAMEWORK = {
    ...
    'DEFAULT_FILTER_BACKENDS': [
            ...
            'rest_framework.filters.SearchFilter',
        ],
}
```

Go to chapter13_filtering_searching_ordering/api/views.py and add the following lines of code:

```
from rest_framework.filters import SearchFilter

class WatchlistSearchFilterView(generics.ListAPIView):
    queryset = WatchList.objects.all()
    serializer_class = serializers.WatchListModelSerializer
    filter_backends = [SearchFilter]
    search_fields = ['title', 'storyline']
```

Add the corresponding URL in chapter13_filtering_searching_ordering/api/urls.py as below:

```
urlpatterns = [
    ...
    path('watchlist-search-filter/', views.WatchlistSearchFilterView.
    as_view(), name='watchlist-search-filter'),
```

```
    # Using ViewSet
    path("", include(router.urls)),
]
```

In the above example, **filter_backends = [SearchFilter]** indicates which filtering back ends to use for this view. Here, we're using SearchFilter from rest_framework.filters. This enables search functionality based on specified fields. **search_fields = ['title', 'storyline']** specifies which fields in the WatchList model to search against when a search query is provided. The search functionality will try to find matches in the title and storyline fields of WatchList.

How the SearchFilter Works

- The SearchFilter allows you to perform simple searches on the specified fields using a query parameter in the request.
- By default, the search query parameter is used. For example:
    - **Search by Title**

      GET `{{domain}}/api/chapter13_filtering_searching_ordering/watchlist-search-filter/?search=Inception`

      This will return WatchList objects where the title contains the string "Inception".
    - **Search by Storyline**

      GET `{{domain}}/api/chapter13_filtering_searching_ordering/watchlist-search-filter/?search=space`

      This will return WatchList objects where the storyline contains the word "space".
- **Partial and Case-Insensitive Matching**

  By default, searches are case-insensitive and match any substring (i.e., a partial match). This means that the search term "space" would match "Space Odyssey" or "spaceship."

You can also perform a related lookup on a ForeignKey or ManyToManyField with the lookup API double-underscore notation:

```
search_fields = ['username', 'email', 'profile__profession']
```

For JSONField and HStoreField fields, you can filter based on nested values within the data structure using the same double-underscore notation:

```
search_fields = ['data__breed', 'data__owner__other_pets__0__name']
```

Default Search Behavior

1. **Case-Insensitive Partial Matches**

   By default, searches using SearchFilter are case-insensitive and perform a partial match search using the icontains lookup. This means that the search term will match any part of the text in the specified fields.

   For example, if you search for "john" in a field like username using search_fields = ['username'], it will match "JohnDoe", "superjohn123", and "littlejohn".

2. **Multiple Search Terms**

   The search parameter can contain multiple terms separated by whitespace or commas. In such cases, the filter will only return results that match **all** of the provided terms somewhere in the specified fields.

   ```
   GET /api/users/?search=john,doe
   ```

   This would return users where both "john" and "doe" appear somewhere in the search_fields specified (e.g., a username like "JohnDoe").

3. **Handling Quoted Phrases**

   If the search term contains quoted phrases with spaces, the entire phrase is treated as a single search term.

   ```
   GET /api/articles/?search="machine learning"
   ```

   This search will look for the exact phrase "machine learning" within the fields specified.

Prefixing Field Names to Modify Search Behavior

To modify the search behavior, you can add specific prefixes to fields in the search_fields attribute:

- **^ (Starts-with Search Using istartswith)**

  When you use the ^ prefix, it performs a "starts-with" search. This means the search term must appear at the beginning of the text in the specified field.

  Example:

  ```
  search_fields = ['^username']
  ```

  A search for "admin" would match "administrator" but not "superadmin".

- **= (Exact Matches Using iexact)**

  The = prefix enforces an exact match (case-insensitive).

  Example:

  ```
  search_fields = ['=email']
  ```

  Searching for "user@example.com" would only match if the email field exactly equals "user@example.com".

- **$ (Regex Search Using iregex)**

  The $ prefix enables regular expression searches. This allows for more complex search patterns.

  Example:

  ```
  search_fields = ['$username']
  ```

  This would enable searches using regex patterns.

- **@ (Full-Text Search)**

  The @ prefix is currently only supported with PostgreSQL's full-text search capabilities.

  Example:

  ```
  search_fields = ['@content']
  ```

This performs a full-text search on the content field.

- **Default (No Prefix)**

  If no prefix is specified, the default behavior is to use a partial match search (icontains), which matches anywhere within the text, case-insensitively.

  Example:

  ```
  search_fields = ['name']
  ```

This matches any occurrence of the search term within the name field.

Overriding the Default Search Parameter

By default, the query parameter used for search is search. You can change this globally in your settings using the SEARCH_PARAM setting.

Example:

```
# settings.py

REST_FRAMEWORK = {
    'SEARCH_PARAM': 'query'
}
```

The search query would now look like:

```
GET /api/items/?query=example
```

Let's apply the above concept to our project. Go to chapter13_filtering_searching_ordering/api/views.py and add the following lines of code:

```
class WatchlistAdvacedSearchView(generics.ListAPIView):
    queryset = WatchList.objects.all()
    serializer_class = serializers.WatchListModelSerializer
    filter_backends = [SearchFilter]
    search_fields = [
        'title',  # Default behavior: partial match, case insensitive
        '^title',  # Starts-with search for titles
```

```
        '=platform__name',  # exact match for platform name
        '$storyline'  # regex search on storyline
    ]
```

Add the corresponding URL in chapter13_filtering_searching_ordering/api/urls.py as below:

```
urlpatterns = [
    ...
    path('watchlist-advanced-search/', views.WatchlistAdvacedSearchView.
    as_view(), name='watchlist-advanced-search'),
    ...
]
```

By default, searches use a case-insensitive "contains" filter. This means that if you search for "space," it would match any WatchList entries where the title or storyline contains "space" (e.g., "Outer Space Adventures"). If the query string contains multiple search terms separated by spaces or commas, DRF will attempt to find matches where all terms are present in at least one of the specified fields.

For example:

```
GET {{domain}}/api/chapter13_filtering_searching_ordering/watchlist-
advanced-search/?search=space,adventure
```

This will only return results where both "space" and "adventure" are found within the title or storyline.

"^title" indicates that searches on title should only return results where the title field starts with the provided search term.

For example:

```
GET {{domain}}/api/chapter13_filtering_searching_ordering/watchlist-
advanced-search/?search=Star
```

The above example, it matches: "Star Trek," "Star Wars". But it does not match: "The Stars Are Bright".

The search behavior may be specified by prefixing field names in search_fields with one of the following characters (which is equivalent to adding __<lookup> to the field). In the above view, '=platform__name' means that only exact matches (case-insensitive) on the platform field will be considered.

For example:

```
GET {{domain}}/api/chapter13_filtering_searching_ordering/watchlist-advanced-search/?search=netflix
```

The search can handle quoted phrases as single terms.

For example:

```
GET {{domain}}/api/chapter13_filtering_searching_ordering/watchlist-advanced-search/?search= "space adventure"
```

This will treat "space adventure" as a single term and match it in the title or storyline fields.

Dynamically Changing Search Fields

Sometimes, you may want to dynamically determine which fields to search based on request parameters. The SearchFilter is a powerful, flexible tool for searching across fields in a model. It supports different matching strategies with prefixes, can handle complex multi-term queries, and allows for dynamic control of search behavior. With customization options like dynamic search fields and adjustable query parameters, it offers fine-grained control over how searches are performed on your data. This can be achieved by subclassing SearchFilter and overriding the get_search_fields() method.

Let's implement this concept in our project. Go to chapter13_filtering_searching_ordering/api/views.py and add the following lines of code:

```
class CustomSearchFilter(SearchFilter):
    def get_search_fields(self, view, request):
        # Dynamically adjust search fields based on a query parameter
        if request.query_params.get('title_only'):
            return ['title']
        return super().get_search_fields(view, request)

# Applying the custom filter
class WatchlistDynamicSearchFieldView(generics.ListAPIView):
    queryset = WatchList.objects.all()
    serializer_class = serializers.WatchListModelSerializer
    filter_backends = [CustomSearchFilter]
    search_fields = ['title', 'storyline']
```

Add the corresponding URL in chapter13_filtering_searching_ordering/api/urls.py as below:

```
urlpatterns = [
    ...
    path('watchlist-dynamic-search-field/', views.WatchlistDynamic
    SearchFieldView.as_view(), name='watchlist-dynamic-search-field'),
    ...
]
```

In this example, if a client makes a request with the query parameter title_only, only the title field will be searched:

```
GET {{domain}}/api/chapter13_filtering_searching_ordering/watchlist-
dynamic-search-field/?title_only=1&search=space
```

Otherwise, the default search_fields are used.

OrderingFilter

The OrderingFilter in Django REST Framework (DRF) is a filtering back end that enables dynamic ordering of querysets based on specified model fields. This allows clients to control the order of results returned by an API by using a query parameter, typically **ordering**.

How OrderingFilter Works

1. **Setting Up the Filter Back End**: Add OrderingFilter to your view's filter_backends or set it globally in the REST_FRAMEWORK settings.

2. **Defining ordering_fields**: Specify the fields that the API will allow for ordering. These fields should correspond to the fields in the model (including related model fields, using double-underscore notation).

3. **Query Parameter: Ordering**—Clients can specify one or more fields in the query parameter ordering to determine the sort order.
   - Prefixing a field with—reverses the order (descending).
   - Multiple fields can be separated by commas for hierarchical ordering.

Let's understand this concept by implementing it for our project. Go to chapter13_filtering_searching_ordering/api/views.py and add the following lines of code:

```
class WatchListOrderingView(generics.ListAPIView):
    queryset = WatchList.objects.all()
    serializer_class = serializers.WatchListModelSerializer
    filter_backends = [OrderingFilter]
    ordering_fields = ['title', 'imdb_rating', 'created', 'episodes',
'platform__name']
```

Add the corresponding URL in chapter13_filtering_searching_ordering/api/urls.py as below:

```
urlpatterns = [
    ...
    path('watchlist-ordering/', views.WatchListOrderingView.as_view(),
    name='watchlist-ordering'),
    ...
]
```

Example Queries

1. **Order by Title (Ascending)**

   GET `{{domain}}/api/chapter13_filtering_searching_ordering/watchlist-ordering/?ordering=-title`

   Results are ordered alphabetically by title.

2. **Order by IMDB Rating (Descending)**

   GET `{{domain}}/api/chapter13_filtering_searching_ordering/watchlist-ordering/?ordering=-imdb_rating`

Results are ordered by imdb_rating in descending order.

3. **Order by Multiple Fields**

   GET {{domain}}/api/chapter13_filtering_searching_ordering/watchlist-ordering/?ordering=created,-title

   Results are ordered by the **created date (ascending)** first and then by **title (descending)** within the same created date.

4. **Order by Related Field**

   GET {{domain}}/api/chapter13_filtering_searching_ordering/watchlist-ordering/?ordering=platform__name

   Results are ordered by the name of the related StreamPlatform.

Specifying Which Fields May Be Ordered Against

It's recommended that you explicitly specify which fields the API should allow in the ordering filter. You can do this by setting an ordering_fields attribute on the view, like so:

```
class WatchListOrderingView(generics.ListAPIView):
    queryset = WatchList.objects.all()
    serializer_class = serializers.WatchListModelSerializer
    filter_backends = [OrderingFilter]
    ordering_fields = ['title', 'imdb_rating', 'created', 'episodes',
    'platform__name']
```

This helps prevent unexpected data leakage, such as allowing users to order against a password hash field or other sensitive data.

If you *don't* specify an ordering_fields attribute on the view, the filter class will default to allowing the user to filter on any readable fields on the serializer specified by the serializer_class attribute.

If you are confident that the queryset being used by the view doesn't contain any sensitive data, you can also explicitly specify that a view should allow ordering on *any* model field or queryset aggregate by using the special value '__all__'.

Let's go to chapter13_filtering_searching_ordering/api/views.py and add the following lines of code:

```
class WatchListFullOrderingView(generics.ListAPIView):
    queryset = WatchList.objects.all()
    serializer_class = serializers.WatchListModelSerializer
    filter_backends = [OrderingFilter]
    ordering_fields = '__all__'  # Allow ordering on all fields
```

Add the corresponding URL in chapter13_filtering_searching_ordering/api/urls.py as below:

```
urlpatterns = [
    ...
    path('watchlist-full-ordering/', views.WatchListFullOrderingView.
    as_view(), name='watchlist-full-ordering'),
    ...
]
```

Example query:

```
GET {{domain}}/api/chapter13_filtering_searching_ordering/watchlist-full-
ordering/?ordering=platform__name
```

This request orders the result by the related StreamPlatform's name.

Use ordering_fields to avoid exposing sensitive fields like created_by, updated_by, or any hidden internal fields. Use ordering_fields = '__all__' cautiously, ensuring no sensitive or unnecessary fields exist in the queryset. Validate serializer or queryset thoroughly to avoid exposing unwanted data.

Specifying a Default Ordering

When using the OrderingFilter back end, you can define a default ordering for your API results by setting the **ordering** attribute on the view. This is different from specifying order_by on the initial queryset. Setting the **ordering** in the view allows for easier context passing to templates or serializers. It also helps the browsable API visually indicate which column is used for ordering. It also ensures a predictable sort order even if no ordering parameter is provided by the client.

Let's go to chapter13_filtering_searching_ordering/api/views.py and add the following lines of code:

```
class WatchlistOrderedView(generics.ListAPIView):
    queryset = WatchList.objects.all()
    serializer_class = serializers.WatchListModelSerializer
    filter_backends = [OrderingFilter]
    ordering_fields = ['title', 'imdb_rating', 'created', 'category']
    # Allowed ordering fields
    ordering = ['imdb_rating']  # Default: Order by IMDB rating (ascending)
```

Add the corresponding URL in chapter13_filtering_searching_ordering/api/urls.py as below:

```
urlpatterns = [
    ...
    path('watchlist-ordered/', views.WatchlistOrderedView.as_view(),
    name='watchlist-ordered'),
    ...
]
```

For the above view, by default, results are sorted by imdb_rating (lowest to highest). But API clients can override this.

For example:

```
GET {{domain}}/api/chapter13_filtering_searching_ordering/watchlist-
ordered/?ordering=-title
```

Order by title in descending order.

```
GET {{domain}}/api/chapter13_filtering_searching_ordering/watchlist-
ordered/?ordering=category,imdb_rating
```

Order by category, then imdb_rating.

This implementation ensures results are always sorted by imdb_rating if no ordering parameter is provided, and only fields explicitly allowed in ordering_fields can be used for sorting.

Custom Generic Filtering

In Django REST Framework, you can create custom filtering logic by subclassing BaseFilterBackend and overriding its filter_queryset method. This concept has many benefits. The custom back end can be applied to multiple views without duplicating logic. You can restrict the visibility of objects based on the request, user, or other conditions. Custom back ends can be packaged as reusable libraries for use across projects.

Let's implement custom filtering for our project. Let's create chapter13_filtering_searching_ordering/api/filters.py and add the following lines of code:

```
from rest_framework.filters import BaseFilterBackend

class IsReviewOwnerFilterBackend(BaseFilterBackend):
    """
    Filter that only allows users to see their own reviews.
    """
    def filter_queryset(self, request, queryset, view):
        return queryset.filter(review_user=request.user)
```

The above approach overrides the filter_queryset() method of BaseFilterBackend and applies a filter (queryset.filter(review_user=request.user)) to return only objects where the review_user field matches the logged-in user. This restricts the queryset to include only objects owned by the logged-in user. It also ensures **data isolation and security** so that users cannot see reviews submitted by others. This filter back end is modular and can be reused across multiple views that need similar ownership restrictions.

Go to chapter13_filtering_searching_ordering/api/views.py and add the following lines of code:

```
from chapter13_filtering_searching_ordering.api.filters import
IsReviewOwnerFilterBackend

class UserReviewListView(generics.ListAPIView):
    """
    View to list all reviews created by the logged-in user, with optional
    filtering by watchlist.
    """
    queryset = Review.objects.all()
```

```
    authentication_classes = [TokenAuthentication]
    permission_classes = [IsAuthenticated]
    serializer_class = serializers.ReviewModelSerializer
    filter_backends = [IsReviewOwnerFilterBackend, SearchFilter]
    search_fields = ['watchlist__title']
```

In the above example, specifying **IsReviewOwnerFilterBackend** restricts the queryset to reviews belonging to the logged-in user and also enables searching within the filtered reviews.

The line search_fields = ['watchlist__title'] specifies that the client can search reviews by the title field of the related WatchList model (accessed via the watchlist foreign key). Example: ?search=Inception will return reviews for watchlists with "Inception" in their title.

Add the corresponding URL in chapter13_filtering_searching_ordering/api/urls.py as below:

```
urlpatterns = [
    ...
    path('user-review-list/', views.UserReviewListView.as_view(),
    name='user-review-list'),
    ...
]
```

We can use the above endpoint as below:

GET {{domain}}/api/chapter13_filtering_searching_ordering/user-review-list/

All reviews created by the logged-in user, serialized as JSON.

GET {{domain}}/api/chapter13_filtering_searching_ordering/user-review-list/?search=Matrix

Only reviews for watchlists with "Matrix" in the title, created by the logged-in user.

For the API requests without a token, it gets an **HTTP 401 Unauthorized** response.

This design has many advantages. It ensures users can only access their own data and prevents accidental or malicious exposure of other users' reviews.

It allows optional, flexible search functionality to improve user experience. It also aligns with best practices for API security and data privacy.

This combination of security, search, and user-specific data access makes the implementation both robust and user-friendly.

Customizing the Interface

The Django REST Framework (DRF) provides a browsable API interface that allows developers and users to interact with the API. Custom filters, such as those inheriting from **BaseFilterBackend**, can be enhanced to display a user-friendly interface in the browsable API by overriding the **to_html()** method. This renders an HTML representation of the filter to display in the browsable API. It is useful for providing a visual interface for filtering options. The **to_html()** method returns a string containing rendered HTML that is displayed in the browsable API. The HTML should present a user-friendly way for users to interact with the filter options.

This approach is used to display drop-downs for predefined choices (e.g., categories) and render text boxes for free-text search. It is also used for displaying filters dynamically based on user context or data.

Let's go to chapter13_filtering_searching_ordering/api/filters.py and add the following lines of code:

```
from django.utils.safestring import mark_safe

class WatchlistCategoryFilter(BaseFilterBackend):
    """
    Filter to allow filtering Watchlist objects by category.
    Also includes a customized HTML interface for the browsable API.
    """

    def filter_queryset(self, request, queryset, view):
        category = request.query_params.get('category', None)
        if category:
            return queryset.filter(category=category)
        return queryset

    def to_html(self, request, queryset, view):
        # Get unique categories from the queryset
```

```
        categories = queryset.values_list('category', flat=True).distinct()
        # Generate dropdown HTML
        html = "<label for='category'>Category:</label>"
        html += "<select id='category' name='category'>"
        html += "<option value=''>All</option>"
        for category in categories:
            html += f"<option value='{category}'>{category}</option>"
        html += "</select>"
        return mark_safe(html)  # Mark the string as safe HTML
```

Go to chapter13_filtering_searching_ordering/api/views.py and add the following lines of code:

```
from chapter13_filtering_searching_ordering.api.filters import
IsReviewOwnerFilterBackend, WatchlistCategoryFilter

class WatchlistCategoryFilterView(generics.ListAPIView):
    """
    API endpoint to list Watchlist objects, with filtering by category.
    Includes a browsable API interface for category selection.
    """
    queryset = WatchList.objects.all()
    serializer_class = serializers.WatchListModelSerializer
    authentication_classes = [TokenAuthentication]
    permission_classes = [IsAuthenticated]
    filter_backends = [WatchlistCategoryFilter, SearchFilter]
    search_fields = ['title', 'storyline']
```

Add the corresponding URL in chapter13_filtering_searching_ordering/api/urls.py as below:

```
urlpatterns = [
    ...
    path('watchlist-category-filter/', views.WatchlistCategoryFilterView.
    as_view(), name='watchlist-category-filter'),
    ...
]
```

In the above example, when a client sends a query parameter like ?category=MOVIE, the WatchlistCategoryFilter filters the queryset to include only items with the specified category. If no category parameter is provided, it returns all items.

In the browsable API, users will see a drop-down populated with the unique categories from the database. Selecting a category from the drop-down applies the corresponding filter.

Example Workflow

1. **Browsable API Interface**

   When accessing the browsable API:

   - A drop-down is displayed with all available categories (MOVIE, SERIES, etc.).
   - Users can select a category and click "Apply" to filter the results.

2. **API Requests**

   GET `{{domain}}/api/chapter13_filtering_searching_ordering/watchlist-category-filter/`

   Returns all watchlist items

   GET `{{domain}}/api/chapter13_filtering_searching_ordering/watchlist-category-filter/?category=MOVIE`

   Returns only watchlist items where category=MOVIE

   GET `{{domain}}/api/chapter13_filtering_searching_ordering/watchlist-category-filter/?category=SERIES&search=Adventure`

   Returns watchlist items where category=SERIES and the title or storyline contains "Adventure"

This implementation has many advantages. The drop-down in the browsable API makes filtering intuitive for users. The **to_html()** method generates options based on the current data in the database, ensuring relevance. The custom filter can be reused across multiple views for similar functionality. It also improves the developer experience when testing or exploring the API.

CHAPTER 14

Pagination

Pagination in Django REST Framework (DRF) is a mechanism for dividing large datasets into smaller, manageable pages. This makes it easier to work with large APIs by breaking the data into consumable chunks and providing navigation options, such as "Previous" and "Next" links.

Why Use Pagination?

Implementing pagination for the API has many benefits in real-world applications. Some of the benefits are as below:

1. **Optimized Performance**
    - Large datasets can slow down systems when processed or returned in their entirety. Pagination limits the amount of data sent per request, reducing response times and server load.
    - It prevents server and client timeouts by handling queries in smaller, manageable chunks.
    - Limits resource usage by fetching and processing data incrementally, ensuring high performance even in resource-intensive environments.

2. **Enhanced User Experience**

    Sending smaller, paginated data sets improves usability for applications, especially in resource-constrained environments like mobile or web apps. For example, paginated tables or feeds are easier to navigate and consume.

G. Patil, *Django REST APIs Demystified*, https://doi.org/10.1007/979-8-8688-1850-9_14

3. **Efficient Resource Usage**

   Fetching and rendering smaller subsets of data reduces memory, CPU, and bandwidth consumption, which is crucial in both APIs and large-scale enterprise systems.

4. **Improved Search and Filtering**

   Breaks down large result sets into manageable pages, especially useful in search-heavy applications like ecommerce or CRM platforms.

5. **Scalability**

   As datasets grow, pagination ensures that systems remain responsive and performant without significant architectural changes.

6. **Better Data Handling**

   In applications with frequent updates or concurrent changes (e.g., real-time logs or financial transactions), pagination (like cursor-based) maintains consistency and avoids duplications or omissions.

7. **Compliance and Logging**

   Enterprises can better track, audit, and log data access by identifying which subset of the data was requested, improving traceability and monitoring.

Pagination in both DRF and enterprise applications is a cornerstone of **performance**, **user experience**, and **scalability**. By controlling the flow of data, it keeps systems efficient, responsive, and adaptable to growing datasets and complex enterprise needs. Whether you're building APIs for small-scale projects or architecting large-scale enterprise solutions, pagination is a best practice that ensures long-term reliability and usability.

How Pagination Works in DRF

DRF includes pagination links in the response content by default, which allow clients to navigate through pages.

```
{
    "count": 100,
    "next": "http://example.com/api/items/?page=2",
    "previous": null,
    "results": [
        {
            "id": 1,
            "name": "Item 1"
        },
        {
            "id": 2,
            "name": "Item 2"
        }
    ]
}
```

Although not the default behavior in DRF, pagination links can also be included in HTTP response headers (e.g., Content-Range or Link). Pagination is automatically applied to **generic views** or **viewsets** but not for regular APIView. For APIView, you need to handle pagination manually. To disable pagination for a specific view or the entire API, set the pagination class to None.

Preparing for This Chapter

Create a new app with the name **chapter14_pagination** with the steps specified in the **Project Setup** section in Chapter 3.

Go to drfproject/settings.py and add the following lines of code:

```
INSTALLED_APPS = [
    ...
    "chapter14_pagination",
]
```

Go to chapter14_pagination/api/serializers.py and the following lines of code:

```
from rest_framework import serializers
from chapter3_project_setup.models import WatchList, StreamPlatform, Review

class WatchListModelSerializer(serializers.ModelSerializer):
    class Meta:
        model = WatchList
        fields = "__all__"
        ref_name = 'C14WatchListModelSerializer'

class StreamPlatformModelSerializer(serializers.ModelSerializer):
    class Meta:
        model = StreamPlatform
        fields = "__all__"
        ref_name = 'C14StreamPlatformModelSerializer'

class ReviewModelSerializer(serializers.ModelSerializer):
    user = serializers.StringRelatedField()
    class Meta:
        model = Review
        fields = "__all__"
        ref_name = 'C14ReviewModelSerializer'
```

Go to chapter14_pagination/api/urls.py and add the following lines of code:

```
from django.urls import path, include
from rest_framework.routers import DefaultRouter

from . import views

router = DefaultRouter()

urlpatterns = [

    # Using ViewSet
    path("", include(router.urls)),
]
```

Go to chapter14_pagination/api/views.py and add the following lines of code:

```
from rest_framework import viewsets
from rest_framework.authentication import TokenAuthentication
from rest_framework.permissions import IsAuthenticated
from chapter3_project_setup.models import WatchList
from chapter14_pagination.api import serializers
```

Go to drfproject/urls.py and add the following lines of code:

```
urlpatterns = [
    ...
    path('api/chapter14_pagination/', include('chapter14_pagination.api.urls')),
]
```

Default Pagination Classes in DRF

Django REST Framework (DRF) provides the following inbuilt pagination classes.

PageNumberPagination

This is the simplest pagination style in DRF. It works by dividing the dataset into discrete pages, where clients can navigate between pages using page numbers.

Key Features of PageNumberPagination

1. **Default Page Size**

   You can specify the number of results per page globally or override it per view.

2. **Page Query Parameter**

   The client specifies which page to retrieve using a query parameter (default is ?page=2).

3. **Customization**

   - Allow clients to set a custom page size via a query parameter.
   - Limit the maximum page size to prevent server overload.

Configure Global Pagination Settings

You can set up global pagination in the settings.py file to apply PageNumberPagination across all views. Let's go to drfproject/settings.py and add the following lines of code:

```
REST_FRAMEWORK = {
    ...
    'DEFAULT_PAGINATION_CLASS': 'rest_framework.pagination.
    PageNumberPagination',  # Use PageNumberPagination globally
    'PAGE_SIZE': 3,  # Default number of results per page
}
```

In the above settings, DEFAULT_PAGINATION_CLASS enables pagination globally using PageNumberPagination. PAGE_SIZE parameter specifies how many records to include on each page (default: 5).

Go to chapter14_pagination/api/views.py and add the following lines of code:

```
class WatchListGlobalPageNumberPaginationViewSet(viewsets.ModelViewSet):
    authentication_classes = [TokenAuthentication]
    permission_classes = [IsAuthenticated]  # Ensure that the user is
                          authenticated
    queryset = WatchList.objects.all()
    serializer_class = serializers.WatchListModelSerializer
```

Add the corresponding URL in chapter14_pagination/api/urls.py as below:

```
router = DefaultRouter()
# Using ViewSet
router.register(r"watchlist-pagenum-global-setting", views.
WatchListGlobalPageNumberPaginationViewSet, basename="watchlist-pagenum-
global-setting")
```

Now when you make a request `{{domain}}/api/chapter14_pagination/watchlist-pagenum-global-setting/`, it returns the first page of results (three items per page) in the below format:

```
{
    "count": 12,
```

```
    "next": "http://127.0.0.1:8000/api/chapter14_pagination/watchlist-
            pagenum-global-setting/?page=2",
    "previous": null,
    "results": [
        {
            "id": 49,
            "title": "Movie1",
            "storyline": "Movie1-Story",
            "active": true,
            "imdb_rating": 2.0,
            "created": "2024-10-26T20:06:27.406145Z",
            "episodes": 0,
            "category": "MOVIE",
            "platform": 1
        },
        ...
    ]
}
```

Clients can use the page query parameter to fetch specific pages using requests like `{{domain}}/api/chapter14_pagination/watchlist-pagenum-global-setting/?page=2`.

You can also create a custom pagination class if the global settings do not meet the specific needs of the view. Before that, we go through different configuration attributes available in the **PageNumberPagination** class that may be overridden to modify the pagination style.

django_paginator_class

This refers to the underlying Django Paginator class. Default is **django.core.paginator.Paginator**. Typically, you don't need to override this unless you require highly customized pagination logic.

page_size

A numeric value indicating the page size. If set, this overrides the PAGE_SIZE setting. Defaults to the same value as the PAGE_SIZE settings key.

page_query_param

This is a string value indicating the name of the query parameter to use for the pagination control. This is the name of a query parameter that allows the client to set the page size on a per-request basis. Defaults to None, indicating that the client may not control the requested page size.

Example: **GET** /api/items/?page_size=10

Here, we are using page_size instead of page.

max_page_size

This attribute sets the maximum page size the client can request (only relevant if page_size_query_param is set). It is useful to prevent clients from requesting excessively large pages that might degrade performance.

last_page_strings

A list or tuple of string values indicating values that may be used with the page_query_param to request the final page in the set. Defaults to ("last").

Example: GET /api/items/?page=last.

Template

This attribute specifies the template used for rendering pagination controls in the browsable API. This may be overridden to modify the rendering style or set to None to disable HTML pagination controls completely. By default, it is set to "rest_framework/pagination/numbers.html".

Let's implement custom pagination for our project. Let's create a file chapter14_pagination/api/pagination.py and add the following lines of code:

```
from rest_framework.pagination import PageNumberPagination

class WatchListPageNumberPagination(PageNumberPagination):
    # django_paginator_class = None  # Use the default Django paginator.
    page_size = 5  # Default number of items per page.
    page_query_param = 'p'  # Change query parameter for the page to 'p'.
    page_size_query_param = 'page_size'  # Allow clients to request custom
                            page sizes.
```

```
    max_page_size = 20  # Prevent excessively large page sizes.
    last_page_strings = ('end',)  # Clients can use 'end' to access the
                        last page.
    template = None  # Disable HTML pagination controls in the
                     browsable API.
```

Go to chapter14_pagination/api/views.py and add the following lines of code:

```
from chapter14_pagination.api.pagination import
WatchListPageNumberPagination

class WatchListCustomPageNumberPaginationViewSet(viewsets.ModelViewSet):
    authentication_classes = [TokenAuthentication]
    permission_classes = [IsAuthenticated]  # Ensure that the user is
                         authenticated
    queryset = WatchList.objects.all()
    serializer_class = serializers.WatchListModelSerializer
    pagination_class = WatchListPageNumberPagination
```

Add the corresponding URL in chapter14_pagination/api/urls.py as below:

```
router = DefaultRouter()
# Using ViewSet
...
router.register(r"watchlist-pagenum-custom-setting", views.
WatchListCustomPageNumberPaginationViewSet, basename="watchlist-pagenum-
custom-setting")
```

You can try the below requests:

- Fetch First Page (Default Behavior)

  GET {{domain}}/api/chapter14_pagination/watchlist-pagenum-custom-setting/

  Authorization: Token <your-token>

- Fetch a Custom Page Size

  GET {{domain}}/api/chapter14_pagination/watchlist-pagenum-custom-setting/?p=1&page_size=10

Authorization: Token <your-token>

- Access the Last Page

GET {{domain}}/api/chapter14_pagination/watchlist-pagenum-custom-setting/?p=end

Authorization: Token <your-token>

LimitOffsetPagination

This is a pagination style provided by Django REST Framework that allows clients to control both the number of items returned per page (**limit**) which is equivalent to the page_size and the starting position in the dataset (**offset**) using query parameters. This pagination style mirrors the syntax used when looking up multiple database records.

This pagination style is particularly useful when clients need precise control over the amount of data they retrieve and its position in the overall dataset, such as in large datasets where data needs to be fetched in chunks.

Example: **GET** /api/items/?limit=10&offset=20

The above request retrieves ten items, starting from the 21st record (zero-based index).

If a limit is not provided, the default page size is used (as configured in the pagination class or settings). If offset is not provided, it defaults to 0 (starting from the beginning of the dataset). Similarly, the response contains metadata about the dataset and paginated results as below:

```
{
    "count": 100,  # Total number of items
    "next": "http://127.0.0.1:8000/api/items/?limit=10&offset=30",
    "previous": "http://127.0.0.1:8000/api/items/?limit=10&offset=10",
    "results": [ ... ]  # The actual data
}
```

Setup: Enabling LimitOffsetPagination Globally

This approach follows the same approach as PageNumberPagination. By adding the following to your settings.py:

```
REST_FRAMEWORK = {
    'DEFAULT_PAGINATION_CLASS': 'rest_framework.pagination.LimitOffset
    Pagination',
    'PAGE_SIZE': 10,  # Optional: Default number of results if limit is not
    provided
}
```

The DEFAULT_PAGINATION_CLASS key specifies that all views should use LimitOffsetPagination by default. If the client doesn't provide the limit query parameter, DRF will fall back to the value specified in PAGE_SIZE. If you don't set PAGE_SIZE, the client **must** provide a limit parameter, or no pagination will occur.

Per-View Configuration

If you want only specific views to use LimitOffsetPagination, you can set the pagination_class attribute on the view. Before getting into customizing LimitOffsetPagination, let's understand what configuration attributes are available to override.

default_limit

The default number of items to return if the limit parameter is not provided. It defaults to the value of PAGE_SIZE in settings or None.

Example: default_limit = 10

limit_query_param

You can change the name of the query parameter used for the limit using this attribute. It defaults to "limit".

For example, if you set limit_query_param = "custom_limit", the client can query like: **GET** `/api/items/?custom_limit=10&offset=5`.

offset_query_param

You can change the name of the query parameter used for the offset using this attribute. It defaults to "offset".

For example, if you set offset_query_param = "start", clients can query like: **GET** `/api/items/?limit=10&start=5`.

max_limit

The maximum number of items a client can request. It prevents overly large queries that might impact server performance. It defaults to None (no limit).

For example, if you set max_limit = 50, even though the client requested 100 items like **GET** `/api/items/?limit=100&offset=0`, it returns 50 items only since the limit is capped at 50.

Template

The name of a template to use when rendering pagination controls in the browsable API. This may be overridden to modify the rendering style or set to None to disable HTML pagination controls completely. It defaults to "rest_framework/pagination/numbers.html".

For example:

```
template = "my_app/custom_pagination_template.html"
```

Let's implement the above concept for our project. Go to chapter14_pagination/api/pagination.py and add the following lines of code:

```
from rest_framework.pagination import PageNumberPagination,
LimitOffsetPagination

class CustomLimitOffsetPagination(LimitOffsetPagination):
    default_limit = 5  # Default limit if the client does not specify a
    limit parameter
    max_limit = 20  # Maximum limit that a client can request
    limit_query_param = 'custom_limit'  # Custom query parameter name
    for limit
    offset_query_param = 'custom_offset'  # Custom query parameter name
    for offset
    last_page_strings = ('end', 'final')  # Custom string values to request
    the last page
    template = None  # Disable HTML pagination controls in the
    browsable API.
```

Go to chapter14_pagination/api/views.py and add the following lines of code:

```
from chapter14_pagination.api.pagination import
WatchListPageNumberPagination, CustomLimitOffsetPagination

class WatchListLimitOffsetPaginationViewSet(viewsets.ModelViewSet):
    authentication_classes = [TokenAuthentication]
    permission_classes = [IsAuthenticated]  # Ensure authenticated access
    queryset = WatchList.objects.all()
    serializer_class = serializers.WatchListModelSerializer
    pagination_class = CustomLimitOffsetPagination  # Apply the custom
    pagination
```

Add the corresponding URL in chapter14_pagination/api/urls.py as below:

```
router = DefaultRouter()
# Using ViewSet
...
router.register(r"watchlist-limit-offset", views.
WatchListLimitOffsetPaginationViewSet, basename="watchlist-limit-offset")
```

In the above example, if the client doesn't provide a custom_limit query parameter, five items will be returned by default. The max_limit attribute prevents the client from requesting more than 20 items in a single query, even if a higher custom_limit is specified. The changes made to the query parameter names to custom_limit and custom_offset make the API easier to customize for client-side developers.

For example: **GET** `{{domain}}/api/chapter14_pagination/watchlist-limit-offset/?custom_limit=10&custom_offset=5`

Returns ten items, starting from the sixth item (offset is zero-based).

Clients can use **end** or **final** as the value of custom_offset to retrieve the last page of the results.

For example: **GET** `{{domain}}/api/chapter14_pagination/watchlist-limit-offset/?custom_offset=end`

Returns the final page of results.

CursorPagination

The cursor-based pagination presents an opaque "cursor" indicator that the client may use to page through the result set. This pagination style only presents forward and reverse controls and does not allow the client to navigate to arbitrary positions.

Cursor-based pagination requires that there be a unique, unchanging ordering of items in the result set. This ordering might typically be a creation timestamp on the records, as this presents a consistent ordering to paginate against.

Cursor-based pagination is more complex than other schemes. It also requires that the result set presents a fixed ordering and does not allow the client to arbitrarily index into the result set. However, it does provide the following benefits:

- Provides a consistent pagination view. When used properly, CursorPagination ensures that the client will never see the same item twice when paging through records, even when new items are being inserted by other clients during the pagination process.
- Supports usage with very large datasets. With extremely large datasets, pagination using offset-based pagination styles may become inefficient or unusable. Cursor-based pagination schemes instead have fixed-time properties and do not slow down as the dataset size increases.

Details and Limitations

The proper use of cursor-based pagination requires a little attention to detail. You'll need to think about what ordering you want the scheme to be applied against. The default is to order by "-created". This assumes that **there must be a "created" timestamp field** on the model instances and will present a "timeline" style paginated view, with the most recently added items first.

You can modify the ordering by overriding the "ordering" attribute on the pagination class or by using the OrderingFilter filter class together with CursorPagination. When used with OrderingFilter, you should strongly consider restricting the fields that the user may order by.

The proper usage of cursor pagination should have an ordering field that satisfies the following:

- Should be an unchanging value, such as a timestamp, slug, or other field that is only set once, on creation.
- Should be unique, or nearly unique. Millisecond precision timestamps are a good example. This implementation of cursor pagination uses a smart "position plus offset" style that allows it to properly support not-strictly-unique values as the ordering.
- Should be a non-nullable value that can be coerced to a string.
- Should not be a float. Precision errors easily lead to incorrect results. Hint: Use decimals instead. (If you already have a float field and must paginate on that, an example CursorPagination subclass that uses decimals to limit precision is available here.)
- The field should have a database index.

Using an ordering field that does not satisfy these constraints will generally still work, but you'll be losing some of the benefits of cursor pagination.

For more technical details on the implementation we use for cursor pagination, the "Building cursors for the Disqus API" blog post gives a good overview of the basic approach.

Set Up: Global Configuration

To enable globally, define the DEFAULT_PAGINATION_CLASS in the REST_FRAMEWORK settings:

```
REST_FRAMEWORK = {
    'DEFAULT_PAGINATION_CLASS': 'rest_framework.pagination.
    CursorPagination',
    'PAGE_SIZE': 10,  # Sets the default page size
}
```

Set Up: Per-View Configuration

If you want only specific views to use CursorPagination, you can set the pagination_class attribute on the view. Before getting into customizing CursorPagination, let's understand what configuration attributes are available to override. The CursorPagination class allows you to customize its behavior and appearance through several configurable attributes. Below is an explanation of each attribute and its role in defining the pagination style.

page_size

This attribute defines how many results are displayed per page. If not explicitly set, it uses the PAGE_SIZE value defined in the REST_FRAMEWORK settings. Override this to set a fixed page size specific to the pagination class. For example:

```
page_size = 5  # Display 5 records per page
```

cursor_query_param

This attribute sets the name of the query parameter used for the cursor in URLs. By default, it is always set to "cursor". You can change this value to customize the URL query parameter if the default "cursor" is not descriptive enough or conflicts with another parameter.

Example:

```
cursor_query_param = 'custom_cursor'  # Query parameter becomes ?custom_
cursor=<value>
```

Ordering

This attribute determines the ordering of the paginated results. It should be a string, or a list of strings, indicating the field against which the cursor-based pagination will be applied. For example: ordering = 'slug'. By default, this attribute is set to the -created field. This value may also be overridden by using OrderingFilter on the view. Use this attribute to specify fields to sort results, like a timestamp, id, or any unique and non-changing field.

This field has specific requirements to satisfy. This field should be unique or nearly unique (e.g., timestamps) and should be indexed and immutable to ensure consistent behavior.

For example:

```
ordering = 'title'  # Order by title (ascending)
ordering = ['-created', 'id']  # First by creation time (descending),
then by ID
```

Template

The name of a template to use when rendering pagination controls in the browsable API. This may be overridden to modify the rendering style or set to None to disable HTML pagination controls completely. Defaults to "rest_framework/pagination/previous_and_next.html".

For example:

To disable HTML controls, set the template attribute as below.

```
template = None
```

To use a custom template, set the template attribute as below:

```
template = 'my_custom_pagination_template.html'
```

To apply CursorPagination to specific views, use the pagination_class attribute. Let's implement the concept in our project. Let's go to chapter14_pagination/api/pagination.py and add the following lines of code:

```
from rest_framework.pagination import PageNumberPagination,
LimitOffsetPagination, CursorPagination

class CustomCursorPagination(CursorPagination):
    page_size = 5  # Display 5 items per page
    cursor_query_param = 'watchlist_cursor'  # Use 'watchlist_cursor' in
    query params
    ordering = '-created'  # Order by the `created` field (most recent first)
    template = None  # Disable HTML pagination controls in the
    browsable API
```

Go to chapter14_pagination/api/views.py and add the following lines of code:

```
from chapter14_pagination.api.pagination import (WatchListPageNumberPagination,
                                                 CustomLimitOffsetPagination,
                                                      CustomCursorPagination)

class WatchListCursorPaginationViewSet(viewsets.ModelViewSet):
    queryset = WatchList.objects.all()
    serializer_class = serializers.WatchListModelSerializer
    pagination_class = CustomCursorPagination
```

Add the corresponding URL in chapter14_pagination/api/urls.py as below:

```
router = DefaultRouter()
# Using ViewSet
...
router.register(r"watchlist-cursor", views.
WatchListCursorPaginationViewSet, basename="watchlist-cursor")
```

When you request without a cursor as below:

```
GET {{domain}}/api/chapter14_pagination/watchlist-cursor/
```

This gives a response in the below format:

```
{
    "next": "http://127.0.0.1:8000/api/chapter14_pagination/watchlist-
    cursor/?watchlist_cursor=cD0yMDI0LTExLTI5KzE0JTNBNDIlMOEzNy42NjEwNjUlMk
    IwMCUzQTAw",
    "previous": null,
    "results": [
        {
            "id": 60,
            "title": "The Matrix",
            "storyline": "The Matrix-Story",
            "active": true,
            "imdb_rating": 8.7,
            "created": "2024-11-29T14:44:12.959493Z",
            "episodes": 0,
```

```
            "category": "MOVIE",
            "platform": 1
        },
        ...
    ]
}
```

When you request with a cursor as below:

```
GET {{domain}}/api/chapter14_pagination/watchlist-cursor/?watchlist_cursor=
cDOyMDIOLTExLTI5KzEOJTNBNDIlMOEzNy42NjEwNjUlMkIwMCUzQTAw
```

This gives a response in the below format:

```
{
    "next": "http://127.0.0.1:8000/api/chapter14_pagination/watchlist-
    cursor/?watchlist_cursor=cDOyMDIOLTExLTE3KzIxJTNBNTAlMOEyOS4wNDYyNjIlMk
    IwMCUzQTAw",
    "previous": "http://127.0.0.1:8000/api/chapter14_pagination/watchlist-
    cursor/?watchlist_cursor=cjOxJnA9MjAyNCOxMSOyOSsxNCUzQTQyJTNBMDQuMTI5OT
    czJTJCMDAlMOEwMA%3D%3D",
    "results": [
        {
            "id": 55,
            "title": "Angry Men",
            "storyline": "Angry Men-Story",
            "active": true,
            "imdb_rating": 9.0,
            "created": "2024-11-29T14:42:04.129973Z",
            "episodes": 0,
            "category": "MOVIE",
            "platform": 1
        },
        ...
    ]
}
```

Overall, CursorPagination offers an efficient and consistent approach for navigating large datasets by relying on an opaque cursor. By leveraging its configurable attributes (page_size, cursor_query_param, ordering, and template), you can tailor pagination to fit your API's specific needs. With proper planning, CursorPagination ensures scalability and prevents issues like duplicate results, even with dynamic or large datasets.

Custom Pagination Styles

Customizing the pagination style in Django REST Framework (DRF) allows you to modify how paginated responses are structured. By inheriting from pagination. BasePagination or one of its subclasses, such as PageNumberPagination, you can implement specific response formats or handle pagination differently.

The following are the key methods for implementing custom pagination.

- **paginate_queryset(self, queryset, request, view=None)**

  This method slices the original queryset to include only the items for the requested page. It should return an iterable object containing the subset of the data for the requested page. In this method, you can add custom logic for determining how to paginate the queryset. It may also set the state on the pagination instance, which can be reused in the get_paginated_response method.

- **get_paginated_response(self, data)**

  This method generates the final paginated response. It receives the serialized page data and returns a Response object. It mainly customizes the structure of the response, e.g., adding metadata like links, total counts, or modifying the data format.

This concept has many advantages. You can structure paginated responses to match your API design preferences, improving client-side parsing. You can easily include extra fields like page size, page range, custom messages, or other details in the response. Once created, the custom pagination class can be reused across multiple views or APIs. Tailor the response structure to match client expectations or align with third-party standards.

Let's implement this concept in our project. Go to chapter14_pagination/ api/pagination.py and add the following lines of code:

```
from rest_framework.pagination import (PageNumberPagination,
                                        LimitOffsetPagination,
                                        CursorPagination,
                                        BasePagination)

class CustomBasePagination(BasePagination):
    """
    Custom pagination class to implement a unique pagination style.
    """
    page_size = 5  # Default number of items per page

    def paginate_queryset(self, queryset, request, view=None):
        """
        Slice the queryset based on custom pagination logic.
        """
        self.page_size = int(request.query_params.get('page_size', self.
        page_size))  # Allow dynamic page size
        self.page_number = int(request.query_params.get('page', 1))  # Get
        the current page number
        self.start_index = (self.page_number - 1) * self.page_size  #
        Calculate the starting index
        self.end_index = self.start_index + self.page_size  # Calculate the
        ending index

        # Slice the queryset for the current page
        self.total_items = len(queryset)
        if self.start_index >= self.total_items:
            return []

        return queryset[self.start_index:self.end_index]

    def get_paginated_response(self, data):
        """
        Return a custom response structure for the paginated data.
        """
```

```
        return Response({
            'meta': {
                'current_page': self.page_number,
                'page_size': self.page_size,
                'total_items': self.total_items,
                'total_pages': (self.total_items + self.page_size - 1)
                // self.page_size,  # Calculate total pages
            },
            'data': data  # Paginated results
        })
```

Go to chapter14_pagination/api/views.py and add the following lines of code:

```
from chapter14_pagination.api.pagination import (WatchListPageNumberPagination,
                                                 CustomLimitOffsetPagination,
                                                  CustomCursorPagination,
                                                  CustomBasePagination)

class WatchListCBPaginationViewSet(viewsets.ModelViewSet):
    queryset = WatchList.objects.all()
    serializer_class = serializers.WatchListModelSerializer
    pagination_class = CustomBasePagination
```

Add the corresponding URL in chapter14_pagination/api/urls.py as below:

```
router = DefaultRouter()
# Using ViewSet
...
router.register(r"watchlist-custom-base", views.
WatchListCBPaginationViewSet, basename="watchlist-custom-base")
```

Features of the above implementation:

- **Dynamic Page Size**

  The client can specify a custom page_size using the query parameter (e.g., ?page_size=5). The default page size is 5 if page_size is not provided.

- **Pagination Metadata**

  Includes **current_page**, **page_size**, **total_items**, and **total_pages** in the response.

- **Custom Logic**

  Pagination logic is handled by slicing the queryset based on start_index and end_index. If the requested page exceeds the total items, it returns an empty list.

- **Reusable Class**

  The CustomPagination class can be used with other views by simply setting pagination_class.

When querying the WatchList API endpoint, the client can pass page and page_size as query parameters.

For example: **GET**: `{{domain}}/api/chapter14_pagination/watchlist-custom-base/?page=1&page_size=3`

The above request returns a response in the below format:

```
{
    "meta": {
        "current_page": 1,
        "page_size": 3,
        "total_items": 12,
        "total_pages": 4
    },
    "data": [
        {
            "id": 49,
            "title": "Movie1",
            "storyline": "Movie1-Story",
            "active": true,
            "imdb_rating": 2.0,
            "created": "2024-10-26T20:06:27.406145Z",
            "episodes": 0,
            "category": "MOVIE",
            "platform": 1
```

```
        },
        {
            "id": 50,
            "title": "Movie2",
            "storyline": "Movie2-Story",
            "active": true,
            "imdb_rating": 2.0,
            "created": "2024-10-26T23:24:31.683138Z",
            "episodes": 0,
            "category": "MOVIE",
            "platform": 1
        },
        {
            "id": 51,
            "title": "Holiday",
            "storyline": "Romantic movie",
            "active": true,
            "imdb_rating": 4.0,
            "created": "2024-11-17T21:50:29.046262Z",
            "episodes": 0,
            "category": "MOVIE",
            "platform": 1
        }
    ]
}
```

As stated before, we can also inherit one of the subclasses of Basepagination such as PageNumberPagination. Let's also implement this concept in our project.

Go to chapter14_pagination/api/pagination.py and add the following lines of code:

```
class CustomPNPagination(PageNumberPagination):
    """
    Custom pagination style with 'next' and 'previous' links nested inside
    a 'links' key.
    """
    def get_paginated_response(self, data):
```

```
        return Response(OrderedDict([
            ('links', {
                'next': self.get_next_link(),
                'previous': self.get_previous_link()
            }),
            ('count', self.page.paginator.count),
            ('page_size', self.page_size),
            ('results', data),
        ]))
```

Go to chapter14_pagination/api/views.py and add the following lines of code:

```
from chapter14_pagination.api.pagination import (WatchListPageNumberPagination,
                                                  CustomLimitOffsetPagination,
                                                  CustomCursorPagination,
                                                  CustomBasePagination,
                                                  CustomPNPagination)

class WatchListCPNPaginationViewSet(viewsets.ModelViewSet):
    queryset = WatchList.objects.all()
    serializer_class = serializers.WatchListModelSerializer
    pagination_class = CustomPNPagination
```

Add the corresponding URL in chapter14_pagination/api/urls.py as below:

```
router = DefaultRouter()
# Using ViewSet
...
router.register(r"watchlist-custom-pn", views.
WatchListCPNPaginationViewSet, basename="watchlist-custom-pn")
```

In the above Custom pagination class, change the default pagination output to include the next and previous links inside a nested links key. The **get_next_link** and **get_previous_link** are the built-in methods that return the next and previous page URLs, respectively. They're included under a links key for better organization. The **OrderedDict** is used to ensure a consistent order of keys in the response (links, count, page_size, results). Also included is page_size to display how many items are shown per page.

When the client made a request: **GET** `{{domain}}/api/chapter14_pagination/watchlist-custom-pn/` returns a response in the below format:


```
{
    "links": {
        "next": "http://127.0.0.1:8000/api/chapter14_pagination/watchlist-
        custom-pn/?page=2",
        "previous": null
    },
    "count": 12,
    "page_size": 3,
    "results": [
        {
            "id": 49,
            "title": "Movie1",
            "storyline": "Movie1-Story",
            "active": true,
            "imdb_rating": 2.0,
            "created": "2024-10-26T20:06:27.406145Z",
            "episodes": 0,
            "category": "MOVIE",
            "platform": 1
        },
        {
            "id": 50,
            "title": "Movie2",
            "storyline": "Movie2-Story",
            "active": true,
            "imdb_rating": 2.0,
            "created": "2024-10-26T23:24:31.683138Z",
            "episodes": 0,
            "category": "MOVIE",
            "platform": 1
        },
        {
            "id": 51,
```

```
            "title": "Holiday",
            "storyline": "Romantic movie",
            "active": true,
            "imdb_rating": 4.0,
            "created": "2024-11-17T21:50:29.046262Z",
            "episodes": 0,
            "category": "MOVIE",
            "platform": 1
        }
    ]
}
```

The client can send the page number for a specific page as below:

GET {{domain}}/api/chapter14_pagination/watchlist-custom-pn/?page=2 returns response as below:


```
{
    "links": {
        "next": "http://127.0.0.1:8000/api/chapter14_pagination/watchlist-
        custom-pn/?page=3",
        "previous": "http://127.0.0.1:8000/api/chapter14_pagination/
        watchlist-custom-pn/"
    },
    "count": 12,
    "page_size": 3,
    "results": [
        {
            "id": 52,
            "title": "Inception",
            "storyline": "A thief who steals corporate secrets through the
            use of dream-sharing technology is given the inverse task of
            planting an idea into the mind of a C.E.O., but his tragic past
            may doom the project",
            "active": true,
            "imdb_rating": 5.0,
            "created": "2024-11-17T21:54:09.569418Z",
            "episodes": 0,
```

```
            "category": "MOVIE",
            "platform": 1
        },
        {
            "id": 53,
            "title": "The Shawshank Redemption",
            "storyline": "The Shawshank Redemption Story",
            "active": true,
            "imdb_rating": 5.0,
            "created": "2024-11-29T10:53:30.248607Z",
            "episodes": 0,
            "category": "MOVIE",
            "platform": 1
        },
        {
            "id": 54,
            "title": "The Godfather",
            "storyline": "The Godfather-Story",
            "active": true,
            "imdb_rating": 9.2,
            "created": "2024-11-29T11:04:33.112452Z",
            "episodes": 0,
            "category": "MOVIE",
            "platform": 1
        }
    ]
}
```

You can also configure the above Pagination globally on the settings file as below:

```
REST_FRAMEWORK = {
    'DEFAULT_PAGINATION_CLASS': ' chapter14_pagination.api.pagination.
    CustomPNPagination',
    'PAGE_SIZE': 10  # Default number of items per page
}
```

CHAPTER 15

Versioning

Versioning in Django Rest Framework (DRF) allows API developers to manage and serve different versions of their APIs. This is particularly useful for maintaining backward compatibility, allowing older clients to continue functioning while newer clients can use updated features. DRF provides several strategies for implementing versioning, enabling flexibility in how versions are handled.

APIs evolve over a period due to changes in requirements. You may want to add or modify the functionality without breaking the existing clients. That's where versioning comes to help. It also helps in maintaining multiple API versions simultaneously. DRF provides built-in support for versioning, allowing developers to specify the current version of the API and handle requests for different versions using version-aware logic. Versioning is determined by the **client's request**. Versions can be specified in the URL, query parameters, headers, or a custom scheme.

Versioning may not be necessary for systems with long-term stability requirements or if you have limited clients and you have full control over APIs for them.

Versioning with REST Framework

Versioning with Django REST Framework (DRF) enables the API to handle different client needs over time by making backward-compatible changes while evolving functionality. Here's a detailed breakdown of how versioning impacts the API and practical tips for using it effectively.

Key Concepts in DRF Versioning

1. **request.version**

   When versioning is enabled, request.version contains the version string extracted from the incoming client request. If versioning is not enabled, request.version will return None.

G. Patil, *Django REST APIs Demystified*, https://doi.org/10.1007/979-8-8688-1850-9_15

2. **Varying API Behavior Based on Version**

   You can define version-specific behavior, such as returning different serializers, applying different business logic, or even serving entirely different endpoints.
   Example: Switching serializers based on the API version as below:

   ```
   def get_serializer_class(self):
       if self.request.version == 'v1':
           return AccountSerializerVersion1
       return AccountSerializer
   ```

3. **Reversing URLs for Versioned APIs**

   The reverse function from rest_framework.reverse ensures that the URL generated matches the versioning scheme of the request.
   For example:

   ```
   from rest_framework.reverse import reverse

   url = reverse('bookings-list', request=request)
   ```

   - For **NamespaceVersioning**, this would resolve to `http://example.org/v1/bookings/`.
   - For **QueryParameterVersioning**, this would resolve to `http://example.org/bookings/?version=1.0`.

4. **Versioned APIs and Hyperlinked Serializers**

   When using hyperlinked serializers with URL-based versioning, you must pass the request context to the serializer.

   For example:

   ```
   def get(self, request):
       queryset = Booking.objects.all()
       serializer = BookingsSerializer(queryset, many=True,
                    context={'request': request})
       return Response({'all_bookings': serializer.data})
   ```

   This ensures that generated URLs in the serialized response include the correct version.

Configuring the Versioning Scheme

To configure versioning schemes in Django REST Framework (DRF), you use the DEFAULT_VERSIONING_CLASS setting or configure versioning at the individual view level.

Global Configuration

You can define the default versioning scheme globally in your settings.py file:

```
REST_FRAMEWORK = {
    'DEFAULT_VERSIONING_CLASS': 'rest_framework.versioning.Namespace
    Versioning',
    'DEFAULT_VERSION': 'v1',
    'ALLOWED_VERSIONS': ['v1', 'v2'],
    'VERSION_PARAM': 'version',
}
```

In the above example, **DEFAULT_VERSIONING_CLASS** specifies the global versioning scheme for your API. The following are the common options:

- NamespaceVersioning
- QueryParameterVersioning
- URLPathVersioning
- HeaderVersioning
- AcceptHeaderVersioning

Note that unless it is explicitly set, the value for DEFAULT_VERSIONING_CLASS will be None. In that case, the request.version attribute will always return None.

DEFAULT_VERSION sets the default version when the client does not explicitly provide one. For example, if no version is supplied in the request, request.version will default to 'v1.'

ALLOWED_VERSIONS is a list of versions allowed by the API. If the client requests a version not in this list, an error is raised.

Example: ['v1,' 'v2'].

VERSION_PARAM allows to specify the name of the query parameter or header field to use when specifying the API version. It defaults to 'version.'

Per-View Configuration

You can also set the versioning scheme on an individual view. Typically, you won't need to do this, as it makes more sense to have a single versioning scheme used globally. But if you do need to do so, use the **versioning_class** attribute.

For example, with QueryParameterVersioning:

```
from rest_framework.views import APIView
from rest_framework.versioning import QueryParameterVersioning

class ProfileList(APIView):
    versioning_class = QueryParameterVersioning

    def get(self, request):
        if request.version == 'v1':
            return Response({"message": "Using Version 1"})
        elif request.version == 'v2':
            return Response({"message": "Using Version 2"})
        else:
            return Response({"message": "Unknown Version"})
```

Customizing the Versioning Class

You can also set your versioning class plus those three values on a per-view or per-viewset basis by defining your own versioning scheme. You can create a custom versioning scheme by subclassing any of the existing versioning classes or by extending BaseVersioning and using the **default_version**, **allowed_versions**, and **version_param** class variables.

For example, if you want to use URLPathVersioning:

```
from rest_framework.versioning import URLPathVersioning
from rest_framework.views import APIView

class CustomURLPathVersioning(URLPathVersioning):
    default_version = 'v1'
    allowed_versions = ['v1', 'v2']
    version_param = 'api_version'

class CustomView(APIView):
```

```
    versioning_class = CustomURLPathVersioning

    def get(self, request):
        return Response({
            "version": request.version,
            "message": f"Hello from API version {request.version}!"
        })
```

In the above example, **default_version** specifies the default version when no version is supplied. The **allowed_versions** restricts the versions allowed in the request. The **version_param** renames the parameter used for versioning (e.g., in a URL or query string).

Preparing for This Chapter

Create a new app with the name **chapter15_versioning** with the steps specified in the **Project Setup** section in Chapter 3.

Go to drfproject/settings.py and add the following lines of code:

```
INSTALLED_APPS = [
    ...
    "chapter15_versioning",
]
```

Create chapter15_versioning/api/serializers.py and add the following lines of code:

```
from rest_framework import serializers
from chapter3_project_setup.models import WatchList, StreamPlatform, Review

class WatchListModelSerializer(serializers.ModelSerializer):
    class Meta:
        model = WatchList
        fields = "__all__"
        ref_name = 'C16WatchListModelSerializer'

class StreamPlatformModelSerializer(serializers.ModelSerializer):
    class Meta:
        model = StreamPlatform
```

```
        fields = "__all__"
        ref_name = 'C16StreamPlatformModelSerializer'

class ReviewModelSerializer(serializers.ModelSerializer):
    user = serializers.StringRelatedField()
    class Meta:
        model = Review
        fields = "__all__"
        ref_name = 'C16ReviewModelSerializer'
```

Create chapter15_versioning/api/urls.py and add the following lines of code:

```
from django.urls import path, include
from rest_framework.routers import DefaultRouter

from . import views

router = DefaultRouter()

urlpatterns = [

    # Using ViewSet
    path("", include(router.urls)),
]
```

Go to chapter15_versioning/api/views.py and add the following lines of code:

```
from rest_framework import viewsets
from django.contrib.auth import get_user_model
from rest_framework.response import Response
from rest_framework.reverse import reverse
from rest_framework.versioning import (URLPathVersioning,
                                       NamespaceVersioning,
                                       QueryParameterVersioning,
                                       AcceptHeaderVersioning)
from chapter3_project_setup.models import WatchList
from chapter15_versioning.api import serializers
```

Go to drfproject/urls.py and add the following lines of code:

```
urlpatterns = [
    ...
    path('api/chapter15_versioning/', include('chapter15_versioning.api.
    urls')),
]
```

Types of API Versioning

DRF provides the following built-in versioning types.

URLPathVersioning

In this versioning scheme, the version of the API is specified as part of the URL path. This approach allows the client to clearly specify which version of the API they are using by including the version identifier in the URL.

This scheme requires the client to specify the version as part of the URL path. For example:

To access version v1 of the bookings resource:

```
GET /v1/bookings/ HTTP/1.1
Host: example.com
Accept: application/json
```

To access version v2 of the bookings resource:

```
GET /v2/bookings/ HTTP/1.1
Host: example.com
Accept: application/json
```

The API URLs are defined with a **version** keyword argument in the URL path using regular expressions. For example:

```
urlpatterns = [
    re_path(
        r'^(?P<version>(v1|v2))/bookings/$',
        bookings_list,
```

```
        name='bookings-list'
    ),
    re_path(
        r'^(?P<version>(v1|v2))/bookings/(?P<pk>[0-9]+)/$',
        bookings_detail,
        name='bookings-detail'
    )
]
```

Here, (?P<version>(v1|v2)) captures the version part of the URL and passes it as a version argument to the view.

In this versioning scheme, the version is visible and self-explanatory in the URL. The clients can easily switch between versions by modifying the URL. But this versioning scheme also has some limitations. Including the version in the path can make URLs longer and more verbose, and as new versions are added, managing older versions in the URL structure can become cumbersome. But it is well suited for small APIs with a limited number of versions and use it when there are clear version boundaries (e.g., v1, v2) and minimal need for complex versioning logic.

Let's implement this concept in our project.

Go to chapter15_versioning/api/views.py and add the following lines of code:

```
class WatchListUrlPathVersioningViewSet(viewsets.ModelViewSet):
    queryset = WatchList.objects.all()
    serializer_class = serializers.WatchListModelSerializer
    versioning_class = URLPathVersioning

    def get_serializer_class(self):
        if self.request.version == 'v1':
            return serializers.WatchListModelSerializer  # Define this
            serializer for v1
        return serializers.WatchListEnhancedSerializer  # Define this
        serializer for v2
```

Add the corresponding URL in chapter15_versioning/api/urls.py as below:

```
router = DefaultRouter()
# Using ViewSet
```

```
router.register(r"watchlist-urlpath", views.
WatchListUrlPathVersioningViewSet, basename="watchlist-urlpath")

urlpatterns = [
    # Define versioned paths using a regex for versioning
    re_path(r'^(?P<version>(v1|v2))/', include(router.urls)),

    # Using ViewSet
    path("", include(router.urls)),
]
```

In the above example, we have added an additional serializer **WatchListEnhancedSerializer** to choose when v2 versioned requests are made to the server. The pattern in URL (?P<version>(v1|v2)) matches the v1 or v2 part of the URL, and the router includes the WatchListUrlPathVersioningViewSet.

In the **WatchListUrlPathVersioningViewSet**, the versioning_class is set to **URLPathVersioning**. The **request.version** is extracted from the URL path using the (?P<version>) regex in the URL pattern. The **get_serializer_class** method chooses the appropriate serializer based on the request.version. The **re_path** captures the version (v1 or v2) in the URL, allowing DRF to determine the version. **WatchListModelSerializer** is used for v1 (all fields), and **WatchListEnhancedSerializer** is used for v2 (selected fields).

To access the v1 API endpoint, the request shall be in the format:

```
GET {{domain}}/api/chapter15_versioning/v1/watchlist-urlpath/
```

Its response will be in the below format:

```
{
    "count": 12,
    "next": "http://127.0.0.1:8000/api/chapter15_versioning/v1/watchlist-
    urlpath/?page=2",
    "previous": null,
    "results": [
        {
            "id": 49,
            "title": "Movie1",
            "storyline": "Movie1-Story",
```

```
            "active": true,
            "imdb_rating": 2.0,
            "created": "2024-10-26T20:06:27.406145Z",
            "episodes": 0,
            "category": "MOVIE",
            "platform": 1
        },
        ...
    ]
}
```


To access the v2 API endpoint, the request shall be in the format:

```
GET {{domain}}/api/chapter15_versioning/v2/watchlist-urlpath/
```

Its response will be in the below format:


```
{
    "count": 12,
    "next": "http://127.0.0.1:8000/api/chapter15_versioning/v2/watchlist-
    urlpath/?page=2",
    "previous": null,
    "results": [
        {
            "title": "Movie1",
            "storyline": "Movie1-Story",
            "platform": 1,
            "category": "MOVIE"
        },
        ...
    ]
}
```


NamespaceVersioning

NamespaceVersioning is a versioning strategy where the API version is determined by the namespace associated with the URL pattern that matches the incoming request. To the client, this approach behaves the same as URLPathVersioning, but it is more manageable in Django applications as it uses URL namespacing rather than URL keyword arguments.

This method is particularly beneficial for large-scale projects where organizing and managing versioned endpoints is a priority. In this versioning scheme, the **request.version** attribute is derived from the **namespace** of the matching URL. Each version of the API is defined under a distinct namespace in Django's URL configuration.

How URLs Work with NamespaceVersioning

Assuming the API is hosted at `http://example.com`:

- A request to `/v1/bookings/` will use the v1 namespace.
- A request to `/v2/bookings/` will use the v2 namespace.

Example Client Requests:

```
GET /v1/bookings/ HTTP/1.1
Host: example.com
Accept: application/json
```

This versioning scheme is ideal for large projects with multiple versions of the API and allows easy addition of new versions by duplicating URL namespaces. It also keeps versioning logic isolated within URL configurations. Client interaction is consistent regardless of the versioning scheme.

Let's understand this concept in more detail by implementing this concept into our project. Let's go to chapter15_versioning/api/views.py and add the following lines of code:

```
class WatchListNamespaceVersioningViewSet(viewsets.ModelViewSet):
    queryset = WatchList.objects.all()
    serializer_class = serializers.WatchListModelSerializer
    versioning_class = NamespaceVersioning

    def get_serializer_class(self):
        if self.request.version == 'v1':
            return serializers.WatchListModelSerializer  # Define this
            serializer for v1
        return serializers.WatchListEnhancedSerializer  # Define this
        serializer for v2
```

Go to chapter15_versioning/api/urls.py and add the following lines of code:

```
router = DefaultRouter()
# Using ViewSet
...
router.register(r"watchlist-namespace", views.
WatchListNamespaceVersioningViewSet, basename="watchlist-namespace")
```

Let's go to drfproject/urls.py and add the following lines of code:

```
urlpatterns = [
    ...
    path('api/v1/chapter15_versioning/', include(('chapter15_versioning.
    api.urls', 'chapter15_versioning'), namespace="v1")),
    path('api/v2/chapter15_versioning/', include(('chapter15_versioning.
    api.urls', 'chapter15_versioning'), namespace="v2")),
]
```

In the above example, URLs are defined at the project level; the URLs are routed to /v1/ and /v2/, where the namespace is defined. When the client requests api/v1/chapter15_versioning/ or api/v2/chapter15_versioning/, the namespace determines the request.version value as v1 or v2. In the **WatchListNamespaceVersioningViewSet**, the get_serializer_class() checks the request.version and returns the correct serializer (WatchListModelSerializer for v1 and WatchListEnhancedSerializer for v2).

To access the v1 API endpoint, the request shall be in the format:

```
GET {{domain}}/api/v1/chapter15_versioning/watchlist-namespace
```

Its response will be in the below format:

```
{
    "count": 12,
    "next": "http://127.0.0.1:8000/api/v1/chapter15_versioning/watchlist-
    namespace/?page=2",
    "previous": null,
    "results": [
        {
            "id": 49,
            "title": "Movie1",
```

```
            "storyline": "Movie1-Story",
            "active": true,
            "imdb_rating": 2.0,
            "created": "2024-10-26T20:06:27.406145Z",
            "episodes": 0,
            "category": "MOVIE",
            "platform": 1
        },
        ...
    ]
}
```

To access the v2 API endpoint, the request shall be in the format:

```
GET {{domain}}/api/v2/chapter15_versioning/watchlist-namespace
```

Its response will be in the below format:

```
{
    "count": 12,
    "next": "http://127.0.0.1:8000/api/v2/chapter15_versioning/watchlist-
    namespace/?page=2",
    "previous": null,
    "results": [
        {
            "title": "Movie1",
            "storyline": "Movie1-Story",
            "platform": 1,
            "category": "MOVIE"
        },
        ...
    ]
}
```

NamespaceVersioning vs. URLPathVersioning

Feature	NamespaceVersioning	URLPathVersioning
Version Placement	Defined in the namespace (v1, v2)	Part of the URL path (/v1/...)
Setup Complexity	Moderate	Simple
Scalability	Better for large projects	Best for small projects
Maintainability	Easier to maintain in modular systems	Can become cluttered with many regex patterns
Flexibility	Tied to Django's URL namespaces	Flexible URL design with regex
Client Clarity	Slightly less clear (namespace-based)	Clearer to clients (URL-based)
Integration	Works seamlessly with Django features	Requires custom regex patterns
Use Case	Large-scale apps with multiple apps and versions	Small to medium apps with few versions

How to Use

1. **Choose NamespaceVersioning if:**
    - Your project has many apps and multiple versions.
    - You want to leverage Django's URL namespaces for better maintainability.
    - You prefer keeping versioning logic centralized in the project-level urls.py.
2. **Choose URLPathVersioning if**
    - Your project is small or medium-sized with straightforward versioning needs.
    - You want the API version to be an explicit part of the URL path.
    - You are comfortable managing regex patterns for URLs.

Both methods are valid, and the choice largely depends on the size and complexity of your project.

QueryParameterVersioning

In this versioning scheme, the API version is specified as a query parameter in the request URL. This approach allows clients to send the version information as part of the query string.

When a client makes a request, it includes the version information as a query parameter, such as

```
GET /bookings/?version=1.0 HTTP/1.1
Host: example.com
Accept: application/json
```

In this case, the version parameter is version=1.0 and the **request.version** attribute in DRF will return the string 1.0.

This versioning approach is simple for clients to append the version to the query string. It keeps the main URL structure clean while still providing versioning. It is easy to test and debug by modifying the URL in a browser or a tool like Postman.

It also has some disadvantages. The query parameters can sometimes interfere with caching mechanisms. Including version information in query parameters does not strictly adhere to RESTful principles. The query parameter name (version) could conflict with other query parameters in the API.

QueryParameterVersioning is ideal when you want a simple, nonintrusive way to specify API versions. It is also ideal when your clients are mainly browsers or testing tools like Postman. Clients can maintain clean URLs using this approach if it is their priority.

Let's implement this concept in our project. Go to chapter15_versioning/api/views.py and add the following lines of code:

```
class WatchListQueryParameterVersioningViewSet(viewsets.ModelViewSet):
    queryset = WatchList.objects.all()
    serializer_class = serializers.WatchListModelSerializer
    versioning_class = QueryParameterVersioning
```

```
    def get_serializer_class(self):
        if self.request.version == '1.0':
            return serializers.WatchListModelSerializer  # Define this
            serializer for v1
        return serializers.WatchListEnhancedSerializer  # Define this
        serializer for v2
```

Add the corresponding URL in chapter15_versioning/api/urls.py as below:

```
router = DefaultRouter()
# Using ViewSet
...
router.register(r"watchlist-queryparam", views.WatchListQueryParameter
VersioningViewSet, basename="watchlist-queryparam")
```

In the above example, **QueryParameterVersioning** allows the client to specify the API version using a query parameter (version). The get_serializer_class() method in your WatchListQueryParameterVersioningViewSet ensures that the correct serializer is used based on the requested version.

To access the version 1.0 API endpoint, the request shall be in the format:

```
GET {{domain}}/api/chapter15_versioning/watchlist-queryparam?version=1.0
```

Its response will be in the below format:

```
{
    "count": 12,
    "next": "http://127.0.0.1:8000/api/chapter15_versioning/watchlist-query
    param/?page=2&version=1.0",
    "previous": null,
    "results": [
        {
            "id": 49,
            "title": "Movie1",
            "storyline": "Movie1-Story",
            "active": true,
            "imdb_rating": 2.0,
            "created": "2024-10-26T20:06:27.406145Z",
```

```
            "episodes": 0,
            "category": "MOVIE",
            "platform": 1
        },
        ...
    ]
}
```

To access the other version of the API endpoint, the request shall be in the format:

```
GET {{domain}}/api/chapter15_versioning/watchlist-queryparam?version=2.0
OR
GET {{domain}}/api/chapter15_versioning/watchlist-queryparam
```

Its response will be in the below format:

```
{
    "count": 12,
    "next": "http://127.0.0.1:8000/api/chapter15_versioning/watchlist-
            queryparam/?page=2",
    "previous": null,
    "results": [
        {
            "title": "Movie1",
            "storyline": "Movie1-Story",
            "platform": 1,
            "category": "MOVIE"
        },
        ...
    ]
}
```

You can test versioned endpoints by appending the version query parameter to the URL (?version=1.0, ?version=2.0, etc.).

AcceptHeaderVersioning

AcceptHeaderVersioning is a versioning scheme in DRF where the API version is determined by the Accept header of the incoming HTTP request. Instead of encoding the version in the URL or query parameters, the client specifies the version as part of the media type in the Accept header. The version is included as a media type parameter that supplements the main media type.

The Accept header typically looks like this:

```
GET /bookings/ HTTP/1.1
Host: example.com
Accept: application/json; version=1.0
```

The version parameter in the Accept header is extracted by DRF's **AcceptHeaderVersioning** class. The value of version becomes accessible via request.version.

In this version approach, versioning information is not embedded in the URL path or query string. It relies on the standard HTTP Accept header, making it consistent with RESTful principles. It follows HTTP standards by relying on the Accept header for content negotiation. It allows for complex negotiation between the client and server for various versions.

This versioning approach also has disadvantages. Clients must explicitly set Accept headers, which is not as straightforward as URL-based versioning. It is harder to test directly in browsers or simple tools, as they don't allow easy customization of headers. Debugging may be more challenging because version information is not visible in the URL.

This versioning approach is useful when APIs follow strict RESTful design principles and in situations where clean URLs are a priority. It is also useful in scenarios where the client base is advanced and capable of handling custom headers. It needs systems that require **content negotiation** for media types and versions.

AcceptHeaderVersioning provides a standards-compliant way to version APIs. While it may require more effort for client-side integration and debugging, it keeps APIs clean and aligns with REST principles. If simplicity and ease of testing are a priority, other schemes like URLPathVersioning may be better suited.

Let's implement this versioning approach in our project. Go to chapter15_versioning/api/views.py and add the following lines of code:

```
class WatchListAcceptHeaderVersioningViewSet(viewsets.ModelViewSet):
    queryset = WatchList.objects.all()
    serializer_class = serializers.WatchListModelSerializer
    versioning_class = AcceptHeaderVersioning

    def get_serializer_class(self):
        if self.request.version == '1.0':
            return serializers.WatchListModelSerializer  # Define this
            serializer for 1.0
        return serializers.WatchListEnhancedSerializer  # Define this
        serializer for 2.0 or other versions
```

Go to chapter15_versioning/api/urls.py and add the following lines of code:

```
router = DefaultRouter()
# Using ViewSet
...
router.register(r"watchlist-acceptheader", views.WatchListAcceptHeader
VersioningViewSet, basename="watchlist-acceptheader")
```

To access the version 1.0 API endpoint, the request shall be in the format:

```
GET {{domain}}/api/chapter15_versioning/watchlist-acceptheader/
Accept: application/json; version=1.0
```

Its response will be in the below format:


```
{
    "count": 12,
    "next": "http://127.0.0.1:8000/api/chapter15_versioning/watchlist-
            acceptheader/?page=2",
    "previous": null,
    "results": [
        {
            "id": 49,
            "title": "Movie1",
            "storyline": "Movie1-Story",
            "active": true,
            "imdb_rating": 2.0,
```

```
            "created": "2024-10-26T20:06:27.406145Z",
            "episodes": 0,
            "category": "MOVIE",
            "platform": 1
        },
        ...
    ]
}
```

To access version 2.0 or other versions of the API endpoint, the request shall be in the format:

```
GET {{domain}}/api/chapter15_versioning/watchlist-acceptheader/
Accept: application/json; version=2.0
```

Its response will be in the below format:

```
{
    "count": 12,
    "next": "http://127.0.0.1:8000/api/chapter15_versioning/watchlist-
            acceptheader/?page=2",
    "previous": null,
    "results": [
        {
            "title": "Movie1",
            "storyline": "Movie1-Story",
            "platform": 1,
            "category": "MOVIE"
        },
        ...
    ]
}
```

HostNameVersioning

This versioning scheme allows you to determine the API version based on the hostname (or subdomain) of the incoming request. This is particularly useful if you have different subdomains or hostnames serving different versions of your API. It requires the client to specify the requested version as part of the hostname in the URL.

The hostname or subdomain in the incoming request determines the API version. For example:

- For the hostname **v1.example.com**, the API version will be **v1**.
- For the hostname **v2.example.com**, the API version will be **v2**.

The **request.version** attribute will reflect the version determined from the hostname. This versioning scheme can be awkward to use in debug mode, as you will typically be accessing a raw IP address such as 127.0.0.1. It is difficult to test this functionality in the development environment. Hostname-based versioning can be particularly useful if you have requirements to route incoming requests to different servers based on the version, as you can configure different DNS records for different API versions.

Make requests using different hostnames or subdomains:

- Request for Version 1 (v1.example.com)

```
GET /api/watchlist-hostname/
Host: v1.example.com
Accept: application/json
```

- Request for Version 2 (v2.example.com)

```
GET /api/watchlist-hostname/
Host: v2.example.com
Accept: application/json
```

HostNameVersioning determines the API version based on the hostname or subdomain of the incoming request. This method is useful for organizations that can manage their DNS configuration and want clear API version separation. It requires proper DNS or web server configuration to route requests for specific subdomains.

Custom Versioning Schemes

In **Django REST Framework (DRF)**, a **custom versioning scheme** allows you to define a custom mechanism for determining the API version from a client request. While DRF provides several built-in versioning schemes (e.g., URLPathVersioning, NamespaceVersioning, AcceptHeaderVersioning), you can implement a custom versioning strategy by subclassing BaseVersioning.

A **custom versioning scheme** is useful when your versioning requirements don't align with the built-in schemes. For instance:

- You want to retrieve the version from a custom header (e.g., X-API-Version).
- You have a unique way of embedding version information in the request or environment (e.g., in cookies or user metadata).
- You need highly customized URL structures.

To create a custom versioning scheme, you need to subclass BaseVersioning and then override the **.determine_version()** method, which determines the version from the request. Optionally, override the **.reverse()** method if you want to modify URL lookups for versioned endpoints. The .determine_version(request, *args, **kwargs) method should return the determined version as a string or None if no version is found.

Using a custom versioning scheme, you can implement any versioning logic required by your application or clients. You can easily adapt to nonstandard versioning methods used by client applications. You can also add custom validation rules or complex logic.

A custom versioning scheme is mainly used when none of DRF's built-in versioning schemes meet your requirements. It is suitable if you have legacy APIs with nonstandard versioning methods. It is also suitable if you want to adopt unconventional versioning methods (e.g., version embedded in cookies).

Let's implement a custom versioning scheme in our project. Create a file chapter15_versioning/api/versioning.py and add the following lines of code:

```
class XAPIVersionScheme(BaseVersioning):
    def determine_version(self, request, *args, **kwargs):
        # Extract the version from the custom header 'X-API-Version'
        return request.META.get('HTTP_X_API_VERSION', None)
```

```
    def reverse(self, viewname, args=None, kwargs=None, request=None,
    format=None):
        # Append version to the URL as a query parameter for demonstration
        URL = super().reverse(viewname, args, kwargs, request, format)
        version = self.determine_version(request)
        if version:
            return f"{url}?version={version}"
        return url
```

Go to chapter15_versioning/api/views.py and add the following lines of code:

```
from chapter15_versioning.api.versioning import XAPIVersionScheme

class WatchListCustomVersioningViewSet(viewsets.ModelViewSet):
    queryset = WatchList.objects.all()
    versioning_class = XAPIVersionScheme  # Use the custom versioning class

    def get_serializer_class(self):
        # Check the requested version and return the appropriate serializer
        if self.request.version == '1.0':
            return serializers.WatchListModelSerializer  # Basic serializer
            for version 1.0
        elif self.request.version == '2.0':
            return serializers.WatchListEnhancedSerializer  # Enhanced
            serializer for version 2.0
        return serializers.WatchListModelSerializer  # Default serializer
        if no version is provided

    def list(self, request, *args, **kwargs):
        # Example response includes a reverse URL for demonstration
        example_url = reverse('watchlist-custom-list', request=request)
        return Response({
            "version": request.version,
            "example_url": example_url,
            "data": super().list(request, *args, **kwargs).data
        })
```

Add the corresponding URL in chapter15_versioning/api/urls.py and add the following lines of code:

```
router = DefaultRouter()
# Using ViewSet
...
router.register(r"watchlist-custom", views.WatchListCustom
VersioningViewSet, basename="watchlist-custom")
```

In the above example, the custom class XAPIVersionScheme is defined. The method **determine_version()** in the custom class determines and returns the version based on the incoming request. It uses the request.META dictionary to fetch the HTTP_X_API_VERSION header (e.g., "1.0" or "2.0"). If the header is missing, it defaults to None. The reverse() method modifies the behavior of the reverse() function to ensure that versioning is reflected in the URLs and appends the version as a query parameter (e.g., ?version=1.0) if a version is present.

Overall, in the above example, the **XAPIVersionScheme** class determines the API version from the X-API-Version header. The **get_serializer_class()** method dynamically selects the serializer based on the version. The custom reverse() method ensures that the version information is included in the generated URLs. The list() method demonstrates how to include version-related information in API responses.

To access the version 1.0 API endpoint, the request shall be in the format:

```
GET {{domain}}/api/chapter15_versioning/watchlist-custom/
X-API-Version: 1.0
```

Its response will be in the below format:

```
{
    "version": "1.0",
    "example_url": "http://127.0.0.1:8000/api/chapter15_versioning/
                    watchlist-custom/?version=1.0",
    "data": {
        "count": 12,
        "next": "http://127.0.0.1:8000/api/chapter15_versioning/watchlist-
                custom/?page=2",
        "previous": null,
```

```
        "results": [
            {
                "id": 49,
                "title": "Movie1",
                "storyline": "Movie1-Story",
                "active": true,
                "imdb_rating": 2.0,
                "created": "2024-10-26T20:06:27.406145Z",
                "episodes": 0,
                "category": "MOVIE",
                "platform": 1
            },
            ...
        ]
    }
}
```

To access the version 2.0 API endpoint, the request shall be in the format:

```
GET {{domain}}/api/chapter15_versioning/watchlist-custom/
X-API-Version: 2.0
```

Its response will be in the below format:

```
{
    "version": "2.0",
    "example_url": "http://127.0.0.1:8000/api/chapter15_versioning/
                    watchlist-custom/?version=2.0",
    "data": {
        "count": 12,
        "next": "http://127.0.0.1:8000/api/chapter15_versioning/watchlist-
                custom/?page=2",
        "previous": null,
        "results": [
            {
                "title": "Movie1",
                "storyline": "Movie1-Story",
```

```
                "platform": 1,
                "category": "MOVIE"
            },
            ...
        ]
    }
}
```

CHAPTER 16

Testing

Testing is a crucial aspect of web development, ensuring that your Django Rest Framework (DRF) API functions correctly and efficiently. It helps identify and fix bugs early in the development process, preventing issues from reaching production. Robust test coverage gives developers confidence in the stability and reliability of their code.

Testing in Django REST Framework (DRF) ensures that your API behaves as expected, handles various edge cases, and continues to function correctly when you make changes. It builds on Django's testing framework, extending it with tools specifically for API testing. It also involves verifying the behavior of your API endpoints, serializers, views, and custom features such as versioning. DRF provides tools to simplify testing by building on Django's testing framework, which is based on Python's **unittest** module.

DRF provides specific tools to perform the tests:

- **APIClient**

  A flexible testing client that allows for making API requests, including adding headers, authentication tokens, and more.

- **APITestCase**

  DRF provides **APITestCase**, which extends Django's TestCase class and includes utilities specifically for API testing. Use **self.client** (an instance of APIClient) to simulate requests like GET, POST, etc.

- **RequestFactory**

  Useful for testing views directly. This allows you to create requests and test individual views instead of going through the URL router.

Test files can be created in two ways. You can create tests.py for each application, or you can also organize multiple test files within the tests/ folder for better structure. But make sure that all test files created within the tests/ folder shall be prefixed with test_.

G. Patil, *Django REST APIs Demystified*, https://doi.org/10.1007/979-8-8688-1850-9_16

Preparing for This Chapter

Create a new app with the name **chapter16_testing** with the steps specified in the **Project Setup** section in Chapter 3.

Go to drfproject/settings.py and add the following lines of code:

```
INSTALLED_APPS = [
    ...
    "chapter16_testing",
]
```

Create chapter16_testing/api/serializers.py and the following lines of code:

```
from rest_framework import serializers
from django.contrib.auth import get_user_model
from chapter3_project_setup.models import WatchList, StreamPlatform, Review

class WatchListModelSerializer(serializers.ModelSerializer):
    class Meta:
        model = WatchList
        fields = "__all__"

class StreamPlatformModelSerializer(serializers.ModelSerializer):
    class Meta:
        model = StreamPlatform
        fields = "__all__"

class ReviewModelSerializer(serializers.ModelSerializer):
    user = serializers.StringRelatedField()
    class Meta:
        model = Review
        fields = "__all__"
```

Create chapter16_testing/api/urls.py and add the following lines of code:

```
from django.urls import path, include
from rest_framework.routers import DefaultRouter
from chapter16_testing.api import views

router = DefaultRouter()
```

```
urlpatterns = [

    # Using ViewSet
    path("", include(router.urls)),
]
```

Go to drfproject/urls.py and add the following lines of code:

```
urlpatterns = [
    ...
    path('api/chapter16_testing/', include('chapter16_testing.api.urls')),
]
```

Go to chapter16_testing/api/views.py and add the following lines of code:

```
from rest_framework import viewsets
from rest_framework.response import Response
from rest_framework.authentication import TokenAuthentication
from rest_framework.permissions import IsAuthenticated

from chapter3_project_setup.models import WatchList, StreamPlatform, Review
from chapter16_testing.api import serializers
```

Also, make sure REST_FRAMEWORK settings are only set as below in the drfproject/settings.py file:

```
REST_FRAMEWORK = {
    'DEFAULT_AUTHENTICATION_CLASSES': (
        'rest_framework.authentication.BasicAuthentication',
        'rest_framework.authentication.TokenAuthentication',
    ),
}
```

APIRequestFactory

This is a utility provided by Django REST Framework (DRF) for creating HTTP requests for testing purposes. It builds on Django's standard **RequestFactory** and adapts it to the specific needs of APIs, such as handling JSON data, supporting content negotiation, and working with REST framework views.

The **APIRequestFactory** behaves almost identically to Django's built-in RequestFactory, which simulates HTTP requests for testing purposes. However, it is enhanced for testing REST APIs. It supports all standard HTTP methods: .get(), .post(), .put(), .patch(), .delete(), .head(), and .options().

You can use the factory methods to create requests to API endpoints.

For example:

```
from rest_framework.test import APIRequestFactory

factory = APIRequestFactory()
request = factory.post('/api/notes/', {'title': 'new idea'})
```

The **APIRequestFactory** provides various features. We go through each of them.

Format Argument

The format argument simplifies generating requests with specific content types. It supports the following formats:

- **multipart**: Default, used for form submissions or file uploads
- **json**: Commonly used for APIs to send data as JSON

Example:

```
# Create a JSON POST request
factory = APIRequestFactory()
request = factory.post('/api/notes/', {'title': 'new idea'}, format='json')
```

This avoids the need to manually encode the request body or set content types explicitly. For example, without the format argument, you would need to do this:

```
import json

request = factory.post(
    '/api/notes/',
    json.dumps({'title': 'new idea'}),
    content_type='application/json'
)
```

PUT and PATCH with Form Data

Unlike Django's **RequestFactory**, which only supports encoding form data for .post() requests, **APIRequestFactory** can handle form data for .put() and .patch() requests.

For example:

```
# Using APIRequestFactory
factory = APIRequestFactory()
request = factory.put('/api/notes/1/', {'title': 'update title'})
```

If you were using Django's **RequestFactory**, you'd need to manually encode the form data like this:

```
from django.test.client import encode_multipart, RequestFactory

factory = RequestFactory()
data = {'title': 'update title'}
content = encode_multipart('boundary123', data)
content_type = 'multipart/form-data; boundary=boundary123'

request = factory.put('/api/notes/1/', content, content_type=content_type)
```

Forcing Authentication

In API testing, authenticating requests is often necessary. The **force_authenticate()** method allows you to bypass normal authentication mechanisms and directly set the user or token for a request.

For example:

```
from rest_framework.test import APIRequestFactory, force_authenticate
from django.contrib.auth.models import User

factory = APIRequestFactory()
user = User.objects.create_user(username='testuser', password='testpass')

# Simulate a GET request
request = factory.get('/api/notes/')
force_authenticate(request, user=user)  # Authenticate the request
```

This is particularly useful for testing restricted views, as it eliminates the need to create actual authentication headers. You can also authenticate using a token as below:

```
force_authenticate(request, user=user, token=user.auth_token)
```

CSRF Validation

By default, requests created with **APIRequestFactory** skip CSRF validation, which simplifies testing. If CSRF validation is required, it can be enabled using the enforce_csrf_checks=True flag as below:

```
factory = APIRequestFactory(enforce_csrf_checks=True)
```

In Django's RequestFactory, CSRF validation is handled by middleware, which isn't triggered when directly testing views. In DRF, CSRF validation occurs at the view level, and **APIRequestFactory** disables it by default.

Now we have gone through all the main features of testing and the **APIRequestFactory** class available in DRF. Let's implement these concepts into our project.

Let's go to chapter16_testing/api/views.py and add the following lines of code:

```
class WatchListViewSet(viewsets.ModelViewSet):
    authentication_classes = [TokenAuthentication]
    permission_classes = [IsAuthenticated]
    queryset = WatchList.objects.all()
    serializer_class = serializers.WatchListModelSerializer

class StreamPlatformViewSet(viewsets.ModelViewSet):
    authentication_classes = [TokenAuthentication]
    permission_classes = [IsAuthenticated]
    queryset = StreamPlatform.objects.all()
    serializer_class = serializers.StreamPlatformModelSerializer

class ReviewViewSet(viewsets.ModelViewSet):
    http_method_names = ["get", "post", "delete"]
    authentication_classes = [TokenAuthentication]
    permission_classes = [IsAuthenticated]
    queryset = Review.objects.all()
    serializer_class = serializers.ReviewModelSerializer
```

Go to chapter16_testing/api/urls.py and add the following lines of code:

```
router = DefaultRouter()
# Using ViewSet
router.register(r"watchlists", views.WatchListViewSet,
basename="watchlists")
router.register(r"stream-platforms", views.StreamPlatformViewSet,
basename="stream-platforms")
router.register(r"reviews", views.ReviewViewSet, basename="reviews")
```

In the above example, we are creating model view sets for each of the models. These are normal model viewsets, as you went through them in Chapter 7 on ViewSets. The only additional change we have made is for ReviewViewSet to allow only **get**, **post**, and **delete** methods using the **http_method_names** parameter. This won't allow the client to use the **put** and **patch** methods.

Since we are writing multiple scenarios of tests, let's organize them in the folder called tests within the application. You need to make it as package to help to import by creating __init__.py file.

Let's create chapter16_testing/tests/api/test_all_models_baseTests.py and add the following lines of code. Please note the relative path on creating folders and files:

```
from rest_framework.test import APIRequestFactory
from rest_framework.test import force_authenticate
from rest_framework import status
from rest_framework.test import APITestCase
from rest_framework.authtoken.models import Token
from django.contrib.auth import get_user_model
from django.urls import reverse
from chapter3_project_setup.models import WatchList, StreamPlatform, Review
from chapter16_testing.api.views import WatchListViewSet  # Import your
ViewSet here
import unittest

User = get_user_model()

class WatchListViewSetAPITest(unittest.TestCase):
    """Tests for WatchListViewSet using APIRequestFactory."""
```

```
    def setUp(self):
        # Create user and token
        self.factory = APIRequestFactory(enforce_csrf_checks=True)
        self.user = User.objects.create_user(username="testuser",
                    password="testpassword")

        # Create test data for WatchList and StreamPlatform
        self.streamplatform = StreamPlatform.objects.create(
            name="Netflix",
            about="Netflix Streaming Platform",
            website="https://netflix.com"
        )

        self.watchlist = WatchList.objects.create(
            title="Test WatchList",
            storyline="Test storyline",
            platform=self.streamplatform,
            category="Drama"
        )

    def tearDown(self):
        self.streamplatform.delete()
        self.watchlist.delete()
        self.user.delete()

    def test_list_watchlist_authenticated(self):
        """Test the list endpoint with authenticated user."""
        # Create request
        request = self.factory.get("/api/chapter16_testing/watchlists/")
        force_authenticate(request, user=self.user)

        # Initialize the view and get the response
        view = WatchListViewSet.as_view({"get": "list"})
        response = view(request)

        self.assertEqual(response.status_code, status.HTTP_200_OK)
        self.assertEqual(len(response.data), WatchList.objects.count())
```

```
    def test_list_watchlist_unauthenticated(self):
        """Test the list endpoint without authentication."""
        request = self.factory.get("/api/chapter16_testing/watchlists/")
        view = WatchListViewSet.as_view({"get": "list"})
        response = view(request)

        self.assertEqual(response.status_code, status.HTTP_401_UNAUTHORIZED)
        self.assertEqual(response.data, {"detail": "Authentication
        credentials were not provided."})

    def test_create_watchlist_authenticated(self):
        """Test creating a new WatchList with authenticated user."""
        data = {
            "title": "New WatchList",
            "storyline": "New storyline",
            "platform": "1",
            "category": "MOVIE",
        }

        request = self.factory.post("/api/chapter16_testing/watchlists/",
                  data, format="json")
        force_authenticate(request, user=self.user)

        view = WatchListViewSet.as_view({"post": "create"})
        response = view(request)

        self.assertEqual(response.status_code, status.HTTP_201_CREATED)
        self.assertEqual(response.data["title"], data["title"])

    def test_create_watchlist_unauthenticated(self):
        """Test creating a new WatchList without authentication."""
        data = {
            "title": "New WatchList",
            "storyline": "New storyline",
            "platform": "1",
            "category": "MOVIE",
        }
```

```
        request = self.factory.post("/api/chapter16_testing/watchlists/",
                  data, format="json")
        view = WatchListViewSet.as_view({"post": "create"})
        response = view(request)

        self.assertEqual(response.status_code, status.HTTP_401_
        UNAUTHORIZED)
        self.assertEqual(response.data, {"detail": "Authentication
        credentials were not provided."})

    def test_update_watchlist_authenticated(self):
        """Test updating an existing WatchList with authenticated user."""
        data = {"title": "Updated WatchList"}

        request = self.factory.patch(f"/api/chapter16_testing/watchlists/
        {self.watchlist.id}/", data, format="json")
        force_authenticate(request, user=self.user)

        view = WatchListViewSet.as_view({"patch": "partial_update"})
        response = view(request, pk=self.watchlist.id)

        self.assertEqual(response.status_code, status.HTTP_200_OK)
        self.watchlist.refresh_from_db()
        self.assertEqual(self.watchlist.title, data["title"])

    def test_delete_watchlist_authenticated(self):
        """Test deleting an existing WatchList with authenticated user."""
        request = self.factory.delete(f"/api/chapter16_testing/watchlists/
        {self.watchlist.id}/")
        force_authenticate(request, user=self.user)

        view = WatchListViewSet.as_view({"delete": "destroy"})
        response = view(request, pk=self.watchlist.id)

        self.assertEqual(response.status_code, status.HTTP_204_NO_CONTENT)
        self.assertFalse(WatchList.objects.filter(id=self.watchlist.id).
        exists())

    def test_delete_watchlist_unauthenticated(self):
        """Test deleting an existing WatchList without authentication."""
```

```
        request = self.factory.delete(f"/api/chapter16_testing/watchlists/
                  {self.watchlist.id}/")
        view = WatchListViewSet.as_view({"delete": "destroy"})
        response = view(request, pk=self.watchlist.id)

        self.assertEqual(response.status_code, status.HTTP_401_
        UNAUTHORIZED)
        self.assertEqual(response.data, {"detail": "Authentication
        credentials were not provided."})
```

In the above example, we have created a list of tests to validate the functionality of the WatchListViewSet. It uses the **unittest** library for structuring and organizing tests, **APIRequestFactory** to create API requests for testing the views, and the **force_ authenticate** method to simulate an authenticated user for the requests. It shows how to use **APIRequestFactory** and **force_authenticate** methods to perform tests.

The DRF test suite provides the built-in methods while performing tests. The commonly used methods are **setup()**, which is used to prepare the test environment before each test, and **tearDown()**, which is used to clean up test data after each test.

The above example provides a test approach to test each method of **WatchListViewSet**. You can run the test using the Django test runner using the command: **python manage.py test**.

The above example tests show how to use **APIRequestFactory** and **force_ authenticate** methods to perform tests. We can improve these tests using the **APIClient** class provided by DRF.

APIClient

The APIClient class is part of Django Rest Framework's test suite and is designed to extend Django's existing Client class. It provides a comprehensive way to interact with and test your API endpoints. It supports the same request methods as Django's Client class such as .get(), .post(), .put(), .patch(), .delete(), .head(), and .options().

For example:

```
from rest_framework.test import APIClient

client = APIClient()
```

```
# Sending a POST request with JSON data
response = client.post('/notes/', {'title': 'new idea'}, format='json')

# Sending a GET request
response = client.get('/notes/1/')
```

You can specify the request format, such as 'json', 'xml', or 'multipart'. This ensures that your API receives data in the expected format.

The APIClient class provides built-in methods for testing. The following are the commonly used built-in methods and key features.

login()

This method allows you to authenticate requests using **session-based authentication** (similar to Django's standard login method). This is useful for APIs that work in tandem with web interfaces that use session authentication.

For example:

```
client = APIClient()

# Login with session-based authentication
client.login(username='lauren', password='secret')

# Logout to end the session
client.logout()
```

When logged in, all subsequent requests by the client are authenticated in the context of the logged-in user.

This method is used for the APIs that use **session-based authentication**, often tied to web interfaces. For example, testing AJAX requests with logged-in users.

credentials(**kwargs)

This method is used to set custom headers (e.g., Authorization) for authentication. This is appropriate for APIs that use token-based or OAuth authentication.

For example:

```
from rest_framework.authtoken.models import Token

client = APIClient()

# Obtain the token for a user
token = Token.objects.get(user__username='lauren')

# Set the token in the Authorization header
client.credentials(HTTP_AUTHORIZATION='Token ' + token.key)

# Stop including credentials in requests
client.credentials()
```

Calling .credentials() again will overwrite the previous credentials. To unset existing credentials, call .credentials() with no arguments.

This method is used for the APIs that require custom headers for authentication. For example, token-based authentication, OAuth1a, or OAuth2.

Let's implement the above concept in our project. Go to chapter16_testing/tests/api/test_all_models_baseTests.py and add the following lines of code:

```
# Test StreamPlatformViewSet
class StreamPlatformViewSetTest(APITestCase):
    def setUp(self):
        # Create test user and token for authentication
        self.user = User.objects.create_user(username="example",
                    password="Password@123")
        self.client.login(username=self.user.username, password=self.user.
        password)
        self.token = Token.objects.get(user__username=self.user)
        self.client.credentials(HTTP_AUTHORIZATION='Token ' + self.
        token.key)

        # Create test data for StreamPlatform
        self.streamplatform = StreamPlatform.objects.create(
            name="Netflix",
            about="Netflix Streaming Platform",
            website="https://netflix.com"
        )
```

```
    def tearDown(self):
        self.streamplatform.delete()
        self.user.delete()
        self.client.logout()

    def test_streamplatform_get_all(self):
        #reverse arguments are reverse(basename-list)
        response = self.client.get(reverse("stream-platforms-list"))
        self.assertEqual(response.status_code, status.HTTP_200_OK)
        self.assertEqual(len(response.data), 1)

    def test_streamplatform_get_all_unauthenticated(self):
        self.client.credentials() #unauthenticate the user
        #reverse arguments are reverse(basename-list)
        response = self.client.get(reverse("stream-platforms-list"))
        self.assertEqual(response.status_code, status.HTTP_401_
        UNAUTHORIZED)

    def test_streamplatform_get_single(self):
        #reverse arguments are reverse(basename-detail)
        response = self.client.get(reverse("stream-platforms-detail",
                    args=(self.streamplatform.id,)))
        self.assertEqual(response.status_code, status.HTTP_200_OK)
        self.assertEqual(response.data["name"], self.streamplatform.name)

    def test_streamplatform_create(self):
        data = {
            "name": "Amazon Prime",
            "about": "Amazon's streaming service",
            "website": "https://primevideo.com"
        }
        response = self.client.post(reverse("stream-platforms-list"), data)
        self.assertEqual(response.status_code, status.HTTP_201_CREATED)
        self.assertEqual(StreamPlatform.objects.count(), 2)

    def test_streamplatform_update(self):
        data = {"name": "Updated Platform"}
```

```
        response = self.client.patch(reverse("stream-platforms-detail",
                   args=(self.streamplatform.id,)), data)
        self.assertEqual(response.status_code, status.HTTP_200_OK)
        self.streamplatform.refresh_from_db()
        self.assertEqual(self.streamplatform.name, "Updated Platform")

    def test_streamplatform_delete(self):
        response = self.client.delete(reverse("stream-platforms-detail",
                   args=(self.streamplatform.id,)))
        self.assertEqual(response.status_code, status.HTTP_204_NO_CONTENT)
        self.assertFalse(StreamPlatform.objects.filter(id=self.
        streamplatform.id).exists())
```

In the above example, we have used the **APITestCase** class which provides an integrated client (**APIClient**) for testing. This approach sends requests using the **self.client** provided by **APITestCase**. It tests the entire API layer, including URL routing, middleware, and authentication mechanisms. It simulates real-world client behavior. We have used the **reverse()** method for API URL construction.

Let's compare the above two approaches.

APIRequestFactory vs. APIClient

Feature	WatchListViewSetAPITest (APIRequestFactory)	StreamPlatformViewSetTest (APITestCase)
Test Framework	Unittest	APITestCase
Request Construction	Manual using APIRequestFactory. Example: factory.get().	Automated using self.client. Example: self.client.get().
Authentication	Handled using force_authenticate.	Handled via self.client.credentials() or self.client.login().
View Access	Directly invokes views with as_view().	Accesses views through the URL routing system.

(continued)

Feature	WatchListViewSetAPITest (APIRequestFactory)	StreamPlatformViewSetTest (APITestCase)
Routing and Middleware	Bypassed. Tests views in isolation.	Included. Tests the entire API layer.
Setup Complexity	Higher: Need to manage requests, CSRF, and view invocation.	Lower: DRF test client abstracts these details.
Test Focus	Isolated view logic. Tests view methods in detail.	End-to-end API behavior, including middleware and authentication.
Example Test (GET All)	Constructs a request and directly calls WatchListViewSet.as_view({"get": ...})	Calls self.client.get(reverse ("stream-platforms-list")).
Use Case	Testing internal view behavior, especially for custom logic.	Testing full API behavior as seen by a client or external user.

In all the previous example tests, we have implemented tests for each method. But we can further optimize functionality using an inheritance approach by creating a BaseViewSetTest class for common functionality and also further optimize the test approach.

Using factory_boy

factory_boy is a Python library used for creating test fixtures (or test data) in a declarative and flexible way. It simplifies the process of generating objects with pre-populated fields for use in testing. This is particularly useful in scenarios where tests require a lot of mock data, such as unit tests for APIs, models, or services.

Instead of manually creating objects in tests (which can be repetitive and error-prone), factory_boy automates this process and provides tools to customize the generated data. Once a factory is defined for a model, it can be reused across multiple tests to generate instances with consistent structure but different values. You can define factories for related models, and factory_boy can automatically generate related objects (e.g., SubFactory).

Let's implement this concept in our project. Install the **factory_boy** package into your virtual environment. Create a folder called **factories** within the tests folder and chapter16_testing/tests/factories/streamplatform_factories.py and add the following lines of code:

```
import factory
from chapter3_project_setup.models import StreamPlatform

class StreamPlatformFactory(factory.django.DjangoModelFactory):
    class Meta:
        model = StreamPlatform

    # Generate fake data for each field
    name = factory.Faker("company")  # Fake company names as streaming
           platform names
    about = factory.Faker("text", max_nb_chars=150)  # Random text up to
            150 characters
    website = factory.Faker("url")  # Random valid URL
```

Create a file chapter16_testing/tests/factories/watchlist_factories.py and add the following lines of code:

```
import factory
from chapter3_project_setup.models import WatchList
from chapter16_testing.tests.factories.streamplatform_factories import
StreamPlatformFactory
from faker import Faker

fake = Faker()

CATEGORY_CHOICES = (
    ("MOVIE", "MOVIE"),
    ("SERIES", "SERIES"),
)

class WatchListFactory(factory.django.DjangoModelFactory):
    class Meta:
        model = WatchList

    # Generate fake data for each field
```

```
    title = factory.Faker("sentence", nb_words=3)  # Random title
            with 3 words
    storyline = factory.Faker("paragraph", nb_sentences=2)  # Random
                storyline with 2 sentences
    platform = factory.SubFactory(StreamPlatformFactory)  # Related
               StreamPlatform instance
    active = factory.Faker("pybool")  # Randomly True or False
    imdb_rating = factory.Faker("pyfloat", left_digits=1, right_digits=1,
                  min_value=0.0, max_value=10.0)  # Random IMDb rating
    created = factory.Faker("date_time_this_decade", tzinfo=None)  # Random
              date-time within this decade
    episodes = factory.Faker("random_int", min=1, max=100)  # Random number
               of episodes
    category = factory.LazyFunction(lambda: fake.random.choice([choice[0]
               for choice in CATEGORY_CHOICES]))  # Random category
```

Let's use these created factories in our tests. Let's create a file chapter16_testing/tests/api/test_all_models_baseViewSetTest.py and add the following lines of code:

```
from copy import deepcopy
from rest_framework.test import APITestCase
from rest_framework.authtoken.models import Token
from rest_framework import status
from django.urls import reverse
from chapter3_project_setup.models import WatchList, StreamPlatform, Review
from chapter16_testing.tests.factories.watchlist_factories import
WatchListFactory
from chapter16_testing.tests.factories.streamplatform_factories import
StreamPlatformFactory
from tests.factories.user_factories import UserFactory

sorted_streamplatform_keys = [
    'about',
    'id',
    'name',
    'website'
]
```

```
sorted_watchlist_keys = [
    'active',
    'category',
    'created',
    'episodes',
    'id',
    'imdb_rating',
    'platform',
    'storyline',
    'title'
]

sorted_review_keys = [
    'active',
    'created',
    'description',
    'id',
    'rating',
    'review_date',
    'review_user',
    'update',
    'watchlist'
]

# Base Test Class
class BaseViewSetTest(APITestCase):
    """
    Base test class for ViewSets to handle authentication, common setup,
    and client initialization.
    """
    def setUp(self):
        # Create test user and token for authentication
        self.user = UserFactory()
        self.client.login(username=self.user.username, password=self.user.
        password)
        self.token = Token.objects.get(user__username=self.user)
```

```
        self.client.credentials(HTTP_AUTHORIZATION='Token ' + self.
        token.key)

        # Create test data for WatchList, StreamPlatform, and Review
        self.streamplatform = StreamPlatformFactory()
        self.watchlist = WatchListFactory()

    def tearDown(self):
        self.streamplatform.delete()
        self.watchlist.delete()
        self.client.logout()

    def authenticate_client(self):
        """Helper method to ensure the client is authenticated."""
        self.client.credentials(HTTP_AUTHORIZATION="Token " + self.token.key)

    def unauthenticate_client(self):
        """Remove authentication credentials from the client."""
        self.client.credentials()  # Removes token from client

# Test WatchListViewSet
class WatchListViewSetTest(BaseViewSetTest):
    def test_watchlist_get_all(self):
        response = self.client.get("/api/chapter16_testing/watchlists/")
        self.assertEqual(response.status_code, status.HTTP_200_OK)
        self.assertEqual(sorted(response.data[0].keys()), sorted_
        watchlist_keys)

    def test_watchlist_get_all_unauthenticated_user(self):
        self.unauthenticate_client()
        response = self.client.get("/api/chapter16_testing/watchlists/")
        self.assertEqual(response.status_code, status.HTTP_401_
        UNAUTHORIZED)
        self.assertEqual(response.data, {"detail": "Authentication
        credentials were not provided."})

    def test_watchlist_get_single(self):
        response = self.client.get(f"/api/chapter16_testing/watchlists/
                   {self.watchlist.id}/")
```

```
        self.assertEqual(response.status_code, status.HTTP_200_OK)
        self.assertEqual(response.data["title"], self.watchlist.title)

    def test_watchlist_create(self):
        data = {
            "title": "Movie1",
            "storyline": "Movie1 Story",
            "platform": 1,
            "category": "MOVIE",
            "imdb_rating":4.0,
            "active": True,
        }
        response_data = deepcopy(data)
        response_data["episodes"]=0
        response = self.client.post("/api/chapter16_testing/
                    watchlists/", data)
        self.assertEqual(response.status_code, status.HTTP_201_CREATED)
        del response.data["id"]
        del response.data["created"]
        self.assertEqual(response.data, response_data)

    def test_watchlist_update(self):
        data = {"title": "Updated WatchList"}
        response = self.client.patch(f"/api/chapter16_testing/watchlists/
                    {self.watchlist.id}/", data)
        self.assertEqual(response.status_code, status.HTTP_200_OK)
        self.watchlist.refresh_from_db()
        self.assertEqual(self.watchlist.title, "Updated WatchList")

    def test_watchlist_delete(self):
        response = self.client.delete(f"/api/chapter16_testing/watchlists/
                    {self.watchlist.id}/")
        self.assertEqual(response.status_code, status.HTTP_204_NO_CONTENT)
        self.assertFalse(WatchList.objects.filter(id=self.watchlist.id).
        exists())
```

```
# Test StreamPlatformViewSet
class StreamPlatformViewSetTest(BaseViewSetTest):
    def test_streamplatform_get_all(self):
        #reverse arguments are reverse(basename-list)
        response = self.client.get(reverse("stream-platforms-list"))
        self.assertEqual(response.status_code, status.HTTP_200_OK)
        self.assertEqual(sorted(response.data[0].keys()), sorted_
        streamplatform_keys)

    def test_streamplatform_get_single(self):
        #reverse arguments are reverse(basename-detail)
        response = self.client.get(reverse("stream-platforms-detail",
                   args=(self.streamplatform.id,)))
        self.assertEqual(response.status_code, status.HTTP_200_OK)
        self.assertEqual(response.data["name"], self.streamplatform.name)

    def test_streamplatform_create(self):
        data = {
            "name": "Amazon Prime",
            "about": "Amazon's streaming service",
            "website": "https://primevideo.com"
        }
        response = self.client.post(reverse("stream-platforms-list"), data)
        self.assertEqual(response.status_code, status.HTTP_201_CREATED)
        del response.data["id"]
        self.assertEqual(response.data, data)

    def test_streamplatform_update(self):
        data = {"name": "Updated Platform"}
        response = self.client.patch(reverse("stream-platforms-detail",
                   args=(self.streamplatform.id,)), data)
        self.assertEqual(response.status_code, status.HTTP_200_OK)
        self.streamplatform.refresh_from_db()
        self.assertEqual(self.streamplatform.name, "Updated Platform")

    def test_streamplatform_delete(self):
        response = self.client.delete(reverse("stream-platforms-detail",
                   args=(self.streamplatform.id,)))
```

```
        self.assertEqual(response.status_code, status.HTTP_204_NO_CONTENT)
        self.assertFalse(StreamPlatform.objects.filter(id=self.
        streamplatform.id).exists())
```

In the above example, the **BaseViewSetTest** class acts as a base class to centralize common setup and teardown functionality for test cases. It reduces redundancy in test code by handling authentication and initialization of test data. It also uses created factories for **Watchlist** and **StreamPlatform** models.

Let's implement unit test cases for the **user_app** application as well. Let's go to user_app/tests.py and add the following lines of code:

```
from django.urls import reverse
from django.contrib.auth import get_user_model

from rest_framework import status
from rest_framework.test import APITestCase
from rest_framework.authtoken.models import Token

User = get_user_model()

class RegisterTestCase(APITestCase):

    def test_register(self):
        data = {
            "username": "testcase",
            "email": "testcase@example.com",
            "password": "NewPassword@123",
            "password2": "NewPassword@123"
        }
        response = self.client.post(reverse('register'), data)
        self.assertEqual(response.status_code, status.HTTP_201_CREATED)

class LoginLogoutTestCase(APITestCase):

    def setUp(self):
        self.user = User.objects.create_user(username="test",
                                             password="user@test")

    def tearDown(self):
        self.user.delete()
```

```
    def test_login(self):
        data = {
            "username": "test",
            "password": "user@test"
        }
        response = self.client.post(reverse('login'), data)
        self.assertEqual(response.status_code, status.HTTP_200_OK)

    def test_logout(self):
        self.client.login(username=self.user.username, password=self.user.
        password)
        self.token = Token.objects.get(user__username=self.user)
        self.client.credentials(HTTP_AUTHORIZATION='Token ' + self.
        token.key)
        response = self.client.post(reverse('logout'))
        self.assertEqual(response.status_code, status.HTTP_200_OK)
```

The above code is a test suite for the **user_app** application, specifically for the registration, login, and logout functionality. The test cases are defined using **APITestCase** from DRF to test API endpoints. The **RegisterTestCase** ensures that users can successfully register. The **LoginLogoutTestCase** tests both login and logout functionality. These tests interact with the API endpoints to confirm they return appropriate status codes based on expected behavior.

Mocking External Dependencies

In all the above cases, we performed unit tests for views which do not have external dependencies. But what if views have external function calls? To test these types of views, the **unittest** module comes to help and mock them.

unittest.mock.patch is a powerful utility in Python's unittest.mock module that allows you to replace (or mock) parts of your application during testing. This is particularly useful when you want to isolate the code under test by mocking out dependencies like external services, database queries, or specific functions that you don't want to execute in a test environment.

Patch temporarily replaces the target you specify with a mock object (or a replacement object of your choice) during the scope of a test. After the test completes, the original object is restored.

For example:

1. Replace a function or method call with a mock.
2. Replace an object in a module.
3. Prevent external HTTP calls by mocking them.

How to Use Patch

1. **As a Decorator**

   Use patch as a decorator for test functions. The patched object is passed as an argument to the test function.

   ```
   from unittest.mock import patch

   def external_service():
       return "Real Data"

   @patch('__main__.external_service')  # Mock the external_service
   function
   def test_mock_service(mock_service):
       mock_service.return_value = "Mock Data"  # Define return value
       for the mock
       result = external_service()
       assert result == "Mock Data"
   ```

2. **As a Context Manager**

   Use patch as a context manager to mock objects only within a specific block of code.

   ```
   from unittest.mock import patch

   def external_service():
       return "Real Data"

   def test_mock_service():
   ```

```
    with patch('__main__.external_service') as mock_service:
        mock_service.return_value = "Mock Data"
        result = external_service()
        assert result == "Mock Data"

    # After the `with` block, the original function is restored
    assert external_service() == "Real Data"
```

3. **Using patch.object**

   Mock attributes or methods of specific objects.

```
from unittest.mock import patch

class Example:
    def method(self):
        return "Real Method"

def test_patch_object():
    example = Example()
    with patch.object(Example, 'method', return_value="Mock
    Method"):
        assert example.method() == "Mock Method"

    # After the `with` block, the original method is restored
    assert example.method() == "Real Method"
```

4. **Using Patch with Multiple Targets**

   Mock multiple objects simultaneously by applying multiple decorators.

```
from unittest.mock import patch

@patch('module.function_a')
@patch('module.function_b')
def test_multiple_mocks(mock_function_b, mock_function_a):
    mock_function_a.return_value = "Mock A"
    mock_function_b.return_value = "Mock B"
    assert module.function_a() == "Mock A"
    assert module.function_b() == "Mock B"
```

Let's implement the above concept in our project.

Let's create a file chapter16_testing/api/utils.py to implement external functions as below:

```
def fetch_watchlist_data():
    """
    Simulates fetching data from an external service for the watchlist.
    """
    return [{"id": 1, "title": "Movie A"}, {"id": 2, "title": "Movie B"}]

def fetch_user_recommendations(user_id):
    """
    Simulates fetching user-specific recommendations from another external
    service.
    """
    return [{"id": 3, "title": "Movie C"}, {"id": 4, "title": "Movie D"}]

def validate_external_watchlist_data(data):
    """
    Simulates validating watchlist data using an external service.
    """
    if data.get("title") == "Invalid Movie":
        return False  # Simulate invalid data from an external service
    return True

def notify_external_service(watchlist_item):
    """
    Simulates notifying an external service after successfully creating a
    watchlist item.
    """
    # Simulate sending data to an external service
    return {"status": "success", "id": watchlist_item.id}
```

Go to chapter16_testing/api/views.py and add the following lines of code:

```
from rest_framework.views import APIView
from rest_framework import status
from chapter16_testing.api import utils
```

```
class WatchlistExternalView(APIView):
    """
    API view to handle watchlist data and user-specific recommendations.
    """

    def get(self, request):
        """
        Handle GET requests to return watchlist data and recommendations.
        """
        try:
            watchlist_data = utils.fetch_watchlist_data()  # External
            function 1
            user_recommendations = utils.fetch_user_recommendations
                                   (request.user.id)  # External function 2

            response_data = {
                "watchlist": watchlist_data,
                "recommendations": user_recommendations
            }

            return Response(response_data, status=status.HTTP_200_OK)

        except Exception as e:
            return Response({"error": str(e)}, status=status.HTTP_500_
            INTERNAL_SERVER_ERROR)

    def post(self, request):
        """
        Handle POST requests to create a new watchlist item.
        """
        # Validate incoming data using external function
        if not utils.validate_external_watchlist_data(request.data):
            return Response({"error": "Invalid watchlist data"},
            status=status.HTTP_400_BAD_REQUEST)

        serializer = serializers.WatchListModelSerializer(data=request.data)
        if serializer.is_valid():
            watchlist_item = serializer.save()
```

```
        # Notify an external service after creation
        notification_response = utils.notify_external_service
        (watchlist_item)
        return Response({
            "watchlist_item": serializer.data,
            "notification": notification_response
        }, status=status.HTTP_201_CREATED)

    return Response(serializer.errors, status=status.HTTP_400_BAD_
    REQUEST)
```

Add the corresponding URL in chapter16_testing/api/urls.py as below:

```
urlpatterns = [
    # Define versioned paths using a regex for versioning

    path('watchlist-external/', views.WatchlistExternalView.as_view(),
    name='watchlist-external'),
    ...
]
```

In the above view, the get() method has two external dependencies such as **fetch_watchlist_data** and **fetch_user_recommendations**. The **post()** method also depends on **validate_external_watchlist_data** and **notify_external_service**. These methods need to be mocked for unit testing of this view. Let's implement mocking of these external functions.

Create a file chapter16_testing/tests/api/test_watchlist_external_view.py and add the following lines of code:

```
from unittest.mock import patch
from rest_framework.test import APITestCase
from rest_framework import status
from django.urls import reverse
from chapter16_testing.tests.factories.streamplatform_factories import
StreamPlatformFactory

class WatchlistExternalViewGetTests(APITestCase):

    get_url = reverse("watchlist-external")
```

```
    @patch('chapter16_testing.api.views.utils.fetch_watchlist_data')
# Mock fetch_watchlist_data
    @patch('chapter16_testing.api.views.utils.fetch_user_recommendations')
# Mock fetch_user_recommendations
    def test_watchlist_external_get_success(self, mock_fetch_user_
    recommendations, mock_fetch_watchlist_data):
        # Arrange
        mock_fetch_watchlist_data.return_value = [
            {"id": 1, "title": "Mock Movie A"},
            {"id": 2, "title": "Mock Movie B"}
        ]
        mock_fetch_user_recommendations.return_value = [
            {"id": 3, "title": "Mock Movie C"},
            {"id": 4, "title": "Mock Movie D"}
        ]

        # Act
        response = self.client.get(self.get_url)

        # Assert
        self.assertEqual(response.status_code, status.HTTP_200_OK)
        self.assertEqual(response.json(), {
            "watchlist": [
                {"id": 1, "title": "Mock Movie A"},
                {"id": 2, "title": "Mock Movie B"}
            ],
            "recommendations": [
                {"id": 3, "title": "Mock Movie C"},
                {"id": 4, "title": "Mock Movie D"}
            ]
        })
        mock_fetch_watchlist_data.assert_called_once()
        mock_fetch_user_recommendations.assert_called_once()

class WatchlistExternalViewPostTests(APITestCase):

    post_url = reverse("watchlist-external")
```

```
def setUp(self):
    self.streamplatform = StreamPlatformFactory()

def tearDown(self):
    self.streamplatform.delete()

@patch('chapter16_testing.api.views.utils.validate_external_watchlist_
data')  # Mock validation function
@patch('chapter16_testing.api.views.utils.notify_external_service')
# Mock notification function
def test_watchlist_external_post_success(self, mock_notify_external_
service, mock_validate_external_watchlist_data):
    # Arrange
    mock_validate_external_watchlist_data.return_value = True
    # Simulate valid external validation
    mock_notify_external_service.return_value = {"status": "success",
    "id": 1}  # Simulate successful notification

    data = {
        "title": "Valid Movie",
        "storyline": "Movie4 Storyline",
        "active": True,
        "platform": self.streamplatform.id,
        "imdb_rating": 2.0,
        "episodes": 0,
        "category": "MOVIE"
    }

    # Act
    response = self.client.post(self.post_url, data)

    # Assert
    self.assertEqual(response.status_code, status.HTTP_201_CREATED)
    self.assertEqual(response.data["watchlist_item"]["title"],
    "Valid Movie")
    self.assertEqual(response.data["notification"]["status"],
    "success")
```

```
        # Ensure mocked functions were called
        mock_validate_external_watchlist_data.assert_called_once()
        mock_notify_external_service.assert_called_once()

    @patch('chapter16_testing.api.views.utils.validate_external_
    watchlist_data')
    def test_watchlist_external_post_invalid_data(self, mock_validate_
    external_watchlist_data):
        # Arrange
        mock_validate_external_watchlist_data.return_value = False
        # Simulate invalid external validation

        data = {
            "title": "Invalid Movie",
            "description": "This movie will fail validation",
            "imdb_rating": 3.5
        }

        # Act
        response = self.client.post(self.post_url, data)

        # Assert
        self.assertEqual(response.status_code, status.HTTP_400_BAD_REQUEST)
        self.assertEqual(response.data["error"], "Invalid watchlist data")

        # Ensure validation function was called
        mock_validate_external_watchlist_data.assert_called_once()

    @patch('chapter16_testing.api.views.utils.validate_external_
    watchlist_data')
    @patch('chapter16_testing.api.views.utils.notify_external_service')
    def test_watchlist_external_post_serializer_invalid(self, mock_notify_
    external_service, mock_validate_external_watchlist_data):
        # Arrange
        mock_validate_external_watchlist_data.return_value = True
        # Simulate valid external validation
```

```
    data = {
        "description": "Missing required title field",
        # Missing 'title'
        "imdb_rating": 4.0
    }

    # Act
    response = self.client.post(self.post_url, data)

    # Assert
    self.assertEqual(response.status_code, status.HTTP_400_BAD_REQUEST)
    self.assertIn("title", response.data)  # Check that the error
    contains 'title'

    # Ensure notification function was not called
    mock_notify_external_service.assert_not_called()
```

In the above tests, separate test classes are defined to handle GET (WatchlistExternalViewGetTests) and POST (WatchlistExternalViewPostTests) requests. Each class ensures the external API interactions are tested in isolation by mocking the related functions. Functions like **fetch_watchlist_data**, **fetch_user_recommendations**, **validate_external_watchlist_data**, and **notify_external_service** are mocked to simulate external behaviors without invoking actual external services. This ensures the tests are fast and reliable.

RequestsClient

This is a utility provided by Django REST Framework (DRF) that allows you to test your API by making real HTTP requests, similar to how external clients (e.g., front-end apps, third-party integrations) would interact with your API. It uses the popular Python requests library under the hood and mimics real-world API interactions.

Unlike Django's built-in test client, RequestsClient works at the HTTP level, requiring fully qualified URLs and simulating actual requests, headers, authentication, and cookies. This makes it useful for validating your API exactly as it would be experienced by external consumers.

By using RequestsClient, you're interacting with the API the same way external services would. This ensures you're testing not just the view logic but the entire API interface, including headers, authentication, and serialization. Since it works with fully qualified URLs, you can run tests against a live or staging environment. This is useful for validating the live service in an automated way. It forces you to avoid direct database interactions (e.g., Customer.objects.count()), ensuring your tests remain strictly API-focused. Any setup or assertions need to be performed through API calls.

For example:

```
from rest_framework.test import RequestsClient

# Initialize the client
client = RequestsClient()

# Make a GET request
response = client.get('http://testserver/users/')
assert response.status_code == 200
```

Fully qualified URLs are required (http://testserver is typically used for local tests).

Headers and Authentication

Custom headers and authentication can be added just like with the requests library as below:

```
from requests.auth import HTTPBasicAuth

client = RequestsClient()

# Add basic authentication
client.auth = HTTPBasicAuth('username', 'password')

# Add custom headers
client.headers.update({'x-custom-header': 'value'})

# Perform a request
response = client.get('http://testserver/endpoint/')
assert response.status_code == 200
```

CSRF Handling

If you're using SessionAuthentication, CSRF tokens must be included for non-GET requests (e.g., POST, PUT, PATCH, DELETE).

For example:

```
client = RequestsClient()

# Obtain CSRF token via a GET request
response = client.get('http://testserver/homepage/')
csrftoken = response.cookies['csrftoken']

# Include CSRF token in the headers for the next request
response = client.post(
    'http://testserver/endpoint/',
    json={'key': 'value'},
    headers={'X-CSRFToken': csrftoken}
)
assert response.status_code == 201
```

There are some limitations on using RequestsClient for the tests. Since RequestsClient works at the HTTP level, it may be slower than Django's built-in test client, which interacts directly with the view layer. Writing tests may require more effort because setup, teardown, and assertions need to be performed via API calls, not direct model queries. When running tests against a staging or production server, careful attention is required to avoid affecting live customer data.

When to Use

RequestsClient can be used in the following scenarios:

- When you want to test your API as a consumer would see it
- When testing cross-service interactions or third-party integrations
- For creating end-to-end tests that validate live or staging environments
- For stricter tests that avoid shortcuts like direct database access

CoreAPIClient

This is a client for interacting with APIs that expose a schema in the Core API format. It was designed to make interacting with APIs structured around Core API schemas easy and intuitive. This client is particularly useful for testing or consuming APIs where a Core API schema is available.

Although the coreapi package has been deprecated in favor of alternatives like OpenAPI and drf-spectacular for schema generation, CoreAPIClient is still relevant in certain legacy projects or where Core API is still being used.

You can fetch an API schema and use it to interact with endpoints. The schema defines all available actions, making the API self-documenting and discoverable. No need to hard-code endpoint paths. Everything can be resolved dynamically from the schema. All interactions follow the Core API conventions, providing a standard way of handling requests. It simplifies writing tests for APIs that expose Core API schemas by allowing high-level interaction with the API. Instead of working directly with HTTP methods (e.g., GET, POST), it lets you use schema-defined "actions" such as list or create, reducing manual work. You can dynamically discover endpoints and their parameters using the schema.

To use the coreAPIClient, you need to install it on your virtual environment using the command: pip install coreapi.

Here's a step-by-step example of how to use CoreAPIClient:

```
from coreapi import Client as CoreAPIClient

# Step 1: Fetch the API schema
client = CoreAPIClient()
schema = client.get('http://testserver/schema/')  # Replace with your
schema URL

# Step 2: Interact with the API using actions
# Create a new organisation
params = {'name': 'MegaCorp', 'status': 'active'}
client.action(schema, ['organisations', 'create'], params)

# List all organisations
data = client.action(schema, ['organisations', 'list'])
assert len(data) == 1
assert data == [{'name': 'MegaCorp', 'status': 'active'}]
```

Headers and Authentication

You can set authentication headers or credentials to interact with protected APIs.

For **BasicAuthentication**, it can be set as below:

```
from requests.auth import HTTPBasicAuth
from coreapi import Client as CoreAPIClient

client = CoreAPIClient()
client.session.auth = HTTPBasicAuth('username', 'password')
client.session.headers.update({'Custom-Header': 'value'})

# Use the client with authentication
schema = client.get('http://testserver/schema/')
```

For APIs that use **token-based authentication**, it can be set as below:

```
client.session.headers.update({'Authorization': 'Token your_api_token'})
```

CSRF Tokens (Session Authentication)

If the API uses SessionAuthentication, include a CSRF token for modifying requests as below:

```
client = CoreAPIClient()

# Obtain CSRF token
schema = client.get('http://testserver/schema/')
csrftoken = client.session.cookies.get('csrftoken')

# Include the token in subsequent requests
client.session.headers.update({'X-CSRFToken': csrftoken})

# Perform an action
params = {'name': 'New Organisation', 'status': 'active'}
client.action(schema, ['organisations', 'create'], params)
```

Dynamic Discovery

With CoreAPIClient, you can dynamically explore and use the schema without prior knowledge of endpoint paths or actions:

```
from coreapi import Client as CoreAPIClient

client = CoreAPIClient()

# Fetch schema
schema = client.get('http://testserver/schema/')

# List all available actions
print(schema.keys())  # E.g., ['organisations']

# Explore an action
action = schema['organisations']['create']
print(action.fields)  # Displays required parameters
```

Comparison with RequestsClient

Feature	CoreAPIClient	RequestsClient
Schema Dependency	Requires a Core API schema for interaction	Works with raw URLs. No schema needed
Action-Based	Uses schema-defined actions like list, create	Interacts directly with HTTP methods
Ease of Use	Higher-level API interaction via schema actions	More flexible but lower-level API interaction
Dynamic Discovery	Can dynamically discover endpoints and parameters	Requires prior knowledge of endpoints
Flexibility	Tied to Core API schema; limited for custom APIs	Works with any API, schema or not

When to Use

CoreAPIClient can be used in the following scenarios:

- **Schema-Driven API Testing**

  Use CoreAPIClient if your API exposes a Core API schema and you want to validate the schema alongside your API functionality.

- **Dynamic Discovery**

  When you don't know the full API structure upfront and want to explore it programmatically.

- **Action-Based Workflows**

  When you want to work with higher-level actions (create, list) instead of raw HTTP methods.

CHAPTER 17

Documenting APIs

Documenting a REST API is of paramount importance for several reasons. First and foremost, it serves as a clear and comprehensive guide for developers and users, providing them with essential information on how to interact with the API and its endpoints. A well-documented API eliminates confusion, reduces learning curves, and accelerates the development process. Moreover, documentation enhances collaboration among team members, ensuring that everyone is on the same page and can work seamlessly together. It also facilitates integration with other systems, making it easier for external developers to utilize the API effectively.

At times, developers may find themselves reluctant to invest time and effort in documenting their REST APIs, especially when under tight deadlines or overwhelmed with other tasks.

In the Django ecosystem, tools like **DRF-Spectacular** and **drf-yasg** are widely used to generate and maintain OpenAPI/Swagger-compliant documentation for APIs built with Django REST Framework (DRF).

Preparing for This Chapter

Create a new app with the name **chapter17_documenting** with the steps specified in the **Project Setup** section in Chapter 3.

Go to drfproject/settings.py and add the following lines of code:

```
INSTALLED_APPS = [
    ...
    "chapter17_documenting",
]
```


G. Patil, *Django REST APIs Demystified*, https://doi.org/10.1007/979-8-8688-1850-9_17

Create chapter17_documenting/api/serializers.py and the following lines of code:

```
from rest_framework import serializers
from chapter3_project_setup.models import WatchList

class WatchListModelSerializer(serializers.ModelSerializer):
    class Meta:
        model = WatchList
        fields = "__all__"
        ref_name = 'C17WatchListModelSerializer'
```

Create chapter17_documenting/api/urls.py and add the following lines of code:

```
from django.urls import path, include
from rest_framework.routers import DefaultRouter
from chapter16_testing.api import views

router = DefaultRouter()

urlpatterns = [

    # Using ViewSet
    path("", include(router.urls)),
]
```

Go to drfproject/urls.py and add the following lines of code:

```
urlpatterns = [
    ...
    path('api/chapter17_documenting/', include('chapter17_documenting.
    api.urls')),
]
```

Go to chapter16_testing/api/views.py and add the following lines of code:

```
from rest_framework import viewsets

from chapter3_project_setup.models import WatchList
from chapter17_documenting.api import serializers
```

drf-spectacular

drf-spectacular is a modern, powerful library for generating OpenAPI 3 schemas from Django REST Framework (DRF) projects. It prioritizes extensibility, customizability, and compatibility with tools for client generation. This library is widely considered the recommended approach for creating OpenAPI schemas in DRF-based APIs.

Key Features of drf-spectacular

1. **OpenAPI 3.x Support**

   drf-spectacular is designed specifically for OpenAPI 3, the latest version of the OpenAPI specification. OpenAPI 3 provides improved support for complex APIs, reusable components, and advanced data validation compared to Swagger 2.0.

2. **Extensibility**

   Supports custom decorators and configuration options to extend or modify schema generation to suit your needs. You can define custom schemas for parameters, responses, authentication, or views.

3. **Customizability**

   Allows developers to easily override default behavior for schema generation. Decorators like @extend_schema and @extend_schema_view enable developers to fine-tune the schema for specific endpoints.

4. **Client Generation**

   The generated OpenAPI 3 schema is compatible with tools like swagger-codegen or openapi-generator, which can generate API client libraries in multiple programming languages.

5. **Built-In Interactive Documentation**

   Provides seamless integration with Swagger UI and Redoc for interactive, visually appealing API documentation. Both tools allow live testing of API endpoints.

6. **Internationalization (i18n)**

   Supports multilingual documentation by leveraging Django's built-in internationalization framework.

7. **Versioning Support**

   Works with DRF's API versioning system to generate schemas for different API versions.

8. **Authentication**

   Supports common authentication methods like **JWT**, **OAuth2**, **API Key**, and custom schemes. Authentication schemes are automatically documented in the generated schema.

9. **Polymorphism**

   Handles complex request/response structures, such as dynamically generated data types or polymorphic serializers. Polymorphism is critical when an API can return multiple types of data for a single endpoint.

10. **Parameters**

    Supports documentation for query, path, header, and request body parameters. Allows explicit parameter documentation using OpenApiParameter.

11. **Plug-Ins for Popular Libraries**

    It provides out-of-the-box support for popular Django libraries like

    - **Django Filters**: Automatically documents filtering options
    - **Django Polymorphic**: Adds polymorphic serializer support
    - **Django Simple JWT**: Provides JWT authentication support
    - **Django Guardian**: Includes permission-based schemas

12. **Reusable Components**

    Supports defining reusable components for request bodies, responses, headers, and security schemes. This reduces duplication in the schema and simplifies complex APIs.

13. **Validation**

    Validates the generated schema to ensure it conforms to the OpenAPI 3 specification.

14. **Dynamic Requests and Responses**

    Supports APIs with dynamic request/response formats by leveraging DRF serializers and explicit schema definitions.

Let's use this tool for our project.

The DRF library (`https://drf-spectacular.readthedocs.io/en/latest/readme.html#installation`) has provided a very clear and concise section on installation and setup.

After a correct installation and setup, add the URLs in drfproject/urls.py as below:

```
from drf_spectacular.views import SpectacularAPIView, SpectacularRedocView,
SpectacularSwaggerView

urlpatterns = [
    ...
    #drf-spectacular URLs
    path('api/schema/', SpectacularAPIView.as_view(), name='schema'),
    path('api/schema/swagger-ui/', SpectacularSwaggerView.as_view(url_
    name='schema'), name='swagger-ui'),
    path('api/schema/redoc/', SpectacularRedocView.as_view(url_
    name='schema'), name='redoc'),
    ...
]
```

With this configuration, if you start the server and access it in your browser at `api/schema`, you will be redirected to download a YAML file that contains the documentation automatically generated by the library. This is how the file looks:

```
openapi: 3.0.3
info:
  title: Your Project API
  version: 1.0.0
  description: Your project description
paths:
  /api/chapter10_permissions/{id}/reviews/:
    get:
      operationId: chapter10_permissions_reviews_list
      parameters:
      - in: path
        name: id
        schema:
          type: integer
        required: true
      tags:
      - chapter10_permissions
      security:
      - basicAuth: []
      - tokenAuth: []
      responses:
        '200':
          content:
            application/json:
              schema:
                type: array
                items:
                  $ref: '#/components/schemas/ReviewModel'
          description: ''
  /api/chapter10_permissions/reviews/{id}/:
    get:
      operationId: chapter10_permissions_reviews_retrieve
      parameters:
      - in: path
        name: id
        schema:
          type: integer
        required: true
      tags:
      - chapter10_permissions
      security:
      - basicAuth: []
      - tokenAuth: []
      responses:
```

Also, you can open in the browser a Swagger UI if you go to `api/schema/swagger-ui/` that has this aspect:

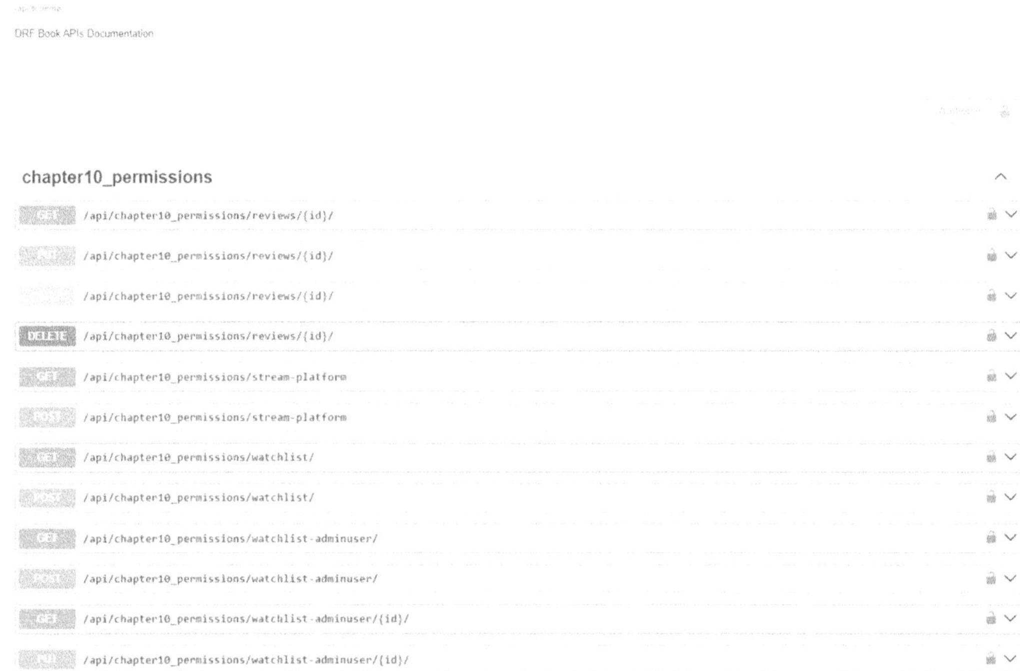

And finally, if you access to `api/schema/redoc/` you will see the Redoc mode of your documentation:

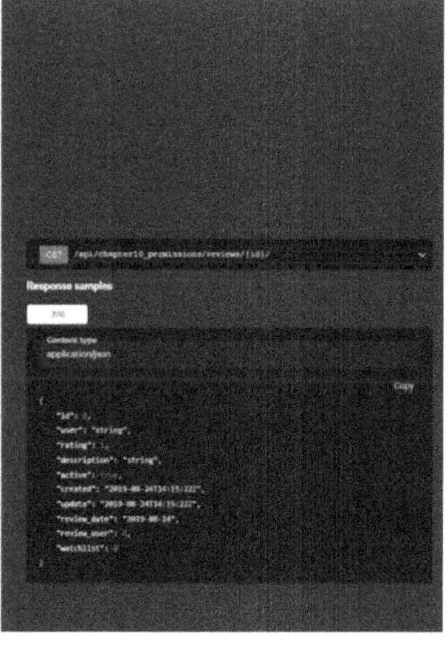

Customization by Using @extend_schema

The **@extend_schema** decorator provided by drf-spectacular is a powerful tool for customizing the OpenAPI schema generated for your Django REST Framework (DRF) APIs. By default, drf-spectacular generates an OpenAPI schema based on your viewset configurations, serializers, and DRF settings. However, there are situations where the default schema generation doesn't meet your requirements. For these cases, the @ extend_schema decorator allows you to customize the schema at a granular level.

You can override the default serializers used for requests and responses, allowing you to define specialized serializers for specific endpoints or methods.

Features and Use Cases of @extend_schema

1. **Customize Input (Request) and Output (Response) Serializers**

   You can override the default serializers used for requests and responses, allowing you to define specialized serializers for specific endpoints or methods.

2. **Define Additional Parameters**

   Add custom query parameters or other parameters (e.g., headers, cookies) to the schema for documentation purposes.

3. **Add Examples for Requests and Responses**

   Include examples for a better understanding of the API's behavior in the generated documentation.

4. **Specify Authentication Classes**

   Override the default authentication mechanism for specific views or endpoints.

5. **Control Descriptions and Operation Names**

   Customize the textual descriptions and operation IDs for endpoints.

6. **Full Manual Overrides**

   Completely bypass the auto-generated schema and define a raw OpenAPI specification for full control.

Key Arguments in @extend_schema

1. **request**

   Specifies the serializer to use for requests (or None for no request body).

   ```
   request=MyRequestSerializer
   ```

2. **responses**

   Defines the expected response structure, status codes, and their associated serializers.

   Example:

   ```
   responses={
       200: MyResponseSerializer,
       400: "Invalid input provided."
   }
   ```

3. **parameters**

   Adds additional parameters such as query parameters, headers, or cookies. Use OpenApiParameter to define these.

   Example:

   ```
   parameters=[
       OpenApiParameter(name='search', type=str,
   location=OpenApiParameter.QUERY, description='Search keyword')
   ]
   ```

4. **examples**

   Provides examples for requests or responses. Use OpenApiExample to define examples.

   Example:

   ```
   examples=[
       OpenApiExample(
           name="Example 1",
   ```

```
            summary="Example of a successful response",
            value={"id": 1, "name": "Example Watchlist"}
        )
    ]
```

5. **description**

   Overrides the method's docstring and provides a custom description for the endpoint.

6. **operation_id**

   Defines a custom operation ID for the endpoint, which can be useful for generating unique client-side functions.

7. **auth**

   Overrides the authentication classes for a specific view.

8. **operation**

   Allows you to completely replace the generated OpenAPI operation specification with a raw dictionary.

Let's implement this concept into our project. Go to chapter17_documenting/api/views.py and add the following lines of code:

```
from rest_framework import viewsets
from drf_spectacular.utils import extend_schema, OpenApiParameter,
OpenApiExample
from drf_spectacular.types import OpenApiTypes

from chapter3_project_setup.models import WatchList
from chapter17_documenting.api import serializers

class WatchListViewSet(viewsets.ModelViewSet):
    """
    A ViewSet for managing the WatchList.
    """
    queryset = WatchList.objects.all()
    serializer_class = serializers.WatchListModelSerializer
```

```
@extend_schema(
    request=serializers.WatchListModelSerializer,
    responses={201: serializers.WatchListModelSerializer},
    description="Create a new WatchList item.",
    examples=[
        OpenApiExample(
            "Create Example",
            summary="Sample WatchList Creation Request",
            description="A sample request to create a new
            watchlist item.",
            value={
                "title": "Example Movie",
                "storyline": "A brief storyline of the movie.",
                "active": True,
                "imdb_rating": 7.5,
                "platform": 1,
                "category": "MOVIE"
            }
        )
    ]
)
def create(self, request):
    """
    Create a new watchlist item with custom behavior.
    """
    return super().create(request)
```

In the above code, using **extend_schema** adds detailed documentation for the create method of a WatchList API. If you open Swagger UI on a browser, the corresponding method displays as below:

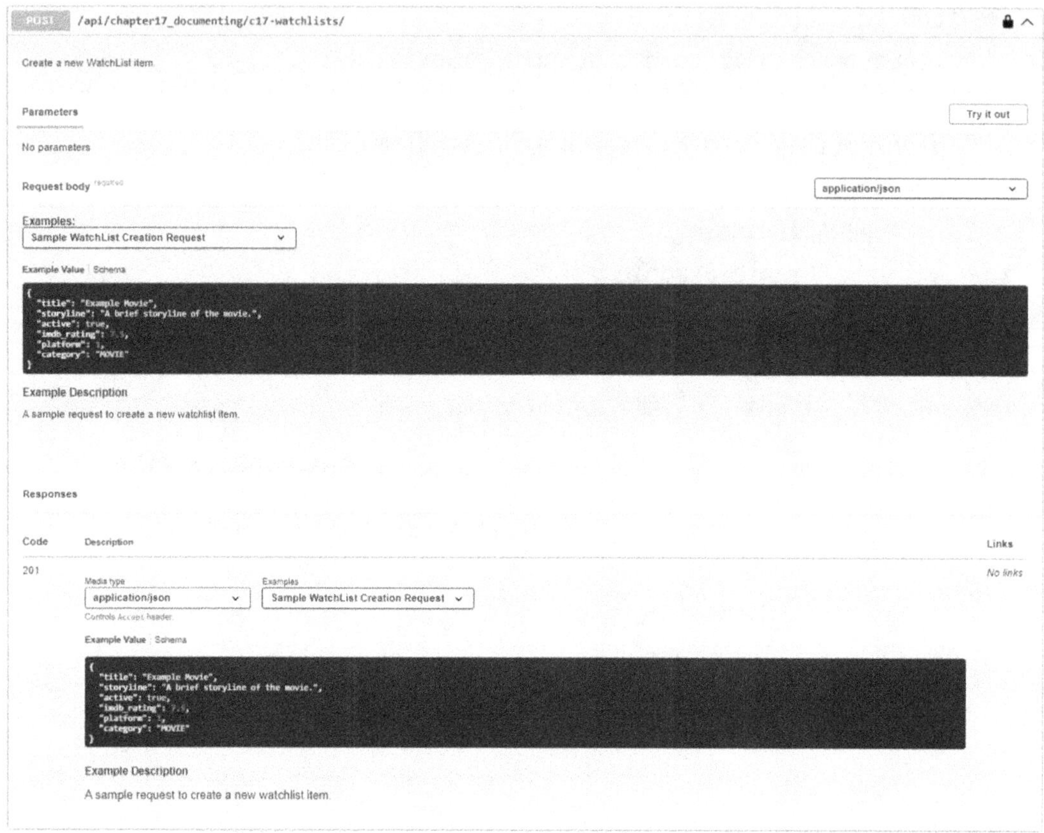

We can also extend the schema for list method as below:

```
class WatchListViewSet(viewsets.ModelViewSet):
    """
    A ViewSet for managing the WatchList.
    """
    queryset = WatchList.objects.all()
    serializer_class = serializers.WatchListModelSerializer

    ...

    @extend_schema(
        parameters=[
            OpenApiParameter(name='platform', description='Filter by
            platform ID', required=False, type=OpenApiTypes.INT),
```

```
            OpenApiParameter(
                name='imdb_rating_min',
                type=OpenApiTypes.NUMBER,
                location=OpenApiParameter.QUERY,
                description='Filter by minimum IMDb rating',
                examples=[
                    OpenApiExample(
                        'Example Rating Filter',
                        summary='Filtering example',
                        description='Filter items with IMDb rating
                                     >= 8.0.',
                        value=8.0
                    )
                ]
            )
        ],
        description="Retrieve a list of WatchList items, optionally
        filtered by platform or IMDb rating.",
        responses={
            200: serializers.WatchListModelSerializer(many=True),
            400: "Invalid query parameters."
        },
    )
    def list(self, request):
        """
        Custom list endpoint for WatchList.
        """
        return super().list(request)
```

In the above code, we have added in the parameters a list of **OpenApiParameter** elements. Let's see the updated documentation for the list method:

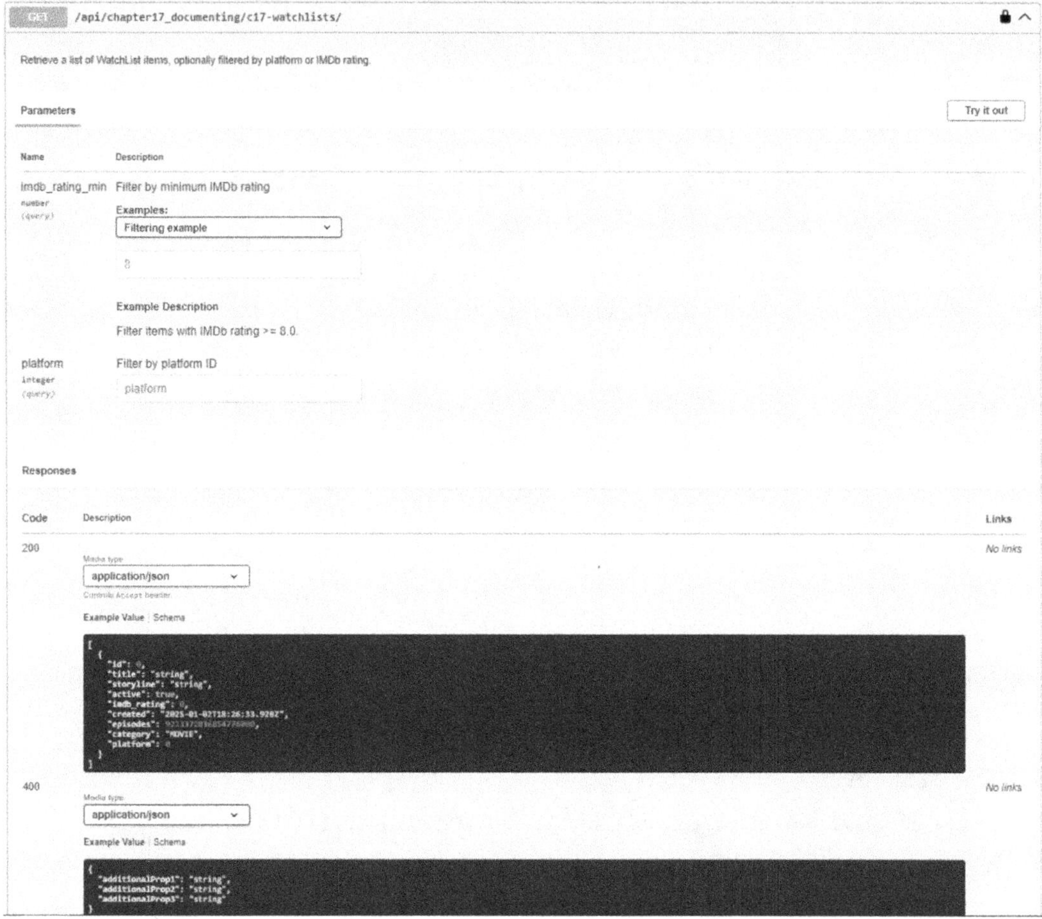

drf-yasg

The drf-yasg stands for Django REST Framework—Yet Another Swagger Generator. It is a library that generates **Swagger (OpenAPI 2.0)** or Redoc documentation for your Django REST Framework (DRF) APIs. Unlike Django's built-in schema generator, drf-yasg is built independently and focuses on providing a highly customizable and developer-friendly experience for creating comprehensive API documentation.

Key Features of drf-yasg

1. **OpenAPI 2.0 Specification**

   Implements the OpenAPI 2.0 spec (formerly Swagger), covering features like

- **Nested Schemas**: Easily model complex JSON objects
- **Named Models**: Identifies and reuses common models throughout the API
- **Response Bodies**: Describes detailed structures of API responses
- **Validation Support**: Captures field constraints such as enum, min, max, pattern, etc.

2. **Interactive Documentation**

   Automatically generates interactive Swagger UI or ReDoc documentation, allowing developers to

   - Browse available endpoints.
   - Try out requests directly from the documentation (e.g., sending test API requests).
   - View examples of requests and responses.

3. **Code Generation Friendly**

   Outputs fully OpenAPI 2.0-compliant documentation that can be used with tools like swagger-codegen to auto-generate API client SDKs (e.g., for Python, JavaScript, Java, etc.)

4. **Extensive Customization**

   Allows full customization of the schema generation using DRF serializers, views, and decorators

5. **Dynamic Validation**

   Automatically introspects DRF views, serializers, and validators to build an accurate API schema

Let's use this tool for our project.

The DRF library (`https://github.com/axnsan12/drf-yasg/?tab=readme-ov-file#installation`) has provided a very clear and concise section on installation and setup.

After a correct installation and setup, add the URLs in drfproject/urls.py as below:

```
from drf_yasg.views import get_schema_view
from drf_yasg import openapi

schema_view = get_schema_view(
   openapi.Info(
      title="DRF Book APIs",
      default_version='v1',
      description="DRF Book APIs Documentation",
      terms_of_service="https://www.google.com/policies/terms/",
      contact=openapi.Contact(email="contact@snippets.local"),
      license=openapi.License(name="BSD License"),
   ),
   public=True,
   permission_classes=(permissions.AllowAny,),
)

urlpatterns = [
    path('admin/', admin.site.urls),
    ...
    #drf-yasg URLs
    path('swagger<format>/', schema_view.without_ui(cache_timeout=0),
    name='schema-json'),
    path('swagger/', schema_view.with_ui('swagger', cache_timeout=0),
    name='schema-swagger-ui'),
    path('redoc/', schema_view.with_ui('redoc', cache_timeout=0),
    name='schema-redoc'),
    ...
]
```

Now run the Django server, and you can open in the browser a Swagger UI if you go to `/swagger` that has this aspect:

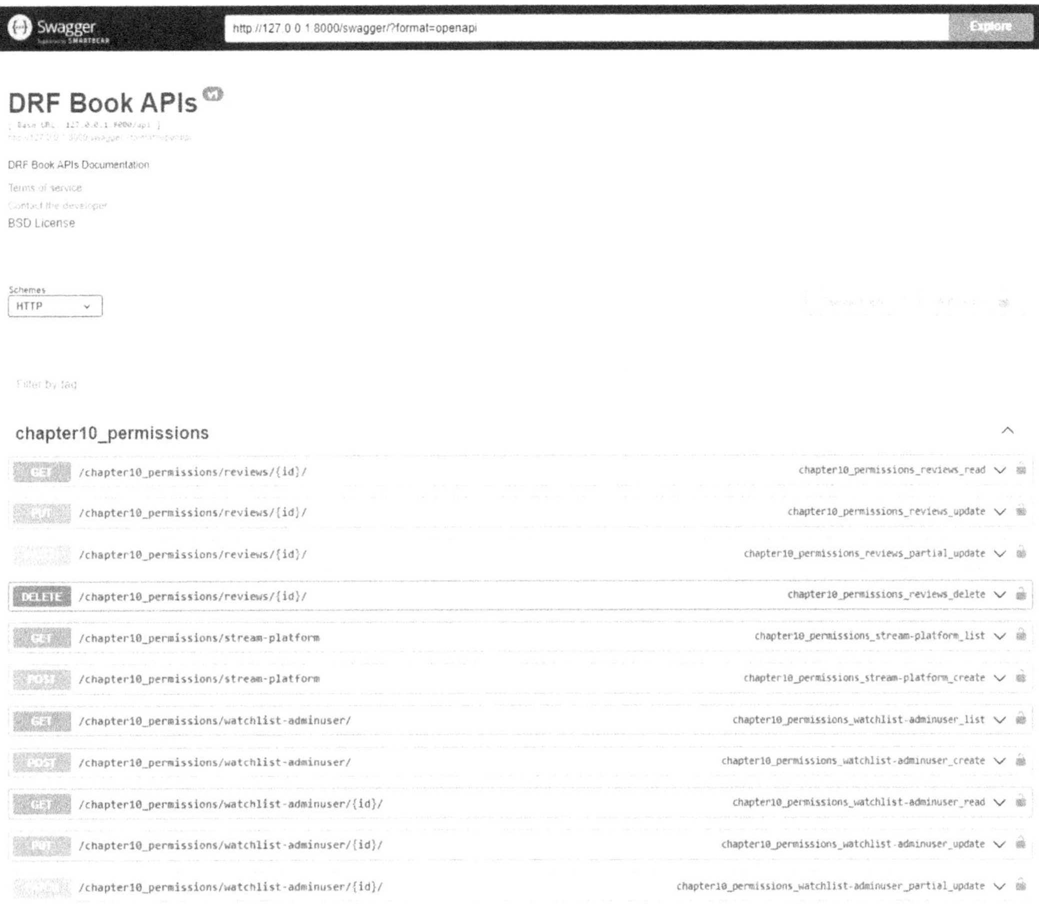

You can see serializer fields when you opened individual method as below:

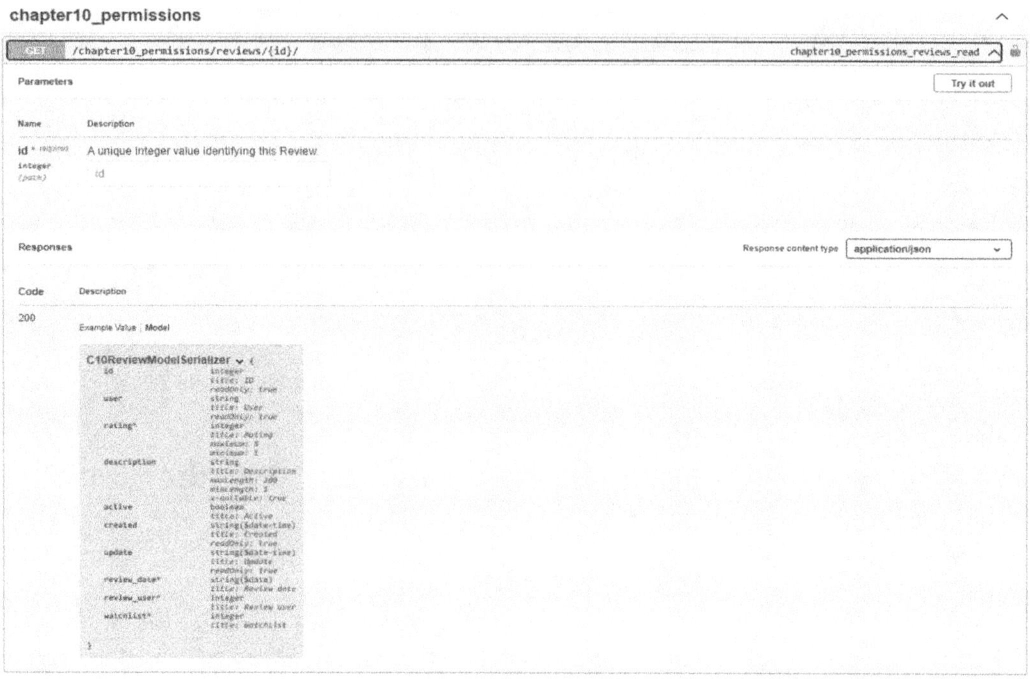

chapter10_permissions

GET /chapter10_permissions/reviews/{id}/ chapter10_permissions_reviews_read

Parameters

Try it out

Name	Description
id * required integer (path)	A unique integer value identifying this Review. id

Responses

Response content type: application/json

Code	Description
200	Example Value | Model

```
C10ReviewModelSerializer {
    id                integer
                      title: ID
                      readOnly: true
    user              string
                      title: User
                      readOnly: true
    rating*           integer
                      title: Rating
                      maximum: 5
                      minimum: 1
    description       string
                      title: Description
                      maxLength: 200
                      minLength: 1
                      x-nullable: true
    active            boolean
                      title: Active
    created           string($date-time)
                      title: Created
                      readOnly: true
    update            string($date-time)
                      title: Update
                      readOnly: true
    review_date*      string($date)
                      title: Review date
    review_user*      integer
                      title: Review user
    watchlist*        integer
                      title: Watchlist
}
```

Index

G. Patil, *Django REST APIs Demystified*, https://doi.org/10.1007/979-8-8688-1850-9

D

E

F

G

H, I

J, K

L

M

N

O

P, Q

R

S

T

U

U

V

W

X, Y, Z

GPSR Compliance
The European Union's (EU) General Product Safety Regulation (GPSR) is a set of rules that requires consumer products to be safe and our obligations to ensure this.

If you have any concerns about our products, you can contact us on

ProductSafety@springernature.com

In case Publisher is established outside the EU, the EU authorized representative is:

Springer Nature Customer Service Center GmbH
Europaplatz 3
69115 Heidelberg, Germany

www.ingramcontent.com/pod-product-compliance
Lightning Source LLC
LaVergne TN
LVHW081345060526
838201LV00050B/1715

* 9 7 9 8 8 6 8 8 1 8 4 9 3 *